THE OTHER FEW

THE OTHER FEW

BY

Larry Donnelly DFM

THE CONTRIBUTION MADE BY BOMBER AND COASTAL AIRCREW TO THE WINNING OF THE BATTLE OF BRITAIN

RED KITE

Author's Acknowledgements

When I first mentioned to my RAF and ex-RAF friends my idea of writing a book about 'The Other Few - the contribution of bomber and coastal aircrew to the winning of the Battle of Britain' the reception more than stimulated my enthusiasm for taking up the task. As I am ex-bomber aircrew myself and had participated in the Battle; I considered it a privilege to be able to devote myself to the project.
Over the past three years I have accepted the assistance of many friends and acquaintances too numerous to mention individually, but I must single out those who more than deserve it.

First I wish to express my sincere thanks and appreciation to Marshal of the Royal Air Force, Sir Michael Beetham (ex-Chief of Air Staff) for his most his most appropriate Foreword, something I will cherish.

Among other stalwart supporters are Andrew Jackson and Rupert ('Tiny') Cooling who flew Wimpeys during the Battle and who supplied photographs and material. Also to Mike Henry and Hugh Lynch-Blosse, 'Blenheim Boys' whose books provided material. Peter and Jill Rutter, expert voluntary researchers, who spent hours researching the Battle of Britain archives of the Royal Air Force Museum. Frank Tams 'The Trenchard Brat' for photos and material. Mrs. V Watson, for providing extensive material concerning her late husband, Flight Lieutenant E. Watson MM, (Blenheim Evader). Mr. Gerry Walters for providing the story of his late brother's involvement in the Battle. All the Coastal Command and Maritime Association personnel who were so forthcoming and helpful, especially Ian Chisholm and John Cairns. And I can't leave out my old Sunderland crewmate Pete Jensen, RAAF, for filling in the Sunderland gaps. My grateful thanks go to the survivors of 'The Other Few' and their descendants for their reports and personal experiences, their letters and photographs.
To any I have missed out - my apologies and sincere thanks.

First Published in 2004 by;
Red Kite
PO Box 223
Walton on Thames
Surrey
KT12 3YQ
www.redkitebooks.co.uk
email info@redkitebooks.co.uk

ISBN 0-9546201-2-7

Jacket painting by Mark Postlethwaite GAvA
www.posart.com
email mark@redkitebooks.co.uk

I have been lucky to be able to draw upon the knowledge of a team of researchers and authors who have been able to contribute material from their own fields of knowledge:

Simon Parry - Editor and casualty research
Mark Postlethwaite – Designer and picture research
John Foreman – Luftwaffe fighter claims

Additional material and photographs have been provided by:

Theo Boiten
Stephen Flower
Martin Goodman
Alistair Goodrum
Chris Goss
Zdenek Hurt
Andy Saunders
Ray Sturtivant
Philippa Wheeler
Roy Conyers Nesbit
Andy Thomas
Simon Gifford
Jiri Rajlich
Ron Mackay
ww2images.com
Colin Rawlins
Bob Pearce
Max Meyer
Ron Low

Notes for casualty listings

As with any work attempting to cover such a complex subject, guidelines had to be set to establish the criteria for inclusion. The purpose of this work is to detail the efforts and sacrifices of the aircrews to prevent an invasion of Britain. Therefore it was decided to include only losses of men and machines incurred during operations over Europe, where fatal casualties were sustained or aircraft destroyed. Incidents where minor damage to aircraft occurred or where non-fatal injuries were sustained are not normally listed. Non-operational and training losses, whether from operational or non-operational units, have also been omitted. There are some events that fall into the inevitable grey area between these categories; where such incidents have been encountered a decision had to be made based on the known circumstances of the loss.

Printed in England by
The Cromwell Press
White Horse Business Park
Trowbridge
Wilts

Foreword

by

Marshal of the Royal Air Force
Sir Michael Beetham GCB CBE DFC AFC

Of all the battles of World War 2, the Battle of Britain is probably the best known to the British public. It was, of course, a major turning point in that the relentless German advance across Europe was halted and, as a nation, we were saved from defeat. Significantly, it was the first battle to be won by air power alone in that, although the Army and Navy played their part, it was on the sidelines and the battle was won by the Royal Air Force.

The Battle has been extensively covered by historians and the media but the focus, in the public mind at least, has always been on 'The Few' of Fighter Command helped no doubt by Winston Churchill's epic and well deserved tribute. This book, which meticulously catalogues the part played by Bomber Command and Coastal Command – 'The Other Few' – needed to be written because their roles were a vital and indispensable contribution to victory, a contribution which has never been adequately publicly recognised.

The book goes some way to redress the balance whilst taking nothing away from the magnificent achievements of Fighter Command. It has been carefully researched with each day's operational activity covered in detail but in a manner which is easy to read.

I commend it not only to historians but also to anyone who is interested in the whole story of the Battle.

Contents

INTRODUCTION

On 18th June 1940, Winston Churchill, the Prime Minister, made the following declaration:

"The Battle of France is over. I expect the Battle of Britain is about to begin. Upon this battle depends the survival of Christian civilisation. Upon it depends our own way of British life, and the long continuity of our institution and our Empire. The whole fury and might of the enemy must be very soon turned upon us. Hitler knows that he will have to break us in this island or lose the war. If we can stand up to this, all Europe may be free and the life of the world may move forward into broad sunlit uplands. But if we fail, then the whole world - including the United States, including all that we have known and cared for - will sink into the abyss of an age more sinister, and perhaps more protracted, by the light of perverted science. Let us therefore brace ourselves to our duties, and so bear ourselves that if the British Empire and its Commonwealth last for a thousand years, men will still say, 'This was their finest hour'."

As he predicted, the battle was joined. All the armed forces were involved, but the Royal Air Force bore the brunt repelling sustained air attacks on Britain and simultaneously carrying out a bomber offensive against the assembling German invasion armada of some 1600 ships and barges. The cost in aircrew lives was a heavy one. In the Battle of Britain Memorial Chapel in Westminster Abbey, the Roll of Honour records the names of the 1,497 aircrew who were killed in the Battle (513 fighter aircrew, 34 Fleet Air Arm aircrew, 719 bomber aircrew and 231 coastal aircrew).

Every year on 15 September (Battle of Britain Day) the deeds of the gallant Few of Fighter Command are deservedly remembered and revered, but those of their Bomber and Coastal Command comrades who also took part in the Battle are somehow pushed into the background. It is also worth noting that the Bomber and Coastal aircrew, despite being continuously engaged in action, were not given the same honourable entitlement of the Battle of Britain clasp to the 1939/45 Star as were their Fighter Command comrades when the campaign medals were awarded. Few seem to appreciate that the victory of the Battle of Britain and the frustration of Hitler's plan to invade our country was jointly achieved. While Fighter Command squadrons denied the German Luftwaffe air superiority by shooting down their attacking fighters and bombers over Britain, Bomber and Coastal Command aircraft attacked the German occupied airfields, the shipping being assembled as an invasion fleet in the German and ports of occupied Europe, as well as other relevant targets such as aircraft factories, oil storage depots, canals and aqueducts all necessary to provide support for Hitler's invasion plan. German ports and coastal waters were mined from the air, while our convoys were protected from sea and air attack.

Fighter Command repulsed the efforts of the Luftwaffe to achieve the air superiority needed to support an invasion. On the 15 September, the day selected by Hitler for the commencement of the invasion, the heaviest losses were inflicted on the Luftwaffe. This failure to overpower Fighter Command, combined with the effective bombing of the invasion armada, forced Hitler to postpone his invasion, code-named '*Sealion*' and finally to abandon it altogether. The Bomber Command raids on Berlin, which commenced on the 25th/26th August, (something which Goering boasted could never happen) also proved to be an influential factor which affected the decision to switch the Luftwaffe from attacking our airfields in daylight to night attacks on our cities to cut down losses, In doing so they unknowingly gave respite to the sorely pressed fighter squadrons. Thus the invasion of Britain, which was Hitler's key objective, was prevented by the joint efforts of the aircrew of Fighter, Bomber and Coastal Commands. The gallant exploits of the Fighter Command aircrew during the Battle were made evident to the public by the reports in the press and on the wireless; also by the sight of the vapour trails high above them during the air battles. But unseen beyond our shores were the continuous day and night operations being carried out by our Bomber and Coastal Command aircrew. Perhaps it was because they were based near sleepy villages and hamlets far from the Metropolis, and operated out of sight, that they received so little recognition, except for the laconic daily reports on the wireless. The crews were mostly young men with a zest for living, but who were prepared to carry out their hazardous tasks regardless of the risk. Highlighting this is not meant to be churlish or to detract any glory from the magnificent 'Few' of Fighter Command, but to remind us of the achievements and sacrifices of 'The Other Few'.

The following chapters are a day-to-day record of the operations they carried out throughout the Battle, with, where possible, accounts and reports by the crews involved.

Note: Throughout the Battle the claims of both the Luftwaffe and the RAF of the numbers of aircraft destroyed were controversial. Those quoted in the following chapters are from the best available sources.

Wrecked German aircraft at the end of the Battle of Britain.

An abandoned RAF Spitfire lies in the sands near Dunkirk.

The Battle of France was over and France had signed an Armistice with Germany. The retreat from Dunkirk and the miraculous rescue of most of the British Expeditionary Force, together with surviving personnel and machines of the RAF's Advanced Striking Force had been accomplished.

The Battle of France had been the RAF's first real test in battle and the cost in men and machines was high. Well over 900 aircraft and 1,382 personnel (including 915 aircrew) had been lost in just six weeks. The aircraft losses comprised 454 fighters (Hurricanes, Spitfires and Defiants) 409 bombers (Blenheim, Battle, Wellington, Whitley and Hampden) plus thirty-five Army Co-op Lysanders, twenty Coastal Command Hudsons and fifteen Fleet Air Arm Swordfish and Skuas. Although outnumbered, the RAF fighters had fought valiantly and with some assistance of the French Air Force had inflicted on the Luftwaffe its first heavy losses. The Germans were to admit later the loss of one thousand and sixty-five aircraft of all types.

The Fairey Battles and Blenheims, also outnumbered, were overwhelmed by the Luftwaffe fighters and the murderous Flak protecting targets. Some of the best and bravest RAF aircrew, most of them pre-war regulars, were lost. A testimony to their bravery was the posthumous award of the first RAF Victoria Crosses of World War II to Flying Officer D. E. Garland and his observer, Sergeant T. Gray of No. 12 Fairey Battle Squadron of the Advanced Air Striking Force in France. He had led a formation of five aircraft which attacked a vital bridge over the Albert Canal in Belgium. The success of the operation was attributed to Flying Officer Garland, as formation leader, and the coolness and resource of Sergeant Gray, who navigated their aircraft in such a manner that the whole formation was able to attack the target in spite of heavy losses. Four aircraft failed to return, including that of Flying Officer Garland. It is tragic to record that no award or recognition was given to their wireless operator/air-gunner, Leading Aircraftsman L. Reynolds, who was killed with them.

One of the many Fairey Battles that fell during the Fall of France. This example being from 150 Squadron.

An RAF Anson joins a French flying boat on patrol over the Channel in Spring 1940.

Although some official sources give the start of The Battle of Britain as July 10th, Bomber and Coastal Commands were involved earlier. On June 20th the Air Ministry anticipated that Hitler, now having conquered most of Western Europe, would concentrate on invading Britain. A directive was issued instructing Bomber and Coastal Commands to attack targets in Germany and the Occupied Countries and carry out tasks which would have the most effect in combating the expected pre-invasion assault on Britain. The so-called 'heavies', the Wellingtons of 3 Group, the Whitleys of 4 Group and the Hampdens of 5 Group, were to concentrate on relevant targets such as aircraft factories, aircraft storage depots and oil refineries in Germany at night. The Blenheims of 2 Group were to concentrate on carrying out daylight raids on airfields in France, the Low Countries and Norway. It beggars belief that they were still persisting with this disastrous policy of unescorted daylight sorties that had resulted in such heavy losses at the beginning of the war and the recent Battle of France.

As the Germans were now in possession of the whole coastline of Western Europe from the North Cape to Bordeaux, they could use the ports from which to operate their U-Boats and surface raiders to attack our shipping supply lines. The Luftwaffe could also use the French airfields to support the attacks taking place west of Ireland.

Coastal Command, with a meagre force of approximately 500 aircraft (some of them obsolete), had the daunting task of meeting this threat. However, from receipt of the Air Ministry Directive, the Command's Anson, Blenheim, Hudson, Sunderland, Stranraer, Whitley and Lysander squadrons with support of detachments of Swordfish and Albacores from the Fleet Air Arm and Spitfires from the Photographic Development Unit, faced up to their many commitments.

The enemy coasts and ports were to be patrolled twice every twenty-four hours and throughout the hours of darkness there was to be a continuous reconnaissance of the ports from the Hook of Holland to Ostend in case of a surprise attack. Protection was to be provided for coastal convoys and Channel shipping. Lysanders operating in pairs were to patrol the coastline from Land's End to Duncansby Head, to search for and prevent any clandestine activity undertaken by the Germans to infiltrate espionage agents. On June 30th the Air Ministry decreed that a minimum of three aircraft per squadron were to be bombed up and crewed to be kept on anti-invasion standby. On July 2nd, Hitler asked his High Command how long it would take the Luftwaffe to gain superiority over the RAF. He was given the reply that it would take only four days to remove fighter protection from Britain; and an additional three weeks to destroy the remainder of the RAF. He then decided that if Britain refused to meet his terms for peace, the

Bombs are loaded aboard a Dornier Do17 in preparation for a bombing raid on Enlgand.

invasion would take place and he outlined the directive to his High Command. From that date until the end of the first week in August, the Luftwaffe would probe British defences by attacking coastal shipping and by carrying out sporadic raids against selected industrial targets by both day and night.

Six weeks before the actual invasion the Luftwaffe was to launch a major offensive to smash British coastal defences, break up initial resistance and destroy the reserves behind the main defences as well as preventing attacks on the German invasion force.

The Luftwaffe forces for the planned assault were to be:
Luftflotte 2 and 3: based in northern Germany, the Netherlands, Belgium and north-eastern France.
Luftflotte 5: based in Denmark and Norway.

The approximate number of aircraft available would be 3,500 of all types. *Luftflotte 2* was to operate east of a line approximately Le Havre - Oxford - Birmingham - Manchester, while Luftflotte 3 was to operate west of the line.
Convergent raids by *Luftflotte 2* and 3, particularly at night, were to be planned to split the defences.
Luftflotte 5 was to operate against targets in northern England and Scotland and also carry out attacks against shipping, with the object of forcing defending forces to be transferred from the south.

During the third week of July, the Luftwaffe was ordered to full readiness and the final detailed invasion operation orders were worked out.

Above: A Wellington is prepared for a forthcoming bombing raid on Germany.

In the meantime in England, fears of invasion were increasing rapidly. The Prime Minister, Winston Churchill, told the Cabinet on July 3rd that there was a growing feeling that an invasion attempt may be imminent. He considered that the coming week might be critical and that the RAF bombing attacks should switch from the German aircraft industry to the bombing of enemy harbours and shipping. The following day Air Marshal Portal, C-in-C Bomber Command, was sent a new directive from the Air Ministry. Photographic Reconnaissance Spitfires operating under the control of Coastal Command had picked up the first signs of movement of invasion barges towards Dutch and Belgian ports. Bomber Command was instructed to shift bombing priority from airfields and aircraft plants to German shipping and invasion craft. The heavies were to concentrate their attacks on the ports of Kiel and Hamburg, where it was thought that warships such as the *Scharnhorst* and *Gneisenau* were lying. In addition, the Hampden mining force was to be increased to three squadrons.

Laying mines from the air was one of the most hazardous of air operations. The Hampden was the only RAF Bomber Command aircraft capable of carrying and dropping the 1,500lb 'M' mines. To be dropped and operate successfully the mines had to be dropped into a depth of water of between 5 and 12 fathoms (10 to 24 metres) and from

Below: Air Marshal Portal, C-in-C Bomber Command.

2 Group Blenheims of 40 Squadron, photographed in June 1940 as their operational strategy was being formulated for the forthcoming battle.

heights of between 400 and 1,000 feet. Operating at this low level in the dark or being blinded by searchlights was, to put it mildly, very 'dicey'. The Germans reacted to the threat of minelaying by locating batteries of 20 and 30mm cannon along the river banks and port inlets in the areas they considered vulnerable. They supplemented these defences with off-shore Flak ships bristling with Flak guns of all calibres.

2 Group Blenheims were to concentrate their attacks on the self-propelled barges that would be an important part of the invasion fleet. However, on July 13th, because there was no great concentration of shipping and invasion barges, the bombing priorities reverted to those outlined in the directive of June 20th.

The 2 Group targets would again be the concentrations of enemy aircraft on the aerodromes of France and Belgium and shipping in Norwegian ports. Because of the vulnerability of aircraft engaged in daylight operations, the attacks were to be made sporadically and only when suitable cloud cover was available. This was easier said than done, especially when on some operations the cloud cover changed when the crews were well on their way to their target. On some occasions the crews 'pressed on' and suffered losses from defending fighters. 2 Group was also instructed to employ up to forty-eight Blenheims per day, operating them individually or in small formations. Every effort was to be made to spread the attacks so that the calls on the defending fighters were widespread and numerous, thus keeping the fighters dispersed and less concentrated.

All the bomber groups were told by Bomber Command; 'You must be prepared to divert your squadrons to repel any invasion at short notice'.

July 1940

The opening shots

Monday 1st July

MAINLY SUNNY IN THE SOUTH, CLOUDIER IN THE NORTH.

A 10 RAAF Squadron Sunderland P9604 taxies back to its mooring. The previous Sunderland off the production line, P9603 was in action today, sinking a U-Boat.

ENEMY AIR ACTIVITY

The Luftwaffe limited its operations to isolated raids against ports and a dive bombing attack on the convoy Jumbo. A Heinkel 59 was intercepted and shot down over the North Sea off Hartlepool.

COASTAL COMMAND

Flight Lieutenant *'Hoot'* Gibson and his crew in Sunderland P9603, 10 RAAF Squadron, Mountbatten, briefed to carry out an anti-submarine patrol, were informed that the *SS Zarian* had been torpedoed 250 miles west of Ushant. Gibson was ordered to provide escort for the rest of the convoy while *HMS Gladiolus* and *HMS Rochester* searched for the U-Boat. Other vessels had been dispatched to tow the crippled *SS Zarian* into Falmouth.
Just before dawn Gibson's crew located the torpedoed ship with a destroyer standing by. After *SS Zarian* had been hit, the U-Boat had been attacked by *HMS Gladiolus* with depth charges and was thought to have been damaged. This was indeed the case and the U-Boat had surfaced, hoping to escape at high speed. Gibson joined the search and when about 30 miles from the torpedoed vessel his First Pilot (Flying Officer Havyatt) sighted a disturbance on the water. Gibson concluded that this was the U-Boat preparing to dive and attacked dropping four anti-submarine bombs just ahead of the submarine which was at periscope level. He assessed that his attack had further damaged the U-Boat as it came to the surface at a steep angle, so he carried out a second attack, his bombs falling forty yards from the conning-tower. *HMS Rochester* was now approaching and opened fire at eleven hundred yards range. However, the U-Boat commander *Kapitanleutnant* Heinz Scherringer, had already given the order to scuttle. The conning-tower opened and the crew scrambled out as the sub pitched up and settled by the stern. Gibson's report transmitted to Group was a model of brevity, "Have attacked enemy U-Boat - Surfaced - Sunk - Survivors".
At 07.00 hours the exultant Sunderland crew watched as the U-Boat survivors, 41 of them, were rescued by *HMS Rochester*. The credit for sinking U-26 was subsequently equally divided between *HMS Gladiolus* and Flight Lieutenant Gibson's crew: Flying Officer G. Havyatt (*First Pilot*), Sergeant H. O'Connor (*Observer*), Corporal J. Burnham (*1st. Fitter*), LAC. W. Vout (*2nd. Fitter*), Corporal J. Grubb (*W/T Operator*), LAC. K. Phillips (*W/T Operator*), LAC. de Wynne (*Rigger*), LAC. Couldrey (*Air/Gunner - Rear*).
Flight Lieutenant *'Hoot'* Gibson was awarded the DFC.
U-26 had sunk eight ships during six patrols since the beginning of the war.
An Anson crew of 608 Squadron, Thornaby, spotted a half submerged Heinkel 59 float-plane off Hartlepool; claimed as the first fighter success of the Battle!

BOMBER COMMAND

Six Blenheims of 15 Squadron, Wyton, carried out a photographic reconnaissance of the French coast in the vicinity of Calais in daylight. Although it was cloudy, the sortie was deemed to be partially successful.

Night Operations

Thirty Hampdens twenty-four Wellingtons and thirteen Whitleys carried out night attacks against targets at Kiel, Hamburg, Osnabrük and Duisburg, while six other Hampdens carried out minelaying. Fifty-three of the force claimed to have bombed successfully.
One of the Hampdens attacking the *Scharnhorst* at Kiel was flown by Flying Officer Guy Gibson of 83 Squadron, who dropped the first 2,000lb bomb of the war. He released it on his sixth shallow dive attempt, but the bomb overshot the warship and exploded in the town of Kiel.

Previous page: A 10 RAAF Squadron Sunderland over Rame Head near Plymouth, heading out on a routine patrol.

OPERATIONAL LOSSES

Hampden P1171 of 83 Squadron, Scampton, hit by Flak attacking Kiel and crashed in the target area killing the entire crew: Pilot Officer D. Redmayne, Sergeant C. Lee, Sergeant O. S. Gander and Sergeant G. E. Little. They are buried in the Kiel War Cemetery.

Whitley N1461 of 58 Squadron, Linton-on-Ouse, was shot down attacking the *Scharnhorst* at Kiel. The aircraft crashed near the Kiel dockyard, killing four members of the crew: Pilot Officer C J. T. Jones, Flying Officer. L. H. McFarlane, Sergeant D. Lieshman and Sergeant H. E. A. Craven. They are buried in the Kiel War Cemetery. The fifth member of the crew, Sergeant J. P. Caldwell, was taken prisoner.

Above and below: The wreckage of Pilot Officer Redmayne's Hampden P1171 OL-P, which was shot down during the raid on Kiel. All four crew members were killed.

Tuesday 2nd July

SUNNY WITH MOSTLY CLEAR SKIES.

ENEMY AIR ACTIVITY

A quiet day for the Luftwaffe crews with only two aircraft missing from operations.. A Do215 reconnaissance aircraft was shot down by Spitfires and a Do17 was lost to AA fire.

COASTAL COMMAND

1. Hudsons of 220 Squadron, Thornaby, 224 and 233 Squadrons, Leuchars, operating in daylight attacked enemy merchantmen and escorting destroyers off Lotberg and Lister (Norway), despite opposition from fighters and Flak.
2. A Sunderland of 204 Squadron, Sullom Voe, on convoy patrol, reported that the *SS Andora Star* had been sunk 100 miles from Bora Head and that Royal Navy ships were picking up survivors from thirteen lifeboats.
3. An Anson of 48 Squadron, Thorney Island, on convoy protection in the English Channel, reported that the convoy (C177) was being attacked by enemy bombers.
4. A High Speed Launch operating in the North Sea, looking for a downed Whitley crew, picked up three Germans, Leutnant Gottfried Schrootes, Unteroffizier Siegfried Soert and Oberfeldwebel Rudolph Worms, from their dinghy in which they had been for twenty-eight hours after ditching on return from a bombing raid on Hartlepool.

Night Operations

1. After dark, twelve Swordfish of 825 (FAA) Squadron operating from RAF Detling attempted to bomb barges in the River Maas (Holland). Only three were successful., two failed to return and three crashed on return, one near Harwich, another at Birchington and the third on Horrocks Island.
2. Another six Swordfish of 812 (FAA) Squadron operating from RAF North Coates, also detailed to bomb the same River Maas target, had difficulty and only one was able to bomb.
3. Five Albacores of 826 (FAA) Squadron, operating from RAF Bircham Newton, attacked shipping in the Hook of Holland.

BOMBER COMMAND

Eleven Blenheims of 82 Squadron, Watton, were briefed to attack targets along the Dortmund-Ems Canal in daylight, but because of the lack of suitable cloud cover ten returned. The remaining crew pressed on but unfortunately failed to return. *Two Blenheims were claimed by Bf109E pilots, one by Oberleutnant Leo Eggers of 2./JG 21 at 11.44 hours northwest of Horn, and by Feldwebel Jakob Schmitt of 2./JG 51, 30 kilometres south of Den Helder, at 11.55 hours.*

Night Operations

On this night six Blenheims were included with the night bombing force with fourteen Hampdens, twenty-four Wellingtons and sixteen Whitleys briefed to bomb targets at Evere, Hingene, Hamm, Hamburg, Osnabrük, Soerst, Scherte, Köln, Dortmund and Rotterdam. Six other Hampdens were detailed to drop mines in German waters. Forty-four of the bombing force claimed successful attacks.

OPERATIONAL LOSSES

Swordfish L2829 of 825 Squadron Fleet Air Arm, failed to return. The body of Leading Airman H. W. Burt lies in the Amsterdam New Eastern Cemetery.

Swordfish L7646 of 825 Squadron Fleet Air Arm, failed to return. The bodies of Sub Lieutenants B. P Grigson and F. L. Lees both lie in the Rozenburg General Cemetery, Holland.

Blenheim P6895 of 82 Squadron, Watton, target Dortmund-Ems Canal, crashed near Veenhuizen, Holland. The crew; Squadron Leader H. F. Chester, Sergeant H. Histon and Sergeant R. J. McAllister were all killed and are buried in the local churchyard.

825 Squadron lost two of their Swordfish biplanes to enemy action today, a further three crashed upon their return.

A 44 Squadron Hampden crew study part of their cargo for the forthcoming night's operation.

ENEMY AIR ACTIVITY

KG30 lost three Ju88s in separate interceptions in the the north of England. In the south, Do17s attacked Manston in a minor raid and mines were laid in the Thames Estuary.

COASTAL COMMAND

1. 53 and 59 Blenheim Mk.IV Squadrons were seconded to Coastal Command, 53 to RAF Detling and 59 to RAF Thorney Island, from where they immediately commenced offensive operations. From then on they were in the forefront of the Battle.

2. Hudsons of 206 Squadron, Bircham Newton, dive-bombed a factory at Ijmuiden in daylight and successfully escaped the unwelcome attentions of an intercepting Bf109s.

3. Another Hudson, also of 206 Squadron, bombed a target at Texel on the Frisian Islands in daylight.

BOMBER COMMAND

The Blenheims of 2 Group had a busy and mostly successful day carrying out photo reconnaissance and bombing raids on various targets in daylight at Kiel, the Ruhr, and Occupied airfields at Evere, Bethune and Abbeville. Also invasion barges in the River Lek near Rotterdam were bombed for the first time. Out of thirty-five aircraft involved in these sorties, twenty- four claimed success.

Night Operations

A total of thirty 'heavies' eighteen Hampdens and twelve Whitleys carried out night bombing attacks on communications at the Dortmund-Ems Canal, Soest, Munster, Grimburg, Merville airfield and invasion barges at Rotterdam, while six other Hampdens carried out minelaying.

OPERATIONAL LOSSES

Hampden P4352 of 44 Squadron, Waddington, detailed to plant mines in the Great belt, was lost in the North Sea. Three members of the crew, Pilot Officer D. A. Todd, Sergeant E. T. Apperson and Sergeant A. Baird are commemorated on the Runnymede Memorial. The body of the fourth member, Flight Lieutenant W. S. Bull was washed ashore on the west coast of Denmark and is buried in Lyngvig churchyard. *This aircraft was possibly claimed by a Bf109 pilot from I./JG 76 near Haarlem.*

Thursday 4th July

RAIN COVERING MOST OF THE COUNTRY AT SOME TIME.

Today was a bad day for 206 Squadron, losing two of its VX coded Hudsons to German fighters during a search for a downed Hampden crew.

ENEMY AIR ACTIVITY

A heavy raid on Portland by Ju87 Stukas resulted in the first VC of the Battle being awarded posthumously to Acting Seaman Jack Mantle, a gunner on *HMS Foyle Bank*. Later raids were also aimed against naval targets.

COASTAL COMMAND

1. At 10.48 hours, an Anson of 612 Squadron, Dyce, bombed an oil streak from a suspected U-Boat while on patrol. No positive result.
2. At 13.10 hours another Anson of 612 Squadron, Dyce, while on patrol twenty-eight miles from Cape Wrath, carried out an attack on what was thought to be a U-Boat. Again there was no positive result.
3. An Anson of 48 Squadron escorting a westbound Channel convoy, reported at 12.45 hours that the convoy was being attacked by fifteen enemy aircraft and that two vessels had been abandoned. Two more attacks took place at 14.43 hrs and 15.00 hours. Three more ships were set on fire.
4. Twenty miles from Bergen (Norway) a Hudson of 224 Squadron, Leuchars, attacked an enemy vessel, claiming hits.
5. Another Hudson, this time from 233 Squadron, Leuchars, attacked four small ships bearing 182 degrees from Alsboen Light, also claiming hits.

BOMBER COMMAND

Twenty Blenheims of 2 Group were detailed to carry out daylight attacks on marshalling yards at Hamm and Soerst, industrial targets at Hanover and Emerich, airfields at Evere and Schipol and shipping west of Den Helder. Eleven claimed to have bombed successfully, one was shot down.

Night Operations

On the night of the 4th/5th thirty-six Wellingtons, twelve Whitleys and nineteen Hampdens carried out bombing raids against targets in Germany. Wellingtons attacked Bremen, Hamm, Scherte, Köln, Osnabrük, Wenzendorf, Emden and Wesel. The Whitleys bombed the shipyards at Hamburg, while the Hampdens attacked the *Scharnhorst* in Kiel Harbour and aqueducts on the Dortmund-Ems Canal. Another six Hampdens planted mines.

OPERATIONAL LOSSES

Hudson P5162 of 206 Squadron, Bircham Newton, missing from a North Sea search for the 44 Squadron Hampden P4352. The crew; Pilot Officer S. J. Lester, Pilot Officer J. E. MacKinnon, Sergeant K. S. Bushell and Sergeant K. E. Lewis are all recorded on the Runnymede Memorial.

Hudson N7368 of 206 Squadron, Bircham Newton, missing from the search as P5162. The crew; Pilot Officer S. R. Henderson DFC, Sergeant G. H. Goldsmith, LAC J. L. Williamson and Sergeant G. C. Sumner, are all recorded on the Runnymede Memorial.
Both of the above two Hudsons were engaged by Messerschmitts of 3./JG 51 at 09.07 hours to the northwest of Terschelling. One fell to Leutnant Rudolf Busch and the other to Unteroffizier Heinz zur Lage.

Blenheim L8866 of 18 Squadron, West Raynham, detailed for operations in north-western Germany, crashed west of Rotterdam shot down over the Mass estuary at 12.10 hours by a Bf109 flown by Unteroffizier Günther Behse of 2./JG 76. This was the first squadron casualty since rejoining 2 Group after the Battle of France. Flight Lieutenant I. C. B. Worthington-Wilmer, Sergeant J. G. Stanley and Sergeant G. E. Maydon were all killed and are buried at Oostvoorne Cemetery.

Hampden P4361 of 144 Squadron, Hemswell, shot down by Flak at Kiel near the target. The crew; Flying Officer E. B. Lancaster, Pilot Officer J. H. Gilling, Sergeant P. F Bailey and Sergeant I. A. I. J. Nicol, were all killed and are buried in the Kiel War Cemetery.

The Blenheim fighter squadrons attached to Coastal Command were very busy today, protecting convoys and RN shipping off the coast of England.

ENEMY AIR ACTIVITY

A very quiet day with the only action of note being a minor dogfight between a handful of Spitfires and Bf109s over the Pas de Calais.

COASTAL COMMAND

1. Sunderland P9623 of 210 Squadron, Oban, on convoy patrol was ordered at 13.45 hours to leave the convoy to attack a suspected U-Boat. At 14.45 hours the crew found a sinking ship which it patrolled until rescue arrived.
2. Blenheim TR-E of 59 Sqn flown by Flying Officer G.T.Palmer) was attacked by 3 Bf109s off Dungeness, but escaped. *Feldwebel Willi Gasthaus of 4./JG 51 claimed a Blenheim south of Dungeness.*

Night Operations

Nos. 235, 236,248, 254 and 263 Blenheim fighter Squadrons attached to Coastal Command from Fighter Command did sterling work providing cover over UK convoys and RN ships in the English Channel and the North Sea, as well as giving support to Hudsons carrying out bombing raids against targets in enemy-held territory. They operated from St. Eval, Thorney Island, Detling, Bircham-Newton, Dyce and Sumburg, being moved around as required.

BOMBER COMMAND

Fifteen Blenheims of 2 Group were detailed to carry out daylight operations. One aircraft of 15 Squadron, Wyton, to carry out photo-reconnaissance of canals in Holland, two of 107 Squadron, Wattisham, to attack Flushing airfield, three of 114 Squadron and three of 139 Squadron, Horsham St Faith, to attack the marshalling yards at Hamm and Soest and three each from 18 and 101 Squadrons, West Raynham, to attack oil and aircraft targets in north-west Germany. Eight crews claimed successful sorties.

Night Operations

1. Twenty Wellingtons, fifteen Hampdens and twelve Whitleys carried out night raids. The Wellingtons bombed the marshalling yards at Hamm, docks at Emden, the shipyards at Kiel and installations on Schipol airfield. Whitleys bombed the docks at Wilhelmshaven and Hamburg and the airfield at Merville. Hampdens bombed Kiel dockyard and the Dortmund-Ems Canal while twelve other Hampdens planted mines. Forty of the force of forty-seven claimed to have bombed successfully.

OPERATIONAL LOSSES

Blenheim N6140 of 101 Squadron, West Raynham, crashed into the sea. This was the squadron's first operation after relinquishing its training role. Of the crew, Wing Commander J. H. Hargroves and Sergeant E. W. Smith are buried at the Kiel War Cemetery and Sergeant R. M. Livermore is recorded on the Runnymede Memorial. *This aircraft was intercepted some 40 kilometres west of Amrum Island by Feldwebel Junge of I./JG 52 and was shot down at 19.45 hours.*

Blenheim R3804 of 114 Squadron, Horsham St Faith, was lost attacking Soest. This was the squadron's first loss being practically wiped out during the Battle of France. The crew; Pilot Officer A. Stewart, Sergeant G. Rimmer and Sergeant R. J. S. Ellicott were all killed and are buried in the Reichswald Forest War Cemetery. *The Blenheim fell victim to Oberleutnant Hubertus von Holtey of II./JG 26, who shot it down 10 kilometres southwest of Münster at 14.15 hours.*

Wellington R3170 of 99 Squadron, Newmarket, shot down attacking the shipyards at Kiel. The crew; Pilot Officer R. A. G. Willis, Pilot Officer Perkins, Sergeant K. A. R. MacArthur and Sergeant C. J. Scanlon were taken prisoner, but Sergeant G. F. Sexton was killed and is buried in the Amsterdam New Eastern Cemetery.

Saturday 6th July

DULL AND OVERCAST, RAIN IN THE NORTH.

ENEMY AIR ACTIVITY

Another quiet day with only reconnaissance aircraft operating over the UK.

COASTAL COMMAND

1. Two Blenheims of 254(F) Squadron took off from Sumburg at 08.30 hours to back a Fleet Air Arm Skua raid on Bergen by acting as air escort to the cruisers *Southampton* and *Coventry* and four destroyers. Fifty miles from Stavanger they rendezvoused with the naval Force but at 10.00 hours, four miles further north, they were 'jumped' by four Bf110s which carried out stern attacks out of sun. The Blenheims had no chance, being completely surprised. L8842, the aircraft piloted by Sergeant Tubbs, was hit in the port petrol tank and the starboard oil tank and he was forced to ditch his Blenheim near the destroyer *HMS Cossack*. Blenheim N3604, being flown by Pilot Officer Pattison, was shot down and crashed into the sea on fire.
2. Five Blenheims of 53 Squadron, Detling, attacked invasion barges at Ijmuiden claiming success.
3. Sunderland P9601 of 10 (RAAF) Squadron and 'E' of 210 Squadron operating from Oban dropped bombs and depth charges on a suspected U-Boat, but there was no visible result.
4. A Photographic Development Unit Spitfire operating with Coastal Command, piloted by Fight Lieutenant Wilson, secured pictures of Hardanger Fjord from 34,000 ft.

Blenheims of 254 Squadron approach the Norwegian coast on one of their many patrols in this area during the Battle of Britain period.

BOMBER COMMAND

1. Nineteen Blenheims of 2 Group were detailed to carry out daylight attacks on airfields in France and Belgium and on invasion barges at Zwolle (Holland) but only three bombed because of the lack of suitable cloud cover.

Night Operations

1. The weather at night was filthy, but twenty-two Wellingtons were detailed to attack the docks and petrol stores at Emden, Bremen and Hamburg. Severe icing was experienced and only six were able to bomb.
2. Ten Whitleys were dispatched to bomb warships believed to be in Kiel harbour, but also because of the adverse weather only three bombed.
3. Eleven Hampdens planted mines in German waters.

OPERATIONAL LOSSES

Blenheim R3662 of 18 Squadron, West Raynham, detailed to attack airfields in France, failed to return. The crew; Pilot Officer B. A. Davidson, Sergeant J. Gilmour and Sergeant R. J. Fisk, were taken prisoners of war. *Caught west of Rotterdam by a Bf109E of 2./JG 54, this bomber was claimed by Feldwebel Alfred Schunk*

Blenheim L8842 of 254 Squadron, Sumburg, was shot down off Stavanger by four Bf110s of *3./ZG76* and was credited to Leutnant Zickler. A ditching was carried out and the crew, Sergeant A. W. Tubbs, R. A. MacVeigh and A. C. Johnston were picked up by a boat from *HMS Cossack*. Unfortunately Sergeant MacVeigh died from his wounds and was buried at sea. Sergeants Tubbs and Johnston were put ashore at Rosyth.

Blenheim N3640 of 254 Squadron, Sumburg, was shot down near Stavanger by Bf109s of 4./JG77 and crashed into the sea on fire, victim to Oberleutnant Wilhelm Moritz. The crew consisted of Pilot Officer V. J. Pattison, Sergeant R. D. Maclaren and Sergeant A. P. Savage. Pilot Officer Pattison's body was not recovered, but the two NCOs were picked up by HMS Fortune and put ashore at Rosyth. Sergeant MacLaren suffered burns to his hands and arms but Sergeant Savage was uninjured.

Wellington R3236 of 37 Squadron, Feltwell, took off at 22.00 hours to attack Bremen and was last heard on W/T at 00.55 hours SW of Borkum (Frisian Islands). The crew; Flying Officer D. W. Lindsay, Pilot Officer R. A. A. Ball, Sergeant A. Aitken Sergeant J. H. Waterfall DFM, and Sergeant A. Glen were subsequently reported buried in Sage War Cemetery, Oldenburg, west of Bremen.

Whitley N1523 of 102 Squadron, Driffield, detailed to attack Kiel failed to return. The crew; Pilot Officer J. M. Lewis, Pilot Officer D. F. M. MacKarness, Sergeant J. Fisk, Sergeant L. Askham and Sergeant S. Fieldhouse were all captured, but in 1943 Pilot Officer Lewis was struck by a train and killed. He is buried in Poznan Old Garrison Cemetery, Poland.

Sunday 7th July

Today was a busy day for all of the Hudson squadrons. Here a 224 Squadron Hudson cruises over the sea in search of enemy shipping.

ENEMY AIR ACTIVITY

Activity was centered around a convoy steaming up the English Channel. Luftwaffe aircraft shadowed the convoy all day until a heavy raid was launched in the evening by Do17s of KG2. One ship was sunk and three others damaged as the convoy passed Dover.

COASTAL COMMAND

This proved to be a busy day for Hudson squadrons.

1. At 05.20 hours aircraft of 220 Hudson Squadron, Thornaby, attacked three small mine-sweepers 12 miles NNW of Terschelling.
2. Aircraft '7' and 'M' Hudsons of 233 Squadron, Leuchars, attacked shipping off Obrestad.
3. Aircraft 'W' of 233 Squadron, Leuchars, attacked a group of three destroyers and six motor vessels forty miles off Karmo. They luckily escaped the attentions of an intercepting Bf110.
4. Sunderland P9600 10 (RAAF) Squadron on patrol found a Swedish motor vessel which had been torpedoed. The Sunderland 'stood by' while an RN destroyer affected rescue.
5. Sunderland N9048 10 (RAAF) squadron found a sinking Portuguese tanker and lifeboat. The Sunderland reported and gave cover.

Night Operations

Six Blenheims of 53 Squadron, Detling, carried out a night attack on shipping at Brest.

Two Blenheims of 59 Squadron, Thorney Island, attacked the motor vessel Condorcet near Brest.

BOMBER COMMAND

1. Twenty-four Blenheims of 2 Group were detailed to reconnoitre and attack airfields and invasion barges in France and Belgium. Adverse weather conditions resulted in only three bombing, two failing to return and the rest aborting.

Night Operations

1. Twelve Wellingtons, twelve Whitleys and eighteen Hampdens carried out night raids. The Wellingtons attacked docks at Wilhelmshaven and the marshalling yards at Osnabrük and Gremberg. The Whitleys attacked the shipyards at Kiel and the marshalling yards at Hamm. The Hampdens attacked Frankfurt, Soest, Duisburg and Dortmund-Ems. A further eleven Hampdens carried out mine-laying.

Sunderland P9600 RB-E of 10 (RAAF) Squadron which came across a torpedoed Swedish vessel on this day.

Sunday 7th July

OPERATIONAL LOSSES

Blenheim R3896 of 15 Squadron, Wyton, detailed to reconnoitre the Ghent region (Belgium) crashed near Bruges. The crew; Pilot Officer H. C. M. Bamber, Sergeant J. Holdsworth and Sergeant G. Reid were all killed and buried in the Bruges General Cemetery. *This was almost certainly the bomber claimed by Feldwebel Georg Kiening of 6./JG 54.*

Blenheim P4843 of 82 Squadron, Watton, detailed for operations in NW Germany failed to return. The crew; Sergeant F. Hutton, Sergeant C.W. Pickering and Sergeant J. A. Rogers were subsequently reported as killed. All are buried in the Reichswald Forest War Cemetery. *They fell to a Bf109 of 3./JG 26 flown by Feldwebel Fw Wilhelm Müller for his fourth victory.*

Hampden P4390 of 61 Squadron, Hemswell, detailed to attack targets on the Dortmund-Ems Canal was shot down by Flak at Nordhorn, Germany. Three of the crew, Flight Lieutenant E. C. S. Fewtrell, Sergeant E. V. Gawith and Sergeant K. B. Wood were taken prisoner, but Pilot Officer J. Eadie was killed and is buried in the Reichswald Forest War Cemetery. Sergeant Wood was later repatriated.

Hampden L4066 of 83 Squadron, Scampton, detailed to attack Frankfurt crashed three miles NE of Clacton, Essex. Three of the crew, Pilot Officer O. H. Launders, Sergeant C. R. Hallet and Sergeant B. Kinton were killed in the crash. The fourth member, Sergeant L. Howard, survived the crash but died later from his injuries.

SHOT DOWN

Sergeant Ken Wood
Wireless Operator Hampden P4390 61 Sqn

I arrived at 61 Squadron early in 1940 as Sgt. Wop/Ag. later W/O. After a number of operations - Bremen, Kassel, North Sea enemy shipping etc., our crew consisting of pilot-Flt Lt 'Fanny' Fewtrell, nav-P/O Eadie, lower rear gunner-Sgt. Gawaith and myself, were briefed to drop a mine in the aqueduct on the Dortmund-Ems canal, supposedly from 50ft but in fact, just skimming the water.

We followed the canal for miles and reached the target without incident. However, with bomb doors open and the drop point coming up, we were suddenly met with 4x20mm anti-aircraft batteries; and they didn't miss! Eadie dropped the mine and at that moment our port engine was hit fair and square.

Fanny managed to pull up to a dangerous 'bale-out' height and we evacuated without delay. Unfortunately, P/O Eadie didn't manage to get through the escape hatch in the nose and sadly perished when the plane crashed a couple of miles away. The rest of us travelled around unable to move far because 'Fanny' hurt his back when he baled out and inevitably we were picked up by the local police at the crash site.

I subsequently spent almost five years in various prison camps, but that's another story.....

The upper rear gunner's position in a Hampden, manned by the wireless operator.

A Spitfire of the Photographic Development Unit, (PDU) which was renamed today as the more commonly known Photographic Reconnaisance Unit, (PRU).

ENEMY AIR ACTIVITY

Convoy attacks continued with fighter versus fighter combats increasing, resulting in the loss of four Bf109s to RAF fighters.

COASTAL COMMAND

The Spitfire Photographic Development Unit was renamed and would now function under Coastal Command as the Photographic Reconnaissance Unit.

1. Sunderland L5800 of 201 Squadron, Sullom Voe, co-operated with an RN destroyer attacking a U-Boat, but without result.
2. Hudson 'O' of 233 Squadron, Leuchars, attacked a force of four destroyers and a motor vessel one hundred and eleven miles from Lister Light (Norway).
3. Hudson 'M' also of 233 Squadron attacked two mine-sweepers seven miles from Lisdenes.
4. Hudson 'D' of 220 Squadron, Thornaby, attacked three fishing vessels, thirty-two miles from Lotberg.
5. Hudson 'F' of 206 Squadron, Bircham Newton, attacked the motor vessel Willemsoord off the Dutch coast.
6.A Hudson of 206 Squadron fought Bf109s near Willemsoord and escaped and a Blenheim was claimed by Ofw. Maximilian Stotz of 4./JG 54 south of Rotterdam.

BOMBER COMMAND

1. Forty-four Blenheims of 2 Group carried out daylight raids against airfields at Ledegham, Soissons, Douai and barge concentrations at Goringhem, Pappendreck and Zwolle. Lack of suitable cloud cover resulted in only twenty-four of the forces carrying out their tasks.

Night operations

A total of fifty-two aircraft carried out night operations. Twenty-eight Wellingtons attacked shipyards at Hamburg, oil targets at Wilhelmshaven, Marshalling yards at Hamm and industrial targets at Essen and Düsseldorf. Twelve Whitleys attacked the shipyards at Kiel and Evere airfield. Five of them from 10 Squadron were carrying out the squadron's last raid from Dishforth. It was planned they would return to the new base of Leeming, where they would have the 'luxury' of using concrete runways instead of the mud and grass of Dishforth. Thirty four out of the bombing force bombed. Twelve Hampdens carried out minelaying.

OPERATIONAL LOSSES

Whitley N1496 of 10 Squadron, detailed to attack Kiel shipyards, was shot down into the sea off Heligoland by Feldwebel Herrmann Förster of 8./NJG 1. The crew; Flight Lieutenant D. A. Ffrench-Mullen, Pilot Officer W. A. K. Carr, Sergeant P. R. Donaldson, AC1 A. G. W. Miller and Sergeant J. P. Atkinson were subsequently reported as PoWs. They did not get back to Leeming, but they survived their incarceration.

Tuesday 9th July

MAINLY SUNNY IN THE SOUTH, CLOUDIER IN THE NORTH.

A 21 Squadron Blenheim photographed during the summer of 1940. The squadron suffered appaling losses on this day during a disastrous daylight raid on the Norwegian airfield at Stavanger.

ENEMY AIR ACTIVITY

Two large raids of over 70 aircraft were launched against convoys in the Channel. A third raid later in the day saw Portland once again receiving the attention of Ju87 Stukas.

COASTAL COMMAND

1. Flying Officer Taylor in Spitfire R6598 of the Photographic Reconnaissance Unit, Heston, took off, refuelled at Coltishall, then carried out the longest PR sortie to date, photographing Bremen, Delmenhorst, Leeuwarden and Wilhelmshaven.
2. Ansons of 612 Squadron Dyce, searched for the Finnish ship *Lahti,* and investigated a Dutch ship which had left its convoy under suspicious circumstances. They also searched for the survivors of a downed Blenheim.
3. Blenheims of 53 Squadron, Detling, attacked E-Boats in Boulogne Harbour.

Night operations

1. Hudsons of 220 Squadron, Thornaby, 224 Squadron, Leuchars, and 269 Squadron, Wick, carried out a night strike against bridges and an ammunition dump near Bergen.

BOMBER COMMAND (WITH COASTAL COMMAND SQUADRONS)

1. Twelve Blenheims from 21 and 57 Squadrons, Lossiemouth, attacked Stavanger airfield in daylight. Seven failed to return.
2. Three Blenheims of 82 Squadron, Watton, were detailed to carry out meteorological reconnaissance in daylight. Only one was able to carry out its task because of the lack of suitable cloud cover protection.
3. Two Blenheims of 110 Squadron, Wattisham, were detailed to carry out Meteorological Reconnaissance over Holland in daylight, but were unable to do so because of the lack of suitable cloud cover protection.
4. Two Blenheims of 114 Squadron, Horsham St Faith, detailed to attack an aircraft factory in daylight failed to do so because of the lack of suitable cloud cover protection.
5. Six Blenheims of 15 and 40 Squadrons, Wyton, were dispatched to attack French airfields. Only one was successful because of lack of cloud cover.
6. Another Blenheim of 40 Squadron, Wyton, was detailed to reconnoitre the Calvados area but failed to return.

Night Operations

1. Twenty-seven Wellingtons were detailed to carry out night attacks on shipyards at Bremen and marshalling yards at Hamm, Osnabrük and Soest. The weather was atrocious and they were recalled, but eight pressed on and bombed.
2. Sixteen Hampdens were detailed to attack the *Tirpitz* at Wilhelmshaven and canals in NW Germany. Fifteen bombed.
3. Another twelve Hampdens were detailed for minelaying. Ten were successful. The Whitleys had a night off - thanks to the weather.

OPERATIONAL LOSSES

Blenheim R3637 of 59 Squadron, Thorney Island, blew up at 03.00 hours on patrol near Cardiff. Pilot Officer A. D. Hopkin, Sergeant T. J. Rowles and Sergeant J. Falconer are all commemorated on the Runnymede Memorial.

Hudson N7377 of 233 Squadron, Leuchars, failed to return from a sortie. Shot down by Oberfeldwebel Schob of 3./ZG76 off Shetland. The crew; Pilot Officer L. J. E. Ewing, Pilot Officer R. M. Buchanan, Sergeant D. C. Sinclair and Sergeant R. G. Ireland all missing believed killed and commemorated on the Runnymede Memorial.

Sunderland N6133 of 201 Squadron, Sullom Voe, failed to return from patrol. Shot down by Leutnant Böhmel of 3./ZG76, 90 miles SW of Sumburgh Head, Shetland. The crew; Flight Lieutenant J. D. Middleton, Pilot Officer D. M. Harry, Pilot Officer J. Seeds, Sergeant L. E. Worthington, LACs M. J. E. Jarvis, J. H. Lane, R. H. F. Hammond and J. F. Hindle and AC1s J. B. Belderson and P. Clark are all missing believed killed and commemorated on the Runnymede Memorial.

Blenheim L8836 of 40 Squadron, Wyton, presumably lost over the English Channel. The bodies of Squadron Leader R. H. Batt DFC and Sergeant P. F. Miles were recovered and identified by *HMS Brilliant* before being committed back to the sea. The third member, Sergeant A. Spencer DFM was never found. All are commemorated on the Runnymede Memorial. *This was credited to Unteroffizier Eduard Hemmerling of 6./JG 51, who claimed it northwest of Cap Griz Nez at 07.55 hours.*

A SURVIVOR'S TALE

Sgt James Dunnet, Blenheim Observer 57 Sqn.

I remember vividly limping back over the North Sea on one engine and hoping that we would not have to ditch. As we were gradually losing height, I gave the pilot a course for Dyce (Aberdeen). Coming into land, some fool in an Anson started to take off right in front of us. My pilot yanked down the emergency nine boost lever and hauled back on the stick. There was no way he could control the tremendous torque from the one engine, and the Blenheim just rolled over. It was a strange experience for me. Just before we hit the ground, my pilot shouted 'Goodbye' and crossed his arms over his face. Sitting beside him, I watched the ground rush up and the, now well known, slow motion effect materialised. I watched the nose of the plane hit the ground and the Mk 9 bombsight crumble towards me. I thought, 'This is how I'm going to die'. I had no fear. It was a total disassociation of personality, complete detachment. Then I was conscious of being racked from side to side, tremendous noise, stones, dirt, all sorts of rubble flying about, then nothing but the realisation that I was still alive. All the crew survived.

Stavanger Raid

Blenheim L8872 of 21 Squadron took off from Lossiemouth at 08.00 hours to bomb Stavanger and was lost without trace. The crew; Flight Lieutenant J. W. D. Murray, Sergeant W. Hartley and Sergeant G. E. Duck are commemorated on the Runnymede Memorial.

Blenheim N3619 of 21 Squadron lost without trace on the same operation. The crew; Pilot Officer W. D. Macley, Sergeant W. L. Rawson and Sergeant J. B. Dorrington are commemorated on the Runnymede Memorial.

Blenheim R3732 also of 21 Squadron on the Stavanger operation crashed into the sea. The crew; Wing Commander L. C. Bennett is buried at Lonstrup Churchyard Denmark, while the names of Sergeant A. T. Summers and Sergeant C. J. Burt are on the Runnymede Memorial.

Blenheim R3822 of 21 Squadron also lost on the Stavanger operation without trace. The crew; Pilot Officer J. A. Heath-Brown, Sergeant W. A. Hamlyn and Sergeant E. Williams are commemorated on the Runnymede Memorial.

Blenheim. R3876 of 21 Squadron also on the Stavanger operation, crashed into the sea. The crew; Sergeant J. B. M. Brown is buried in the Trondheim (Stavne) Cemetery, Norway. Sergeant C. D. Stevens and Sergeant J. Morton have no known graves and are commemorated on the Runnymede Memorial.

Blenheim R3750 of 57 Squadron, Lossiemouth, also lost without trace on the Stavanger operation. The crew; Pilot officer R. A. Hopkinson, Sergeant J. G. Andrew and Sergeant G. A. Miles are commemorated on the Runnymede Memorial.

Blenheim R3847 of 57 Squadron, Lossiemouth, also lost without trace on the Stavanger operation. The crew; Sergeant F. G. Mills, Sergeant S. J. Newcombe and Sergeant T. J. Jervis are commemorated on the Runnymede Memorial.

The above losses emphasise the futility of unescorted bomber operations in daylight.
Their opponents were Bf109E pilots from II./JG 77 and Bf110C crews from I./ZG 76 The JG 77 pilots made eight claims: Leutnant Horst Carganico of the Gruppenstab and Oberleutnant Berthold Jung of 5 Staffel claimed two apiece, While Oberleutnant Heinz Deuschle, Feldwebel Werner Petermann, Oberfeldwebel. Robert Menge and Gefreiter Rudolf Schmidt, all of 5./JG 77, claimed one each. Another was claimed by a Bf110 pilot, Unteroffizier Fresia of I./ZG 76.

Wednesday 10th July

RAIN EVERYWHERE BUT THE SOUTH-EAST.

An 82 Squadron Blenheim is prepared for its next sortie.

ENEMY AIR ACTIVITY

This was the day, according to official sources, when the Battle of Britain really began and the Luftwaffe launched heavy bombing attacks on our shipping off the south Kent coast. The bombers were escorted by fighters with the aim of luring our fighters into combat. A particularly heavy attack developed later in the day, but only one vessel, the motor vessel *Waterloo* was sunk north-east of Smith's Knolls Bay. Shipping in Falmouth harbour and industrial targets at Swansea was also bombed by a force of sixty-three Ju88s. The motor vessel *Tascalusa* was sunk and the *British Chancellor* was damaged at Falmouth. Civilian casualties were suffered during the attack on Swansea.

During the day's fighting Fighter Command lost one Spitfire and destroyed eight Luftwaffe aircraft.

COASTAL COMMAND

1. Two Blenheims of 59 Squadron, Thorney Island, carried out a reconnaissance of the French coast between Le Havre and Cherbourg. One crashed on return, in Shropshire.
2. Hudson 'T' of 22 Squadron, Leuchars, on North Sea patrol, encountered and engaged a Do18, eighty-two miles east of Kinnaird's Head. After a brief engagement during which the Hudson *WOp/AG* was wounded the enemy aircraft turned tail.
3. Hudson 'K' of 206 Squadron, Bircham Newton, engaged raiders attacking the south bound east coast convoy it was escorting.
4. An Anson crew of 612 Squadron, Dyce, on convoy escort reported that the Dutch motor vessel Alwaki was listing and had drawn away from the convoy. An hour and a half later another Anson crew reported the ship to be sinking fifteen miles east of Cape Wrath. Three lifeboats full of survivors were picked up by another motor vessel.

Night operations

1. Anson 'F' of 500 Squadron, Detling, carried out a night reconnaissance over Dunkirk and Dieppe. It crashed on return.

BOMBER COMMAND

Forty Blenheims were detailed to carry out various tasks in daylight. Their targets included airfields at Glissy (Amiens), St. Omer, Stavanger (Norway), docks at Bremen, industrial targets in the Ruhr and meteorological reconnaissance over Holland. It turned out to be an unproductive and, for 107 Squadron, most unfortunate day. Out of the forty aircraft participating, only five completed the tasks, thirty abandoned them and five failed to return.

It was tragically reminiscent of previous daylight raids which were inflicted on the Blenheim crews who were unable to cope with German fighters and Flak. It is sad to report that the crews, whose courage and raw guts were unsurpassed, were lost like this time after time. The 107 Squadron detail to bomb Glissy airfield is an example.

The squadron force of six aircraft was led by Squadron Leader Harold Percival Pleasance with his crew of Pilot Officer Etherington (*Observer*) and Sergeant Price (*WOp/AG*). They took off at 11.40 hours from Wattisham and set course for Glissy, the base of *I/Zerstorergeschwader 2* that was equipped with Bf110s. After two hours the Blenheim formation approached their target at 7,000 feet, as they did so the German Flak defences opened up putting up a wall of tracer, incendiary and shrapnel shells.

The Blenheims fought to keep in formation but were driven apart as they got near to the airfield. Etherington saw four Bf110s parked on the north side of the of the field as his bombs exploded near one of the hangars. As the scattered Blenheims turned away from the target they were set upon by nine Bf109s. Sergeant Price opened fire as two of them singled out his machine. The other seven Messerschmitts engaged the rest of the formation. As Pleasance headed north the two fighters continued to attack him, scoring hits. They finally broke off when they were some thirty miles out over the Channel. Pleasance set course for Wattisham where they landed three hours and ten minutes after taking off. As they surveyed the damage inflicted on their Blenheim they waited for their comrades to return or news that they had landed at other airfields, but none came. They were the only crew to get back.

The force had been engaged by Bf109E pilots from 9./JG 3, who claimed Blenheims as follows between 14.25 and 14.40 hours: Hauptmann Dr Albrecht Ochs, Leutnant Franz Achleitner (two) plus Oberfeldwebel Hans Heitmann and Unteroffizier Otto Wessling (one each), all near Arras, Unteroffizier Helmut Struve and Feldwebel Hans Stechmann one apiece near Le Touquet. A little later Leutnant Lenz of I.(J)./LG 2 claimed another west of Le Touquet.

Night Operations
All night operations were cancelled because of adverse weather.

Five Blenheims of 107 Squadron were lost today attacking Glissy airfield in what again bordered on a 'suicide' mission.

OPERATIONAL LOSSES

Blenheim R3881 'A' of 59 Squadron, Thorney Island, crashed on the Clee Hill, Shropshire. The crew; Pilot Officer J. Rex, Sergeant J. S. Jeffery, and Sergeant J. W. Liddle, were all killed.

Anson 'F' of 500 Squadron, Detling, crashed at Sternham near Detling. The crew; Sergeants J. Wilson, W. G. Shier, L. F. J. O'Kelly and H. G. Worton were all killed.

Blenheim L9468 of 107 Squadron, Wattisham, lost attacking Glissy airfield. The aircraft crashed at Aigneville, SW of Abbeville. The crew; Pilot Officer H. L. Atkin-Berry, Sergeant R. D. Cook and Sergeant F. Mercer were all killed.

Blenheim R3916 of 107 Squadron, Wattisham, shot down attacking Glissy airfield. The crew; Pilot Officer J. P. North-Lewis, Sergeant R. V. Lonsdale and Sergeant B. R. George were subsequently reported as PoWs.

Blenheim R3815 of 107 Squadron, Wattisham, lost attacking Glissy airfield. The crew; Pilot Officer E. A. Wray, Sergeant G. T. Drew and Sergeant S. M. Wood, lost without trace. They are all commemorated on the Runnymede Memorial.

Blenheim P6894, 107 Squadron, Wattisham, lost attacking Glissy airfield. The aircraft crashed at Cavillon, WNW of Amiens. The crew; Pilot Officer T. W. Maslin, Sergeant G. T. Truscott and Sergeant S. E. Hinton were killed and all are buried in the Communal Cemetery at Cavillon.

Blenheim R3606, 107 Squadron, Wattisham, shot down attacking the airfield at Glissy. The crew; Sergeant S. L. Bain, Sergeant G. C. G. Hawkins and Sergeant G. A. Allison were all made PoWs. Sergeant Hawkins was killed on 19th April 1945 by Allied fighter-bombers when marching. He is buried in the Berlin 1939/1945 War Cemetery.

Thursday 11th July

LOW CLOUD IN THE SOUTH, HEAVY RAIN AND THUNDER IN THE NORTH.

Left: The Heinkel 59 shot down by P/O Webb's Anson sits on the waves after a succesful forced landing. Note the broken port float and the crew boarding their dinghy under the fuselage.

ENEMY AIR ACTIVITY

The Luftwaffe carried out a number of raids on targets in the south and east during the morning. A force of approximately fifty aircraft approached Portland from the Channel Islands. Ten of the raiders were claimed to have been destroyed.

COASTAL COMMAND

1. At 06.00 hours, the Sunderland crew of N9050 of 10 RAAF Squadron, Mount Batten, on patrol reported a Norwegian motor vessel sinking and that the crew were in two lifeboats.
2. At 06.51 hours, the crew of Sunderland 'H' of 210 Squadron, Oban, dropped four 250lb AS Bombs on a U-Boat at 49042'N/08018'W.
3. Two Blenheims of 59 Squadron ('E' and 'P'), Thorney Island, looking for E-Boats in the English Channel discovered and attacked a Do17 twenty miles off Cherbourg. The combat ended when the enemy aircraft left the area trailing black smoke. The Blenheim crews claimed that it was unlikely that the bomber would get back to base and that it was highly likely that the rear gunner was either wounded or dead.
4. During the morning, Flight Sergeant Webb and his crew, Pilot Officer Swift (*navigator*), Sergeant Botha (*gunner*), and AC. Holiday (*WOp*) in an Anson of 217 Squadron, St. Eval, were detailed to intercept an enemy aircraft, believed to be twenty miles from Start Point.

The Anson was originally designed as a navigation trainer and communications aircraft, but come the war it was equipped with a gun turret on the mid-upper fuselage armed with a single 303 VGO machine gun and another hand-held VGO in the navigator's position. It was also fitted to carry two hundred pounds of bombs. Its cruising speed was only 135 mph but even so several of the Anson equipped squadrons committed them to combat operations and on several occasions they gave a good account of themselves and they also suffered casualties.

At 10.11 hours Flight Sergeant Webb and his crew intercepted a German He59 float plane of the *Seenotflugcommando 1*. Webb's gunners, Pilot Officer Swift and Sergeant Botha opened fire on it and after expending a considerable amount of ammunition which scored hits, caused the He59 to land on the sea. As the crew evacuated the aircraft and boarded a rubber dinghy, AC. Holiday informed St. Eval by W/T. Two destroyers put out from Plymouth and three Blenheims of 236 Squadron took off from St. Eval to escort them. On the way, Pilot Officer Riley (one of the 236 escorts) sighted and engaged a Ju88. Riley's gunners used up all their ammunition claiming hits, but the bomber escaped.
Thirty minutes later, Pilot Officer MacDonough and his crew in another one of the escorting Blenheims sighted and attacked another enemy bomber, but had to break off the fight when return fire damaged a wing and an engine. The incident finally ended when the destroyers reached the area and took the He59 crew into captivity.
5. A Blenheim of 53 Squadron, Detling, on coastal surveillance of French ports, braved the defences of Boulogne and dropped two 250lb bombs on a lock where twenty barges were tied up, then dived over the harbour at low level; machine gunned a flying-boat and dropped the remaining bombs on the Marine Parade, causing fires.
6. During the period 22.30 hrs to 23.40 hours, three Blenheims of 53 Squadron (N, P and F) carried out a night strike against shipping in Boulogne harbour.

BOMBER COMMAND

Forty Blenheims were detailed to attack various targets in daylight, but because of the unfavourable conditions most abandoned their tasks. Those who pressed on carried out single attacks on the airfields at Boulogne and Schipol. Of the five 82 Squadron aircraft detailed to attack the airfield at St. Omer, four turned back. The fifth crew pressed on and was shot down, falling to either Unteroffizier Robert Fuchs or Unteroffizier Kurt Hübel 7./JG 51

Night operations

Sixty-four 'heavies' were detailed to carry out night raids: Thirty-seven Wellingtons to Osnabrük, Hamm, Soest, Mannheim and one to Stettin; Eighteen Hampdens to Wanne-Eickel, Mundenheim and the Dortmund-Ems Canals; Eight Whitleys went to Leverkusen and Köln. The adverse weather conditions made navigation and target identification very difficult, but forty-five of the force bombed either primaries or alternatives. The 115 Squadron Wellington from Marham, which was supposed to carry out night photography, was burnt out when the photoflash was accidentally set off when loading. Three airmen were injured in the fire.

OPERATIONAL LOSSES

Anson N5220 'D' of 500 Squadron, Detling, failed to return from a patrol over the North Sea. Shot down by He111s at Pernis, Holland. The crew; Pilot Officer A. W. A. Whitehead, Pilot Officer A. R. Mathias and AC1 W. C. Hubbard were killed and are buried in the Crooswijk Cemetery, Rotterdam. Sergeant H. W. J. Smith was taken prisoner.

Blenheim L9474 'L' of 53 Squadron, Detling, target Leiden, abandoned at 21.03 hours on return over Essex and crashed at Bulphan. Wing Commander Edwards and his crew landed safely by parachute.

Blenheim R3690 of 82 Squadron, Watton, detailed to attack the airfield at St. Omer, was shot down near the target by Bf109s flown by Leutnant Stailer and Unteroffizier Hubel of III./JG51. The crew; Pilot Officer J. H. T. Palmer, Sergeant K. Howard, and Sergeant K. W. J. Farley were taken prisoner, but Palmer died on 6 December 1942 and is now buried in the Berlin 1939/1945 War Cemetery.

Hampden P4366 of 144 Squadron, Hemswell, detailed to attack Wanne-Eickel was hit by Flak and crashed near Kessel, Holland. The crew; Pilot Officer I. M. Hossack, Sergeant E. B. H. France, Sergeant E. D. Leamy and Sergeant C. Rose, were all killed and are buried in the Jonkerbos War Cemetery, Nijmegen.

Wellington L7805 of 149 Squadron, Mildenhall, detailed to bomb naval installations at Bremen, failed to return. The crew; Pilot Officer J. S. Torgalson, Pilot Officer J. A. Rose, Sergeant J. W. Craig, Sergeant J. V. Futcher, Sergeant C. Suggett and Pilot Officer C. W. Howie were all killed and are buried in the Reichswald Forest War Cemetery.

Whitley N1424 of 58 Squadron, Linton-on-Ouse, target Leverkusen, crashed near Antwerp, Belgium, killing the entire crew: Sergeant F. Young, Sergeant D. B. Hopes, Sergeant L. Isherwood, Sergeant B. M. Bennett and Sergeant N Emmerson are all buried in the local Schoonselhof Cemetery.

Pilot Officer N H Webb

Nelson Henry Webb joined the RAF in 1932 as an Aircraft Apprentice and trained as a Wireless Mechanic at the Electrical and Wireless School at RAF Cranwell. He graduated in 1935 and after a brief spell with No. 9 Squadron he was posted to 214 (Virginia) Squadron with which he re-mustered as WOP/AG. After eighteen months he was posted to Iraq and joined 70 (Valentia) Squadron. In 1937 he was elected for training as an airman (sergeant) pilot and returned to England to train on Tiger Moths at Perth. He gained an above average assessment and was sent in June 1938 to 9 FTS for multi engine training. On completion of the course he was awarded his wings in September 1938 and promoted to sergeant.

He completed advanced training in photography, reconnaissance, bombing and gunnery for which he received above average assessment and a rarely awarded distinguished pass. He was posted to No. 217 (Anson) Squadron, Coastal Command in May 1939. With the threat of war, training was stepped up and when it broke out on the 3rd September 1939, he started his operational career on the following day with the first of his many coastal patrols.

By February 1940 he had completed thirty-three convoy patrols and been awarded a MID. During July he and his crew shot down a German He59 float-plane. Although it was displaying a Red Cross it was carrying out reconnaissance over our convoys and was considered by Air Ministry to be hostile.

He continued escort duties during the Battle of Britain and on two occasions carried out bombing and strafing attacks on surfaced U-Boats forcing them to crash dive. In September he was awarded the Distinguished Flying Medal and commissioned. During the month, along with other members of No. 217 they carried out a night attack on shipping in Brest Harbour. Despite the cloud cover they bombed from between four and ten thousand feet, but results were not observed. This was Webb's 80th operational 'trip' and his final sortie in Ansons.

He converted onto Beauforts and resumed operations on the 1st December with another raid on Brest. He followed this with six similar attacks on the Atlantic ports including Lorient and Brest (again). On the 17th. December he took part in a raid from low level and saw his bombs burst in the target area. He then flew over the enemy airfield at Merignac, where he and his gunner strafed a number of FW200 Condors.

On the 20th December, Webb and his crew took off on his 115th operation. They failed to return. His aircraft crashed near Lorient. Pilot Officer N. H. Webb, DFM, MID, Sergeant Tiplady and Sergeant Milligan were all buried with full Military Honours in Lanester Cemetery.

ENEMY AIR ACTIVITY

Low Clouds and stormy conditions over the British Isles deterred the Luftwaffe from bombing inland targets. Instead the convoy *'Booty'* steaming off the Essex coast towards the Thames Estuary came under heavy attack. Further north in Scotland a shipyard at Aberdeen was bombed. One of the attacking He111s from 9./KG26 was brought down and crashed into a newly completed ice rink which collapsed around it and buried both the machine and crew.

COASTAL COMMAND

1. Sunderland N9049 captained by Squadron Leader Pearce, 10 RAAF Squadron, Mount Batten, took off at 07.15 hours and carried out a reconnaissance of Bordeaux and St. Nazaire securing photographs. The flying boat was slightly damaged by Flak, but got back safely, landing at 19.00 hours, a 'flog' of eleven hours forty-five minutes spent mainly in enemy controlled airspace.
2. At 08.40 hours the crew of Anson 'L' 500 Squadron, Detling, captained by Pilot Officer Pain, was escorting convoy *'Booty'* when it was attacked by nine He111s. Despite the odds and its limited armament, the Anson crew took on the attackers and claimed to have shot one down before the Hurricanes of 17 Squadron arrived and shot down two more of the He111s.
3. Another Anson of 500 Squadron was escorting convoy F21 when it came under attack by six He111s and three Bf109s.
4. The Blenheims of 53 Squadron, Detling, and 59 Squadron, Thorney Island, were busy searching and striking. Aircraft 'U' of 53 Squadron, reconnoitring Belgian canals, found fifty barges north of Bruges and on the Ostend-Bruges canal as for south as Passchendaele. Barges were moored three deep on the south bend which stretched for eight miles. 'U' carried on to Dunkirk where they bombed three motor vessels before being driven off by five Bf109s. Blenheim 'U' of 59 Squadron bombed Cherbourg and suffered Flak damage. It was then attacked by no less than twelve Bf109s who pursued them and only broke off their attacks when they were five miles from the Isle of Wight.

BOMBER COMMAND

The weather conditions were considered unsuitable for daylight bombing operations by 2 Group Blenheims and only two reconnaissance sorties were carried out by 107 Squadron, Wattisham, to Bruges and Ostend.

Night operations

1. The adverse weather conditions continued and night operations by Wellingtons and Hampdens were cancelled, but twenty-four Whitleys were detailed, despite the weather, to carry out raids on the dockyards at Kiel and petrol storage sheds at Emden. One of the twelve for Emden failed to get off because of engine failure. The other eleven crews pressed on. When ten of them returned they reported a successful attack, as forty 5001b and fifty-nine 250 lb bombs had been dropped in the target area. Fires were started which could be seen seventy miles away.

The eleventh aircraft of 102 Squadron, captained by Sergeant Langton, was hit by Flak and the port engine put out of action. He set course for home gradually losing height and managed to keep his stricken bomber in the air for three and a half hours, before he was forced to ditch it in the North Sea, thirty-eight miles from Cromer. The wireless operator got off a last SOS for a radio fix before they went in. Langton carried out a successful ditching in the most difficult circumstances; on one engine, in the dark and into a turbulent sea. But *Sod's Law* took over when the crew scrambled out of the Whitley and launched the dinghy - it inflated upside down. Despite the conditions they got it righted and scrambled aboard. Luckily they did not have long to wait for rescue because, an hour later, they were picked by a trawler and taken into Yarmouth. Later, at debriefing, they reported that the Whitley had floated for twenty minutes after ditching. This was good news, for up to now it had been generally assumed that the Whitleys' propensity for floating resembled that of a house brick!

2. The raid on the dockyards at Kiel was unfortunately hindered by the obscuring cloud. Only four of the crews detailed were able to drop their bombs in the target area. Of the others, one returned early and the remaining seven, unable to find alternative targets, brought their bombs back.

OPERATIONAL LOSSES

Blenheim 'J' of 59 Squadron crashed on landing at Thorney Island as a result of the Flak damage and the combat with the German fighters. Of the crew, Pilot Officer R.W. Ayres was unharmed, but Sergeants Webb and Roper were wounded.

Above: Pilot Officer Ayres (left), Sgt. Webb (top) and Sgt. Roper (bottom) the 59 Sqn crew involved in the crash landing at Thorney Island.

Whitley N1502 of 102 Squadron, Driffield, ditched in the North Sea thirty-eight miles from Cromer. The crew; Sergeant R. T. Langton, Squadron Leader C. S. Bryan, Sergeant C. P. Coad, Sergeant G. Gibson and Sergeant C. Wood were rescued uninjured.

Saturday 13th July

Two Hudsons of 220 Squadron on patrol.

ENEMY AIR ACTIVITY

The weather once again dominated the pattern of operations. Conditions were so bad in the north of England that even the most 'press on' coastal crews were prevented from getting airborne. Further south it was better and the Luftwaffe continued attacks against coastal shipping. Off Portland and Dover convoys were bombed. Other raids were carried out against east coast and Isle of Wight installations. Fighter Command engaged eighteen of the enemy off Calais and claimed to have destroyed five of them.

COASTAL COMMAND

Although the weather curtailed the anti-invasion and anti-submarine patrols in the far north, operations further south continued.

1. The crew of Hudson 'F' of 220 Squadron, Thornaby, sighted and attacked two mine sweepers off the island of Terschelling at 05.38 hours. They made three dive-bombing and machine gun strafing attacks. In their last attack the bomb fell and exploded against the port bow of the ship it was attacking and caused it to heel over violently.

2. Several other crews on patrol saw enemy bombers attacking convoys. They were powerless to prevent them, but reported that the bombs missed their targets - a slight consolation.

3. Sunderland N9050 'D' of 10 RAAF Squadron, Mount Batten, captained by Squadron Leader *'Hoot'* Gibson was attacked by a Bf110 while on patrol eighty miles off Bishop's Rock at 15.00 hours. The flying boat sustained hits which punctured the port fuel tanks, but the Sunderland return fire caused the Messerschmitt to break off the attack with smoke pouring from its port engine. There were no casualties aboard the Sunderland, which got back to base safely.

4. At 15.34 hours Sunderland N9048 of 10 RAAF Squadron, Mount Batten, captained by Flight Lieutenant Cohen drove off an He111 approaching the convoy they were protecting.

5. Hudson 'B' of 220 Squadron, Thornaby, on patrol 113 miles from Flamborough Head on a bearing of 050 degrees, found a capsized He115, which had failed to get back from a reconnaissance sortie over the Thames Estuary. It was later established that Leutnant Dr. Steinert and Oberleutnant Zur See Hilderbrand were two crew members of the Reconnaissance unit 3./906. Another member of the crew, an SNCO, was rescued later by the German Air Sea Rescue Service, (*Seenotdienst*).

Night Operations

1. Blenheims of 53 Squadron, Detling, and 59 Squadron, Thorney Island, carried out a night strike against barges moored in the canals near Bruges. One of the 59 Squadron crews crashed into the sea of Shoreham on return and Pilot Officer Clark and his crew were killed. No other casualties were recorded.

BOMBER COMMAND OPERATIONS

1. Twenty-two 2 Group Blenheims were dispatched in daylight to carry out attacks on airfields in France, oil and industrial plants in the Ruhr and the ship-building yard at Hamburg. Once again lack of suitable cloud cover hindered their activities and twelve of them abandoned their tasks. Two crews of 82 Squadron got through to Monheim. One attacked an oil plant, but its bombs fell short. The other crew failed to return, as did another of the same squadron whose target was Hamburg. Other individual crews bombed barges at Bruges, the airfield at Evere and alternative targets.

Night Operations

1. Night attacks were scheduled for thirty Wellingtons to attack Bremen Duisburg-Ruhort, Hamm and Soest. The majority of crews claimed to have bombed the primaries or alternatives.

Saturday 13th July

An unusual view of a Whitley showing the isolated rear gunner's position.

2. Twenty-three Whitleys were detailed to attack Grevenbroich and Monheim. Twenty claimed to have bombed, but three were damaged by Flak. One of them, N1365 of 77 Squadron, Driffield, captained by Flying Officer J. A. Piddington, was hit by Flak over the target which resulted in on engine seizing up when they were over Holland. Piddington nursed the aircraft on its good engine over the North Sea and when they reached the English coast he ordered his observer, WOP/AG and rear gunner to bale out. They landed safely and Piddington, assisted by his second pilot, landed the aircraft successfully at Martlesham Heath.

The second Whitley, N1521, captained by Pilot Officer R. B. McGregor, also of 77 Squadron, was coned by searchlights and badly shot up causing them to jettison their bombs. They struggled back and managed a safe landing at Duxford in their damaged aircraft.

The third Whitley to be damaged by Flak was P4969 of 51 Squadron, Dishforth, captained by Flying Officer G. A. Lane, who managed to get his aircraft back to carry out a successful landing at Honington.

3. Forty-three Hampdens were detailed to attack the Dortmund-Ems Canal, Hamburg and Deichshausen, while another twelve were scheduled to sow mines in the Elbe Estuary. The Hampden force was hampered by low cloud and rain in their target area and only twenty-six bombed primaries, two bombed alternatives and fifteen brought their bombs back.

OPERATIONAL LOSSES

Blenheim R3665 'P' of 59 Squadron, Thorney Island, target Bruges. Fell into the sea 2 miles south of Saltdean, Sussex, at 02.22 hours. The bodies of Pilot Officer H. A. Clark, Sergeant D. D. Morton and Sergeant F. Clayton were all recovered from the sea.

Hudson N7231 of 220 Squadron, Thornaby, hit a balloon cable at Boldon Colliery, near Newcastle. The crew; Pilot Officer G. W. F. Carey, Pilot Officer P. K. Vartan, Sergeant V. G. Gent and Sergeant G. A. Matthews were all killed.

Blenheim R3701 of 82 Squadron, Watton, lost over the sea. The crew was Flight Lieutenant P. H. Lewis, Sergeant H. W. Richardson and Sergeant J. Newberry. The body of Sergeant Richardson was washed onto the Dutch island of Schiermonnikoog, where he is buried in the Vredenhof Cemetery. The bodies of Lewis and Newberry were not recovered and their names are on the Runnymede Memorial.

Blenheim R3756 of 82 Squadron, Watton, detailed to attack the shipyard at Hamburg, failed to return. Two members of the crew, Sergeant D. A. Adams and Sergeant A. Avery were later reported as PoWs, while the third, Sergeant A. Evans, is buried in the Hamburg Cemetery, Ohlsdorf.

**Three claims for Blenheims shot down were submitted by Bf109 pilots. Leutnant Gustav Denk of 6./JG52 claimed he had shot one down northwest of the island of Borkum, while Oberleutnant Schumann claimed he had shot one down at Brunsbüttelkoog and Leutnant Hermann Behrend of Stab./JG 1 claimed one in the same general area.*

Sunday 14th July

During the early days of the Battle of Britain, the Luftwaffe concentrated its efforts against convoys sailing off the coast of England. This day was typical with a formation of Stukas attacking this convoy off Dover.

ENEMY AIR ACTIVITY

Averse weather conditions, rain and low cloud hampered both the RAF and Luftwaffe flying operations, the Luftwaffe being restricted to an attack on our shipping off Dover in the afternoon. Some RAF reconnaissance and protection patrols over the North Sea were also affected.

COASTAL COMMAND

1. One search and strike patrol which did take place was flown by Hudsons of 220 Squadron, Thornaby.
2. Five Blenheims of 53 Squadron, Detling and six of 59 Squadron, Thorney Island, attempted to carry out the largest coastal strike of the day against oil and petrol storage tanks on the Ghent-Selzaette Canal. One 53 Squadron aircraft was lost and one of 59 Squadron was attacked by four Bf109s forty miles south of Selsey Bill. The navigator was wounded and the aircraft badly damaged, but the crew, captained by Pilot Officer Sanders, got it back to Thorney Island where it crash landed. There were no additional casualties.

BOMBER COMMAND

1. Six Blenheims of 114 Squadron, Horsham St. Faith, were dispatched in daylight to bomb targets in the Ruhr, while one of 110 Squadron, Wattisham, was detailed to carry out a photoreconnaissance of Kiel. Lack of suitable cloud cover forced both tasks to be abandoned.

Night operations

Night raids were carried out by thirty-five Wellingtons on Gelsenkirchen, Hamburg, Bremen, Hamm, Soest and Cologne. Twenty-two Whitleys went to Diepholz and Paderborn, while twelve Hampdens bombed Wezendorf and nine more laid mines in German waters. Most of the crews found their primary targets and claimed excellent results.

OPERATIONAL LOSSES

Blenheim N3551 of 53 Squadron, Detling, target Ghent, crashed at Eeklo, Belgium. Two of the crew, Flying Officer A. D. Panton DFC, and Sergeant A. E. Farrow were taken prisoner, but the third member, Sergeant L. H. Stride, was killed.

Wellington L7792 of 37 Squadron, Feltwell, lost attacking Hamburg. Three of the crew, Sergeant J. F. McCauley, Sergeant S. C. Kirkbride and Sergeant C. F. Read, were killed and are buried in the Becklingen War Cemetery, Saltau. The other members, Sergeant T. Johnson and Sergeant G. J. W. Grimson were taken prisoner.

Monday 15th July

DULL WITH LOW CLOUD.

ENEMY AIR ACTIVITY
Flying operations by both the RAF and the Luftwaffe continued to be restricted by the persistent rain and low cloud. A small battle took place over a convoy off the Thames Estuary and another was fought over a convoy near the Isle of Wight. Also South Wales and South West England were subject to sporadic German raids when bombs were dropped.

COASTAL COMMAND
1. Despite the weather some search and reconnaissance flights were carried out, but little was achieved. A single Hudson bombed Willemsford with four 200lb GP bombs and four incendiaries which started a large fire.
2. Other crews reported on the position of balloon barrages and shipping movements. Photographs taken on the 14th over Wilhelmshaven revealed that the warships *Admiral Scheer* and *Tirpitz* were berthed at Austrustungshaven and the Bauhaven respectively.
3. Sunderland P9063 of 10 RAAF Squadron, Mount Batten, captained by Flight Lieutenant Birch, while on convoy protection patrol at 14.30 hours, south of Bishop Rock sighted a ship being attacked by five He111s. Birch climbed the Sunderland up to 2,000 feet in an attempt to interrupt the attack, but was unable to do so. After completing their attack the Heinkels turned to the Sunderland whose front gunner opened fire causing one of them to turn, exposing its underside to further fire before reached the safety of cloud. The other Heinkels came in to attack the flying-boat, but were discouraged by fire from the four guns in its rear turret. They retired to a safe distance and shadowed the Sunderland for about ten minutes before leaving the area. While the Sunderland had suffered no damage one of the ships in the convoy, the 1,359 ton motor vessel, *City of Limerick*, sank later as a result of the Heinkels' attack.

BOMBER COMMAND
1. Seventeen Blenheims, three of 110 Squadron, Wattisham, twelve of 107 Squadron Wattisham and two of 18 Squadron, West Raynham were scheduled to carry out daylight raids on airfields in France and industrial targets in the Ruhr. All but four returned early because of adverse weather conditions. Two of the remaining crews pressed on and bombed Evreux and the other two bombed Lisieux, where incendiaries were seen to fail around a twin-engined aircraft.

Night operations
1. The night raids for the Blenheim, Wellington and Whitley squadrons were scrubbed because of adverse weather, but those for the 5 Group Hampdens went ahead as planned - twenty to bomb and twelve to carry out mine-laying. Bad weather, thunderstorms and low cloud caused navigation and target recognition difficulties, but six of the bombing force found and bombed the Misburg oil refinery at Hanover, where fires were started. The other crews bombed alternative targets; Paderborn aircraft park, Osnabrük, Dortmund, De Kooy and Nordeney airfields and blast furnaces at Hoorn and Hamborn. The mining force successfully laid mines in the Sound of Copenhagen. All aircraft returned safely.

OPERATIONAL LOSSES

None recorded

A single Hudson bombed Willemsford and started a large fire today.

Tuesday 16th July

The wreck of an 18 Sqn Blenheim (probably L9191) lies in a French field. Careful study of the photo would suggest that this was one of those abandoned during the Fall of France.

ENEMY AIR ACTIVITY

The weather conditions again precluded any operations of consequence in the early part of the day. In the evening a Luftwaffe raid was intercepted by our fighters off the Isle of Wight.

COASTAL COMMAND

Reconnaissance sorties were hampered by the poor visibility and only the following incidents were reported.

1. A Hudson crew had a brief but inconclusive engagement with an enemy aircraft seventy miles north-west of Kinnaird's Head.
2. Another Hudson crew came upon six submarines and thirteen mine-sweepers eighty-four miles north-east of Horns Reef at 19.00 hours. The attack that the Hudson crew carried out was unsuccessful as the submarines escaped by diving and the bombs aimed at the mine-sweepers missed.
3. Off the Shetland Isles a further Hudson rounded up ships of a scattered convoy and guided them on their way.
4. Off Barra Head, a Sunderland crew reported seeing a tanker in a convoy on fire.
5. Sunderland P9601 of 10 RAAF Squadron, Mount-Batten, carried out a depth charge attack on a suspected U-Boat 50.00'N/060.00'W, without obtaining a result.

BOMBER COMMAND

1. Fifteen Blenheim crews of 82 and 18 Squadrons were detailed to carry out daylight attacks on airfields and invasion barges in France early in the morning. Because of the appalling weather only four pressed on - the other eleven turned back. One of the four crews dropped bombs on St. Inglevert airfield and another found and attacked barges (estimated as two to three hundred moored three abreast) in the canals between Armentieres and Merville. One of their 250lb bombs scored a direct hit on a barge that sank in the canal. One aircraft of 18 Squadron was wrecked when it forced landed near Welwyn Garden City on return. Fortunately only one of the crew was slightly injured. Another aircraft of 18 Squadron failed to return.

Night operations

Because of the atrocious weather conditions all the night raids by the 'heavies' were cancelled - even the owls were walking. However, the 'M' Balloon Unit released fifty-six of their balloons (carrying 200,000 propaganda leaflets) which they hoped would drift over France and deposit the leaflets in the area abounded by St. Omer, Douai and Cambrai.

OPERATIONAL LOSSES

Blenheim L9251 of 18 Squadron, West Raynham, force landed near Welwyn Garden City returning from operations. Only one crew member of Pilot Officer Jones's crew was slightly injured.

Blenheim P6933 of 18 Squadron, West Raynham, on a sortie to attack French airfields was shot down northeast of Brugge by Feldwebel Georg Kiening 6./JG 54. The Blenheim crew, Sergeant A. St.J. Bunker is buried at Cement House Cemetery, Langemark-Poelkapelle, Belgium. Sergeant P. R. Harris and Sergeant J. F. Hatch are buried at Flushing (Vlissingen) Northern Cemetery.

Wednesday 17th July

CLOUDY WITH SOME RAIN.

A 59 Squadron Blenheim sits in the summer sun at Thorney Island.

ENEMY AIR ACTIVITY

Bad weather continued throughout the day, rain and drizzle restricting visibility. Luftwaffe operations were on a limited scale with scattered raids plotted from the Scottish to the Kent coasts.

COASTAL COMMAND OPERATIONS

The main incident of the day concerned a Blenheim of 59 Squadron, Thorney Island, captained by Pilot Officer Jackson. The crew was detailed to carry out an armed reconnaissance in daylight over Le Havre and Cherbourg and took off at 08.42 hours. By the afternoon the return ETA had expired and it was suspected the Blenheim might have come down in the sea. A flight of three Blenheims of 236 Squadron, 59 Squadron's sister squadron at Thorney Island, were sent out during the afternoon to sweep the area between Selsey Bill, Dungeness and Le Havre in the hope of finding the 59 Squadron crew. At 14.30 hours they sighted three German bombers identified as Ju87s or Ju88s and attacked them. The rear gunner of one of them was silenced and black smoke poured from another as the formation dived low over the sea and headed back for France. The downed 59 Squadron Blenheim was not found. Subsequent intelligence revealed it had been shot down by a Bf109 into the sea near Cherbourg at 14.30 hours.

2. That evening, six Blenheims of 53 Squadron, Detling, and four of 59 Squadron, Thorney Island, were sent to attack petrol storage tanks at Ghent. Six failed to find the target and the remainder bombed targets of opportunity.

BOMBER COMMAND OPERATIONS

1. Thirteen Blenheim crews of 2 Group were dispatched to carry out daylight attacks on airfields and barges. Only two managed to bomb barges at Enkhuizen on the Bruges Canal.

Night Operations

1. Because of the weather conditions night operations were restricted to seven Wellingtons tasked to attack an oil target at Gelsenkirchen, but only three bombed. There were no losses, but one aircraft of 149 Squadron crash landed at Mildenhall on return.

2. Another contribution to the night's operations was seven Blenheims sent to attack French airfields. Only one bombed the airfield at Morlaix, but a 15 Squadron crew attempted what was claimed as the first 'intruder' patrol over an airfield near Caen - without success.

3. Minelaying by three Hampdens in Friedrichshafen Bay was the only other operation of the night.

OPERATIONAL LOSSES

Blenheim R3694 of 59 Squadron, Thorney Island, on armed reconnaissance over Le Havre and Cherbourg, was shot down into the sea by a Bf109. It was claimed by Leutnant Hans-Folkert Rosenboom of III./JG27 off Cherbourg at 11.30 hours. Pilot Officer A. K. Jackson and Sergeant R. V. Kingshott were posted missing. Sergeant J. A. Hunter's body was recovered from the sea and buried at Cayeux-sur-Mer.

An Avro Anson of 500 Squadron had a running battle with a swarm of Messerschmitt Bf110s, claiming one as destroyed.

ENEMY AIR ACTIVITY

The weather improved, but only slightly, with rain and low cloud persisting which hindered operations. However at 09.30 hours British radar detected a build-up of some thirty German aircraft near Calais. The early warning enabled three fighter squadrons to head off the force, but not before the East Goodwin Light Vessel had been sunk.

COASTAL COMMAND OPERATIONS

1. In spite of the bad weather very few patrols and reconnaissance sorties were cancelled and the Blenheim, Hudson and Anson crews were able to bring information to up-date the movement of enemy shipping and barge concentrations around the coasts of North Europe. A PRU Spitfire carried out a low level photographic sortie over Flushing during which it avoided the attentions of an intercepting Ju88.

2. Two of the Blenheim fighter squadrons, 235 and 236, were transferred from Fighter Command to operate with Coastal Command throughout the official period of the Battle of Britain. They did a sterling job, carrying out convoy cover patrols, escorting warships, making reconnaissance flights over the Dutch and Belgian coasts as well as supporting Hudsons on their bombing raids. They were involved during operations on the 18th.

3. At 10.00 hours Pilot Officer Patterson and Pilot Officer Jackson-Smith and their crews of 235 Blenheim Squadron took off from Bircham Newton to patrol a convoy. The weather was very bad with rain and low cloud restricting visibility. Only Pilot Officer Jackson-Smith and his crew returned after completing their task, having no idea what had happened to Pilot Officer Patterson and his crew. They did, however, report that they had been challenged by Hurricanes over the convoy.

4. Three Blenheims of 236 (F) Squadron led by Flight Lieutenant Power took off from St. Eval at 11.20 hours tasked to escort reconnaissance aircraft to Le Havre and Cherbourg. Flying in cloud near Cap de la Hague they came under intense anti-aircraft fire and the formation lost contact with each other. When Flight Lieutenant Power emerged from the cloud there was no sign of the other two aircraft of his formation and he came to the conclusion they may have been hit by flak. However, unknown to him Bf109s of JG2 were patrolling in the area and it is likely they were the victims of Major Wolfgang Schellman and Uffz. Willi Melchert of II Gruppe. Both claimed Blenheims near Le Havre at 13.15 and 13.25 hours respectively. Another 109 pilot, Fw. Georg Kiening of *6./JG 54*, claimed a Blenheim shot down southwest of Vlissingen. (This one could have been a Blenheim lost by 53 or 101 squadrons who were also operating in the area).

5. Sergeant Barr and crew in Anson 'G' of 500 Squadron from Detling were patrolling convoy F524, comprising thirty-four ships steaming thirty miles south east of Harwich when it came under attack from four Bf110s. After machine gunning the convoy the Messerschmitts then attacked the Anson. In his report later Sergeant Barr stated that his gunner and observer had exchanged fire with one of the Bf110s and had scored hits on its starboard engine causing it to plunge into the sea on fire, however Luftwaffe records show no such loss. This incident apparently occurred just before Spitfires arrived on the scene. The German aircraft were clearly from *Erprobungsgruppe 210*, Hauptmann Rubensdörffer and Oberleutnant Habisch each claiming a Blenheim. Rubensdörffer's claim

probably relates to the 236 Squadron loss recorded below, claimed southeast of Orfordness at 12.00 hours, while that by Habisch occurred fifteen minutes later, southeast of Harwich..

6. Anson N5268 of 612 Squadron, Dyce, captained by Flying Officer Isted drove off a Dornier Do17 which was attacking a convoy.

BOMBER COMMAND OPERATIONS

1. Forty-two Blenheims took off to carry out daylight operations including meteorological reconnaissance, attacks against airfields, invasion barges and other targets. Not all of the force was able to complete the allotted tasks, but the airfield at St. Omer and Pernis and ships in Boulogne harbour were bombed. At Boulogne bombs were seen to fall among the ships. Other crews reported seeing what was estimated as 700 to 800 trucks at the Ostend marshalling yard and 300 covered goods trucks west of Cassel. Two Blenheims were lost and another of 18 Squadron was attacked by three Bf109s near St. Omer. Cannon shells shot away part of the rudder controls and trim tabs, but the pilot managed to get his damaged aircraft back to base.

2. At 14.05 hours a 15 Squadron Blenheim took off from Wyton detailed to attack Sterkrade Halter, but when only ten miles over the sea outbound it was set upon by a formation of three Bf110s. The Blenheim gunners opened fire attempting to fend off the attacks, but to no avail and during one attack cannon shells set the inner fuel tanks in the wings on fire. By this time they were two miles from the coast near Norwich, so the Blenheim pilot, Pilot Officer Mahler, courageously dived his blazing aircraft towards the beach where he crash landed it. Miraculously he and his crew managed to scramble out just before the other fuel tanks and remaining ammunition exploded.

Night Operations

1. Night operations for 2 and 4 Groups were cancelled, but seventy-one aircraft comprising Wellingtons of 3 Group and Hampdens of 5 Group were detailed to attack various targets. The Wellingtons were sent to the air depot at Rotenberg, the aircraft park at Diepholz, an airframe factory at Bremen and the marshalling yards at Hamm. The Hampden targets were the Dortmund-Ems Canal, an airframe factory at Gotha, marshalling yards at Soest, an aircraft park at Paderborn and a naval target - the *Admiral Scheer* berthed at Wilhelmshaven. Not all of the Wellingtons achieved their tasks, but three bombed the air depot at Rotenberg, claiming that bombs fell across the target including a direct hit on a hangar. Two other crews attacked the aircraft park at Diepholz, causing fires. One crew attacked the airframe factory at Bremen and their bombs overshot, but still caused fires. Oil refineries at Hannover and Bremen were attacked causing fires. An attack on the marshalling yards at Hamm caused explosions and fires. At Saltau a train was wrecked with large explosions which produced blue and green flashes which lasted for ten minutes. The factory at Ratzeburg was hit by nine 250lb GP bombs and sixty 4lb incendiaries which caused large fires.

The Hampden crews attacking the aircraft park at Paderborn obtained hits on buildings and a station siding at Wewer. Six crews attacked the Krupp works, where there was a large explosion, and another five crews attacked Eschwege airfield, where bombs fell across the hangars causing explosions and fires. Other crews attacked what was described as 'self illuminating targets' such as blast furnaces. Only one Hampden was damaged by Flak in these attacks. It caused severe injuries to the pilot. The navigator took over control and flew the aircraft back to base where the pilot unfortunately succumbed to his injuries.

2. A small contribution to the night's effort was made by three Wellington crews of 15 OTU, who dropped 81,000 leaflets over Le Havre, Rouen, Amiens and Lille.

OPERATIONAL LOSSES

Blenheim IV R3661 of 53 Squadron, Detling, failed to return from a reconnaissance over Flushing. It was subsequently reported as having been shot down by an Me 109 into the mouth of the Scheldt. Flying Officer J. E. Mahony and Sergeant D. A. Keetley were posted as missing in action. The body of Sergeant G. E. Exton was found near Klemskerke.

Blenheim IV(F) N3541 of 235 Squadron, Bircham Newton, lost on a convoy patrol in bad weather off the east coast. Pilot Officer R. L. Patterson, Sergeant L. H. M. Reece and Sergeant R. Y. Tucker were posted as missing in action and are recorded on the Runnymede Memorial.

Blenheim IV(F) L6779 of 236 Squadron, Thorney Island, shot down on an escort sortie to Le Havre by a Bf109. Pilot Officer C. R. D. Thomas was killed and is buried at Quiberville. Sergeant H. D. B. Elsdon was posted as missing in action.

Blenheim IV(F) L6639 also of 236 Squadron, Thorney Island, shot down on the Le Havre sortie by a Bf109 near Cap-de-la-Hague. Pilot Officer R. H. Rigby and Sergeant D. D. MacKinnon were both killed.

Blenheim R3603 of 15 Squadron, Wyton, detailed to attack Sterkrade Holter, was shot down and crash landed on an east coast beach near Norwich. The crew; Flying Officer Mahler, Sergeant Pavely and Sergeant Baker, escaped without injury.

Blenheim P6924 of 101 Squadron, West Raynham, failed to return from a daylight sortie to attack airfields in France. It was lost without trace and the crew; Flying Officer F. E. R. Ducker, Sergeant E. L. Dodd and Sergeant G. E. Bloor, are commemorated on the Runnymede Memorial.

Wellington P9227 of 115 Squadron, Marham, failed to return from attacking Bremen. The crew; Pilot Officer W. H. C. Hunkin, Pilot Officer J. Barker, Sergeant C. Clark, Sergeant J. J. MacGregor, Sergeant A. G. S. Colley and Sergeant H. Dickson were later reported to be PoWs.

Boulton Paul Defiants prepare to enter the Battle. They were soon exposed as 'easy meat' for German fighters and were withdrawn from daylight operations. With no forward firing armament, the Defiant went on to find a new vocation as quite an effective night-fighter.

ENEMY AIR ACTIVITY

The Boulton Paul Defiant was initially successful in combat with the Luftwaffe over the beaches of Dunkirk during the evacuation in May, but it had severe limitations. This day these limitations were exploited by the Luftwaffe when nine Defiants were engaged by a Gruppe of Bf109s from *III Gruppe Jagdgeschwader 51*, which shot down six of them over Dover. The tragedy was the fate of the Defiant gunners who were unable to get free from their turrets when their aircraft were shot down. Getting out of the aircraft was difficult enough in level flight, but it was practically impossible when the 'G' forces experienced in combat were applied and, worst of all, when the aircraft was on fire. Even if they managed to get out and make a successful parachute descent, the elaborate flying suits they wore made survival in water a matter of chance. Although the air trapped in the suit kept the wearer afloat, it had the unfortunate tendency to keep the wearer's head under water! After this action only one gunner was picked up from the sea alive. Later the Defiant was taken off daylight operations and used as a night fighter.

COASTAL COMMAND OPERATIONS

Numerous patrols and reconnaissance flights took place and on one a force two cruisers and six destroyers were sighted in the Skagerrak. Subsequently a strike force of Hudsons was sent out which found two cruisers, eight destroyers and seven motor vessels in a position plotted as being between twenty-eight and sixty-five miles off Horn's Reef.

Night operations

Six Hudsons of 206 Squadron, Bircham Newton, escorted by three Blenheim IV(F)s of 235 Squadron also from Bircham Newton, carried out a night attack against shipping at Emden.

There were no losses reported from any of the coastal day and night sorties.

BOMBER COMMAND OPERATIONS

Sixteen 2 Group Blenheims were sent on daylight operations, but only one bombed a railway viaduct near Vorholle, south of Dortmund. The others were unable to carry out their tasks because of unsuitable weather conditions. There were no losses.

Night operations

Eighty-six aircraft and crews were detailed for night operations, comprising Wellingtons of 3 Group, Whitleys of 4 Group and Hampdens of 5 Group.

1. Eighteen Wellingtons attacked the airframe factories at Bremen, Wismar and Wenzendorf, hitting buildings with their 500lb bombs which caused fires. Others bombed oil refineries at Bremen and Hamburg. Industrial targets at Essen and Oldenburg and eight airfields were also bombed. Squadron Leader J. B. S. Monypenny and his crew of 9 Squadron, Honington, were flying over Munster at 02.00 hours when they had the bad luck to be intercepted by Oberleutnant Werner Streib, Staffelkapitain of *2./NJG1*, in his Bf110 who shot them down in flames as the first officially confirmed victory of the *Nachtjagd*. (Werner Streib became a noted Luftwaffe night fighter 'Ace'.)

Friday 19th July

A Wellington of 149 Squadron, Mildenhall, reported being attacked by two night fighters and the gunners claimed they shot them both down, but this was not confirmed.

2. Thirty Whitley crews were detailed to attack oil storage tanks at Bremen and Gelsenkirchen as well as industrial targets in the Ruhr. Only eight bombed their primary targets, but the others attacked SEMO (Self Evident Military Objectives) or MOPA (Military Objectives Previously Attacked). This was 78 Squadron's first operational sortie of the war. Up to now it had been the non-operational reserve squadron of 4 Group. *The Oberkommando der Wehrmacht* (Army High Command) reported a Whitley shot by a night-fighter near Burgsteinfurt. This was probably Flight Lieutenant Curry and crew of 51 Squadron, who failed to return.

3. Eight Hampden crews were sent to attack the *Admiral Scheer*, which had been reported as being in harbour at Kiel, but only one crew located it and dropped a 2,000lb armour-piercing bomb which missed. Another crew had a 'go' at the *Tirpitz* with four 250lb bombs, while others bombed the dock installations. Six other aircraft attacked Paderborn, De Kooy and Bentheim as well as road and rail junctions at Wewer.

A mining force of five aircraft sowed mines off Friedrichshafen. A wireless message was received from one of them captained by Sergeant Farrand to the effect they had been hit by Flak and landed in Denmark. This was proved later to be incorrect.

OPERATIONAL LOSSES

Hampden L4087 of 44 Squadron, Waddington, detailed for mining operations off Friedrichshafen was hit by Flak and crashed in the sea off Jutland. Two of the crew, Sergeant E. L. Farrand and Pilot Officer B. Green MC, were taken prisoner. Sergeant P. D. Nixon and Sergeant R. T. Miller were killed and are buried in Skagen Cemetery, Denmark.

Wellington L7795 of 9 Squadron, detailed to attack Wismar, was shot down by Werner Streib's Bf110 night-fighter and crashed into Eckernförder Bay, 25 miles north-west Kiel. All members of the crew were killed. Squadron Leader J. B. S. Monypenny, Flight Lieutenant D. D. Middleton, Sergeant F. Watson, Sergeant W. R. Cowell and Sergeant M. Gott are commemorated on the Runnymede Memorial. The other crew member, Pilot Officer H. F. A. Lees is buried in the Kiel War Cemetery. (The Wellington – claimed as a 'Whitley' - actually crashed north of Munster, where the crew were originally buried. They were later exhumed and re-buried at Kiel)

Whitley P5007 of 51 Squadron, Dishforth, detailed to attack Gelsenkirchen, was shot down and crashed near Osnabrük . An unconfirmed report suggests it may have been another victim of Oberleutnant Werner Streib of NJG1. Four members of the crew, Flight Lieutenant S. E. F. Curry, Sergeant A. J. Harris, Sergeant R. N. Lewis and Sergeant J. Tansley were killed and buried in a collective grave at Ibbenburen, but have since been laid to rest in the Reichswald Forest Cemetery. Sergeant G. R. Harvey, the fifth member, was taken prisoner.

Oberleutnant Werner Streib (right) is congratulated by the 'father' of the German night fighter force, Wolfgang Falk. Streib was credited with the first Nachtjagd victory on this night, his unfortunate victim being Wellington L7795 of 9 Squadron flown by Sqn Ldr Monypenny.

Aircrew of 144 Squadron pose for a formal photo in July 1940. Many of these men were to die in the following months as the squadron remained at the forefront of Bomber Command's night offensive.

ENEMY AIR ACTIVITY

The main Luftwaffe action during the day was attacks on the convoy *'Bosom'* as it steamed eastwards from Lyme Bay to Dover. The attacks continued throughout the day ending in a battle off Dover that lasted over an hour. The Luftwaffe losses included two He59 float planes searching for crews lost in the attacks. These aircraft were marked with red crosses and engaged in rescue work, but according to Air Ministry instructions they were legitimate military targets.

COASTAL COMMAND OPERATIONS

1. In addition to the usual patrols and reconnaissance of the French, Belgian and Dutch coasts, a Hudson of 233 Squadron, Leuchars, attacked a wireless station at Utsire on the Norwegian coast. Its four 250lb GP bombs and three incendiaries caused considerable damage including the destruction of the wireless aerial.

2. PR Spitfires of the Photographic Reconnaissance Unit operating from St. Eval and Heston flew sorties throughout the day taking photographs of Brest, Ushant, Lorient and The Scheldt. Two sorties a day by individual Spitfires were now quite frequent, even over Norway from Wick.

3. Three Blenheim crews of 236(F) Squadron, escorted one of 59 Squadron on a reconnaissance between Le Havre and Cherbourg. When they got to Le Havre a cruiser and a destroyer were sighted. They continued on to Cherbourg, but when they were six miles north-east at 18.00 hours, flying at 13,000 feet in brilliant sunshine, three Bf109s appeared. Two of the Blenheims dived in line astern down to 6,000 feet towards the sun in a defensive manoeuvre. For some unknown reason the third Blenheim remained at 13,000 feet where it was attacked by the Messerschmitts. The two other Blenheim crews watched helplessly as one of the attackers, (Hauptmann Eduard Neuman of *Stab./JG27*) opened fire. Pieces were seen coming off the Blenheim's port wing and smoke poured from both engines. It entered a steep spin and crashed into the sea 30 kilometres south of Portland. The two crew failed to escape.

Night operations

1. Night raids were carried out by Blenheims of 59 Squadron and Hudsons of 206 Squadron on oil tanks at Vlaadingen, causing fires.

2. Other Aircraft of the same two squadrons bombed the oil tanks at Ghent and three more Hudsons bombed shipping and the docks at Emden.

3. At 03.19 hours a Hudson crew of 233 Squadron, on a reconnaissance in the Bergen area, attacked a U-Boat with three 2501b. anti-sub bombs. They reported that it heeled over and sank upside down.

BOMBER COMMAND OPERATIONS

1. Twenty-five 2 Group Blenheim crews took off in daylight to carry out various tasks including meteorological reconnaissance, attacks on the airfields in the occupied countries and industrial and naval targets in Germany. All but two returned early because of the lack of suitable cloud cover. Of the remaining two, one attacked the airfield at Flushing, the other, captained by Squadron Leader Stephens of 110 Squadron, took off from Wattisham at 12.00 hours to attack Lunen. It never returned and was later reported to have been shot down near Rotterdam by Hauptmann Von Bonin and Leutnant Kinzinger of *I./JG54* at 13.30 hours.

Night operations

The main targets for the night raids were oil plants at Bremen, Gelsenkirchen and Hamburg, the Dornier aircraft factory at Wismar and warships berthed at Wilhelmshaven.

1. Twenty-four Wellingtons claimed to have started large fires at Bremen and Gelsenkirchen. Twelve other crews failed to find their primary target, but bombed 'self illuminating targets' in the Ruhr.

The German night fighters took advantage of the improved weather and Oberleutnant Ehle of *3./NJG1* claimed to have shot a Wellington down over Munster at 01.40 hours. Oberleutnant Wandam submitted a claim for another Wellington shot down over Borken at 02.27 hours. These could have been the two 3 Group aircraft, one of 37 Squadron, the other of 75 Squadron who did not return.

Another Wellington of 37 Squadron was attacked and its rear gunner killed. It was reported by Flying Officer Williams that his aircraft had been attacked by three He113s. He claimed one of them had been shot down in flames.

Saturday 20th July

The intense flak barrage faced by the 61 Squadron Hampden crews on the night of 20th July. Three of the Hampdens were shot down by this deadly pyrotechnic display.

2. The Whitley crews' targets were the Dornier aircraft factory at Wismar and an industrial plant at Düsseldorf. Eight out of nine crews bombed Düsseldorf, where the opposition was severe and one aircraft was hit by Flak. Of the twelve detailed to attack Wismar, one returned early, eight bombed the primary and three others bombed alternatives. Three aircraft were hit by Flak, but got back safely.

3. It was the task of the Hampden squadrons from Hemswell (61 and 144) to attack the warships at Wilhelmshaven with 'M' bombs (modified mines). These had to be dropped at low level so that they would explode on the sea bed, thus causing damage to the bottom of a ship's hull which was less well protected. The bombs were fitted with parachutes to retard the descent and to improve the dropping accuracy. Three of the 61 Squadron aircraft made diversion attacks to allow the four Hampdens flown by Pilot Officer Davis, Pilot Officer Gould, Pilot Officer Jones and Flight Sergeant Saunders to make their attacks on the *Tirpitz* and *Admiral Scheer*. However, as the four neared Wilhelmshaven they ran into intense Flak and Flight Sergeant Saunders, unable to get to his target of the *Admiral Scheer*, ordered his observer to drop his bombs on a group of ships lying off the mole. He turned for home, and his was the only crew to return. The other three aircraft were shot down. Only four out of the twelve crewmen were reported as having been taken prisoner, the others perished. The 144 Squadron crews, whose target was also at Wilhelmshaven, lost Flight Lieutenant Edwards and his crew who sent out an SOS. It was later reported that they had been hit by Flak and had ditched in the North Sea at 03.22 hours, ninety miles east of Skegness.

4. Twelve other Hampdens were sent to lay mines in the Baltic Sound. One aircraft ran out of fuel on return and crashed near Hunstanton.

OPERATIONAL LOSSES

Blenheim L1300 of 236(F) Squadron, Thorney Island, was shot down by a Bf109 off Cherbourg at 18.30 hours. Sergeant E. E. Lockton and Sergeant H. Corcoran were posted as missing and commemorated on the Runnymede Memorial.

1. **Blenheim R3738 of 110 Squadron,** Wattisham, failed to return from a sortie to Lunen. It was later reported to have been shot down near Rotterdam by I./JG54. The crew of Squadron Leader J. F. Stephens, Sergeant E. C. Parker and Sergeant J. V. West DFM was posted as missing.

Two Blenheims were claimed by II./JG 54 in this area, one by Unteroffizier Oswald Frauendorf of 6 Staffel.

The wreckage of Pilot Officer Jones's Hampden P4344 which was shot down on this night during the disastrous raid against warships in Wilhelmshaven. All the crew survived.

Hampden L4077 of 49 Squadron, Scampton, detailed for minelaying in the Baltic Sound, ran out of fuel on return and crashed near Hunstanton. The crew; Pilot Officer K. W. Mitchie, Sergeant Lowe, AC1. Bellamy and Sergeant F. Corbett, escaped unhurt.

Hampden P4343 of 61 Squadron, Hemswell, detailed to attack warships at Wilhelmshaven was hit by Flak and crashed close to the Kaiser Wilhelm Bridge, Wilhelmshaven. Pilot Officer M. R. Tagg, Sergeant F. S. Waltho and Sergeant A. McN. Cockburn are buried in Sage War Cemetery, Oldenburg. Pilot Officer D. H. Davis was taken prisoner.

Hampden P4344 of 61 Squadron, Hemswell, detailed to attack warships at Wilhelmshaven, was hit by Flak and crash landed near Jever airfield. Pilot Officer K. Jones, Sergeant G. A. Wright, Sergeant R. Bonson and Sergeant D. D. Cain were taken prisoner.

Hampden P4358 of 61 Squadron, Hemswell, detailed to attack warships at Wilhelmshaven was hit repeatedly by Flak and crash landed on fire near Wilhelmshaven. Miraculously three of the crew, Pilot Officer A. H. Gould, Sergeant J. F. Cowan and Sergeant J. N. Prendergrast only suffered cuts and bruises and were taken prisoner. The fourth member of the crew, Pilot Officer D. S. Carnegie, was found dead after his parachute failed to open.

Hampden P4367 of 144 Squadron, Hemswell, ditched 90 miles off the Lincolnshire coast during a mining sortie. The crew; Flight Lieutenant D. H. Edwards, Sergeant B. N. Dingle, Sergeant W. Wylie, Sergeant A. J. Giles are all recorded on the Runnymede Memorial.

Wellington R3210 of 37 Squadron, Feltwell, detailed to attack Gelsenkirchen, failed to return. It is believed to have been shot down by a night fighter. Pilot Officer G. H. Muirhead, Sergeant F. J. B. Winch, Sergeant F. H. E. Phillips and Pilot Officer J. Littlejohn, were all killed and now rest in the Reichswald Forest Cemetery. The other two members of the crew; Sergeant T. E. S. Alderwick and Sergeant J. A. Theed were taken prisoner.

Wellington R3165 of 75 Squadron, Feltwell, detailed to attack Horst, failed to return and it was believed to have been shot down by a night fighter. Flying Officer S. M. M. Watson, Pilot Officer E. C. J. Cameron, Sergeant G. M. Cumming, Sergeant R. A. J. Anderson RNZAF, and Sergeant J. L. Owen RNZAF were all killed and are now buried in the Reichswald Forest Cemetery.

The two Wellingtons above both fell to Luftwaffe nightfighter crews from I./NJG 1. Oberleutnant Walter Ehle destroyed one 12 kilometres northwest of Münster at 01.38 hours, while Oberleutnant Siegfried Wandam broiught the other down north of Borken at 02.33 hours.

Sunday 21st July

CLEAR SKIES IN THE MORNING AND EVENING, BUT CLOUDY AROUND MIDDAY.

Oberleutnant Runde's Messerschmitt Bf110 after it was restored to flying condition at RAE Farnborough. Interestingly, RAF markings have yet to be applied.

ENEMY AIR ACTIVITY

The convoy 'Peewit' steaming westwards from Dover was the main Luftwaffe objective. Three attacks were made on it before violent thunderstorms developed in the afternoon that halted operations. Several barrage balloons came down when struck by lightning.

At Old Sarum in Wiltshire was No.1 Flying Training School where pilots under training received their flying instruction on aircraft such as the obsolescent single engined Hawker Hart. Leading Airman John Arthur Seed from *HMS Daedalus* was on a solo flight in a Hart over Salisbury Plain when he was attacked by a Bf110 flown by Oberleutnant Runde of a long range reconnaissance group on a photographic sortie over the area. The Bf110 easily overtook the ancient Hart and Feldwebel Baden, the 110's gunner, opened fire with his single MG15 machine-gun from his rear cockpit. The helpless and unarmed Hart caught fire and plunged to earth, carrying the young pilot to his death. He was buried at his home town of Preston, Lancashire. However, the incident did not end there. Retribution struck in the shape of three Hurricane pilots of 238 Squadron who pursued Runde as he headed south for the coast. They caught up with him over Sussex and forced him to crash land in a beet field near Goodwood, from where Runde and his gunner Baden were taken prisoner. The Bf110 was later dismantled and taken to RAE Farnborough where it was repaired and flown by the RAF for evaluation and assessment.

COASTAL COMMAND OPERATIONS

1. Seventy-five patrols and escort flights were carried out. On one of the patrols a Hudson crew of 233 Squadron reported sighting a force of one large and five small vessels thirty-four miles off Lister Light. Seven other Hudsons of

'I HAVE CONTROL'

Flying Officer John Wray
Fairey Battle pilot 1FTS

Flying Officer John Wray, an instructor with 1 FTS had good reason to remember 21st July:

"On that day I had, as a trainee, Lieutenant Churchill, a Royal Marine. We were practicing blind-flying in a Battle and he had the canvas covers around his section of cockpit and, of course, couldn't see out.
"We had gone down as far as Southampton and were droning northwards again when I looked back and saw a lone aircraft coming up fast on our starboard side. I thought that it must be an experimental aircraft from Boscombe Down. As it was on its own, it simply never occurred to me that it could be German – but it was!

"It came up on my starboard side, about 100 yards away and I suddenly recognised it as a Messerschmitt 110. I saw a black cross on the side and, before I could take control and break away, the rear gunner lazily swung his machine-gun around and gave us a short burst. That was all that was needed for a Battle; there were a lot of tinkling and banging noises from the nose and the engine simply stopped dead. "I have control" I shouted and Churchill released the controls. I took the battle down and crash-landed it in a field near Stockbridge, getting a bruised fore-head in the process. Churchill didn't realise we'd been shot down until I told him about it once we were safe!"

Wray's victor must have been a reconnaisance aircraft since a Bf110 fighter would certainly have attacked with cannon from astern. No victory claims were recorded by Luftwaffe reconnaissance units. The Bf110 could only have been that flown by Runde on his way to Old Sarum, who thus achieved two victories on the one sortie but was unable to claim them.

224 and 233 Squadrons were dispatched to attack the ships. The first attack by three crews caused a violent explosion in the large ship identified as a tanker and the second wave scored a direct hit on the same vessel. Two of the attacking Hudsons were caught by Bf110 crews from I./ZG 76. One was credited to Oberleutnant Reinhold Echardt, later to become a notable nightfighter pilot, and the second was credited to Unteroffizier Ladwein, both at 13.45 hours, some 150 kilometres south of Kiristiansand.
2. Sunderland N9028 of 204 Squadron, Sullum Voe, captained by Wing Commander Davis OBE, DFC, set out on a long range reconnaissance patrol to Trondheim, Norway. When they reached the Norwegian coast they were unluckily intercepted and shot down by a Bf109 flown by Oberleutnant Lorenz Weber of 8./JG77, the fighter unit charged with the defence of Norway.

Night operations

1. Three Blenheims of 235 Squadron engaged in a reconnaissance over Le Havre had a brief encounter with a Bf109 before it escaped by diving into cloud.
2. Six Blenheims of 53 Squadron were detailed to attack petrol storage tanks at Ghent. Only one bombed, but they were all damaged by the severe Flak.

BOMBER COMMAND OPERATIONS

1. One daylight reconnaissance of Wilhelmshaven was scheduled to be carried out by a Blenheim of 114 Squadron, Horsham St Faith, but was abandoned because of the lack of suitable cloud cover.

Night operations

1. Another large night raid was planned which included Blenheims and Fairey Battles of 103 and 105 Squadrons. This was the first operation to be carried out by Fairey Battles during the Battle of Britain. The Blenheims attacked airfields and the invasion barges in Dutch ports.
2. Thirty-four Wellingtons were detailed. Eight crews attacked the aircraft park and buildings at Rotenburg, where direct hits were claimed on three hangars, a large building and barracks. Flak sites and two trains, one of which came to a halt, were machine gunned. Ten crews attacked a similar target at Göttingen, hitting buildings and starting fires, while others bombed a synthetic oil plant at Gelsenkirchen. During the attack on Bremen, hits were claimed on the docks and a direct hit on the Focke Wulf building caused an explosion.
3. The targets for the twenty-eight Whitleys were the Fiesler aircraft factory at Kassel and the marshalling yards at Hamm and Soest. Twenty crews were dispatched to Kassel, one returned early, but the others claimed hits which resulted in fires and a large explosion. Three fighters were seen but did not attack. Eight other crews bombed Hamm and Soest where they claimed direct hits in spite of the severe opposition. One aircraft failed to return; this was 78 Squadron's first loss since becoming operational only a few days before.
4. Seventeen Hampden crews bomber the Dornier aircraft factory at Wismar, where hits were claimed. Late arrivals over the target reported the remains of buildings were smouldering. Eight other Hampdens laid mines.

The Fairey Battle returned to the front line today after its mauling during the Fall of France.

OPERATIONAL LOSSES

1. Hudson N7305 of 224 Squadron, Leuchars, one of the strike force against shipping off Lister Light, was shot down by Flak ships. Pilot Officer V. C. R. Morrison, Sergeant E. A. Cotton, Sergeant S. W. Curry and Sergeant D. Middleton were all posted missing in action.

2. Hudson N7242 of 233 Squadron, Leuchars, attacking the same target as Pilot Officer Morrison, was also shot down by Flak. Pilot Officer W. L. Ather, Sergeant J. J. Crabtree, Sergeant B. J. Mahon and Sergeant A. W. Lamont were posted as missing in action.

3. Sunderland N9128 of 204 Squadron, Sullom Voe, on a reconnaissance to Trondheim was intercepted and shot down by a Bf109 flown by Oberleutnant Weber of *8./JG77* near Linesøya at 05.15 hours. Wing Commander E. S. C. Davis OBE AFC, Flight Lieutenant F. Phillips DFC, Pilot Officer G. E. MacDonald, Pilot Officer R. T. Pareezer, Sergeant D. P. Dixon, Sergeant W. G. Lillie DFM, Sergeant E. W. Ovens, LAC D. J. Frame, LAC T. P. J. Trickey, AC1 J. A. McL. G White, AC1 L. C. Bennett, AC2 E. Sneyd were posted as missing in action and are recorded on the Runnymede Memorial.
(Pilot Officer MacDonald was an American from Washington State.)

Whitley N1487 of 78 Squadron, Dishforth, detailed to bomb the marshalling yards at Hamm and Soest, failed to return. The crew; Sergeant V. C. Monkhouse, Sergeant C. G. Hill, Sergeant N. H. Burton, Sergeant W. McCrorie and Sergeant J. A. Sulter were all killed and are buried in the Reichswald Forest Cemetery.
This aircraft was intercepted north of Münster and shot down by Oberleutnant Werner Streib of I./NJG 1 at 01.22 hours.

Monday 22nd July

SHOWERY WITH OCCASIONAL SUNNY SPELLS.

ENEMY AIR ACTIVITY

Few Luftwaffe raids took place. One by a Do17P of 4(F)/121 on a reconnaissance sortie resulted in the Dornier being shot down by Hurricanes off Selsey Bill. During another raid, which took place over Scotland, a bomb hit a German Prisoner of War camp and six of the prisoners were killed. A cemetery at Leith was also hit by a bomb that had the macabre result of disgorging the remains of German First World War dead.

COASTAL COMMAND OPERATIONS

116 crews flew on patrols to the enemy coasts. Pilot Officer Winter-Taylor, flying Anson N5366 of 612 Squadron on escort patrol, aided two RN destroyers to attack a suspected U-Boat. The Anson carried out a dive bombing attack and dropped four 100lb anti-submarine bombs just ahead of the rapidly submerging U-Boat. Although there were no signs of success, the RN destroyer crews optimistically believed it had been hit.

Night operations

1. Six Swordfish of 812 (FAA) Squadron carried out a night minelaying sortie.
2. Six Blenheims of 59 Squadron and one Hudson bombed invasion barges at Amsterdam. On return the undercarriage of Blenheim R3639 collapsed on landing at Thorney Island. The aircraft caught fire and burnt out, but fortunately the crew, Pilot Officer Hovenier, Sergeant Magee and Sergeant Scotchmere escaped unhurt. There were no other losses reported.

BOMBER COMMAND OPERATIONS

Although daylight operations were planned for the 2 Group Blenheims they were all cancelled because of the adverse weather conditions.

Night operations

Limited night operations were carried out by the five bomber groups.

1. Six Fairey Battles, three from 103 Squadron and three from 150 Squadron, attacked targets at Rotterdam.
2. Nine Blenheims of 107 Squadron, Wattisham, bombed airfields in France. One failed to return.
3. Seven Wellingtons were detailed to bomb Essen and Düsseldorf. Unsuitable weather conditions resulted in one bombing a primary target, three bombing alternatives and one a 'last gasp' opportunity target. The other two failed to bomb.
4. Twenty-five Whitleys were detailed to bomb various targets, an aircraft factory at Bremen and other industrial targets in the Ruhr. The adverse weather made navigation and target identification difficult but most crews bombed either a primary or an alternative target. One aircraft of 58 Squadron, Linton-on-Ouse, failed to return after it was hit by Flak.
5. Gelsenkirchen was again one of the targets of the Hampden force. Seven of the eight crews detailed claimed to have bombed it, causing explosions and fires - the smoke rising to 5,000 feet.

Another eight Hampden crews bombed the marshalling yards at Hamm and Eschwege. One crew reported firing 300 rounds at a night fighter off Texel, but claimed no definite result. Four other aircraft carried out minelaying.

OPERATIONAL LOSSES

Blenheim L9414 of 107 Squadron, Wattisham, failed to return from a sortie to Creil. It was presumed that it had crashed in the English Channel as the body of Sergeant C. J. Holland was washed onto the south coast. The bodies of the other two crew members, Pilot Officer P. G. A. Watson and Sergeant W. P. O'Heney were never recovered.

Whitley N1472 of 58 Squadron, Linton-on-Ouse, target Paderborn, was hit by Flak and crashed near Detmold. The crew; Sergeant J. B. Jones, Pilot Officer J. D. Smith, Sergeant J. W. Candlish, Sergeant J. K. Easton and Sergeant E. Hill were all killed and are now buried in the Hannover War Cemetery.

L-R; Pilot Officer Houvenier, Sgt. Magee and Sgt. Scotchmere who escaped from their burning 59 Squadron Blenheim R3639 at Thorney Island.

During a 40 minute combat with three Dornier Do18 flying boats, a 269 Squadron Hudson forced one of them to make an emergency landing on the sea with a wounded crew-member aboard.

ENEMY AIR ACTIVITY

The Luftwaffe concentrated on attacking the convoy 'Pilot' which was steaming off the Lincolnshire coast. Two of the raiders were shot down by fighters. Fighter Command is alleged to have recorded that when convoys were attacked the Luftwaffe bombers usually abandoned their attacks as soon as our fighters appeared over the convoy. In mid afternoon a lone Dornier dropped bombs on the old airship hangar at Pulham and another attempted to bomb the Vickers Armstrong aircraft factory at Weybridge, taking the advantage of cloud cover. Its bombs fell on the edge of the landing ground missing the factory.

COASTAL COMMAND OPERATIONS

1. The main action of the day concerned Hudsons. Early in the morning, an aircraft of 269 Squadron, taking off from Wick, collided with a Hurricane of 3 Squadron. Tragically the Hurricane pilot and the crew of the Hudson were killed.
2. Another Hudson of 269 Squadron went on patrol during which a Do18 was sighted and attacked 115 miles east of Karmo. Two more Dorniers joined in the fray that lasted forty minutes. The outcome was that one of the Dorniers was forced to land on the sea. When its crew evacuated their aircraft and boarded their dinghy they signalled in English 'one wounded'. The Hudson, having sustained damage to its hydraulics during the fight, broke off and returned to base where it carried out a safe belly landing.
3. The crew of a 224 Squadron Hudson on patrol from Leuchars sighted six motor vessels escorted by eight destroyers, eighty-eight miles west of Lister Light and shadowed it for two and a half hours. When three Do18s appeared a short combat ensued during which the Hudson's guns jammed, forcing the pilot to abandon the action.
4. The crew of Anson N5366 of 612 Squadron attacked a suspected U-Boat without any positive result.

Night operations

Six Blenheims of 53 Squadron carried out a night attack on invasion barges at Amsterdam and six aircraft of 59 Squadron bombed oil tanks at Flushing.

BOMBER COMMAND OPERATIONS

1. Blenheim crews of 2 Group were detailed to bomb oil targets in Germany in daylight. Eleven of them abandoned their task because of unsuitable weather conditions, but three pressed on and attacked airfields in France while another bombed the docks at The Hague. Sergeant Garvey and his crew, attacking the airfield at St. Omer, had a narrow escape when Flak burst under their aircraft blowing in the side door and windows. The W/T was put out of action, the elevators were damaged and the maps were sucked out of the window. The aircraft then went into a spin, but Sergeant Garvey was able to take recovery action at 1,000 feet. Despite their tribulations he got the aircraft back and carried out a safe landing at base.

Tuesday 23rd July

Night Operations

1. Eighty-five crews of all the bomber groups were detailed to participate in the night operations, but low cloud and fog caused problems. Fairey Battles and Blenheims briefed to attack airfields achieved little. Sergeant Hayward and his crew of 110 Squadron was lost on a sortie to bomb the airfield near Bernburg.

2. Thirty Wellington crews were briefed to bomb targets at Gotha (aircraft factory) and Gelsenkirchen (oil plant). Eight bombed primary objectives while fourteen bombed alternatives. Eight crews failed to attack. An aircraft of 9 Squadron and another of 149 Squadron were attacked by Bf110s. The 149 crew claimed one 'kill' and one damaged, but their navigator was killed during the action.

Two Wellingtons were claimed destroyed off Texel by crews from 5./NJG 2, credits going to Feldwebels Georg Schramm and Wiese.

3. Twenty-four Whitley crews were briefed to attack an aircraft factory at Kassel, an oil refinery at Hamburg and road and rail communications at Osnabrük . One crew returned early, seventeen claimed to have bombed primary targets and the remainder alternatives.

4. The Hampden crews were detailed to attack an aircraft factory at Wenzendorf and the docks at Wilhelmshaven. Six crews attacked Wenzendorf, four attacked the docks at Wilhelmshaven and the remainder bombed Schipol airfield and searchlight and Flak batteries at Ijmuiden.

OPERATIONAL LOSSES

Hudson P5152 of 269 Squadron collided with Hurricane P2862 of 3 Squadron when taking off from Wick. Flight Lieutenant C. D. W. Price, Pilot Officer J. T. T. Fleming, Pilot Officer W. Appleby and Sergeant L. Land were all killed.

Blenheim R3748 of 110 Squadron, Wattisham, briefed to bomb an airfield near Bernburg, crashed into the North Sea off Haamstede (Zeeland) Holland. The crew; Sergeant C. C. Heyward (name recorded incorrectly in ORB), Sergeant L. A. N. Walker and Sergeant I. Winberg were all posted missing and are recorded on the Runnymede Memorial.

Intruder!

Sgt George Dove, Whitley Rear Gunner, 10 Squadron

Any trip over the other side was mostly tension, apprehension and then a sense of relief that another one was over. But our crew did one trip that left us chuckling for days afterwards.

It was whilst we were at R.A.F. Leeming with 10 Squadron, flying Whitley Vs and at that time crews were briefed for a primary and secondary target and, if neither could be found, any target of opportunity could be bombed.

On this particular night we had been given two targets north of the Ruhr and duly took off at dusk on a fine evening, with a good weather forecast ahead. As they always did, the good people of Leeming village were dotted along the hedge bordering the airfield and waved as the laden Whitley lumbered along the grass, (no runways yet as we had opened the brand new station just a few weeks previously). With the tail up and the nose almost touching the deck, which was characteristic of the Whitley (something to do with wing incidence I believe), we lifted over the boundary, did a circuit, and headed out towards Hornsea and the long haul over the North Sea. Once well clear of the coast I gave the usual testing burst from the rear turret, then settled down till landfall over the Dutch coast. Apart from the usual welcome from the flak ships, we crossed the coast without incident and set course for the primary target. Despite the good met. forecast we soon found ourselves in 10/10ths cloud and any hope of finding either target was soon dashed. After sniffing around for an hour looking for a break in the soup, the skipper called up and said: "That's it. we'll head N/West over Holland and home."

The thick cloud persisted until we were well over Holland when it suddenly cleared and there, right ahead of us. was an airfield fully lit up, with aircraft circling with nav. lights on. The navigator took a quick look and checked his map and shouted: "It's Schiphol, the Luftwaffe is doing circuits and bumps." So it was, we could scarcely believe our eyes. We waited for the challenge and the burst of light flak, but nothing happened. The skipper told us he was going down to take a closer look, warily we began to lose height, expecting any moment to be on the wrong end of a burst of coloured tracer, but nothing! We were now down to 600 ft. and we could quite clearly see all German aircraft on the circuit and one taking-off. Everything was switched on - runway, perimeter and hangar lights - they must have been very overconfident.

It was at this point that our pilot, who was a pre-war regular and very much a press-on type, decided to switch on our nav. lights and join the circuit.

Picture, if you will, a Whitley on circuit with assorted Luftwaffe aircraft over a German airfield. You could de-synchronise the engines of a Whitley and the out of phase Merlins did sound rather Teutonic, and so I must assume this is why we were completely undetected. We must have arrived towards the end of the night's exercise, because one by one the aircraft landed, until there was only one left in the circuit, us! The runway controller was flashing us a persistent green to come in. we were astonished at our good fortune. The skipper had by now decided on a course of action. He called on the intercom: "I am going to do a long downwind leg then come back over the hangars low and fast. Navigator drop the bombs on the hangars, and rear gunner spray the airfield as we pass." By chance our bomb load were all delayed action, perfect for the situation. We raced back over the airfield as fast as the Whitley could go, dropped the bombs, and as the airfield came into view I pressed the triggers on the four-gun turret and kept them pressed till we reached the other side.

As we sped out to sea. I gave a running commentary on what was happening, all the lights went out at once, bursts of flak, searchlights and red flares - all too late -we were well on our way home.

When we landed at Leeming and lit our first fag we were all elated and amused, and told our story to a disbelieving debriefing officer. Although we never heard any more about it. I do hope those bombs went off.

It is easy to imagine a 'Mossie' getting away with it, but a WHITLEY?

Wednesday 24th July

The rear turret of a Whitley in which the author spent many uncomfortable hours over enemy territory.

ENEMY AIR ACTIVITY

1. Mining was carried out by He111s in the Mersey while it was still dark and gunners fired on the searchlights which illuminated them. One Heinkel was caught in the beams for three minutes and coastguards at Hoylake and Formby Point claimed it had crashed into the sea as the result of dazzle.
2. A low level 'sneak' raid by a single He111 on Glasgow's Hillington industrial estate caused damage to buildings and injury to eighteen civilians.
3. Over Porthcawl (Wales), three Spitfires of 92 Squadron engaged an attacking Ju88, whose destruction was completed near Lynton by Pilot Officer R. P. Beaumont* of 87 Squadron.

** After a very distinguished war career, Pilot Officer R. P. Beaumont became Chief Test Pilot for English Electric, Warton, testing the Canberra and Lightning.*

4. Later eighteen Do17s escorted by Bf109s attacked a convoy in the Thames Estuary. They were engaged by 54 Squadron and a furious battle ensued during which both sides suffered casualties. At the end of the day it was claimed that ten German aircraft had been destroyed for the loss of two RAF fighters.

COASTAL COMMAND OPERATIONS

The usual patrols took place over the North Sea, but the Hudson crews once again hogged the limelight.

1. Two Hudson crews of 269 Squadron attempted to shoot down a Do18 off the Norwegian coast; they damaged it, but it escaped.
2. Another two crews of 269 Squadron sighted U-Boats eighty-one miles from Muckle Flugga. They attacked one of them but failed to achieve a result.
3. A Blenheim crew of 59 Squadron on patrol off Texel (Frisian Islands) reported seeing several salvage vessels who they presumed were Russian as they were flying red flags!
4. An Anson crew of 612 Squadron searched for survivors of an He111 shot down off the coast of Scotland.

BOMBER COMMAND OPERATIONS

1. Ten Blenheims from 2 Group squadrons were detailed to carry out daylight meteorological reconnaissance and to attack airfields and industrial targets. Nine of them abandoned their tasks because of unsuitable weather conditions. The one who 'pressed on' bombed an airfield at St. Aubin near Dieppe. There were no losses.

Night operations

The weather was filthy, but despite this thirteen Hampdens and twelve Whitleys were detailed for night operations.

1. The thirteen Hampdens whose targets were aircraft factories at Wezendorf and Wismar and the airfield at Evere (Brussels) were beaten by the adverse weather and failed to bomb.
2. The Whitley targets were the battleship *Bismarck*, the liners *Bremen* and *Europa* at Hamburg and the battleship *Tirpitz* located at Wilhelmshaven.

OPERATIONAL LOSSES

None recorded

'BAD WEATHER'

"Our crew was one of those detailed for Hamburg and I was making my 'debut' as first wireless operator - up to now I'd been flying as 'Tail-end Charlie'. As we flew across the North Sea the weather worsened and we were in cloud all the time picking up ice. We pressed on hoping the weather would improve, but we were out of luck and we were still in cloud when we reached our Expected Time of Arrival at the target. We stooged around hoping to find a gap through which to descend and bomb, but were unable to do so. We presumed we must have been in the vicinity of the target because of the Flak bursts in the cloud around us, an alarming spectacle. After some considerable time we gave it up as a bad job and set course for home, still in the murk which persisted practically all the way until we reached base where we landed safely.

"Despite the disappointment of having to abandon our task on my debut, I was pleased to get a personal mention in our Squadron Record Book: 'A number of loop fixes brought this aircraft back with remarkable accuracy'. Another consolation was there no losses from any of the night sorties."

Larry Donnelly

Thursday 25th July

SUNNY WITH CLEAR SKIES, WARM.

A 149 Squadron Wellington waits to receive its bomb-load.

ENEMY AIR ACTIVITY

The fine weather during the morning proved to be an ominous portent for what was to come. The first enemy aircraft were reconnaissance planes searching for shipping. At 10.40 hours the first attack came in the form of Ju87 Stukas attacking Portland. Around noon several bombers and Bf109s approached Dover. They were engaged by 65 Squadron, Flight Sergeant Franklin causing one of the 109s to plunge into the sea. Pilot Officer V. G Daw, of 32 (Hurricane) Squadron mixing it with six Messerschmitts was wounded and force landed his damaged aircraft.

2. At 14.30 hours a convoy of small ships was attacked by Ju87s escorted by Bf109s off Dover. A battle ensued during which two Spitfires were lost. This onslaught was followed by another carried out by thirty Ju88s escorted by fifty plus Bf109s. They were engaged by twelve Hurricane squadrons that were unable to prevent them from sinking five and damaging several other ships of the convoy.

3. Another battle took place at 16.21 hours when 54 and 64 Squadrons endeavoured to protect two RN destroyers which had sunk two E-Boats off Calais. 56 (Hurricane) Squadron and 610 (Spitfire) Squadron joined in the fight which involved one hundred enemy aircraft.

4. Also during the afternoon Ju88s set out to attack the Gloucester aircraft factory at Hucclecote. One of them, flown by Unteroffizier Heine, was intercepted by Pilot Officers Bird and Manlove of No.4 Ferry Pilots Pool who were joined by Flight Lieutenant Prosser-Hanks, a Battle of France veteran now instructing with No.5 OTU. They caught up with Heine over Gloucester where a running fight took place resulting in the Ju88 and a Hurricane falling near the village of Oakridge Lynch. All four of the Ju88 crew baled out, but Pilot Officer Bird was found dead in his Hurricane. It is not clear whether he had collided with the Ju88 or had been shot down by its return fire.

In the most hectic day's fighting so far, sixteen enemy aircraft were claimed to have been destroyed for the loss of six Fighter Command aircraft.

COASTAL COMMAND OPERATIONS

1. At 06.00 hours two Blenheim crews of 59 Squadron on Channel patrol off Portland Bill came across the grim results of an attack on shipping during the previous night. They spotted a lifeboat with 40 to 50 persons on board and directed a naval unit to it which picked up the survivors. Later more lifeboats, unfortunately empty, were spotted fourteen miles off Portland Bill with lifejackets, wreckage and bodies floating in the vicinity.

2. In the afternoon another 59 Squadron Blenheim crew took off from Thorney Island to locate destroyers in the same area, but it was attacked by a Bf109 flown by Unteroffizier Karl Born of *7./JG27* and shot down.

3. Also during the afternoon Pilot Officer Starky and his crew of 53 Blenheim Squadron took off from Detling from which they failed to return.

4. The Photographic Reconnaissance Unit now operating with Coastal Command was carrying out five or six sorties a day and the sorties of the 25th proved to be successful. The flights they accomplished covered Antwerp and the Dutch Coast, Le Havre and Cap Gris Nez.

Night operations

In the early hours of the 26th Pilot Officer Turnbull and his crew of 59 Squadron took off from Thorney Island on a night sortie to bomb Cherbourg. They failed to return.

British servicemen inspect the remains of the Junkers Ju88 near Oakridge Lynch.

CRASH INVESTIGATION

One of the strangest and most confusing incidents of the battle occurred over the village of Oakridge Lynch, between Stroud and Cirencester. Ju88s of *5/KG51 'Edelweiss'* had set off from their base at Metz and flew via Cherbourg to the Gloster aircraft factory at Hucclecote, where Hurricanes were produced. From the training airfields in the West Country fighters scrambled in an attempt to intercept the raiders. From Kemble, Pilot Officer Charles Bird and Manlove of No.4 Ferry Pilots Pool set off in Hurricanes belonging to No.5 MU. They were joined by Flight Lieutenant Peter Prosser Hanks, a Battle of France veteran now instructing with No.5 OTU, in Spitfire P9501.

A 15 year-old schoolboy living at Oakridge Lynch on that Thursday afternoon recalled the memorable day:

'My recollections of that day are still quite clear. In those days grammar schools worked on Saturday mornings and had a half day on Thursday. One of the parachutists landed in the next door garden, adjacent to Oakridge school, he injured his face when he hit the sundial on the lawn, I remember that he seemed very young, perhaps only 18.
'There was certainly machine-gun fire, I later saw several deep marks on the backs of the propeller blades, but there was also a collision in the cloud. A Hurricane fell in a field on Oakridge Common, I remember the ammunition exploding in the subsequent fire. The starboard engine of the bomber was sheared off at the leading edge of the wing and the propeller fell in a field bordering Farm Lane. The Ju88 crashed in a steep valley known locally as Bidcombes. The wreckage was difficult to remove as the area has no vehicular access and it had to be winched out on sledges.
'The other parachutists were spread over several miles. The first came down near Finch's Farm at Tunley and was discovered in a field of corn. The second man came down unhurt and landed close to the Waterlane – Oakridge cross-roads. The final man was killed when his parachute failed to open and he fell in Oldhills Wood.'

It is recorded that one man was taken into custody by a Captain Weston, the village schoolmaster and local Homeguard / LDV leader.

The pilot of the Hurricane P3271 that collided the Ju88 was Pilot Officer Charles Alec Bird from Adle, Yorkshire. Credit for the destruction of this bomber has been given to Peter Prosser Hanks. It has also been published that this Ju88 collided with a Miles Master flown by Sergeant G H Bell of No.5 Flying Training School, but this is not the case.

Thursday 25th July

The tail of a Blenheim shot down on this day, probably that of L9469 or R3763.

BOMBER COMMAND OPERATIONS

1. Four Blenheim crews of 2 Group were dispatched during the day to carry out meteorological reconnaissance and to attack airfields. Three returned having abandoned their tasks because of unsuitable weather. The fourth crew, of 101 Squadron West Raynham, took off at 16.20 hours to carry out a weather reconnaissance over the Channel and Cherbourg. They were intercepted over Cherbourg Leutnant Herbert Wasserzier flying a Bf109 of *7./JG27* and shot down into the sea at 19.25 hours.

Night operations

Although the weather conditions were very bad a maximum effort of night operations was called for. All Groups were involved but the 1 Group Fairey Battle participation was cancelled.

1. Twelve Blenheims of 2 Group were detailed to attack airfields at Jever, De Kooy and Enelde. Two failed to return but the rest claimed to have bombed their targets.

2. The targets for the Wellington were an aircraft factory at Gotha, a synthetic oil plant at Dortmund and the marshalling yards at Scherte, Soest and Hamm. Twenty-seven crews claimed to have bombed primary targets, twelve self-illuminating targets, seven airfields and nine failed to bomb. Two crews failed to return. The crews reported fires and explosions at Dortmund and claimed that the factory at Gotha was hit resulting in flashes illuminating aircraft flying at 7,000 feet. Several of the crews reported intense searchlight and night fighter activity. A crew held in the searchlights near Dortmund evaded a Bf110. Another two crews fired on an Bf110 which appeared to dive out of control and another rear gunner returned the fire from an enemy aircraft which dived steeply away. One Bf110 of *III./NJG1* which crashed near Coesfeld may have been shot down by, or had collided with, one of the Wellingtons which were shot down.

3. Twenty-four Whitleys were detailed for night operations to attack synthetic oil plants at Sterkrade and Boltrope and industrial targets in the Ruhr. Fifteen crews claimed to have bombed the oil plants and reported the opposition as severe. One bomber was hit by Flak and landed at Bircham Newton. Four crews bombed alternative targets. Of the five crews detailed to attack the Ruhr targets, one returned early and four bombed primary targets. One fighter was seen but did not attack.

4. The Hampden force had a variety of targets. Twelve attacked Dortmund-Ems Canal where four special 'M' bombs were dropped. Dortmund continued to be a prime target throughout the war because of its importance as an inland waterway.

PETER PROSSER HANKS

Prosser Hanks was 22 years old in 1940 when he went to France with No.1 Squadron. He claimed six victories in the first five days of May before he was shot down and baled out of his Hurricane. He returned to England and was posted to No.5 OTU at Aston Down as an instructor. In December 1940 he continued operational flying, this time with No.257 Squadron. By the war's end he had been credited with 13 enemy aircraft destroyed and the rank of Group Captain, by coincidence as Station Commander of Aston Down.

The remaining Hampdens bombed the other targets which included Wanne-Eickel and the synthetic oil plant at Castrop-Rauxel. Six crews dropped leaflets. One crew was lost and another crashed at Happisburgh (Norfolk) on return. The following message from the Commander in Chief, Bomber Command, was sent, 'Please convey to all in Nos. 3, 4 and 5 Groups my heartiest congratulations. Despite adverse weather conditions, they have done a wonderful week's work culminating in last night's success.'

Lt Rosler examines the engine of the crashed Blenheim illustrated opposite.

OPERATIONAL LOSSES

Blenheim IV R3836 of 53 Squadron, Detling, failed to return from an attack on invasion barges off Holland. Pilot Officer D. B. Starky (New Zealander) and Sergeant B. Moriarty (Irish) are recorded on the Runnymede Memorial. The body of Sergeant H. W. Hunt (Canadian) was found and buried at Jonkerbos.
This is probably the "Breguet 690" claimed by Unteroffizier Edmund Rossmann of 7./JG 52, some 40 kilometres east of Margate.

Blenheim IV L9473 of 59 Squadron, Thorney Island, was shot down while on an Air Sea Rescue patrol off Portland Bill. Flying Officer H. Haswell (South African), Sergeant R. B. Martin and Sergeant D. B. Simpson were lost and are commemorated on the Runnymede Memorial.

Blenheim IV T1801 of 59 Squadron, Thorney Island, failed to return from a night bombing sortie on Cherbourg. Pilot Officer M. R. Turnbull and Sergeant G. P. Rowe are commemorated on the Runnymede Memorial. The body of Sergeant D. Wallace was washed ashore and buried at Criel-sur-Mer.

Blenheim N6174 of 101 Squadron, West Raynham, lost on a sortie to Cherbourg. Pilot Officer R. E. Short, Sergeant J. Parkinson and Sergeant K. V. Gibson were lost without trace and are commemorated on the Runnymede Memorial

Blenheim L9469 of 15 Squadron Wyton, detailed to attack Wilhelmshaven, is believed to have been shot down over the sea. Pilot Officer C. H. Robinson, Pilot Officer A. L McLaggan and Sergeant L. J. Horton were presumed killed and their names are on the Runnymede Memorial.

Blenheim R3763 of 40 Squadron, Wyton, detailed to attack an airfield at Eelde, Holland was lost. Sergeant P. H. Steele, Sergeant J. Moore and Sergeant R. Peacock were taken prisoner.

Hampden P1321 of 50 Squadron, Lindholme, detailed to attack Castrop-Rauxel was damaged by enemy action and lost an engine over Cuxhaven, but managed to get back over the North Sea only to crash on the beach at Happisburgh (Norfolk). Flying Officer W. A. Mulloy DFC, Sergeant G. R. Watt, Sergeant A. L. Stewart and Pilot Officer T. M. Taylor were all killed

.

Hampden L4094 of 83 Squadron, Scampton, detailed to attack targets on the Dortmund-Ems Canal, crashed at Wesel. Pilot Officer W. O. D. Tweddell DFC, Sergeant G. W. Jones and Sergeant D. G. J. Townsend were killed and are buried in the Reichswald Forest Cemetery. The fourth crew member, Sergeant P. J. Tointon was taken prisoner.

Wellington R3235 of 75 Squadron, Feltwell, detailed to attack Kassel, crashed near Amsterdam. The entire crew, Flying Officer W. H. Coleman DFC (RNZAF), Pilot Officer F. T. Poole, Sergeant N. W. Brown DFM, Sergeant J. Dowds, Sergeant W. E. Nevill and Sergeant W. D. F. Annan (RNZAF) were killed and are buried in the New Eastern Cemetery, Amsterdam.

Wellington P9274 of 99 Squadron, Newmarket, crashed into trees on the airfield boundary after returning with engine failure on a sortie to NW Germany. The crew; Sergeant A. J. Herriot, Sergeant Summer, Sergeant Smith, Sergeant Evans, Sergeant Wright and Sergeant Watkin, are presumed to have escaped unhurt.

Wellington P9275 of 99 Squadron, Newmarket, failed to return from operations over NW Germany. Flying Officer J. L. Scott, Sergeant H. J. Casselden, Sergeant H. F. Heritage, Sergeant A. L. Walker and Sergeant K. R. Sellwood were taken prisoner. The other member of the crew, Pilot Officer B. A. Power was killed and is buried in the Rheinberg War Cemetery.
This aircraft was credited to Leutnant Pack of I./NJG 1, who himself perished with his crew this night. It is possible – indeed probable - that Pack collided with his opponent seven kilometres southwest of Coesfeld at 01.14 hours.

Friday 26th July

SHOWERS AND CLOUD OVER THE WHOLE COUNTRY.

The Fokker T-VIII was one of those rare types that saw service both with the RAF and the Luftwaffe.

ENEMY AIR ACTIVITY

Rain and low cloud reduced enemy activity during the day, but during the night widespread raids took place as far apart as Fraserburgh (Scotland) Bristol and Wales.

COASTAL COMMAND OPERATIONS

An unusual incident occurred in the Irish Sea when a Dutch crew and aircraft crashed into the water whilst patrolling a convoy. The aircraft was a Fokker T-VIIIW twin engined seaplane, once operated by the Royal Netherlands Naval Air Service, but now serving with 320 Squadron based at Pembroke Dock. The wreckage was found floating 13 miles ESE of St Goven's Head, but its four man crew were all killed.

BOMBER COMMAND OPERATIONS

Weather was far from favourable but fourteen Blenheims were detailed to carry out reconnaissance and attacks against Schipol and Waalhaven airfields and the Dortmund power station. Because of the unsuitable conditions only three bombed. There were no losses.

Night operations

The adverse weather also affected night operations. The Wellington squadrons had the night off but eighteen Hampdens and nine Whitleys were dispatched to attack St. Nazaire, Nantes, Hamm and Mannheim. The Hampdens, whose targets were oil installations at St. Nazaire and Nantes, were fortunate to be able to carry out successful attacks in bright moonlight. The Whitley crews were not so lucky. They ploughed through the murk to Mannheim and Hamm, but only three of them were able to bomb and one failed to return.

OPERATIONAL LOSSES

Fokker T-VIIIW AV964 of 320 Squadron, Pembroke Dock, lost on a convoy escort in the Irish Sea. Off E. Martare and Kpl J. G. Ras were brought ashore and are buried at Llanion Cemetery, Pembrokeshire. The bodies of Off J. C. Den Hollander and Sergt-Maj A. de Knegt were not recovered.

Whitley N1377 of 102 Squadron, Driffield, target Mannheim, force landed at 01.30 hours fifteen miles south west of Rotterdam. Pilot Officer R. F. Beauclair, Pilot Officer J. W. Bushell, Sergeant E. A. Caloway, Sergeant C. Wood and Sergeant K. J. Read were all taken prisoner.

Skua L2906 of 801 Squadron Fleet Air Arm lost on operations. The names of Sub Lieutenant A. Hartoch and Naval Airman I. S. Bass appear on the Lee-on Solent memorial

A 102 Squadron Whitley after a forced landing in the UK.

As the skies darken over Waterbeach, the crew of a 99 Squadron Wellington climb aboard via the nose hatch.

ENEMY AIR ACTIVITY

The weather improved in the south and the Luftwaffe took advantage of it sending thirty Stukas escorted by Bf109s to attack a convoy off Swanage. They were intercepted by Spitfires which engaged the escort while Hurricanes engaged the Stukas.

In the afternoon two attacks on Dover took place during which *HMS Codrington* was sunk. In another engagement *HMS Wren* was sunk off Aldeburgh. Night raids took place on Belfast, Gillingham and Maidstone.

COASTAL COMMAND OPERATIONS

Eighty-two crews flew patrols mainly over the North Sea towards Norway. One Hudson attacked a Norwegian motor vessel dropping ten 100lb anti-submarine bombs scoring a direct hit on the stern. The crew was seen to abandon the ship. There were no losses.

BOMBER COMMAND OPERATIONS

Fifteen Blenheim crews were detailed to attack German naval targets in daylight at Wilhelmshaven and barges at Ijmuiden. Only three were able to take advantage of cloud cover and carry out bombing attacks. There were no losses due to enemy action, but an accident occurred at Newton. During the bombing up of a Fairey Battle a bomb fell off and ignited, setting the machine on fire. As the crew and ground staff fought the fire the wreck blew up and killed six men.

Night operations

It was the Whitley crews' turn for a night off.

Twenty-four Wellington crews and seven Hampden crews were dispatched to bomb targets at Bremen, Wilhelmshaven and Hamburg. Two oil refineries were bombed and fires started. The aircraft who failed to bomb the primary targets bombed airfields and other targets of opportunity.

Twelve Hampdens laid mines in German waters and six others from the OTU dropped leaflets over France.

OPERATIONAL LOSSES

Battle L5528 of 150 Squadron, Newton, exploded on the ground. Flying Officer W. M. Blom DFC, Sergeant W. H. J. Franklin BEM, Sergeant C. T. Gould (SAAF), Corporal D. H. Sharp, LAC W. Y. Cann, LAC G. A. Hall and AC1 F. Stewart were all killed.

Sunday 28th July

SUNNY WITH CLEAR SKIES, WARM, GETTING CLOUDY TOWARDS THE EVENING.

A 142 Squadron Fairey Battle. The squadron lost two of these aircraft to enemy action today.

ENEMY ACTIVITY

The weather was fine and a large force of German bombers escorted by Bf109s was detected approaching Dover and intercepted by our Spitfires and Hurricanes. After dark He115 float planes laid mines while He111s and Ju88s carried out widespread bombing attacks.

COASTAL COMMAND OPERATIONS

Ninety-one crews carried out daylight reconnaissance and patrols. A Sunderland crew of 10 RAAF Squadron, Mount Batten, was sent to search for the U-Boat which had torpedoed the *Auckland Star* north-west of Skelligs. Photographic reconnaissance sorties were carried out over Boulogne, Cherbourg and Caen to Cap Gris Nez in France as well as Kristiansund, Stavanger and Bergen in Norway.

Night operations

Three Hudsons of 206 Squadron were dispatched to carry out a night attack on oil tanks at Amsterdam. One aborted but the two others bombed, suffering Flak damage in the process. There were no casualties. Six Blenheims of 59 Squadron were detailed to bomb oil tanks at Cherbourg. Only three were successful. There were no losses from the night operations.

BOMBER COMMAND OPERATIONS

Seven Blenheim crews of 82 Squadron were detailed to attack Leeuwarden airfield in daylight. Because of the lack of suitable cloud cover six turned back, but the seventh flown by Wing Commander Lart and his crew pressed on alone. When they reached their target there were twelve Bf109s parked near the hangars. They quickly released their bombs on them and high-tailed it for home. Bf109s took off to intercept them and four caught up with the Blenheim over Den Helder and began their attacks. Taking evasive action the Blenheim gunners returned their fire and one fighter was seen to go down. Continuing their evasive action and taking advantage of the cloud cover the Blenheim fought off the fighters who eventually broke off their attacks. The Blenheim got back to base, but because of the damage incurred during the fight, when landing its undercarriage collapsed and the aircraft slid along on its belly. When it came to a halt the fortunate uninjured crew carried out a speedy evacuation.

Destruction of this aircraft was credited to Leutnant Herbert Kargel of 4./JG 27 during the battle over Leeuwarden at 20.35 hours.

Night operations

Crews from all five Groups participated in the night operations. Four Fairey Battles were dispatched to attack the airfield at Evere. Only one of the crews reported making an attack and two failed to return, both of them were engaged over Marquise and claimed by *II./JG 26.*

Six Blenheims of 110 Squadron were detailed to attack French airfields. Four claimed to have bombed successfully. The Wellington and Hampden crews whose targets were oil installations at Hamburg, Bremen and Kamen and marshalling yards at Hamm were frustrated by the weather and their attacks were widely scattered. One Hampden failed to return. Twelve others carried out mining sorties. The fourteen Whitleys detailed to attack the Dornier aircraft factory at Wismar and the airfield at Travemünde claimed to have bombed, but because of the weather conditions they were unable to observe their results. The crews reported that enemy aircraft were dropping flares in the area and that night fighters were seen but did not attack.

OPERATIONAL LOSSES

Fairey Battle L5502 of 142 Squadron, Binbrook, attacking airfields in the Brussels region, failed to return. Flight Lieutenant R. H. Edwards, Sergeant R. W. Cornwell and Sergeant R. E. Hotchkiss were taken prisoner. On 26th September 1942 Flight Lieutenant Edwards was shot attempting to escape from a PoW camp near Poznan in Poland . He is now buried in the Poznan Garrison Cemetery.

Fairey Battle L5584 of 142 Squadron, Binbrook, attacking airfields in the Brussels area, was lost without trace. Pilot Officer M. J. A. Kirdy, Sergeant N. Longcluse and Sergeant McG. Hettle are all commemorated on the Runnymede Memorial.

Hampden P4375 of 44 Squadron failed to return. While flying at 8,000 feet over Hamburg it collided with a balloon cable and crashed in the target area. Squadron Leader J. G. Macintyre was killed, but Sergeant V. A. Coveyduck, Sergeant A. Cross and Sergeant J. H. R. Edgar were taken prisoner.

Monday 29th July

ENEMY AIR ACTIVITY

The weather was fine again and a large raid on Dover took place during the morning, followed by raids on Channel convoys in the afternoon. At night there were limited attacks which included the bombing of nine targets in the North East.

COASTAL COMMAND OPERATIONS

The usual daily reconnaissance and convoy patrols were carried out. Sunderland P9602 of 10 RAAF Squadron Mount Batten, en-route for Gibraltar, was attacked by a Do18 at 47.58'N/06.52'W and returned to base. There were no casualties.

Night operations

Night strikes were carried out by 53 and 59 Blenheim Squadrons and 206 Hudson Squadron.

Eight Blenheims of 53 Squadron attacked shipping at Emden. Four Blenheims of 59 Squadron bombed oil tanks at Cherbourg and six Hudsons of 206 Squadron bombed oil tanks at Amsterdam. Two Hudsons suffered Flak damage but there were no casualties or losses.

BOMBER COMMAND OPERATIONS

Fourteen Blenheims were detailed to carry out daylight raids against Bremen and Dutch airfields. Only six bombed and one failed to return.

Night operations

The weather conditions were far from favourable for night operations. All three Battles of 150 Squadron dispatched to attack Waalhaven airfield aborted because of the conditions. Twenty-six Wellingtons were detailed to attack oil targets at Hamburg, Köln and Monheim, but again the weather conditions interfered and only twelve bombed. Twenty-two Hampdens targeted Frankfurt and the Dortmund-Ems canal. Fifteen managed to bomb. Twelve others laid mines in German waters. Eleven out of the sixteen Whitleys dispatched to bomb the marshalling yards at Hamm and installations at Reisholtz, claimed successful attacks. There were no losses.

OPERATIONAL LOSSES

Blenheim R3619 of 82 Squadron, Watton, target Bremen, shot down into the sea. Flight Lieutenant F. W. S. Keighley, and Sergeant J. W. H. Parsons were taken prisoner, but Sergeant K. D. MacPherson was killed and is buried on the island of Texel.

This fell to Leutnant Hans Bosch of Stab II./JG 27 near Texel at 13.07 hours.

Hampden crews climb aboard the transport waiting to take them to their aircraft, not an easy task in full flying clothing!

Tuesday 30th July

Heavy cloud with some rain and drizzle.

An assortment of Blenheims from 110 Sqn, (VE) 15 Sqn, (LS) 82 Sqn (UX) and 107 Sqn (OM) lined up at RAF Wyton in August 1940. The type in the foreground is a Percival Q.6 communications aircraft.

ENEMY ACTIVITY

There was low cloud and drizzle and, taking advantage of the cover it afforded, the Luftwaffe mounted raids over Scotland and a strike on shipping off the Suffolk coast.

That night the Bay of Liverpool was mined extensively. Bombing attacks were mainly directed against targets in Wales and Lancashire.

COASTAL COMMAND OPERATIONS

The Anson, Blenheim, Hudson and Sunderland squadrons continued their patrols and reconnaissance despite the weather. Sunderland 'F' of 10 RAAF Squadron engaged Ju88s attacking shipping at 50.32'N/08.3'W.

BOMBER COMMAND OPERATIONS

Twenty-four 2 Group Blenheims carried out daylight raids on French, Belgian and Dutch airfields, an aircraft park at Paderborn and a synthetic oil plant at Gelsenkirchen. One failed to return from Paderborn.

Night operations

Because of the adverse weather over the continent the only night operations were carried out by fourteen Wellingtons who were dispatched to attack synthetic oil plants at Monheim and Hamburg and marshalling yards at Mönchengladbach. Because of the filthy weather only four bombed their primary target, one bombed the alternative and six bombed self illuminating targets. Three failed to bomb.

OPERATIONAL LOSSES

Blenheim R3764 of 15 Squadron, Wyton, failed to return from attacking Paderborn. It is believed the aircraft crashed in the Scheldt. Pilot Officer P. F. Eames was taken prisoner. Pilot Officer F. H. Jones was killed and is buried at Breskens (Zeeland). Sergeant P. Murphy is commemorated on the Runnymede Memorial.

This probably fell to Uffz Joachim Schreckenberg of 8./JG 54.

The Wellington was tough! This 99 Squadron Wimpey returned to base with over half of its tail missing.

A 15 Squadron Blenheim cruises over the English countryside during the summer of 1940.

ENEMY AIR ACTIVITY

Hazy conditions resulted in the Luftwaffe being limited to single aircraft operations, Bf109s shooting down barrage balloons. At night the activity increased and targets mainly south of a line Newcastle to Liverpool, namely, Ipswich, Croydon, Romford and Gravesend were attacked.

Vegetables

Sgt Joe Taylor, 61 Sqn Hampden

At briefing that evening, we learned that we were to go on a '*gardening*' trip with a '*vegetable*' to the Baltic. At first I was flummoxed. The expressions were gibberish to me and I soon learned that '*gardening*' was laying mines in the sea, and the mines to be laid were '*vegetables*'. These *vegetables* were long cylinders, and the Hampden bomb bays were just large enough to accommodate one. An old R.N. Chief Petty Officer used to fuse them up before loading. It was both alarming and amusing to see him operate with a long string of scissor like trolleys, each supporting one of these tin monsters. The C.P.O. carried his tools and other paraphenalia in an old Gladstone bag. He invariably smoked a pipe. When the time came for his attentions, it was noticeable that the R.A.F. characters seemed to melt away, and little wonder! He would place his bag down beside the *vegetable* to be treated, pick up a screwdriver and spanner, open a flap in the monster's side, stick in his hand complete with spanner and nonchalantly rattle around at some invisible mechanism inside. I suppose he knew what he was doing but we lads in the lighter blue outfits were not so trusting and kept a discreet distance, usually with a hangar in between from his scene of operations.

COASTAL COMMAND OPERATIONS

Patrols, escorts and reconnaissance flights were carried out throughout the period. Anson 'Z' of 500 Squadron carrying out a convoy escort south east of Harwich, was fired on by RN AA ships. Unfortunately for the Anson crew their marksmanship was better than their aircraft recognition and Flight Sergeant Ward, the Anson observer, was wounded in the leg.

Sunderland P9601 of 10 RAAF Squadron, on convoy patrol engaged Ju88s attacking the *SS Moolthan*.

Sunderland 'B' of 10 RAAF Squadron on patrol over the Western approaches attacked a crash-diving U-Boat at 56.08'N/09.37'W, but saw no positive result. Hudsons of 233 Squadron carried out reconnaissance in the Kristiansund area of Norway. One failed to return.

Hudson 'E' of 233 Squadron carried out an attack on a U-Boat during the hours of darkness 160 miles east of St. Abb's Head.

BOMBER COMMAND OPERATIONS

Twenty-eight Blenheims were detailed to carry out daylight raids on enemy airfields and industrial targets in Germany. Because of the lack of suitable cloud cover only eleven bombed, one failed to return. Battles of 12 Squadron were detailed to attack the invasion ports. Unfortunately one was shot down by an RAF night fighter and crashed in the sea off Skegness.

Night operations

Night operations were planned to be carried out by Battle, Blenheim and Hampden squadrons. The Wellington and Whitley crews had the night off. Six Blenheim attacked Le Bourget airfield and six Battles attacked the invasion ports. Eighteen Hampdens attacked various targets in Germany, while another twelve carried out mining in German coastal waters. Two of the mine-laying aircraft failed to return. A third Hampden, P1327 flown by Squadron Leader Oxley, was damaged beyond repair when overstressed over the North Sea.

Wednesday 31st July

A mine is carefully manoeuvered towards the waiting bomb bay of a Hampden. The straps around the end of the weapon are part of a parachute mechanism designed to ensure that the mine entered the water smoothly. The Hampden's large and single-section bomb-bay made it the ideal type to carry out minelaying, a task that it carried out until late 1942.

OPERATIONAL LOSSES

Hudson N7224 of 233 Squadron, Leuchars, failed to return from a sortie in the Kristiansand (Norway) area. Pilot Officer J. H. Horan (Australian), Sergeant W. G. Cameron and Sergeant S. Morgan. Were posted missing and their names are on the Runnymede Memorial. The body of Pilot Officer B. C. Paton was recovered from the sea and buried at Kristiansand.

It is believed that it fell victim to either Unteroffizier Otto Niemayer of 4./JG77 or Oberfeldwebel Georg Bergmann of 9./JG 77, both flying Bf109s and both claiming "Blenheims".

Blenheim R3895 of 114 Squadron, Horsham St. Faith, failed to return from attacking Aalborg. Squadron Leader M. N. McKennedy, Pilot Officer J. B. P. Hanlon and Sergeant G. Reinhart were subsequently reported as prisoners of war.

This appears to have been the Blenheim engaged west of Ijmuiden at 10.15 hours by Feldwebel Helmut Karstadt of II./JG 54.

Battle L5568 of 12 Squadron, Binbrook, detailed to attack invasion ports was shot down by a night fighter from 29 Squadron into the sea off Skegness. Flying Officer B. E. Moss, Sergeant B. C. Long and Sergeant T. J. Radley were all killed. Their bodies were recovered and taken for burial at Binbrook (St. Mary's) churchyard

Hampden L4085 of 44 Squadron, Waddington, returning from a mining operation, got lost and flew across southern England before ditching in Cardigan Bay. Sergeant E. D. Farmer and Sergeant C. E. T. Wood were killed. Sergeant R. D. Hobbs and Sergeant D. Seager survived and were picked up the motor boat *Emerald Star* which also picked up one body. The other body was recovered by the Aberystwyth lifeboat.

Hampden P4383 of 50 Squadron, Lindholme, lost on a minelaying operation. Presumed to have ditched 40/45 miles east of Flamborough Head after all contact had been lost at 04.10 hours. Pilot Officer B. S. Bell's body was washed onto the Dutch coast six weeks later and is buried in Bergen Op Zoom War Cemetery. Sergeant W. E. Miller, Sergeant C. D. Evans and Sergeant D. Tailford are commemorated on the Runnymede Memorial.

August 1940

The main battle is joined

August - The main battle is joined

After the Luftwaffe had spent the month of July carrying out air attacks to probe and assess British air defences Hitler, having had no reply to his so-called 'peace overtures' to the British Government, outlined his plans for '*Adlerangriff*' which was to provide the conditions for the final conquest of England. The Luftwaffe's initial task was to destroy RAF Fighter Command entirely, its flying units, ground installations, supply and its supporting aircraft industry. When this had been achieved the Luftwaffe would assist the Army and Navy in the execution of *Operation 'Sealion'*, (the invasion of England).

Dornier Do17s tighten the formation as they head for their target, the gunners keeping watch for fighters.

On the first day of August, Reichsmarschall Goering held a meeting at The Hague to discuss the forthcoming operations with his Luftwaffe commanders. During the discussion the commanders were hesitant to agree to carry out daylight attacks to destroy the RAF because of the possibility of incurring severe losses. Instead they suggested continuous night bombing attacks, but Goering over-ruled them believing that the RAF had been weakened sufficiently to enable the Luftwaffe to carry out successful attacks in daylight to achieve their objective.

Consequently the '*Adlerangriff*' Directive was issued on 2nd August, delegating Luftflotte 2, commanded by Field Marshal Koshering and Luftflotte 3 commanded by Feldmarschall Sperrle, with the task of destroying the defences protecting the south east of England including London. The attacks were to be carried out in three phases - the first phase to destroy targets within a radius of ninety miles of London - the second phase to destroy targets within sixty to thirty miles of London - and the third, final phase to destroy the targets within a thirty mile circle of London. The Luftwaffe High Command estimated the whole operation could be completed in two to four weeks! On 6th August, Goering initially set the date for the opening of the main attack of Phase 1 as 10th August. Because of unsuitable weather this was postponed to a final date of the 13th August.

In the meantime the Luftwaffe resumed attacks on the English Channel shipping and between the 8th and 11th August, seven motor vessels were sunk and six damaged. In the air battles which took place when RAF fighters protected the shipping the Luftwaffe lost sixty-six aircraft destroyed and ten damaged. RAF losses were forty-five destroyed and seven damaged.

On 12th August, as a prelude to '*Adlerangriff*', the Luftwaffe attacked RAF forward airfields of Manston, Hawkinge and Lympne, putting them temporarily out of action. Six radar stations were also attacked. 13th August was dull and overcast in the morning, delaying the start of heavy attacks which were mounted on the RAF airfields of Detling and Andover, the port of Southampton and our Channel shipping. Widespread attacks continued and at night, the Spitfire factory at Castle Bromwich was damaged.

On 15th August the Luftwaffe suffered its heaviest losses during this 'phase'. Fortunately cloudy weather prevented them from locating and attacking Fighter Command airfields and during their attacks on other targets which were completely irrelevant to Fighter Command operations, the Luftwaffe lost fifty aircraft destroyed and eight heavily damaged. Also suffering from the delusion that northern based fighters would be moved south to bolster the defence against the main attacks in the south, an attack against northern bomber bases was mounted from Norway and Denmark by Luftflotte 5. They paid dearly for their delusion. The force

Previous page: Blenheim V5595 YH-P of 21 Squadron on the beach at Gravelines after being shot down by flak. Miraculously, all the crew survived.

comprised of He111s and Ju88s escorted by Bf110s were intercepted by fighters of 13 Group who destroyed fifteen He111s/Ju88s and seven Bf110s for the loss of one Hurricane. Three more of the Luftwaffe force were damaged with others unlikely to get back to their bases.

Some Ju88s managed to get through the fighter screen to clobber RAF Driffield. They destroyed ten dispersed Whitleys and caused damage and casualties. It is worth noting that this was the first and last mass raid carried out by Luftflotte 5.

Up to and including 18th August the battle to destroy airfields continued. Harwell, Brize Norton, Farnborough, Ford, Gosport, Worthy Down, Eastchurch, Linton-on-Ouse, Dishforth and Andover were attacked - all these airfields were unrelated to the air defence of the UK. For some reason airfields such as Hornchurch, Northolt, Debden, North Weald, Gravesend and West Hampnet were left off the Luftwaffe list. 18th August is looked upon by some as being the climax of the Battle, both sides reaching their highest total of casualties.

On 19th August Goering announced, 'We have reached the decisive period of the air war against England'. He decided that Luftflotte 2 with its bases nearer to south east England were to bear the brunt of the daylight fighting while Luftflotte 3 would undertake night raids, their joint aim being to destroy 11 Group Fighter Command whose bases ringed London.

There was a lull in the fighting from 19th to the 23rd August while the fighter force was reorganised under Luftflotte 2. The second 'Phase' of '*Adlerangriff*' began on 24th August. During one of Luftflotte 3's night attacks on Gravesend and Thameshaven the target was overshot and bombs dropped in the centre of London.

In retaliation RAF Bomber Command bombed Berlin on the night of 25/26th August and on another three nights by the end of the month. The damage caused was not great, but the effect on the morale of the civilian Berliners was considerable, having been assured by Goering that no RAF bombs would fall on Berlin. Hitler's reaction was a severe attack of the 'Rants' during which he stated, 'When they declare they will attack our cities in great strength, then we will erase theirs' and on 31st August he gave permission for reprisal day and night attacks on London to take place. In doing so he diverted attacks from Fighter Command airfields to London, which gave Fighter Command squadrons the 'breathing space' they sorely needed. If the airfield attacks had continued, who knows, the Luftwaffe may have achieved a degree of air superiority. Throughout the month of August, Bomber and Coastal Command squadrons were heavily engaged:

Coastal Command

Spitfires of the Photographic Reconnaissance Unit carried out continuous sorties to provide information and confirmation that the German invasion sources were gathering. Anson squadrons were engaged in convoy protection patrols braving attacks from attacking bombers and fighters. Hudson squadrons carried out day and night reconnaissance patrols and strikes against enemy shipping and ports from Norway down to the French/Spanish border. Blenheim squadrons operated both during the day and night attacking shipping, ports, airfields, fuel installations, and barge concentrations. Blenheim fighter squadrons attached to Coastal Command flew armed reconnaissance, bomber escorts and airfield protection patrols. Sunderland flying boat squadrons were involved in anti-submarine, convoy protection patrols and reconnaissance. Fairey Battle squadrons and Fleet Air Arm Swordfish/Albacore squadrons carried out day and night attacks on E-Boats, seaplanes and invasion barge concentrations.

Bomber Command

2 Group squadrons were, as usual, in the thick of the action carrying out day and night attacks against enemy airfields, ports and invasion shipping in France, Germany, Holland Denmark and Belgium. 82 Squadron again suffered heavy losses on unescorted sorties. On 13th August, the Luftwaffe 'Adlerangriff', the squadron was detailed to carry out a daylight attack on the airfield at Aalborg (Denmark). Twelve Blenheims took off, one returned early and the remaining eleven were massacred. 5 Group Hampdens had an exceptionally busy and notable month of night operations, carrying out bombing attacks on a variety of targets as well as mine-laying activities. Their bombing raids included the first raids on Berlin.

One of their most notable raids took place on the night of 12th/13th August. Five crews from 49 and 83 Squadrons were detailed to attack the Ladbergen Aqueduct on the Dortmund-Ems Canal - a hazardous low-flying operation. Two of the Hampdens were shot down over the target, but Flight Lieutenant R. Learoyd flying as number five dived through the searchlights and Flak to drop his bombs. The result was that the canal was blocked for ten days, delaying the progress of the invasion barges on their way through the inland waterways to the Channel ports. Learoyd's aircraft was badly damaged, but he got it back to base circling until he was able to carry out a safe landing in daylight. For courage he was awarded Bomber Command's first Victoria Cross of WWII. The Wellington squadrons of 3 Group carried out night raids throughout the month, attacking warships berthed in port, shipyards, airfields, marshalling yards and oil installations. They also joined the Hampdens of 5 Group and the Whitleys of 4 Group to carry out the first raids on Berlin. 4 Group Whitley squadrons carried out most of the long range night operations, attacking Augsburg, the first four raids on Berlin*, and six to bomb targets in Italy. Their other targets in Germany included oil and chemical installations and aircraft factories.

** The Berlin raids, together with Fighter Command denying the Luftwaffe air superiority over England, were no doubt crucial factors influencing German policy changing from bombing RAF fighter airfields to British cities.*

Thursday 1st August

WATERY SUNSHINE BECOMING BRIGHTER LATER IN THE DAY.

'B' Flight of 18 Squadron pose for a photograph with one of their Blenheims on 1st August.

ENEMY AIR ACTIVITY

Enemy activity was on a reduced scale and consisted of reconnaissance and raids by single aircraft or small formations. Shipping was attacked and one land target bombed. Fighters claimed four of the raiders. At night the raids were sporadic and widespread over Scotland and England. Bombs were dropped at Montrose, Dundee, Hardington, Armdale and Duns. Single raids were carried out on East Anglia, the Midlands, the South and the South West of England.

COASTAL COMMAND OPERATIONS

1. Twenty-one anti-invasion, seven anti-submarine, ten photographic and six reconnaissance and searches were flown involving eighty-five aircraft.
2. A Hudson of 220 Squadron attacked three armed trawlers and a Danish auxiliary off Terschelling with bombs - no results were observed.
3. A Blenheim on reconnaissance of Cherbourg reported seeing thirty enemy aircraft - twelve near hangars and the others dispersed on the airfield. Later it was attacked by thirteen Blenheim Mk.IV bombers of 59 (B) Squadron escorted by ten Mk.IV fighter Blenheims of 236 Squadron. Hits were obtained on hangars and barrack blocks and fires were started. Enemy aircraft were strafed and an explosion occurred on the airfield. Three aircraft failed to return and two were damaged by Flak.
4. Two east coast convoys were attacked by Ju88s and in one case a motor vessel was damaged before fighters (called up by an escorting Albacore) appeared. In the second case a Hudson drove off the attackers before bombs were dropped.
5. The PRU was active during the day taking photographs of Jersey, Guernsey, The Hook of Holland, La-Rochelle, St. Nazaire, Nantes, Lorient and Brest. Lieutenant Commander Kingdon was lost on a training flight in PR Spitfire K9879 when his oxygen failed. The Spitfire fell from 30,000 feet and crashed near Crewkerne, Somerset.

BOMBER COMMAND OPERATIONS

Twelve 2 Group Blenheims were detailed to carry out daylight attacks on airfields and oil plants. Seven crews abandoned their task because of lack of cloud cover but the others 'pressed on'. Two crews attacked Leeuwarden airfield, but the results were not observed.

One aircraft attacked Haamstede airfield and obtained hits on a new hangar as well as strafing dispersed aircraft and transport. Another crew bombed a Flak ship thirty miles west of Den Helder. One aircraft failed to return.

Night operations

1. Twenty-eight Wellingtons were despatched to carry out night attacks on oil refineries and marshalling yards at Gelsenkirchen, Kamen, Hamburg, Hamm and Mannheim. Thirteen crews claimed to have bombed their primary targets causing damage and starting fires, at Kamen in particular. Others bombed alternatives and one crew claimed to have shot down an enemy aircraft over The Hague.
2. Fifteen Whitleys were detailed to carry out attacks against oil refineries at Reisholtz and Hamburg. One returned early, but nine claimed to have bombed the targets successfully, the others bombed alternatives, such as coke ovens and communications in the Ruhr.

There were no losses and for a change the Hampden boys of 5 Group had the night off, no doubt 'whooping it up' at their favourite watering holes.

Eventually, twin machine guns replaced the single Vickers gun in the Blenheim's upper turret, but they were still no match for the 20mm cannons used by the Bf109 fighters.

OPERATIONAL LOSSES

Blenheim L8792 'A' of 59 Squadron, Thorney Island, failed to return from an attack on Cherbourg. The bodies of the crew were washed ashore in France and buried; Wing Commander R. G. S. Morgan-Weld-Smith at St. Pierre-en-Port, Pilot Officer D. H. Davis AFM at St. Valery-en-Caux, and Sergeant P. Pryde at Veules-les-Roses.

Blenheim (F) N2774 of 236 Squadron, Thorney Island, also escorting 59 Squadron to Cherbourg, failed to return. Pilot Officer B. M. McDonough (Australian) and Sergeant F. A. P. Head were posted as missing in action and recorded on the Runnymede Memorial.

The Luftwaffe unit was 8./JG 27 and Blenheims were credited to Oberleutnants Walter Adolph, Enst Düllberg and Oberfeldwebel Hans Richter.

Blenheim (F) N3601 of 236 Squadron, Thorney Island, escorting the 59 Squadron aircraft to Cherbourg, failed to return. Squadron Leader P. E. Drew lies buried at Biville, and Pilot Officer B. Nokes-Cooper was buried at Bayeux.

Hudson N7314 'B' of 220 Squadron, Thornaby, hit power cables near Maltby, Yorkshire, during a patrol and crash landed. Unfortunately the bomb load exploded killing three of the crew, Flight Lieutenant H. W. A. Sheahan DFC (South African), Pilot Officer C. J. Allsup (Canadian) and Sergeant S. Smith. A fourth man, Sergeant Butler, escaped with injuries

Blenheim R3898 of 114 Squadron, Horsham St. Faith, failed to return from Haamstede. Pilot Officer J. D. Goode, Sergeant E. A. Will and Sergeant V. St.G. Barrow were all killed and are buried in Bergen Op Zoom War Cemetery.

Two Blenheims were claimed by Bf109 pilots, credited to Oblt. Franz Eckerle of 6./JG 54 and Ofw. Michael Hauer of 4 Staffel.

Messerschmitt Bf109s of JG27 during the Battle of Britain.

Friday 2nd August

RAIN AND CLOUD IN THE SOUTH, BRIGHTER TO THE NORTH.

The C/O of 15 Squadron Wing Commander J. Cox (left) prepares to board his Blenheim 'D' with his crew Pilot Officer Camp and Sergeant Treherne for an operational sortie.

ENEMY AIR ACTIVITY

The weather was dull to start off with but improved as the day wore on. When it did, the enemy concentrated on attacking shipping. Off Harwich fighter bombers sank *HM Trawler Cape Finisterre* with a direct hit. The gunners of the *SS Highlander* in a Scottish convoy shot down an He111 which was attacking them and proudly sailed into Leith with it on their deck as a trophy.

During the night ineffective raids were made on Halton, Catterick, Farnborough and Rochford.

COASTAL COMMAND OPERATIONS

1. Eighty-one aircraft flew twenty-one routine patrols and thirty-three special patrols. Seventeen convoys were escorted and eighteen Blenheims were provided as escort for naval operations which were taking place sixty miles off Lowestoft and Cromer.
2. A Hudson of 224 Squadron attacked a U-Boat five miles from Malin Head on a bearing of 286 degrees. Six 250lb AS bombs were used. The Hudson crew claimed the U-Boat was damaged, but this was not confirmed.
3. Other Hudsons made attacks on two more submarines, one in position 160 miles off St. Abbs Head on a bearing of 087 degrees. The second was 135 miles from Lister on a bearing of 233 degrees. Again there were no positive results.
4. A Blenheim detailed to carry out reconnaissance on Trondheim was unable to reach its objective but carried out reconnaissance of the Andalnes and South Romsdals Fjords.
5. Another Blenheim patrolling the French Coast between Dunkirk and Dieppe reported there was no activity, but noted there was an efficient boom in Dieppe Harbour.
6. A third Blenheim failed to return from reconnaissance on Cherbourg.
7. Spitfires of the PRU took photographs of Emden, Wilhelmshaven, and the Frisian Islands from Wangerooge to Borkum.

BOMBER COMMAND OPERATIONS

Thirty-six Blenheims of 2 Group were detailed to carry out daylight attacks on enemy airfields. Twenty-four bombed, ten abandoned because of lack of cloud cover, one was unable to release his bombs and one failed to return.

1. Three aircraft attacked Soesterburg with six 250lb GP, thirty-six 40lb GP, and sixty 4lb incendiaries. Hits were observed on a hangar and the surrounding tarmac.
2. Schipol was attacked by three aircraft that scored hits on runways and hangars with GP bombs. The gunner of one aircraft strafed and damaged two parked aircraft.
3. Leeuwarden was bombed with six 250lb and thirty-six 40lb GP bombs, but no results were seen. During the attack Blenheim 3897 was damaged by a Bf109 and the pilot, Flight Lieutenant Maude, was wounded.
4. Haamstede was attacked by three aircraft using GP and Incendiary bombs but no results were observed, possibly because they were too busy evading the defending Bf109s.
5. Flushing airfield was attacked by one crew who failed to observe the results.
6. At Waalhaven the airfield was bombed with GPs and incendiaries and enemy aircraft on the ground were strafed. Also bombs were dropped on a railway track in

Sergeant George Parr
Blenheim 18 Squadron

Our second mission was to Wenzendorf, an airfield south east of Hamburg, at extreme aircraft range. We had decided to stay over the sea all the way to the Elbe estuary, where I planned to follow the river to Hamburg to ensure target identification. This was not a good idea since we would have had to run the gauntlet of very heavily concentrated AA and probably fighters for some fifty miles.

At first we had complete cover and halfway across the North Sea I asked the pilot to descend below cloud to get a position check on a light ship whose position I had plotted on my chart. The ship appeared right on cue and we popped back into the sheltering cloud while I concealed my delight, hoping to foster an aura of confident efficiency. As it was, the cloud cover gradually decreased and eventually we were flying in blue sky with the German coast visible away to our right. We spotted a seaplane a mile or so on the landward side. It would have been an easy target but the captain decided not to go after it while we still had bombs on board. Soon after, we decided to about turn and go for the secondary target at Leeuwarden, a very busy operational fighter station in Holland.

I calculated our position, set a new course and ETA and we found the cloud cover again, but not before we diverted to fly round the island of Heligoland at about 2000 ft while I took photographs with the hand held Leica camera provided for just such a purpose. Again this was not an exercise to be recommended. Heligoland was heavily defended and we should have been met with heavy fire. As it was, luck was with us. There was an eerie lack of any reaction. Not a shot was fired and we continued serenely on our way. Over Holland we had reasonable cloud cover but kept low enough to pick out landmarks and Leeuwarden was identified without much trouble. Here I made another bad decision. We circled the airfield, which was crowded with aircraft, at about a thousand feet to see where we could inflict the most damage. It was very encouraging to see the people on the streets waving enthusiastically, but by the time we turned in to bomb the biggest concentration of aircraft, several Messerschmitts, some in small groups, were taking off with obvious malicious intent. The old saying about poking a stick in a hornet's nest sprang to mind.

Sergeant George Parr (left) with his fellow crew members and their Blenheim. Pilot (centre) is Flying Officer J A Douch and WOp/AG (right) is Sergeant R J Bassett.

We dropped even lower when Sgt Bassett suddenly shouted, odd as it may seem, 'There are three Messerschmitts behind us. Shall I shoot them down?' For his pains he was curtly told to keep quiet while we were trying to bomb. I dropped all bombs, which were fitted with ten second delay fuses for our safety, in a short stick, and Douch put on full boost for Texel and cloud. At this bombing height it was only necessary to use the bomb sight as a guide, and I am confident that we caused damage. Fortunately we were not stupid enough to go back and take a look. We returned to base without a scratch!

It was over fifty years later that I received this story from German sources, via the research of a Dutch air historian. The military records state that on that day three Messerschmitts were destroyed or severely damaged on the ground at Leeuwarden. Hauptmann Albrecht von Ankum-Frank, the commander of *5/JG 27*, angered that a lone Blenheim was flying round the airfield unmolested, took off with two others in their Messerschmitts to attack the intruder. But it was the Hauptmann who was shot down, dived into the ground and was killed. I have never been able to contact Reg Bassett, but I am sure he would have agreed that this was not bad for starters.

front of a train three miles south of Haarlem. During their attacks they evaded the attentions of two Bf109s.

7. During the attack on Evere airfield hits were observed on a hangar and a railway nearby.

8. Lock-gates and a bridge near Leimuiden were hit, a Flak battery on Knocke airfield was silenced and the airfield at Merville hit with GP bombs and incendiaries.

Night operations

Night operations were carried out by Wellingtons, Whitleys and Hampdens.

1. Twenty-two Wellingtons were detailed to attack an oil refinery at Hamburg, a power station at Bremen, marshalling-yards at Hamm and a storage siding at Scherte. Fifteen of the force attacked the oil refinery at Hamburg where there was an explosion and fires were started. The others failed to find the primary targets and bombed alternatives - Emden Naval dockyards where fires were also started, a factory at Moorburg and the airfield at Amrun. One aircraft crashed in the sea on return.

2. The targets of fourteen Whitleys were the oil refineries at Salzbergen and Emerich.

3. Of the Hampden force, ten attacked the oil refineries at Hannover and Emmerich, starting fires. Others successfully bombed a target at Wanne-Eickel and airfields at Gelsenkirchen and Hannover. Twelve laid mines in Lübeck Bay and the Helsingor area.

Friday 2nd August

OPERATIONAL LOSSES

Blenheim L8794 of 53 Squadron, Detling, was abandoned at night over Bordon, Hampshire. The crew; Squadron Leader D. C. Oliver, Sergeant Dunjey and Sergeant Thirlby landed safely.

Blenheim N3587 of 59 Squadron, Thorney Island, failed to return from Cherbourg after being shot down north of Le Havre at 11.05 hours. Pilot Officer D. A. Drew, Sergeant A. G. Herbert and Sergeant J. R. Close are all buried at Le Havre. *Claimed by by Oberleutnant Paul Temme of Stab I./JG 2.*

Blenheim L8780 of 110 Squadron, Wattisham, attacking Soesterburg, was damaged by Flak which wounded the pilot, Sergeant Hards. The aircraft crash-landed at base on return. *Two Blenheims were credited to Bf109 pilots, Unteroffizier. Hans Schätzel of 4./JG 54 and Feldwebel Fritz Oeltjen of 7./JG 54 each being credited with a victory.*

Blenheim L9422 of 18 Squadron, West Raynham, failed to return. Sergeant J. H. Davies, Sergeant K. R. Bryant and Sergeant W. S. Barrett were killed and are buried in Bergen Op Zoom War Cemetery.

Hampden P4376 of 83 Squadron, Scampton, detailed to attack Hannover, returned early and crashed three miles east of Scampton. Sergeant S. Harpham and Sergeant A. E. Jackson escaped with injuries, but Sergeant R. Beales and Sergeant E. J. Clarke were killed.

Wellington R3202 'J'of 115 Squadron, Marham, detailed to attack Hamburg, ditched off the Island of Rottum. Later, the bodies of Pilot Officer R. T. Gerry, Pilot Officer R. W. Pryor, Pilot Officer S. J. S. Wilde and Sergeant J. Dempsey were washed up on Dutch beaches. The bodies of Flight Sergeant R. J. Ruffell-Hazel DFM and Sergeant J. M. Croft were not recovered and their names are commemorated on the Runnymede Memorial.

"Our crew was on the Salzbergen target. At briefing we were told that the weather conditions weren't good but should improve as we got near the target area where it was forecast it should be fine if hazy. It wasn't long after take-off when we entered cloud and for the next three hours we ploughed through the murk flying blind. However, at the beginning of August a new long-range W/T Direction Finding System was introduced which provided us with W/T fixes and bearings when we were deep in Germany. This new facility helped to reduce the difficulties and fallibilities of Dead Reckoning navigation, especially in conditions we were experiencing. 'GB' our navigator used the bearings I obtained to keep us on track for Salzbergen. The Met. forecast they'd given us at briefing was, for a change, correct and the cloud broke before we reached the target area enabling 'GB' to confirm we were on track. He reported that Salzbergen was ahead where fires were burning and the Flak defences were having a 'go' at the 'early birds'. As we prepared our attack I went down the fuselage to prepare to drop parachute flares as and when required.

"I listened on the intercom as the bomb-aimer set us up for our vulnerable straight and level run-in. In the dark, claustrophobic fuselage I couldn't see much, but looking down the open flare-chute it seemed that the multicoloured Flak was coming straight at us and I could feel the 'bumps and grinds' of the heavy stuff as it exploded nearby.

"We started our bomb-run and the bomb-aimer intoned his litany, 'left, left, steady, right steady' and then 'Bombs Gone.' The wait always seemed to be an eternity.

I immediately launched a flare to indicate the target to crews following us in and returned to the cockpit where I could see what was going on and where I kidded myself there's safety in numbers! By this time the 'Skipper' had opened up the 'taps' (throttles) and was taking evasive action to get us out of the Flak.

"His 'bobbing and weaving' paid off and we escaped unscathed and set course for home. On the way back we were informed that the weather had deteriorated at base and we were diverted to Driffield where we managed to get in before it also closed in. As we waited for the crew transport to take us to de-briefing I recall there wasn't much conversation. I suppose we were simmering down, subconsciously reliving those past few hours when we had been dicing over Germany. The other Whitleys successfully bombed the oil refinery at Emmerich starting fires as well as attacking an airfield near Rheine."

Larry Donnelly
10 Squadron Whitley

Saturday 3rd August

Fairey Albacores of the Fleet Air Arm were sent out on night operations over Dutch ports armed with general-purpose and incendiary bombs.

ENEMY AIR ACTIVITY

Dull weather again affected the Luftwaffe operations and the raids on the Channel shipping during the day were reduced. Some nuisance raids by single aircraft were carried out. There was some night activity which included bombing raids on targets in Scotland, Tyneside, the Humber, Harwich and Crewe. Mine-laying also took place.

COASTAL COMMAND OPERATIONS

Seventy-four aircraft flew twenty-three routine and nineteen special patrols and five photographic sorties as well as providing nineteen convoys with air escort.

1.Hudson aircraft patrolling the Dutch coast early reported there were large fires on the Island of Texel and others near Rotterdam.

2.Blenheims on reconnaissance along the coast of Norway saw a submarine and a large motor vessel ten miles west of Feje Island.

3. Another U-Boat seven miles from Bummelo on a bearing of 275 degrees was attacked by a Blenheim. After dropping HEs and incendiaries on it from one hundred feet a large patch of oil was observed.

4. Three fighter Blenheims of 235 Squadron on patrol attacked an He115 float plane registering many hits forcing it to land on the sea.

5. Photographs were taken by PRU aircraft during sorties in the Brest, Calais to Dunkirk and the St. Eval to Cherbourg areas.

Night operations

1. Four FAA Albacores were detailed to attack fuel tanks at Vlaadingen and Rotterdam. Only one attacked with GP and incendiary bombs causing large fires.

2. Six FAA Swordfish of 812 Squadron, also detailed to bomb Vlaadingen and Rotterdam, were unable to locate their targets. Instead one bombed a searchlight at the Hook of Holland and another bombed the docks at Dordrecht.

3. Only two of six Blenheims detailed to attack shipping at Emden succeeded in locating and bombing, but the results were not observed.

BOMBER COMMAND OPERATIONS

1. Eighteen Blenheims of 2 Group, six each from 107, 114 and 139 Squadrons were despatched to attack airfields at Schipol, Evere, Haamstede, Leeuwarden, Antwerp, Soesterburg, Abbeville, St. Omer, Knocke and Brest, eleven abandoned their tasks because lack of cloud cover. The remainder attacked the following: Schipol, where hangars were hit by bombs and strafed; Abbeville, where bomb hits were observed on a stores park and troops in a convoy were strafed from a height of fifty feet; Haamstede, where hits were made on a hangar and the road leading to the airfield.

Other targets attacked included a train between Gravelines and Dunkirk and twenty barges at Bourburg. Troops seen on a nearby airfield were strafed.

Night operations

1. Twenty-eight Wellingtons were detailed to carry out night attacks on synthetic oil refineries at Gelsenkirchen, Boltrope and Homburg and marshalling yards at Hamm and Soest. Nine bombed primary targets and fourteen bombed alternatives. Fires were started at Gelsenkirchen, Boltrope and Homburg. At Horst an explosion was observed. Five crews did not bomb. A photo-flash set Wellington L7781 on fire when being prepared for operations and its bomb load exploded at Feltwell.

2. Twenty Hampdens were despatched to attack the '*Gneisenau*' berthed in Kiel and the old aqueduct at Dortmund-Ems. Because of the extreme haze the prime targets were not located, nine aircraft bombed the armament base at Kiel where bursts were seen in the target area. The combination of haze and the enemy defences prevented the others from carrying out their attack on the Dortmund-Ems aqueduct.

Twelve other aircraft carried out successful mining operations in the Kiel area and attacks against enemy airfields and sea-plane bases at Husum. Westerland, Amrum, Hornum and Demok. The weather deteriorated on return

causing diversions. One aircraft ran out of fuel and was forced to ditch ten miles east of Skegness.
3. Eleven Whitleys were detailed to carry out attacks on oil refineries at Monheim and Düsseldorf. Nine bombed their targets as briefed and two bombed alternatives.

OPERATIONAL LOSSES

Blenheim L9475 of 53 Squadron, Detling, carrying out a night attack of shipping at Emden, failed to return. The body of Pilot Officer H. C. Corbett was found on the Dutch Coast and is buried at Schoorl. Sergeant S. E. Riddington is buried at Thurmaston, Leicestershire and Sergeant K. W. Crane is remembered on the Runnymede Memorial.

Hudson T9282 of 206 Squadron, Bircham Newton, failed to return from a routine patrol. Pilot Officer J. A. Gilbert, Sergeant B. P. Gannon, Sergeant W. L. Johnston and Sergeant P. W. Swinson were posted as missing in action and are remembered on the Runnymede Memorial.

Swordfish P4007 of 812 Squadron, Fleet Air Arm, attacking Vlaadingen and Rotterdam failed to return. The body of Sub-Lt R. C. Eborn was recovered and lies at Noorwijk, Holland. The name of Lieutenant T. A. Johnston (Royal Marines) appears on the Lee-on-Solent Memorial.

Blenheim L9239 of 139 Squadron, Horsham St. Faith, was presumed lost over the English Channel. The crew; Flying Officer A. R. B. Tedder, Sergeant D. F. Spencer and Sergeant O. P. Evans lie in Bayeux War Cemetery.

Hampden P4351 of 49 Squadron, Scampton, detailed to attack Kiel, ran out of fuel on return and ditched in the North Sea ten miles east of Skegness. The uninjured crew were all rescued, Sergeant J. Unsworth, Sergeant D. S. Imber, Sergeant McDonald, LAC Allwood.

Wellington R3176 of 75 Squadron, Feltwell, attacked Horst. On return the aircraft crashed near Barton-Mills, Suffolk. Squadron Leader W. I. Collett was killed. Pilot Officer Humphries, Sergeant Simpkin, Flight Sergeant Williams, Sergeant Holford and Pilot Officer Ferris sustained injuries.

A Swordfish is loaded with a torpedo, the light bomb racks can be seen under the wings.

A 269 Squadron Hudson undergoes some open-air maintenance. The Hudson squadrons were operating around the clock on coastal patrols at this time, placing enormous pressure on the ground crews to keep them serviceable.

ENEMY AIR ACTIVITY

It was possibly the combination of dull weather and preparations for '*Adlerangriff*' which limited the Luftwaffe operations to attacks on Channel shipping using single aircraft or small formations during the day and sporadic but widespread night raids.

COASTAL COMMAND OPERATIONS

Despite foggy conditions ten anti-invasion, fourteen anti-submarine patrols, and five photographic and four special reconnaissance sorties were carried out involving fifty-five aircraft.

1. Hudson 'E' of 269 Squadron on anti-submarine patrol discovered a large ocean-going U-Boat in a position seventy-two miles from Cape Wrath on a bearing of 348 degrees. The Hudson crew carried out an attack from 400 feet with three 250lb A/S bombs. The first bomb hit the conning-tower, the second the bows and the third fell thirty feet ahead. The stern of the submarine came up at an angle of 40 degrees then gradually sank at that angle leaving a large patch of oil and bubbles.
2. A Blenheim on patrol carried out an attack on eight E-Boats seen making for Le Havre. Near misses with GP and incendiary bombs were claimed.
3. A Blenheim on anti-invasion patrol escorted by three fighter Blenheim of 236 Squadron was attacked by three Bf109s twenty miles north of Le Havre. During the engagement it was claimed that one Bf109 was shot down in flames and another damaged. Blenheim 'D' of 236 Squadron sustained battle damage to Feldwebel Rudolf Täschner of *1./JG 2,* who was credited with its destruction.
4. During PR operations photographs were taken of the following locations: French coast north of Dunkirk to Knocke, Flushing Canal and Dunkirk. Scheldt Estuary and oil stores east of Rotterdam. Boulogne, St. Omer- Calais railways Gris Nez to Ostend. Brest and St. Malo areas.

Night operations

1. A Hudson on a night sortie bombed and machine-gunned one of five fishing boats sixty-three miles from Horns Reef on a bearing of 265 degrees. There were no apparent results.
2. Another Hudson bombed an enemy submarine seventy miles off the Butt of Lewes on a bearing of 347 degrees. The bombs fell ahead of the target but no result was observed.

BOMBER COMMAND OPERATIONS

Because of adverse weather conditions no daylight operations were undertaken by the 2 Group Blenheim squadrons.

Night operations

Because of the filthy weather conditions, eleven Whitleys of 4 Group were the only Bomber Command aircraft to carry out night operations. They were detailed to attack synthetic oil refineries at Sterkrade-Halter and Emmerich. The raid on Sterkrade resulted in explosions and fires. The aerodrome at Krefeld was also attacked where a hangar was hit and fires started. On its return flight one aircraft was intercepted by a Bf110 off the Dutch coast. The Whitley gunners opened fire and the enemy aircraft broke off without attacking.

OPERATIONAL LOSSES

None recorded.

Monday 5th August

CLEAR SKIES AND SUNSHINE, VERY WARM.

ENEMY AIR ACTIVITY

Again the Luftwaffe activity was limited to isolated raids against targets on the South East Coast, Wales and a North East Coast town. Fighters claimed to have shot down four enemy aircraft.

COASTAL COMMAND OPERATIONS

Sixty-seven aircraft took part in forty-nine anti-invasion/anti-submarine and other routine patrols, despite the unfavourable weather conditions. Twenty-six convoys were provided with escorts.

1.A Blenheim on patrol in the Dunkirk to Dieppe area observed barges, motor vessels and seaplanes in Boulogne harbour. Photographs were taken from Dieppe to the outskirts of Calais.

2. Four PRU aircraft took photographs of Ecker Fjord, Flensburg, Heligoland, Emden, Delfzyl, Willemsoord, Ijmuiden and Schipol airfields and the Amsterdam area.

3. Four other aircraft were detailed to photograph Aalborg, Bergen, Fécamp and Kristiansund. Two aircraft failed to photograph the Gironde River and Bergen.

BOMBER COMMAND OPERATIONS

Nine 2 Group Blenheims were detailed to attack Dutch airfields and carry out weather reconnaissance. Five of the aircraft detailed got off, but had to abandon because of adverse weather conditions.

Night operations

Eighty-five Wellingtons, Whitleys and Hampdens were detailed to carry out night operations.

1.Thirty-five Wellingtons took off to attack the '*Gneisenau*' at Kiel, an oil refinery at Hamburg, oil stores at Nordenham, the ship-building yards at Ostermoor, Kiel Canal and an oil refinery at Hamm. Operations were curtailed because of adverse weather, but twenty-three bombed primary and other targets. Explosions and fires were started at the oil refinery at Hamburg and bombs fell in the Altona Docks area. Four fires were observed in the Krupps ship-building yard at Kiel. Airfields at Schipol and Cloppenburg were attacked where explosions took place and fires were started and another aircraft stoked up the fires burning at an oil plant at Nordenham. Wilhelmshaven docks were attacked, but no results were observed because of the intense opposition. Borkum was another target where fires were started at the southern end of the island. Assessment of the results of the attacks on most of the targets was made difficult by the weather conditions, however all aircraft returned safely.

2. Fifteen Whitleys out of twenty-one detailed got off to attack the Dornier airframe factory at Wismar and the naval docks at Kiel.

3. The '*Bismarck*' at Hamburg, the ship-building yards at Bremen, an electrical power station and the '*Tirpitz*' at Wilhelmshaven were the targets of seventeen Hampdens.

All the attacks were carried out and in addition the airfields at Barge and Nordeney were bombed, however because of the haze results were not observed. Twelve other Hampdens successfully mined the Elbe Estuary. On return one Hampden was intercepted near Nordeney. The Hampden gunners claimed the enemy aircraft as a possible.

OPERATIONAL LOSSES

Hudson P5133 of 206 Squadron, Bircham Newton, stalled and crashed at Syderstone, Norfolk, at 18.05 hours after a search patrol. Pilot Officer R. T. Kean DFC (New Zealander), Pilot Officer R. Rustom, Sergeant F. H. Hull and Sergeant D. Mannion were all killed.

A well camouflaged 206 Squadron Hudson.

Our crew was among those detailed to attack the Dornier factory; this would be my twenty-ninth scheduled raid. After starting the war as a somewhat naive eighteen-year-old full of bravado and dreams of glory, I had grown up fast to have a more realistic view on war and survival, but of course like most aircrew I bolstered any flagging of morale with the false supposition, 'It's always the other blokes who get the chop!'. On this 'trip' the weather over the North Sea could have been better, but we were able to pin-point and avoid the heavily defended naval base at Kiel and follow the coast north of Lübeck to Wismar where the Flak and searchlights were already in operation. When everything was set up for our bomb-run I went to the fuselage to standby to drop flares and surplus loose incendiaries. These incendiaries were ostensibly provided for drift assessment purposes, but any left gave me the where-withal to fight my personal war with the Third Reich! It also helped to concentrate my mind as we went through the Flak on our vulnerable straight and level bomb-run. I went through the usual tenterhooks waiting for the bomb-aimer to announce 'Bombs Gone'. It eventually came and we left the target area in double-quick time.

Once again we'd made it unscathed, or so we thought. It was only after getting back to base when our disgruntled ground-crew complained about having to repair Flak damage that we realised we'd been hit, but not seriously. Ignorance is bliss!

Larry Donnelly

10 Squadron Whitley

It was subsequently reported that there had been many bomb bursts in the target area at Wismar and that at the oil depot at Kiel, the other Whitley target, explosions had occurred and fires started. The airfield at Nueminster had also been bombed.

Tuesday 6th August

A 49 Squadron Hampden similar to the one that went missing on a minelaying operation off Frederikshaven on this night.

ENEMY AIR ACTIVITY

Again enemy activity was limited by weather conditions, however the RAF station at Llandow was bombed.
An enemy aircraft reconnoitring East Coast shipping was intercepted and shot down off Lowestoft. Individual raids took place along South and East Coasts, but the prevailing mist and cloud made interceptions difficult.

COASTAL COMMAND OPERATIONS

The usual routine and special patrols were carried out throughout the period.
1. Hudson P5153 of 206 Squadron crashed on landing at Bircham Newton on return from patrol. The bomb load exploded, but there were no casualties.
2. Anson 'H' of 217 Squadron attacked a U-Boat eighty-two miles from Bishop's Rock.
3. Anson 'W' of 502 Squadron on convoy escort reported that the motor vessel '*Boma*' had been torpedoed forty-seven miles north-west of Malin Head.

BOMBER COMMAND OPERATIONS

Forty-one 2 Group Blenheims were despatched during daylight to carry out weather reconnaissance and attacks against enemy airfields. Thirty-nine abandoned because of adverse weather conditions and one because of engine trouble. The 'press on' survivor dropped his bombs on the aerodrome at Le Bourget. Six other Blenheims carried out a sea search. All aircraft returned safely.

Night operations

Because of the atrocious weather conditions it was left to twenty-five Wellington crews of 3 Group and twelve Hampden crews of 5 Group to carry out night operations. Bombing operations by Whitleys and other Hampdens were cancelled.

1. The twenty-five Wellingtons were despatched to attack oil targets at Homburg, Reisholtz and Emmerich and communications targets at Scherte and Hamm. Because of the bad visibility target location was difficult but five managed to attack the primary targets at Homburg, Reisholtz and Scherte. At Homburg there were explosions and five fires were started. At Scherte a fire was started within the target area. Reisholtz was bombed hut the results were not observed.
Sixteen other aircraft carried out successful attacks against the airfields at Krefeld, Gilze-Rijen, Gladbach-Rheydt, Wesel, Ypenburg, Texel, Venlo and Eindhoven, but the results of the attacks on Soesterberg and Schipol were not observed. Four crews failed to bomb.
2. The twelve Hampdens detailed carried out mine laying and reconnaissance of Frederikstad (Norway) and Frederikshaven (Denmark).

OPERATIONAL LOSSES

Hampden P4377 of 49 Squadron, Scampton, was lost without trace from a mining operation off Frederikshaven, (Denmark). Sergeant R. J. Jennings DFM, Sergeant R. F. Batho, Sergeant J. F. Lindsay and Sergeant J. Jones were presumed killed and are commemorated on the Runnymede Memorial.

Wednesday 7th August

CLOUD AND RAIN IN THE EAST, CLEARER IN THE WEST..

ENEMY AIR ACTIVITY

There was very little enemy activity during the day. A few convoys were reconnoitred and one was bombed. In the south and west there was some activity in the Isle of Wight, Bournemouth, Gloucester, Oxford and Reading areas.

COASTAL COMMAND OPERATIONS

Twenty-five anti invasion, sixteen anti submarine patrols five photographic and five special reconnaissance sorties were flown using sixty-seven aircraft. Twenty-one convoys were provided with air escorts.

1. Three Hudsons flew reconnaissance sorties over Stavanger and Bjorne Fjords. One aircraft failed to return. Pilot Officer Burn, pilot of Hudson N7595 of 206 Squadron, had an eventful return to Docking. He overshot his landing in the dark, swung, causing the undercarriage to collapse, then hit a parked aircraft and, after the crew had escaped, the bomb load exploded.
2. A Hudson on routine patrol made an unsuccessful attack on an E-Boat sixty miles from Muckle Flugga on a bearing of 072 degrees.
3. A Blenheim returning from a reconnaissance over Trondheim ditched in the sea near the Farne Islands.
4. Three Blenheims, N3531, N3523 and P9261 of 235(F) Squadron strafed a group of ships off the coast of Denmark.
5. PRU sorties were carried out over Calais-Radio Normandie, Oslo, Aalborg, Nantes, and St. Nazaire without success, but photographs were taken of Bergen through a gap in the clouds.

L-R; Sgt. Don McFarlane, Sgt. Peter Eames and P/O Donald Wellings of 82 Squadron. This crew scored an amazing direct hit on a line of Messerschmitt Bf109s of 4/JG54 during their raid on Haamstede today. As a result, they probably destroyed more Bf109s in one action than most Spitfire pilots managed during the entire Battle of Britain!

BOMBER COMMAND OPERATIONS

Twenty-eight 2 Group Blenheims were detailed to carry out daylight attacks on oil plants and aircraft factories in Germany and enemy occupied airfields in France and Holland. Another aircraft was despatched on a weather reconnaissance. Because of adverse weather conditions all aircraft except two abandoned their tasks. The exceptions bombed the airfields at Querqueville and Haamstede. In addition six other aircraft carried out a North Sea search and reconnaissance. There were no losses.

Night operations

Twenty Wellingtons and seventeen Hampdens were detailed to carry out night bombing attacks. A further twelve Hampdens were detailed for mine-laying.

1. The Wellington targets were the '*Bismarck*' at Hamburg and others at Hamm and Soerst.

Because of bad weather conditions only seven bombed primary targets. Two attacked secondary targets, two opportunist targets, three abandoned their task and six brought their bombs back. However it was claimed that a large fire was started at Homburg and that hits had been scored on the oil plant at Emmerich and an airfield in the vicinity.

2. The *Gneisenau* in Kiel was the prime target of the seventeen Hampdens, but it was not located because of the weather conditions. However, the dockyard installation at Kiel and two airfields were attacked by thirteen of the force.
3. Twelve Hampdens carried out mine-laying and reconnaissance in the Langelands Belt.

There were no losses from operations, but Hampden L4187 of 106 Squadron crashed during night-flying training eight miles south-west of Scunthorpe after the pilot was dazzled by searchlights. Sergeant R. F. Wilson, Sergeant A. S. Dalgress, Sergeant W. C. Goldsmith and Sergeant D. K. Mills were all killed.

OPERATIONAL LOSSES

Blenheim L9456 of 248 Squadron, operating out of Sullom Voe, on an anti invasion patrol to Trondheim ditched in the sea off St. Abb's Head when it ran out of fuel after a flight lasting eight and a half hours. Pilot Officer R. H. Haviland, Pilot Officer M. L. Wells and Sergeant A. Kay were rescued by a trawler. Their aircraft was subsequently salvaged.

Hudson N7282 of 224 Squadron, Leuchars, failed to return from a reconnaissance of the Norwegian Coast. Shot down by Feldwebel Ladwein of I./ZG76 off Bergen at 14.04 hours. Pilot Officer R. B. Forbes (Canadian), Sergeant J. M. Oliver Sergeant G. D. Tennant were posted missing and are commemorated on the Runnymede Memorial. The body of Sergeant S. Grant was recovered from the sea and buried at Stavne Cemetery, Norway.

Thursday 8th August

Hugh George and fellow 15 Squadron Blenheim pilots return after a sortie. In the background is a 57 Squadron Blenheim.

ENEMY AIR ACTIVITY

Enemy activity hotted up. Waves of dive-bombers carried out attacks on Channel convoys. E-Boats joined in the attacks. Considerable damage was inflicted on shipping, but during the ensuing battles the enemy suffered losses in aircraft and surface vessels. Fighter aircraft losses were comparatively light. Enemy aircraft also dropped bombs over a wide area of Britain, but little damage was caused apart from in north-east England where buildings were hit and some casualties were suffered.

COASTAL COMMAND OPERATIONS

Although the weather again affected operations, anti submarine, anti invasion patrols and reconnaissance and search sorties were carried out by seventy-seven aircraft. Air escort was provided for twenty-two convoys.

1. A Blenheim patrolling Dunkirk to Dieppe reported and photographed shipping in Boulogne Harbour.
2. Three Blenheims escorting a convoy in the Channel reported it was attacked by enemy aircraft.
3. 235(F) Squadron sent three Blenheims on reconnaissance over Le Havre, Trouville and the mouth of the River Seine. They reported that there was no shipping in the harbour at Le Havre, but eleven miles from there they were attacked by six Bf110s. During the running fight two of the Blenheims claimed to have shot down one Bf110 in flames while suffering no loss themselves. A Blenheim was claimed by Leutnant Hartmann Grasser of *II./ZG 2* in this area.
4. One PRU aircraft successfully photographed La Rochelle and Bordeaux, but weather conditions foiled attempts to photograph Oslo and the River Gironde from Bordeaux to Le Verdon.

BOMBER COMMAND OPERATIONS

1. Fifteen 2 Group Blenheims were detailed to carry out daylight attacks on enemy held airfields in the occupied territories. All but two crews abandoned their tasks because of lack of suitable cloud cover. Schipol and Valkenburg were attacked by the two 'press on' crews. On the way to attack Rennes one crew reported there were fifty He111s and nine fighters on the aerodrome at Guernsey.
2. Six additional Blenheims carried out a sweep of the northern North Sea, but nothing of interest was discovered.

Night operations

Forty-six aircraft, twenty-eight Wellingtons and eighteen Hampdens were despatched to carry out night operations.

1. Wellington targets were the *Bismarck* at Hamburg and military objectives at Hamm, Soest, Osnabrük and Köln-Eifelter. The adverse weather conditions curtailed their operations and ten brought their bombs back, however, of the remainder, five claimed successful attacks on targets in the Ruhr. Two crews who attacked Hamm at the same time reported explosions and large fires. At Köln-Eifelter a stick of bombs which was dropped along the target started fires which were well established when the aircraft left the area. A bomb hit on the centre of the target at Soest caused a large fire and a line of explosions on what was thought to be an ammunition train. At Osnabrük, bomb flashes and flashes were seen but no results observed. One aircraft bombed the *Bismarck* in Hamburg, resulting in a large explosion. No results were observed from the attacks an electric power station at Bremen or the commercial dockyards at Wilhelmshaven. Several enemy airfields were attacked and propaganda leaflets were dropped
2. The Hampdens, although being hampered by cloud, darkness and haze, carried out attacks on an oil target at Ludwigshaven-Opau and a petrol depot at Frankfurt, but no definite results were claimed. Attacks were also carried out on several aerodromes and searchlight batteries. One Hampden failed to return.
3. The 'M' Balloon Unit released 360,000 leaflets during the night which, if the wind speed and direction remained constant, should have covered an area of the southern Ruhr, Koblenz and Bonn.

OPERATIONAL LOSSES

Blenheim L9472 of 18 Squadron, West Raynham, detailed to attack the airfields at Schipol and Valkenburg, failed to return and was presumed lost over the sea. Sergeant J. H. Saville and Sergeant V. R. T. L and are commemorated on the Runnymede Memorial. Sergeant F. F. Parvin is buried in the Canadian War Cemetery at Bergen Op Zoom. *This is believed to have been the "Handley-Page" reported shot down by Oberleutnant Gerhard Schöpfel of 9./JG 26 off Ramsgate at 12.35 hours.*

Hampden L4053 of 83 Squadron, Scampton, detailed to attack Ludwigshaven, crashed near Mannheim. Two of the crew were injured. Flying Officer I. M. Muir, Sergeant W. Barber, Sergeant J. Leakey and Sergeant F. A. Stone were all taken prisoner.

Friday 9th August

Some sun, but scattered showers over southern counties.

An Avro Anson of 500 Squadron was reported to have been brought down by German searchlights today.

ENEMY AIR ACTIVITY

After the raids on convoys and air battles during the previous day, enemy activity was confined to sporadic bombing by single aircraft and machine-gun attacks by German fighters on balloon defences in the south-east of England. However, at night bombs were dropped over many areas destroying buildings and causing casualties, some of them fatal.

COASTAL COMMAND OPERATIONS

The usual routine and special patrols, as well as reconnaissance and convoy escorts, took place during the period.
1. An Anson of 500 Squadron failed to return from a patrol Hook to Ostend.
2. Six Blenheims of 59 Squadron carried out a dusk raid on the aerodrome at Guernsey. Some damage was caused to the airfield buildings, however some of our aircraft suffered Flak damage during the attack.
3. An additional three aircraft of 59 Squadron accompanied by six of 53 Squadron carried out an attack on oil targets at Flushing.

BOMBER COMMAND OPERATIONS

1. Fifteen Blenheims of 2 Group were despatched on daylight raids to attack enemy occupied airfields in France and the Low Countries, but because of the lack of suitable cloud cover thirteen abandoned. The remaining two attacked the aerodrome at Guernsey and the flying boat base at Brest. The crew who attacked Guernsey claimed to have scored a direct hit on a transport aircraft and hits on the hangars. During the attack the light Flak batteries defending the airfield were machine-gunned. The crew observed that there were thirty to fifty enemy aircraft on the airfield, mostly Bf109s, the remainder were twin-engined transports. The other crew that attacked the flying-boat base at Brest dropped a long stick of bombs which started among the flying-boats and finished among the hangars. The crew reported there were twelve flying-boats moored between jetties at the base.

Night operations

Thirty-eight aircraft were detailed for night operations.
1. Fourteen Wellingtons of 3 Group whose target was an aluminium works at Köln, claimed to have caused explosions and started fires. Ten other aircraft successfully attacked military targets at Hamm, Soest and Ruhrort-Haven. The airfields at Werl, Munster, Gilze-Rijen, Venlo, Schipol and Eindhoven were also bombed. At Eindhoven fires were started and explosions observed.
2. Three Wellingtons of 6 Group dropped propaganda leaflets in the Lille-Amiens-Rouen area.
3. Nine out of fourteen Whitleys attacked the aluminium works at Ludwigshaven, causing fires and explosions. Two other aircraft successfully attacked Tirlemont aerodrome and another airfield twenty miles north of Trier.
All the aircraft on night operations returned safely.

OPERATIONAL LOSSES

Anson N5356 'B' of 500 Squadron, Detling, failed to return from the Hook - Ostend patrol. It was subsequently reported by German sources that it had been brought down by searchlights west of Scheveningen and that two of the crew had been taken prisoner. Pilot Officer H. G. R. Pirie and Sergeant M. A. Prentice are buried at the Bergen-Op-Zoom Canadian War Cemetery. Pilot Officer J. B. S. Brockway and Sergeant S. R. Croft were captured.

Blenheim IV N3590 'F' of 59 Squadron, Thorney Island, failed to return form a reconnaissance of Cherbourg. Pilot Officer H. L. N. Davis and Sergeant G. H. Coulton were posted missing in action and recorded on the Runnymede Memorial. The body of Sergeant B. W. Beaumont was washed ashore and is buried at Hautot-sur-Mer, France.

ENEMY AIR ACTIVITY

10th August was the day intended by Goering to be 'Adlertag' (Eagle Day) the beginning of the all-out Luftwaffe attack on Britain, but once again the Channel weather intervened and enemy activity was reduced to sporadic raiding on a small scale.

COASTAL COMMAND OPERATIONS

1. Hudson 'P' of 220 Squadron on a routine North Sea patrol was attacked by a Blohm and Voss Ha140 seaplane, forty-eight miles from Cromer. The Hudson returned fire and the enemy aircraft broke off the engagement. Both aircraft suffered damage.
2. Another Hudson on reconnaissance of the Dutch Coast attacked a barrage balloon one hundred and thirty miles from Flamborough Head and sighted an unknown aircraft. It did not attack and flew off into cloud. The Hudson crew concluded it was probably friendly and if it was not, thankful for its lack of aggression!
3. A Blenheim on patrol from Le Havre to the mouth of the Seine attacked a merchant vessel, but the result was not observed.
4. Six 2 Group Blenheims operating from Lossiemouth carried out a North Sea search, but nothing of interest was seen.
5. Three PRU Spitfires successfully photographed the Cap Gris Nez area between Calais and Boulogne, Cherbourg, Brest, Fécamp, Radio Normandie, Le Crotoy and Le Touquet. An attempt to photograph Aalborg failed.

Night operations

1. Two Swordfish were detailed to carry out a night reconnaissance of the Ems River, while another four reconnoitred Hubert Gat.
2. Six Blenheims were despatched to carry out a night strike on fuel tanks at Cherbourg. Three bombed the primary target and one an oil tank south of the aerodrome. No results were observed, but fires were seen in the target area.

BOMBER COMMAND OPERATIONS

1. Twenty-two 2 Group Blenheims were despatched in daylight to attack enemy held airfields in France and the Low Countries, but because of the lack of suitable cloud cover only eight bombed aerodromes at Schipol, Waalhaven and Querqueville where hangars were damaged. The landing grounds at Le Bourg, Dinard and Caen as well as the aerodromes at Cherbourg and Flushing were also attacked but results were not observed.

At Flushing one of the Blenheim crews saw an enemy aircraft believed to be a Henschel 126 shot down by its own Flak.

Night operations

A total of sixty aircraft were despatched on night operations.

1. Twenty Wellingtons were detailed to carry out attacks against the shipbuilding yards at Hamburg and marshalling yards and railway sidings at Soest. Weather conditions were far from ideal, but eleven crews bombed the primary target at Hamburg claiming bomb bursts were seen in the vicinity of the *SS Bremen* and *SS Europa*. Some of the other aircraft bombed Hamm, Soest and the naval base at Wilhelmshaven, but the rest who were unable to locate any of the allocated targets bombed targets of opportunity such as aerodromes.
2. Seventeen Hampdens attacked oil targets at Homburg and the inland port of Duisburg-Ruhrort causing explosions and fires. Aerodromes at Duisburg, Gransbergen and Krefeld were also attacked. At Krefeld night flying was in progress and an aircraft was hit on the ground and destroyed. One Hampden failed to return.
3. Twenty Whitleys of 4 Group were given the oil plant at Frankfurt/Main as their prime target. A number of hits were claimed which caused explosions and fires. Other crews who had difficulty in identifying the main target bombed alternatives including a nitrogen plant and power station at Osnabrük, a blast furnace north of Frankfurt and the airfield at Hangelar (Bonn).
4. Three Whitleys of 6 Group were despatched to drop propaganda leaflets over a prescribed area of France.

OPERATIONAL LOSSES

Blenheim R3910 of 82 Squadron, Watton, detailed to attack enemy airfields was presumed lost over the sea. Pilot Officer N. H. H. Smith, Sergeant C. Hamilton and Sergeant J. K. Blazier were presumed killed and recorded on the Runnymede Memorial.

This is almost certainly the Blenheim claimed near Le Havre at 12.33 hours by Oberleutnant Karl-Heinz Metz of 8./JG 2.

Blenheim R3775 of 110 Squadron, Wattisham, also detailed to attack enemy airfields, crashed near Pihen-les-Guines, ten miles south-west of Calais. Pilot Officer A. R. Storrow, Sergeant L. C. Cooke and Sergeant A. J. Underwood were all killed and remain buried in the local cemetery.

Hampden P4368 of 144 Squadron, Hemswell, detailed to attack Homburg, crashed in the Ijsselmeer (Holland). Pilot Officer W. F. Tudhope DFC is buried in Kampen General Cemetery. The names of Sergeant S. L. S. Belton DFM, Sergeant D. MacKay and Sergeant A. J. Griffiths are recorded on the Runnymede Memorial.

Pilot Officer W. F. 'Bill' Tudhope DFC
remembered

My navigator for the first 18 ops of my first tour was an RAF Canadian Bill Tudhope. He was a great chap and a man of many parts. We got on well. Bill was also a pilot but at that time was not experienced enough to have his own crew and aircraft. In the air, he seldom gave me a course to steer in degrees of the compass, instead, to my initial amazement, he used to say *"go a bit more to the left or right"* and when he was satisfied he would say *"that's alright, hold that"*. We did quite a bit of minelaying as far afield as Rostock and Stettin and we always got there and back which speaks volumes for Bill's expertise. (He won a well earned DFC).

Bill eventually got his own crew but sadly was shot down and killed over Holland shortly afterwards.

Sqn Ldr Max Meyer 144 Sqn Hampden pilot.

CLOUDY, GETTING HEAVIER DURING THE DAY.

ENEMY AIR ACTIVITY

There was considerable enemy activity during the day. A heavy attack was made on Portland, four on the Dover balloon barrage and attacks by large formations on convoys in the Thames Estuary and off East Anglia. During the air battles which took place thirty-two enemy aircraft were shot down for the loss of twenty-five RAF fighters.

COASTAL COMMAND OPERATIONS

Eighty-two aircraft carried out anti invasion and anti submarine patrols, searches and reconnaissance as well as providing air escort for twenty-nine convoys. Some of the searches and reconnaissance were affected by adverse weather conditions.

1. A Blenheim escorted by three fighter Blenheims on armed reconnaissance in daylight over Le Havre-Cherbourg bombed oil tanks at Le Havre. Results were not observed, but photographs were taken. Near Fécamp the three escorts were attacked by two Bf109s, one of which was shot down into the sea by the Blenheims.
2. Three PRU aircraft successfully photographed in daylight canals from Nijmegen to Liege, Den Helder, Le Havre to Caudebec and Yvetot, Fécamp, Radio Normandie to Cap Gris Nez, and Le Crotoy to Abbeville.

Night operations

1. Eight Blenheims of 59 Squadron carried out a night strike on an oil store at Cherbourg, starting a large number of fires. One of them also attacked searchlights on the airfield at Cherbourg.
2. Six Blenheims of 53 Squadron were detailed to attack an oil store at Amsterdam, but only one of them bombed. On return Flying Officer Jameson was unable to locate Detling and the crew abandoned T1937 at 01.45 hours on the 12th near Hawkhurst, Kent.
3. Four Swordfish carried out mine laying in Hubert Gat, while another two laid mines in the Ems River.

BOMBER COMMAND OPERATIONS

Seventeen Blenheims of 2 Group were despatched in daylight to attack air parks and occupied airfields. Another six carried out a sea search. Seven of those on bombing strikes abandoned their task because of unsuitable cloud cover conditions, but the remainder carried out the following attacks:

1. One aircraft bombed the airfield at Guernsey and columns of smoke were seen coming from the target area.

The seaplane base at Sylt was an alternative target for the Hampden force on the night of 11th August

2. Brest was attacked by three aircraft where bursts were observed in the seaplane base.
3. At Dinard hits were observed which started fires.
4. Caen was attacked by three aircraft that scored hits on buildings. One Blenheim bombed two destroyers off Den Helder, but no results were observed.

Night operations

Twenty-six Wellingtons, sixteen Whitleys and eighteen Hampdens were despatched to carry out night bombing operations. A further twelve Hampdens were detailed for mine laying and another five from 7 Group to drop propaganda leaflets.

1. The Wellington targets were synthetic oil plants at Castrop-Rauxel and Wanne-Eickel, marshalling yards at Hamm, railway sidings at Soest and military targets in the forest area south-east of the Ruhr. Twenty crews bombed the primary targets starting fires at Castrop, Wanne-Eickel, Hamm and Soest. A power station at Köln and an aerodrome at Herdegen Busch were also bombed. In addition incendiary attacks were made on military targets in the Ruhr forest area. Propaganda leaflets were also dropped.
2. The Hampdens' primary target was a synthetic oil plant at Dortmund. Four of the Hampden force attacked it causing a large explosion followed by a blue flash and fire. The others carried out attacks against the following alternative targets: a factory north of Dortmund, an aerodrome at Metelen, marshalling yards at Düsseldorf and Wanne-Eickel, aerodromes at List and Sonderberg Port, an AA battery at Sylt and the installations at the Hornum seaplane base. In addition to their other tasks, sixteen aircraft made attacks on military targets in forest areas south-east of the Ruhr. Twelve aircraft carried out successful mine laying in the Kiel area.
3. Five aircraft of 4 Group dropped propaganda leaflets in the Caen, St. Malo - Dinant, Lessey - Avroco, Rennes and Brest areas. Sixteen Whitleys were despatched to bomb the synthetic oil plant at Gelsenkirchen and military targets in the forest area south-east of the Ruhr. One crew returned early.

OPERATIONAL LOSSES

Anson K8813 of 217 Squadron, St. Eval, failed to return from patrol. Pilot Officer A. Gordon-Peiniger, Pilot Officer R. M. Coulman, Sergeant E. K. Mellody and Sergeant E. Hopperton were posted as missing in action and are commemorated on the Runnymede Memorial.

An unknown Ju88 crew from Küstenflieger Gruppe 806 engaged an aircraft identified as a "Blenheim" some 80km northwest of Lands End and claimed it destroyed at 16.15 hours. It could have been nothing other than this Anson.

Blenheim T1816 of 53 Squadron, Detling, failed to return from a 'Dundee' patrol Dunkirk to Dieppe. Pilot Officer P. J. Coleman evaded capture. Sergeant I. Inskip was lost and is recorded on the Runnymede Memorial. Sergeant G. M. Bardolph (Canadian) died of his injuries in a German hospital on 17 August.

It is believed to fallen victim to 3./JG 52 and was credited to Oberfeldwebel Willi Grosse.

Blenheim T1850 of 107 Squadron, Wattisham, attacking Dinard, was lost without trace. Squadron Leader J. B. Fyfe DFC, Sergeant P. B. Taylor and Sergeant T. O. Price are all commemorated on the Runnymede Memorial.
This was clearly the aircraft attacked and shot down by Leutnant Erick Bodendieck of 4./JG 53, who engaged it over Dinan and pursued it to the French coast.

Hampden L4036 'R' of 49 Squadron, Scampton, failed to return from Dortmund, reported as having been shot down by Flak. Pilot Officer R. F. Gower, Sergeant A. J. Baum, Sergeant P. W. N. Jelley and Pilot Officer E. A. Harris are all buried in the Reichswald Forest War Cemetery.

Wellington P9244 'E' of 149 Squadron, Mildenhall crashed at Beck Row near the airfield on return from attacking oil targets in Germany. Pilot Officer J. G. Miller, Pilot Officer J. Body, Sergeant J. J. Scott, Sergeant R. J. Cocks, Sergeant J. H. Swift and Pilot Officer R. E. Houseman were all killed when the aircraft collided with a radio mast on its final approach to land.

Whitley P4983 of 51 Squadron, Dishforth, failed to return from Gelsenkirchen. Sergeant J. A. Kearey, Sergeant A. E. Bowes, Sergeant J. F. C. Brown, Sergeant W. H. Mercer and Sergeant E. H. Platts were all subsequently reported as being PoWs.

A Whitley crewman prepares to despatch leaflets

Our crew was involved and at briefing we discovered that the military targets in the forest area of the Ruhr concealed dumps of stores and ammunition. The means to destroy them was the Boffins' latest secret weapon, '*Razzle*' a pill of phosphorous covered in gauze inserted in celluloid leaflets. They were carried in sealed cans of water to prevent them from drying out and becoming combustible. The idea was that after we had bombed our primary target we would fly to the forest area and dump the '*Razzle*'. The leaflets would flutter down to earth, hopefully on the concealed dumps, dry out and instantaneous combustion would take place setting fire to the stores.
We took off at 21.00 hours and set course for Gelsenkirchen. The weather wasn't too bad and after crossing the North Sea we made our way down 'Happy Valley' (the Ruhr) avoiding the defences of searchlights and Flak to our target. There the Flak opposition was severe but we managed to carry out our bomb run and get through practically unscathed; we found out when we got back to base we had suffered some slight Flak damage. We then made our way to drop the '*Razzle*'.

On arrival at the designated area I went to the fuselage as it would be my responsibility to do the dropping. As the aircraft stooged around I diligently poured the contents of the forty-eight cans down the flare-chute. When the last can had been emptied I checked with my shaded torch to make sure none of the leaflets remained in the aircraft. We had been briefed by the Boffins that if any remained we had to prevent them from drying out. The safety device supplied to us to use in such an emergency was, you'd better believe it, a garden water syringe!
Our flight back to base was uneventful and we landed at 05.25 hours and taxied back to dispersal basking in the relief that we'd 'made it', once again. However, our complacency was abruptly shattered by a call from George Dove, our tail-gunner, who reported that the fabric on the aircraft elevators was burning - some of the '*Razzle*' leaflets had lodged in the control hinges and had dried out during our return flight. We lost no time getting to dispersal where our ground crew extinguished the fire.
Larry Donnelly 10 Squadron Whitley

Monday 12th August

SUNNY WITH A LITTLE MIST DISPERSING IN THE MORNING.

...Nothing, not even a Stuka, could dive more slowly than a Blackburn Roc...!

ENEMY AIR ACTIVITY

Large scale enemy raids took place over the south coast during the morning, which extended later to Kent, the Isle of Wight and Portsmouth. A number of buildings including the railway station at Portsmouth were hit. During the air battles, twenty-seven enemy aircraft were destroyed for the loss of twenty RAF fighters.

One naval pilot had a hair-raising experience. Sub Lieutenant A.G.Blake (who would soon be seconded to the RAF and fly Spitfires with 19 Sqn) was on a routine flight from RNAS Lee-on-Solent in a Blackburn Roc dive-bomber. Suddenly he saw, in his rear-view mirror, the square white-painted nose of a Bf109E. Without hesitation he went into a vertical dive, with dive-brakes fully extended. Nothing, not even a Stuka, could dive more slowly than the Roc and the Messerschmitt whistled past him. Blake pulled out just above the waves and the Bf109 pilot, Unteroffizier Gottfried Haferkorn of *2./JG 26*, having last seen the Roc diving vertically at 200 feet, went home to be credited with a "Morane destroyed". Neither Blake nor Haferkorn were to survive the battles to come.

Extensive night bombing took place after dark over England and Wales.

COASTAL COMMAND OPERATIONS

1. An Anson of 48 Squadron carried out two searches for an E-Boat reported off Gunna Island without result.
2. A Walrus flying boat thirty miles north-east of Muckle Flugga was circled by an enemy aircraft (believed to be a Focke Wulf 200 Condor) but for some reason it did not attack.
3. A Blenheim on a special reconnaissance of the Norwegian Coast reported sighting a large motor vessel twenty miles north of Obrestad.
4.PRU aircraft took photographs of the Cherbourg Peninsula, Bordeaux, Paullic Wharf, La Rochelle, La Pallice, Gris Nez, Calais, Boulogne, Den Helder and Kiel. The Spitfire over Kiel reported that the dry docks were occupied (probably by the '*Scharnhorst*' and the '*Gneisenau*'.
5. A photo reconnaissance of the Norwegian Coast was unsuccessful due to lack of cloud cover.

Night operations

1. An offensive sortie was carried out at night by three Blenheims of 53 Squadron and another three of 59 Squadron as well as six Swordfish and six Albacores on the naval base at Den Helder. Six aircraft located and bombed the target. Although results were not confirmed, it was thought that an ammunition dump was hit. Six of the remaining aircraft attacked alternative targets including the harbour at Ijmuiden and Willemsoord and aerodromes at Zuiderland and De Kooy.
2. Three Hudsons on a routine night patrol attacked Den Helder, dropping bombs on the quayside, warehouses and Flak ships. Another crew attacked Willemsoord.

BOMBER COMMAND OPERATIONS

1. Six 2 Group Blenheims operating from Lossiemouth carried out a sea search in daylight, but nothing of interest was sighted.
2. A Blenheim of 82 Squadron was detailed to carry out a daylight photo reconnaissance and to attack the synthetic oil plant at Kamen. It did not get to Kamen but bombed De Kooy aerodrome instead. Results were not observed. There were no losses.

Night operations

Although the weather was not too good over Germany, seventy-nine aircraft were despatched on night operations.

1. Twenty-eight Wellingtons were sent to attack an airframe factory at Gotha and an aircraft park at Diepholz. Nine of the aircraft attacked the factories at Diepholz and Gotha, the last of the crews to attack the targets said it was on fire when they dropped their bombs.

Thirteen other aircraft claimed to have carried out successful attacks on the docks at Amsterdam, the sea-plane base at Borkum, a factory south of Lippstadt, a Flak battery at Langensalza and the aerodromes at Schipol, Kassel and Borkum. Fires and explosions were reported to have occurred at Lippstadt and Borkum.

Hampden P4379 which went missing on this day on a minelaying mission near Salzbergen.

2. Fifteen Whitleys were given the task of bombing the aluminium works at Herringen. Because of the adverse weather conditions making target identification extremely difficult only one managed to bomb the Herringen target. The other crews attacked a blast furnace near Witten, self illuminating targets west of Düsseldorf and Munster as well as an aerodrome near Dortmund. The crews reported that fires were started.

3. The targets for the nineteen Hampdens were an oil refinery at Salzbergen, the old aqueducts on the Dortmund-Ems Canal and military targets in the forest area of Solzau-Ulzen-Cello.

Aircraft of 49 and 83 Squadrons were given the task of carrying out a low-level attack on the important twin aqueducts of the canal near Munster. The intense light Flak defences were very accurate and shot down two of the Hampdens, but the aqueduct was hit and badly damaged. For making an especially determined attack, during which his aircraft was badly damaged, Flight Lieutenant R. A. B. Learoyd of 49 Squadron was subsequently awarded Bomber Command's first Victoria Cross of the war.

The port rudder of one of the Hampdens shot down during the Dortmund-Ems raid.

The other aircraft attacked aerodromes at Texel, Castrup and Lingen, a Flak battery at Cello and military targets in the Saltau-Cello forest area. In addition ten other Hampdens successfully carried out mine-laying operations in the Langelands Belt and Flensburg Fjord. Two aircraft failed to return.

Four aircraft of 7 Group dropped propaganda leaflets over France.

4. Five Blenheims of 2 Group were despatched to carry out a night attack on the airfields at Querqueville, Maupertus, Caen and Dinard. The crews reported hangars were hit and one was left burning. One failed to return.

OPERATIONAL LOSSES

Blenheim R3768 of 15 Squadron, Wyton, detailed to bomb an airfield at Lannion crashed near Fermanville, 14 Km east of Cherbourg. Pilot Officer F. G. H. Dench, Sergeant A. N. Gray and Sergeant E. E. Scrase were killed and are buried in the local cemetery.

Hampden P4335 of 61 Squadron, Hemswell, lost without trace from Salzbergen. Pilot Officer T. C. Cundill, Pilot Officer D. E. Gardener, Sergeant W. B. Taylor and Sergeant D. R. Aldom are all commemorated on the Runnymede Memorial.

Hampden P4379 of 61 Squadron, Hemswell, lost minelaying near Salzbergen. Pilot Officer H. C. Sheldon, Flight Sergeant W. Ward, Sergeant R. McC. Morrison and Sergeant C. E. Thrower are all buried in the Hamburg Cemetery, Oblsdorf.

Hampden P4340 of 83 Squadron, Scampton, attacking Dortmund, was hit by Flak and crashed near Mesum. Flight Lieutenant D. R. Mulligan DFC, and Sergeant W. G. W. Younger were taken prisoner. Sergeant S. D. Hill and Sergeant R. Abel were killed and are buried in the Reichswald Forest War Cemetery.

Hampden P4410 of 83 Squadron, Scampton, detailed to attack Dortmund was lost without trace. Flying Officer E. H. Ross DFC, Sergeant J. L. Dewhurst, Sergeant K. A. Sayer DFM, and Sergeant R. J. Buckley are all commemorated on the Runnymede Memorial.

Monday 12th August

Flight Lieutenant R. A. B. Learoyd VC

The Dortmund-Ems Canal, one of Germany's great inland waterways, was the target of many RAF bombing attacks. It was heavily protected by anti-aircraft guns of all calibres. On the night of the 12th/13th August, a crucial stage in the Battle of Britain, Flight Lieutenant Learoyd was one of the pilots of a force of Nos. 49 Squadron and 83 Squadron Hampdens given the special task of carrying out a low level attack on the important twin aqueducts of the Dortmund-Ems Canal near Munster.

To achieve success it was necessary to approach the target from a direction well known to the enemy through a lane of specially located anti-aircraft defences and in the face of the most intense point blank fire from the guns. The aircraft preceding Flight Lieutenant Learoyd received a hot reception resulting in all of them being hit and two of them being shot down. Ignoring this he made his attack from 150 feet, his aircraft being repeatedly hit with large pieces of the mainplane being shot away. Despite this and the fact that he was almost blinded by the glare of many searchlights, he pressed home his attack, successfully bombing the aqueducts which subsequently affected canal traffic for some considerable time.

He then flew his wrecked aircraft back to base and, as the landing flaps were inoperative and the undercarriage indicators out of action, he waited for dawn in the vicinity of the aerodrome before landing which he accomplished without causing injury to his crew or further damage to the aircraft.

For the high courage, skill and determination which he had displayed on many occasions in the face of the enemy setting an example which was unsurpassed he was awarded the Victoria Cross.

Tuesday 13th August

A Fairey Battle sits in a damaged hangar at Eastchurch after the raid on 13th August.

ENEMY AIR ACTIVITY

'Adlertag' (Eagle Day)

This was designated by Goering to be the day when the Luftwaffe would launch the attacks to wipe out Fighter Command in preparation for *'Operation Sealion'* (the invasion of Britain). Because of an adverse weather forecast in the morning Goering personally postponed it, but his message did not get through to *KG2's* HQ. Consequently Oberst Fink took off with seventy-four of his Do17s and carried out the only raid of the morning. They bombed RAF Eastchurch and Sheerness, inflicting heavy damage, but lost five Do17s destroyed and five seriously damaged.

The weather improved in the afternoon - 'Adlertag' was on again and massive attacks were to be made on RAF airfields. Engagements were fought all over south-east England. RAF Detling was dive-bombed and machine-gunned. Twenty aircraft were destroyed on the ground including four Blenheims of 53 Squadron (R3677, R3819, R3849, T1938). There were also heavy casualties among RAF personnel. Six out of nine Stukas were shot down on their way to attack RAF Middle Wallop. During the day's fighting the Luftwaffe lost thirty-four aircraft, mostly Stuka dive-bombers. The RAF lost thirteen fighters.

COASTAL COMMAND OPERATIONS

Sixty-seven aircraft carried out forty-three anti invasion and anti submarine patrols as well as special reconnaissance. Routine North Sea patrols were extended to the Norwegian and Danish Coasts. Twenty convoys were provided with air escorts. Fairey Battle Squadrons of 1 Group were now operating under Coastal Command control and would do so until the end of August.

1. Three Fairey Battles of 142 Squadron operating from Eastchurch carried out a daylight raid on shipping and barges in Boulogne. No results observed.
2. PRU aircraft took photographs of enemy territory including the coast From Brest to St. Nazaire, the River Seine, Nantes, Rouen, Le Havre, Gris Nez, Larvik, Tonsberg and the coastline from Larvik to Arendal.

BOMBER OPERATIONS

1. Twenty-nine 2 Group Blenheims of 82, 114 and 139 Squadrons were detailed to carry out daylight raids on enemy airfields in the occupied territories. During the course of the day they all got off, but seven abandoned because of lack of cloud cover and technical trouble. One crew returned because of fuel shortage, nine crews bombed and twelve failed to return. Two additional aircraft which took off to carry out a photo-reconnaissance of Kamen and the Dortmund-Ems Canal also abandoned due to a lack of cloud cover.
2. The following targets were attacked:-

Two aircraft bombed the aerodrome and seaplane base at Brest. Bursts were observed near a hangar and two large seaplanes.

Morlaix was bombed by one aircraft. No results were observed.

Caen was bombed by two aircraft. The crews observed hits in the centre of the target and that there were fifteen twin-engined enemy aircraft on the south-east of the airfield.

Two aircraft bombed at Waalhaven and the crews confirmed hits on the target and that there were two twin-engined aircraft on the north side of the airfield.

Tuesday 13th August

A wider view of the photo of Pilot Officer Wellings's crew reveals the Blenheim to be R3821 UX-M. This aircraft was one of the eleven 82 Squadron Blenheims shot down on the Aalborg raid as the squadron was all but wiped out in a day. Pilot Officer Hale and his crew who were flying R3821 were all killed.

The initial target at Dunkirk was abandoned but a cargo ship a mile off shore was attacked and the bombs overshot. At Hingene a successful attack was carried out by one aircraft and the crew reported there was no opposition from Flak or enemy aircraft.

3.Twelve Blenheims were sent to attack Aalborg, *see opposite.*

Night operations

1. Six Blenheims of 2 Group were detailed to carry out night operations against airfields in the occupied territories. The seaplane base at Brest and the aerodrome at Lerbieuc were bombed.

2. Thirty-four Wellingtons of 3 Group were detailed to attack the aluminium works at Gravenbroich and Lunen, an aircraft component factory at Frankfurt and marshalling yards at Hamm and Soest.

Two additional Wellingtons were despatched to take photographs of the naval yard and the synthetic oil plant at Stettin and the seaplane base at Swinemunde. Weather conditions affected the location of the primary targets, however successful attacks were claimed on the Gravenbroich target where there were explosions and fires. An aircraft component factory at Frankfurt was bombed and a large explosion was observed in the target area.

Other aircraft attacked the enemy airfields at Vught and Diest where hits on the hangars caused fires. Also targets such as blast furnaces, searchlight batteries and communications were attacked.

The photographic sortie by the two Wellingtons to Stettin was unsuccessful.

3. Twenty-eight Hampdens of 5 Group were detailed to carry out attacks against airframe factories at Dessau and Bromberg. The crews claimed that both factories had suffered severe damage as many bursts were seen on the targets. At Dessau the power house was claimed to have been destroyed and a big explosion occurred at Bromberg. In addition a number of enemy aerodromes, Flak and searchlight positions were attacked.

4.Thirty-seven 4 Group Whitleys were detailed to attack an aero engine factory at Turin and an airframe factory at Milan. One crew returned early* and another ditched in the Channel off Lympne on return.

In spite of the long night flight to Italy over the Alps, thirty-two of the thirty five aircraft despatched carried out successful high and low level attacks on the Fiat works at Turin where a parachute flare falling on the roof made a good aiming point and illuminated the target. The result was fires and explosions. Hits were also claimed on a blast furnace and on railway lines south of the city.

The attacks on the Caproni works in Milan resulted in explosions and the hangars were seen to be on fire. Fires were also started in the nearby marshalling yard and the road/rail bridge at Cassando D'Adda, carrying the main line to Venice, is believed to have been destroyed.

**Our crew was one of those selected, but we were the one who had to return early. We took off from our forward base of Abingdon at 20.00 hours, crossed the Channel and proceeded over France to the Alps. As we were attempting to climb over the mountains an engine packed in and we had to turn back. As this was my second abortive attempt to bomb Italy I was getting that 'jinxed' feeling. However we got back safely on our one engine, but as far as I was concerned it was a six hour 'flog' for nothing.*

Larry Donnelly

The wreck of R2272 UX-T in Limfjord, Denmark another victim of the Aalborg Raid. Remarkably, the crew of this aircraft all survived.

The Aalborg Raid

This raid by 82 Squadron was a complete disaster. It remains a mystery why this suicidal operation on Aalborg was ordered. It was at the limit of a Blenheim's range and they took off into a cloudless sky even though at briefing it was stressed that if there was less than 5/10ths cloud cover the operation was to be aborted.

They flew in four vics of three across the North Sea, but on reaching the Danish coast one of them dropped out of formation and turned for home. The eleven remaining aircraft cruised on. Unfortunately the lead navigator had brought them on a course that crossed the southern instead of the northern coast of Denmark, which meant they had to fly the length of the country to get to their target of Aalborg.

Flying in clear sunshine at 8,000 feet they flew northwards. They were twenty miles short of Aalborg when they were intercepted and attacked by the first Bf109s who raked the Blenheim formation continuously, only breaking off when the Flak took over as they got near the airfield. The tragic result was that every aircraft of the remaining eleven was shot down by fighters or Flak.

Only nine out of the thirty-three aircrew survived, some of them terribly wounded, to become prisoners of war. One of the survivors, Sergeant Johnnie Oates, flying Blenheim L1889, almost died of his wounds. He had been hedge-hopping to escape the fighters when a wing-tip hit a fence post causing the Blenheim to cartwheel into the ground. Pilot Officer R. M. Biden, his navigator, was thrown clear, miraculously only suffering from shock and a broken wrist. When an ambulance arrived Oates insisted that his navigator occupied a stretcher while he sat on the floor. It was only when they got to the hospital that Oates learnt that his back was broken. Sergeant Bill Magrath, flying with Sergeant Don Blair and Sergeant Greenwood in Blenheim R2772, fared even worse. He suffered a smashed hip, a broken shoulder and the loss of one eye, disabling him for the rest of his life. In November 1941, when he learned that his repatriation on medical grounds had been turned down, he escaped from a transit camp in Rouen and evaded across France via Paris and Marseilles to the Pyrenees. Although lame he crossed the mountains into Spain in the freezing January weather and eventually got back to England. His fortitude and courage earned him the award of the Military Medal, but he was disappointed to learn he was now unfit for further flying duties and would remain on ground duties in his present rank of sergeant. It is ironic that if he had remained as a prisoner of war he would have been promoted and received commensurate rises in pay!

Corporal Reg Charles was an engine fitter on 82 Squadron. He well recalled the disastrous raid on Gembloux on 9th June 1940, when the squadron was virtually wiped out by Messerschmitts and of 13th August he said: "Our aircrews had the custom of giving their wallets to their ground crews before take-off. If they didn't come back, the ground crews could have whatever cash was inside. That was the second time we 'made a few bob'. But it didn't make up for losing the crews. I think our crew knew it was a one-way trip; you could see it in their eyes."

This raid was another indictment against the 'Mahogany Bomber Pilots' of the higher echelons who persisted in ordering these unescorted daylight raids, still believing the archaic policy of 'the bomber will always get through'.

Tuesday 13th August

Eight Blenheims of 82 Squadron lined up in front of the hangars at Watton. By the evening of the 13th August, this apron was deserted as the ground crews waited in vain for the squadron to return from Aalborg.

OPERATIONAL LOSSES

Blenheim R2772 of 82 Squadron, Watton, target Aalborg, shot down in the target area. Sergeant D. Blair, Sergeant W. G. McGrath and Sergeant W. Greenwood were all wounded and made prisoners.

Blenheim R3800 of 82 Squadron, Watton, target Aalborg, shot down in the target area. Flight Lieutenant T. E. Syms and Sergeant K. H. Wright were taken prisoner. Sergeant E. V. Turner was killed and is buried in Vadum Cemetery.

Blenheim R3802 of 82 Squadron, Watton, target Aalborg, shot down in the target area. Flight Lieutenant R. A. G. Ellen and Sergeant V. J. Dance were taken prisoner and Sergeant G. Davies was killed and is buried in Vadum Cemetery.

Blenheim R3821 of 82 Squadron, target Aalborg, shot down in the target area. Pilot Officer E. R. Hale, Sergeant R. G. Oliver and Sergeant A. E. Boland were all killed and are buried in Vadum Cemetery.

Blenheim R3829 of 82 Squadron, target Aalborg, shot down in the target area. Squadron Leader R. N. Wardell was taken prisoner. Flight Sergeant G. P. Moore and Sergeant T. E. Girvan were killed and are buried in Vadum cemetery.

Blenheim R3904 of 82 Squadron, Watton, target Aalborg, shot down in the target area. Pilot Officer B. T. J. Newland was taken prisoner, Sergeant G. C. Ankers and Sergeant K. V. Turner were killed and are buried in Vadum Cemetery.

Blenheim R3913 of 82 Squadron, target Aalborg, shot down in the target area. Pilot Officer C. W. Wigley, Sergeant A. H. Patchett and Sergeant A. F. Morrison were all killed and are buried in Vadum Cemetery.

Blenheim T1857 of 82 Squadron, Watton, target Aalborg, shot down in the target area. Squadron Leader N. C. Jones and Pilot Officer T. J. Cranidge were killed and are buried in Vadum Cemetery. Sergeant J. F. H. Bristow was taken prisoner.

Blenheim T1889 of 82 Squadron, Watton, target Aalborg, shot down in target area. Sergeant J. E. Oates, Pilot Officer R. M. Biden and Sergeant T. Graham were all taken prisoner.

Blenheim T1933 of 82 Squadron, Watton, target Aalborg, shot down in target area. Pilot Officer D. A. J. Parfitt, Sergeant L. R. Youngs and Sergeant K. W. Neaverson were all killed and are buried in Vadum Cemetery.

Blenheim T1934 of 82 Squadron, target Aalborg, shot down in target area. Wing Commander E. C. de V. Lart DSO, Pilot Officer M. H. Gillingham and Sergeant A. S. Beeby DFM, were all killed and are buried in Vadum Cemetery.

Blenheim L9265 of 114 Squadron, Oulton, target Jersey aerodrome, lost without trace. Pilot Officer I. T. H. Carson, Sergeant D. P. Morrissy and Sergeant L. E. Moores are commemorated on the Runnymede memorial. *This is believed to have fallen to Unteroffizier Wilhelm Holdermann of 5./JG 53 in its target area.*

During the day a 139 Squadron Blenheim was damaged by Bf109s, but Flight Lieutenant Pepper DFC brought the aircraft back and force-landed it at Horsham St.Faith. It is likely to been that attacked and claimed destroyed by Unteroffizier Friedrich Geisshardt of 2.(J)/LG 2

Hampden P2077 of 44 Squadron, Waddington, target Bernburg. Hit by Flak and crashed 18 Km east-south-east of Alkmaar (Holland). Pilot Officer H. P. Clarke, Sergeant F. M. Wilkes, Sergeant G. E. Harris and Sergeant J. L. Brooks were all taken prisoner.

Whitley P4965 'H' of 10 Squadron, target Fiat aero engine works, Turin. Badly shot up by a night fighter over the target which put one engine out of action and damaged the starboard aileron. The captain, Pilot Officer 'Pip' Parsons DFC, succeeded in getting his crippled aircraft back over the Alps and France, but while attempting to land on the beach near Lympne the damaged aileron broke off and the aircraft plunged into the sea, killing Pilot Officer E. I. Parsons and his second pilot, Sergeant A. N. Campion. The other crew members, Sergeant Chamberlain, Marshall and Sharpe, escaped from the aircraft. Sergeants Chamberlain and Sharpe were rescued by two fishermen in their boat. Sergeant Marshall was rescued by Miss Peggy Prince who paddled out in her frail canoe. She was subsequently awarded the BEM. The bodies of Pilot Officer Parsons and Sergeant Campion were washed onto the French coast. They are buried in Boulogne's Eastern Cemetery in the Pas-de-Calais.

A wrecked hangar at Middle Wallop after the previous day's heavy raids.

ENEMY AIR ACTIVITY

After the heavy air attacks of the previous day the action was confined to scattered raids on targets in the south-east. A naval action took place in the Channel between RN destroyers and armed German trawlers and E-Boats during which the navy claimed hits on three enemy vessels. In the air fighting which took place the Luftwaffe lost nineteen aircraft destroyed. RAF fighter command lost four fighters.

COASTAL COMMAND OPERATIONS

Despite tasks having to be cancelled because of adverse weather, forty-one anti invasion and anti submarine patrols, special reconnaissance and searches were carried out throughout the period by sixty aircraft. The reconnaissance included two of the Norwegian Coast between Trondheim to Lister Light and Aisboen to Lister Light.

1. The two Blenheim crews who carried out the Trondheim to Lister Light sortie reported seeing thirteen motor vessels and a hospital ship in the vicinity of Royde Fjord and a concentration of small vessels twenty to seventy miles from Aisboen.

2. Sunderland 'J' of 210 Squadron on convoy escort was attacked by a Focke-Wulf 200 Condor, one hundred and thirty miles from Bloody Foreland. The Condor scored hits with cannon fire on the Sunderland's starboard wing and fuel tanks forcing it to abandon its task and return to base. It managed to do so safely and there were no casualties.

Night operations

A Hudson on a reconnaissance flight dived into the ground near its base in Norfolk.

BOMBER COMMAND OPERATIONS

1. A North Sea sweep in daylight was carried out by six 2 Group Blenheims but nothing of interest was seen.

2. Twenty-four Blenheims of 2 Group were detailed to carry out daylight attacks on airfields, air parks, oil targets and airframe factories. Because of the unsuitable weather conditions only three airfields were attacked at Morlaix, St. Omer and Dinard. Hits on the hangars at St. Omer were observed. There were no losses.

Night operations

1. 2 Group detailed thirteen Blenheims to carry out night raids on airfields in France, Holland and Belgium. Six of them attacked the aerodromes at Lisieux, Rouen-Boos, St. Inglevert, Creil and Soesterberg. Two aircraft failed to return.

2. Twelve 3 Group Wellingtons were despatched to attack oil installations at Blaye (west France). Eight crews claimed they were successful in causing explosions in the target area and fires with the smoke reaching 4,000 feet. Three other fires were observed in the vicinity with the smoke getting up to 7,000 feet.

3. The targets for thirty-one Whitleys of 4 Group were oil installations in France and the Caproni aircraft factory at Milan. Ten crews went to an oil target at Bordeaux, twelve to another at St. Nazaire and nine to the Caproni factory. The concentrated attacks on the oil targets by the twenty-two aircraft were claimed by the crews to have been successful as there were direct hits which left the area in flames. The nine 102 Squadron crews attacking the Caproni works also claimed success.

4. Thirty-six Hampdens of 5 Group were detailed to attack oil installations at Pauillac, marshalling yards at Köln/Eifelter, Soest, Hamm and Osnabrük , also a photo-reconnaissance of the Dortmund-Ems Canal. The twenty-two crews who attacked the oil target at Pauillac claimed to have left it in flames. Six crews bombed the marshalling yards at Köln/Eifelter also starting fires. The attacks on the other marshalling yards in the Ruhr were prevented because of the 10/10ths cloud and rain. The photo-reconnaissance of the Dortmund-Ems Canal was also a 'no-go' because of the weather. One aircraft bombed the aerodrome at Cherbourg.

Wednesday 14th August

OPERATIONAL LOSSES

Hudson N7401 of 206 Squadron, Docking, pilot lost control on take-off at night. Pilot Officer H. G. Ballantyne, (New Zealander) Pilot Officer J. O. L. Stephenson (New Zealander) and Sergeant E. Fitzgerald were killed. Sergeant J. Steel survived.

Blenheim P4908 of 40 Squadron, Wyton, target Chartres, failed to return. Sergeant K. Newton, Sergeant F. M. Hotchkiss and Sergeant C. A. McCreary were later reported to be PoWs.

Blenheim R3609 of 40 Squadron, Wyton, also failed to return from Chartres. Pilot Officer G. Parker was made prisoner, but Sergeant G. H. Easton and Sergeant E. Watson evaded capture. Sergeant Watson was awarded the Military Medal when he got back to England.

Blenheim T1882 of 18 Squadron, West Raynham, lost without trace from anti shipping strike. Sergeant H. E. Tyldesley, Sergeant F. L. Smith and Sergeant T. P. J. Byrne are all commemorated on the Runnymede Memorial.

Whitley P4982 of 51 Squadron, Dishforth, on return from Bordeaux flew into balloon barrage cables near Langley, Buckinghamshire, killing the entire crew; Pilot Officer S. P. Swensen, Sergeant A. K. Dawson, Sergeant J. B. O'Brien, Sergeant R. A. W. Tait and Sergeant L. P. Stubberfield.

Whitley P5044 of 77 Squadron, Driffield, target oil depot near Bordeaux, collided on return with balloon cables one mile south-east of Eastleigh, Hampshire. Flying Officer W. A. Stenhouse, Flying Officer R. B. MacGregor, Sergeant C. L. G. Hood, Sergeant J. Burrow and Sergeant H. Davies were all killed.

Ditching the Blenheim

Sergeant K. Newton
Blenheim pilot, 40 Squadron

Sergeant Fitton, Newton's usual navigator, who was replaced by Sergeant Hotchkiss on that night, Sergeant Newton, and Sergeant McCreary.

We left our base at Wyton on the night of 14th August 1940 to bomb an airfield in Normandy, having completed our mission it was on the return that we had navigation problems. It is possible that our fuel system was damaged whilst flying in the area of the Channel Islands where we encountered heavy flak.

Running out of fuel and over the sea I noticed a headland and a lighthouse which was flashing. Leaving this lighthouse on the starboard side and with the engines spluttering we prepared to ditch. Now bear in mind that it was now into the early hours of 15th August, pitch dark, and we had fearful prospects of what might happen to us – it was no time for sight seeing I can tell you. Fortunately the sea was calm; but solid. We seemed to skim and bounce before settling nose first. Water quickly entered the cockpit waist high and I had great difficulty in moving. Sergeant Hotchkiss, the observer, emerged from the nose of the aircraft and seemed OK. Sergeant McCreary, the air gunner, was out and had the dinghy inflated which he manoeuvred onto the mainplane close to the cockpit and I managed with their help to flop into the middle of it.

Thus we left the doomed Blenheim about half to three-quarters of a mile from the shore. We drifted cum paddled our way to the beach where a party of Germans were already appearing. They dragged us out and put us into what appeared to be a signals van and took us into Cherbourg and the *Hospital Maritime.* I was badly injured, having sustained a fractured femur, dislocated shoulder and facial injuries and was detained in hospital. The Germans took the rest of my crew away and I have not been in contact with them from that moment.

K. Newton (1983)

ENEMY AIR ACTIVITY

This turned out to be a most decisive day and some say it was the real start of the battle, when the Luftwaffe concentrated mass attacks on RAF airfields. Enemy attacks began in mid-morning when seventy-two He111s escorted by twenty-one Bf110s of *Luftflotte 5*, operating from Stavanger, attempted to carry out attacks on the north of England, their primary targets being the 4 Group bomber bases. To draw off any fighter opposition a feint attack was launched by a formation of He115 float planes. Because of a navigation error this failed and as the German bomber force approached the British coast it was detected by Radar. Every 13 Group fighter squadron from Catterick in Yorkshire, to Drem in Scotland was scrambled to intercept. Fifteen German aircraft were destroyed for the loss of one RAF fighter. The other main attack force was fifty Ju88s from Aalborg whose primary target was the 4 Group base at Driffield. They were detected and attacked by fighters of 12 Group who destroyed seven Ju88s and severely damaged three more. Some of the surviving raiders got through and clobbered Driffield, destroying nine Whitleys, three hangars, one wing of the Officers' Mess and causing casualties, some of them fatal. At this time airfield defence against low level attacks was woefully lacking, comprising a few light machine-guns, so the Ju88s were able to sweep across Driffield with impunity, bombing and strafing. However, overall it was a small return for their losses. The survivors of both the He111 and Ju88 forces were harried by Fighter Command Blenheims as they attempted to escape across the North Sea. The pilot of one of the attacking Blenheims was wounded by return fire so the air gunner took over and flew the aircraft hack to Driffield where they carried out a successful wheels-up landing. For this exploit Sergeant Dube, the pilot, and Sergeant Bannister the air gunner were subsequently awarded DFMs. After this debacle, *Luftflotte 5* never again launched mass attacks and several of its northern squadrons were transferred south to support the main assaults during the battle.

While 12 and 13 Groups fought off the attack in the north, heavy attacks were taking place in the south. Escorted Stukas bombed Hawkinge airfield and cut off power to the Radar stations at Dover, Rye and Foreness. The mass attacks continued throughout the afternoon and evening against airfields in south-east England and Croydon was bombed in mistake for Kenley. Numerous combats took place. The Luftwaffe lost seventy-one aircraft; the RAF lost twenty-nine. The Luftwaffe's failure to pin-point vital targets wasted most of their efforts, and they lost Hauptman Walter Rubensdörffer, leader of *Eprg210,* who was shot down in flames.

COASTAL COMMAND OPERATIONS

Eighty-seven aircraft carried out sixty-one routine anti invasion, anti submarine patrols, reconnaissance and special sorties. Air escort was provided for twenty convoys.

1. A Hudson on routine patrol reported at 09.00 hours that a 10,000 ton motor vessel of unknown nationality was stationary twelve miles from Lister Light.

The Heinkel 59 that was shot down by Hudson VX-V of 206 Squadron. The He59 had just picked up an He111 crew from the sea when the Hudson attacked and sent them back down again. The German crewmen spent two days at sea before they were rescued by a minesweeper. This photo was taken on the 17th August as the crews were rescued and the battered He59 finally sank beneath the waves.

2. Sunderland 'E' of 204 Squadron on patrol attacked a U-Boat with bombs and depth charges eighteen miles south of the Faroe Islands. There were no visible results.
3. Hudson 'E' of 206 Squadron fought an inconclusive engagement with an He115 for forty minutes, fifty miles from Terschelling.
4. Three Blenheims on a search for enemy shipping attacked twenty-four He111s eighty miles from Horns Reef. One enemy aircraft was seen diving towards the sea with an engine on fire. It was claimed that other enemy aircraft were also damaged.
5. Successful PR sorties were flown over The Hague, Rotterdam, Scheldt, Den Helder, Amsterdam, Ghent, Bruges, Wilhelmshaven, Emden, Kiel, Bremen and Hamburg. There were no losses.

Night operations

1. Three Blenheims of 53 Squadron and three of 59 Squadron who carried out a night strike on Den Helder and Willemsoord claimed direct hits which caused explosions and fires.
2. Minelaying was carried by three Swordfish in the Maas Estuary and by another three at Texel.
3. Hudson 'V' of 206 Sqn on routine night patrol engaged an He59 and shot it down twenty miles from Borkum. It landed on the sea and was last seen on fire at 2230hrs.

Thursday 15th August

One of the 102 Squadron Whitleys destroyed by the bombing of Driffield on 15th August.

BOMBER COMMAND OPERATIONS

1. Eight 2 Group Blenheims were detailed for daylight raids on oil targets in west Germany and airfields in occupied territory. Because of adverse weather these attacks were not possible, but one aircraft detailed to attack Hanover bombed the airfield at De Kooy on return. Results were not observed. There were no losses.

Night operations

1. Eighteen 2 Group Blenheims were despatched to carry out night raids on enemy occupied airfields. Twelve bombed. At Leeuwarden, fires were started in a large hangar and among dispersed aircraft. Successful attacks on the airfields at Forêt de Guines and Chartres were claimed by the crews. The long-range guns at Cap Gris Nez were also bombed but no results were observed. One aircraft failed to return.
2. Forty-three Wellingtons were despatched to attack oil plants, an aluminium works and marshalling yards. Thirty-seven bombed the primary targets, four bombed alternatives and two failed to bomb. The oil plant at Gelsenkirchen was hit and the fires started by the 'early birds' assisted the late comers who used them as aiming points. Fires were also started at the marshalling yards at Hamm and Soest. Other objectives attacked included airfields at Eindhoven and Kevalier and an arms factory at Düsseldorf where bombs were seen to burst in the target area.
3. Twenty-one Hampdens were sent to attack the oil refinery at Reisholtz and the synthetic oil plant at Gelsenkirchen. Attacks on both targets were claimed as successful. Other aircraft bombed the Krupps works at Essen, and dock installations at Emmerich. Leaflets were dropped over northern France by six Hampdens of 7 Group.
4. Because of the of the raid carried out by Luftflotte 5 on RAF Driffield earlier in the day only four Whitleys were detailed. Their targets were the aircraft factory at Turin and the Caproni works at Milan. One crew who bombed the

The Raid on Driffield

Pilot Officer Jim Verran (later Squadron Leader DFC and Bar) of 102 Whitley Squadron recalls the Luftwaffe raid on Driffield.

"I had returned to Driffield in the middle of the night from a raid on Milan. After sleeping it off, I went to the Mess, had lunch and retired to the ante-room to read the newspapers when the air raid siren sounded. The initial reaction was, as usual, lethargic until the bombs started exploding when everyone made a mad dash for the shelter near the Mess. I made it OK, but one fellow officer was blown into the shelter with a window frame around his neck - the result of a bomb which hit the Mess just as we left it."

Another survivor was **Sergeant Arthur Stokes**, WOp/AG also of 102 Squadron, (he completed his 'tour' but was killed during his second tour).

"At about 1.30 pm, my room-mate in the Sergeants' Mess looked out of the window and said, 'What are all these Blenheims flying around here for?' (he was later given extra instruction on aircraft recognition!). Then the bombs started exploding. I left my bed in a hurry - I'd been on the Milan raid and was having a 'lie in'. Our room was on the first floor hut but without hesitation I leapt through the window landing on the grass below. I then 'streaked' across the grass and flung myself into the shelter."

Inside the shelter he discovered he had literally 'streaked' across the grass - he was only wearing his shirt!

factory at Turin claimed their attack caused explosions and fires. Another who bombed the Caproni works at Milan claimed that the fires caused by their attack were visible long after they had left the target. One aircraft failed to return.

Above: More scenes of devastation at Driffield, again, 102 Squadron Whitleys are the main casualties.

Below: The raiders didn't have it all their own way, here the remains of a Messerschmitt Bf110 lie wrapped around a telegraph pole a few hours after the Driffield raid.

OPERATIONAL LOSSES

Fairey Battle L5093 of 12 Squadron was destroyed by enemy bombing at Martlesham Heath. Wing Commander V. Q. Blackden was wounded in his right foot. (Vyvian Quentery Blackden was killed over Holland with 12 Squadron on 10 April 1941.)

Nine Whitleys were destroyed by enemy bombing at RAF Driffield and three airmen killed.
77 Squadron
N1353, N1501, N1506, P5056
102 Squadron
N1378, N1413, N1420, P4945, P5022

Blenheim R3770 of 15 Squadron, Wyton, target the airfield at Forêt de Guines, failed to return and was presumed lost over the sea. Sergeant P. K. Garvey, Sergeant H. Bowers and Sergeant H. Rolls were presumed killed and recorded on the Runnymede Memorial.
Whitley N1497 'B' of 10 Squadron, Abingdon, hit by Flak after bombing the target at Milan. Sergeant Green, Sergeant H. J. Davis, Sergeant A. Millington and Pilot Officer A. E. V. Oliver were taken prisoner. Flying Officer K. H. Higson was killed.

Sergeant Eric Watson
Blenheim gunner 40 Squadron

Eric Watson was a member of the RAF Volunteer Reserve before the war and was called up shortly after the war started. He was sent to 2 Electrical and Wireless School where he trained as a wireless operator. This was followed by air/gunnery and OTU training on Blenheims.

He was posted to No. 40 (Blenheim) Squadron at Wyton with which he started bombing operations on the 11th July against a target in the Seine district. As the Battle of Britain commenced with the threat of invasion he participated in raids against enemy airfields and shipping in the occupied ports. On the night of the 14th/15th August his crew were detailed to attack a target at Chartres. They failed to locate it and set course to bomb the shipping at Le Havre. Shortly after setting course a snag occurred and the aircraft failed to answer the controls. It lost height as the captain endeavoured to regain control, but he was unsuccessful and gave the order to bale out. The crew successfully evacuated the Blenheim at one thousand feet, which crashed and exploded in the fields below.

Sergeant Watson ended up suspended in a tree, but after extricating himself he left the area and spent six hours in a nearby farm building. At dawn he walked to the village where he made contact with the Mayor and his pilot, Pilot Officer Parker. They spent the day in the nearby fields after being given food and cigarettes, while the Germans searched for them and questioned the Mayor who refused to give them any information. In the meantime they were fed by peasants who told them that their observer, Jock Easton, was holed up in a woodcutter's hut three miles south.

At night fall they made contact with Jock and commenced walking south for their ultimate destination of Gibraltar. Watson commenced keeping a notebook recording the events of what was to be an epic evasion. He understated the hazards of being on the run suffering the hardships of hunger, sleeping rough in bad weather, incarcerations in French and Spanish jails. He also risked the possibility of being accused as a spy if he was caught with his notebook which might contain military information.

They walked by night and hid up during the day. At this time there was no organisation as there was later for helping downed fliers, but there were some sympathetic French people who assisted them, on the other hand there were others of a less helpful nature.

On the 21st August they were challenged by German sentries and they split up. Watson caught up with Jock Easton later but Parker was captured and sent off to Germany as a prisoner.

By the 6th September they reached Charteroux where they met two British soldiers on the run, Sergeant Fraser and Driver McKenzie. They weren't together for long as Jock Easton and Sergeant Fraser were arrested by French Gendarmes on 13th September (Sergeant Watson heard later they were interned in Marseilles from where Sergeant Fraser escaped and from where Sergeant Easton was eventually released to arrive in Gibraltar in April 1941).

On the 15th September Sergeant Watson and Driver McKenzie crossed the frontier into Spain where they were arrested by Spanish soldiers who turned them over to the Guardia Civil who put them in the jail at Figuera, to join fifteen English soldiers. Shortly afterwards the British Vice Consul saw them and informed them they would possibly be interned for the duration! From 19th September they were shunted from jail to jail, some worse than others, but on 14th November they reached Gibraltar.

On 19th November they embarked on the *SS Aquila* for Blighty in convoy and arrived in the UK on 4th December, after an eventful voyage with the destroyer escort keeping U-Boats at bay.

Sergeant Dawson was kitted out in new uniform and comprehensively debriefed at the Air Ministry during which he gave full details of his failed operation over Chartres on the 15th/16th August and his subsequent hair raising evasion through France and Spain to Gibraltar. Subsequently he was awarded a well deserved Military Medal.

After leave he volunteered to return to flying in February 1941 and after OTU training rejoined his old squadron who were now flying Wellingtons. He recommenced flying on operations in July 1941, completing twelve 'trips' before going to Malta with No. 40 Squadron in October 1941 to finish his 'tour' with operations over North Africa and Italy.

During his sojourn his phenomenally charmed life stood him in good stead. He was in a cinema when it was bombed and was buried for nine hours before being rescued. He was commissioned, finished his 'tour' and returned to the UK where he carried on flying until he was de mobbed, having carried out eleven operations on Blenheims, thirty-eight on Wellingtons and two on Halifaxes, amassing a total of seven hundred and eighty-four flying hours.

He left the RAF in 1945 as Flight Lieutenant and resumed his pre-war career in accountancy and, as can be expected of a character of such fortitude and determination, he achieved the post of Senior Finacial Advisor to a Commonwealth Government in Africa.

Friday 16th August

ENEMY AIR ACTIVITY

The mass attacks on south-east England continued. Ventnor radar was attacked by Stukas and put out of action for a week. Other Stukas escorted by Bf109s attacked the RAF stations of Thorney Island, Tangmere, Manston, Farnborough and Lee-on-Solent inflicting damage and causing casualties. An audacious evening raid by two Ju88s on RAF Brize Norton, when they lowered their wheels to give the impression they were Blenheims coming in to land, resulted in two hangars being hit in which forty-six aircraft were destroyed and seven damaged. A further eleven aircraft at an MU on the airfield were also destroyed. During the day's heavy fighting forty-four Luftwaffe aircraft were destroyed. RAF Fighter Command lost twenty-two aircraft including one of 249 Squadron flown by Flight Lieutenant J Nicholson who was subsequently awarded the Victoria Cross, the only VC to be awarded to Fighter Command during the war.

Flight Lieutenant J. B. Nicholson, who was awarded Fighter Command's only VC of the Battle of Britain for his actions on this day.

COASTAL COMMAND OPERATIONS

Coastal Command squadrons carried out forty-five anti invasion and anti submarine patrols as well as special sorties. Air escort was provided for twelve convoys. Throughout the day seventy-six aircraft were involved.

1. Sunderland P9624 of 210 Squadron claimed to have sunk a U-Boat one hundred and eighty miles from Bloody Foreland.
2. A Hudson on a reconnaissance of the Norwegian Coast attacked Flak ships entering Stavanger Harbour but no results were observed.
3. A Blenheim on Air Sea Rescue directed a life-boat to a downed airman in the sea off Selsey.
4. The main hangar at Thorney Island was damaged by enemy bombers and two Blenheims (R3835 and T1815) of 59 Squadron destroyed.
5. Aircraft of the Photographic Reconnaissance Unit took photographs of Scheldt to Rotterdam, Le Havre, Bordeaux, Blaye, Pauillac and Verdon.

Night operations

1. Six Swordfish successfully carried out night minelaying in West Scheldt, Flushing and Terschelling Gat.
2. A Sunderland attacked a suspected U-Boat twenty miles from Lundy Island. Two depth charges exploded close to the target but there was no apparent result. From these operations there were no losses.

BOMBER COMMAND OPERATIONS

Six Blenheims of 2 Group carried out an uneventful sea sweep during daylight.

Night operations

1. Two Blenheims were detailed to carry out a night attack on the airfields at Lannion and De Kooy abandoned the other bombed - no result observed.
2. Thirty-seven Wellingtons were despatched on night operations; nine claimed successful attacks on the aircraft component works at Frankfurt, six attacked the aircraft storage depot at Kolleda and claimed direct hits on hangars and buildings, incendiary bombs caused fires. Some other aircraft attacked the Krupps works at Essen. The marshalling yards at Hamm and Soest were bombed but the results were unobserved.
3. The Whitley targets for the night were factories at Jena and Augsburg and the power station at Boblen.

> Our crew was one of the nine despatched to attack the Zeiss works at Jena. We fortunately had an unmolested trip outbound and with the aid of bearings from the D/F station at Butser Hill we located the target. As the opposition was light we attacked from 5,000 feet and, to make sure all our bombs hit the target, we made four separate runs. The return flight was also uneventful and we landed safely at Leeming at 05.30 hours - a round trip of nine hours. Another of our squadron aircraft on the same target was attacked by a Bf110 before they got there. The Whitley tail-gunner returned fire and claimed it as a 'possible'.
>
> ***Larry Donnelly, 10 Squadron Whitley***

The other Whitleys attacking the airframe factory at Augsburg and the oil refinery and power station at Boblen also claimed successful attacks. In addition a chemical factory at Mannheim, a blast furnace at Sonderhausen, a factory at Helbrungen and airfields at Darmstadt Langenberg and a railway junction at Halle were successfully attacked.

4. A concentrated attack by thirty-eight Hampdens on the hydro generation plant at Leuna was claimed as successful despite severe opposition. In addition single aircraft carried out attacks on the aerodromes at De Kooy, Bielefeld and

Friday 16th August

Nordhausen. Railways at Kolleda, Buttstadt, Bittefeld and Merseburg were also bombed.

OPERATIONAL LOSSES

Hampden P1333 'F' of 49 Squadron, Driffield, target Leuna, crashed near Breda, Holland. Sergeant M. G. P. Stetton, Sergeant C. H. Butcher, Sergeant K. N. Farrow and AC2. F. H. Lindesay were all taken prisoner.

Hampden P4291 of 144 Squadron, Hemswell, target Merseburg, crashed in Germany. Pilot Officer H. A. T. Skehill and Sergeant D. Perritt taken prisoner, Sergeant W. A. Hughes and Sergeant R. L. Wake were killed and are buried in the Reichswald Forest War Cemetery.

Hampden P4365 of 144 Squadron, Hemswell, target Merseburg, destroyed in a fatal crash on return to base. Squadron Leader P. H. Rebbeck, Pilot Officer D. Hutchins, Sergeant B. H. Foster and Sergeant H. Dickinson were all killed.

Wellington R3174 'A' of 149 Squadron, Mildenhall, target Kolleda, brought down in Germany. Squadron Leader E. H. T. Thwaites AFC, Pilot Officer D. E. S. Charles and Pilot Officer J. Wilk were killed and are buried in the Durnbach War Cemetery. Flight Lieutenant M. J. Fisher, Sergeant N. J. V. Cownie and Sergeant F. J. Pennicott were taken prisoner.

Whitley P4955 of 10 Squadron, Leeming, target Jena. Hit by Flak over the target and eventually crashed 10 km south-south-west of Breda. Flying Officer W. M. Nixon, Flying Officer P. G. Whitby, Sergeant R. W. Bradley, Sergeant E. R. Holmes and Sergeant A. M. Somerville were all taken prisoner.

Whitley P4986 of 51 Squadron, Dishforth, target Bohlen power station, failed to return. Flight Lieutenant J. S. Scott, Sergeant F. A. Beale, Sergeant R. D. E. Clarke, Sergeant P. D. Salmon and Sergeant H. Haggett were killed and are buried in the Hannover War Cemetery.

Whitley N1382 of 102 Squadron, target Augsburg, crashed in the Walser Valley, Austria. Pilot Officer M. H. Rogers, Sergeant M. W. J. Pollard, Sergeant S. G. Jermond, Sergeant J. Patterson and Sergeant W. F. Haywood were all killed and buried in the Klagenfurt War Cemetery.

Hampden P1333 being bombed up at Scampton. This aircraft was lost on this night when it crashed near Breda in Holland. Sgt. Stetton and his crew were all taken prisoner.

ENEMY AIR ACTIVITY

The Luftwaffe activity during the day was limited to single aircraft seeking coastal shipping and high level reconnaissance flights over London, however night bombing attacks were widespread over Aberavon, Coventry, Liverpool and the Birmingham area. A notable night fighter success was achieved when a Blenheim (L6741 of 29 Squadron) flown by Pilot Officer Rhodes, Sergeant Gregory and Sergeant Ternhill was vectored onto a raider fifteen miles south-west of Gloucester. They followed it persistently and forced it to ditch in the North Sea ten miles from the Cromer Knoll Light. Killed in the encounter was the Gruppenkommandeur of *KG53*.

A Luftwaffe fighter pilot recorded an interesting experience sometime during August (date unknown). Hauptmann Josef Fözö, Gruppenkommandeur of *II./JG 51* was leading a Freijagd (fighter sweep) in cloudy conditions and remembered: *"I somehow got separated from the others in my Stabschwarm in some thick cloud. I emerged below, alone, see a single aircraft in front of me. It was an Oxford or an Anson, something like that. Of course, I couldn't pass up a gift like that! I eased behind him, throttled back, and opened fire. Immediately my Emil yawed violently to starboard and I realised that only the cannon on that side was firing and I was being yawed by the recoil. I tried once again, and the same thing happened. I was about to try a third time but then thought, 'No. They deserve some luck' and I climbed back up into the cloud to find my missing boys. Those Tommies never realised that they had an angel sitting on their wing that day!"*

The PRU lost one of its Spitfires today on a sortie over the Ruhr.

COASTAL COMMAND OPERATIONS

Eighty-six aircraft carried out forty-six anti invasion, anti submarine and fighter escorted offensive sorties. Because of adverse weather routine patrols north of Scotland between the Faroe Islands and the Norwegian Coast were curtailed. Air escort was provided for nineteen convoys.

1. Hudson 'E' of 206 Squadron sighted and carried out an attack on nine armed motor vessels forty-two miles from Horns Reef, but no results were observed.

2. Six Blenheim (F) of 235 and 236 Squadrons escorted Fairey Battles of 12 and 142 Squadrons who bombed shipping in Boulogne. A 12 Squadron Battle P2331 was hit by Flak and crashed on return. There were no casualties.

3. An Anson on patrol reported having observed a U-Boat fifty-two miles from Lundy Island.

4. PRU Spitfires took photographs of the coastlines from Calais to Boulogne and Dunkirk, Cap Gris Nez and the railway from Boulogne to Lumbres. The coast from Hulst to Haamstede, Flushing and Knocke, Blankenberge to Ostend and Dunkirk was also photographed. One Spitfire was reported missing from a PR sortie over Dortmund-Ems.

Night operations

1. Eight Blenheims of 59 Squadron carried out night operations against targets at Rotterdam; One bombed a fuel depot and barges at Vlaadingen. The results were not observed.

BOMBER COMMAND OPERATIONS

1. Blenheim daylight bombing operations were hampered by the weather conditions and only three were despatched to attack the aerodromes at Fécamp, Dieppe and St. Inglevert. Bombs were dropped on Fécamp and Dieppe but the results were not observed.

2. A further six 2 Group Blenheims carried out an uneventful sweep over the North Sea. There were no losses.

Night operations

1. Thirty-six Blenheims were despatched to carry out night attacks on twenty-one airfields. Twenty-nine crews claimed to have carried out successful attacks.

2. The targets of the forty-one Wellingtons detailed were; the synthetic oil plant at Zeitz and the aircraft parks and marshalling yards at Eschwege, Hamm, Soest, Scherte, Osnabrük, Göttingen, Diepholz as well as the airfields at Schipol and Evere. The attack on Zeitz caused an explosion and many fires in the target area. The aircraft storage units at Diepholz, Göttingen and Eschwege also suffered considerable damage, as did the marshalling yards at Hamm and Osnabrük . Boblen power station, railways, roads and several airfields were also bombed. One aircraft encountered a Bf110 forty miles east of Great Yarmouth and shot it down in flames.

3. Twenty Hampdens were despatched to attack the Krupps works at Essen; eleven bombed and hits were observed. Other crews attacked an armament factory Düsseldorf and factories at Emmerich and Buderich, but the results were not observed. Five additional aircraft carried out successful mining in the Elbe Estuary.

OPERATIONAL LOSSES

Blenheim L4833 of 235 Squadron, Thorney Island, crashed in the sea near the airfield after a night patrol. Crew safe.

Blenheim N3540 of 235 Squadron, Thorney Island, undercarriage collapsed on bad landing. Crew safe.

Spitfire K9791 of the PRU, Heston, failed to return from a sortie over the Ruhr. Flight Sergeant J. D. T. Taylor-Gill was taken prisoner.

Sunday 18th August

ENEMY AIR ACTIVITY

The battle to destroy Fighter Command airfields was resumed early in the morning by six high-flying Bf110s of *LG2*. One was shot down over Manston. By midday a raiding force of 350 bombers and fighters crossed the south coast in three waves and headed for targets near London. Fighters from ten of our squadrons were scrambled to engage them. Another force headed for Kenley and Biggin Hill where they carried out high level low level bombing and strafing. Kenley was severely damaged and fires raged for six hours after the raid. Communications to vital group sector stations was disrupted. In the afternoon a radar station at Poling was hit during attacks by seventy Ju87s and twenty-four Ju88s escorted by Bf109s who also attacked the naval station at Ford, RAF Gosport and RAF Thorney Island. Later a large force attempted to bomb North Weald and Hornchurch but most of the bombing was prevented by intercepting fighters making them jettison their bombs before reaching their targets.

At night it was estimated that seventy bombers attacked south Wales, Zealand, Birmingham and Wolverhampton.

The 18th August proved to be toughest and most vital days of fighting during the battle, both sides suffering heavy losses - the Luftwaffe sixty aircraft and RAF Fighter Command thirty-five fighters.

COASTAL COMMAND OPERATIONS

A total of sixty-three aircraft carried out thirty-seven anti invasion, anti submarine and special reconnaissance sorties. Twenty-two convoys were escorted.

1. Nine out of twelve Fairey Battles of 12 and 142 Squadrons, escorted by fighter Blenheims, carried out a daylight sortie and successfully bombed shipping at Boulogne.
2. One Hudson of 220 Squadron on patrol dive-bombed four small armed vessels forty miles from Horns Reef, resulting in near misses.
3. Fighter Blenheims from Thorney Island carried out an armed reconnaissance over Le Havre and Cherbourg
4. Blenheim fighters of 'A' flight 235 Squadron were scrambled to defend Thorney Island. Pilot Officer Peacock in L9446, Pilot Officer Wordsworth in N3533 and Sergeant Nelson in T1869 each claimed to have shot down a Ju88.
5. Three other Blenheims of 235 Squadron on station protection over Bircham Newton engaged twenty Ju87s and six Bf109s and claimed to have shot down two Ju87s and to have damaged another. The leader of the Ju87s was shot down in flames.
6. PRU aircraft took photographs of the Bruges to Ostend Canal, the coastline from Ostend to Dunkirk, Boulogne, Paris, Orleans, the area north of Chateaudun, Sotteville and an airfield south of Rouen. It was reported there was considerable shipping activity at Boulogne.

BOMBER COMMAND OPERATIONS

Because of unfavourable weather there were no daylight operations by 2 Group Blenheims over Germany, however six carried out a sweep over the North Sea but nothing of interest was observed.

Night operations

4 Group Whitleys were the only aircraft to carry out night operations; twenty were despatched to attack an aluminium factory at Rheinfelden and four to the Caproni aircraft factory at Milan. Although the weather over Germany was very bad, ten of the crews claimed hits on the factory at Rheinfelden which left the whole area in flames. Other aircraft started fires at the Electra-chemical plant at Waldshut and an attack on Freiburg aerodrome resulted in an explosion suggesting an ammunition dump had been hit. Another successful attack was claimed on the airfield at Hashemite.

Bad Weather

Our crew was detailed to attack Rheinfelden, but it was not our night. We took off from Leeming at 23.00 hours and had an uneventful flight over the North Sea, but after crossing the enemy coast the weather deteriorated and I could tell from the interference on the W/T we were in for a rough ride. From time to time the darkness was illuminated by brilliant flashes of lightning from towering cumulo-nimbus clouds. We steered clear of them and the heavily defended areas on route. However when our ETA target arrived we were in thick cloud. We stooged back and forth attempting to find a break without success and after spending as much time as we could seeking our primary target we gave it up and set course for an alternative. Our bad luck and the bad weather continued and we were unable to find an alternative even though we spent time up to our PLE (Prudent Limit of Endurance) searching. We set course for home but to pile on the agony our W/T transmitter packed in. Thankfully, G.B. our navigator was on the ball with his dead reckoning and the weather improved over the North Sea. We were able to get back to Leeming and land safely with our bombs still on board, having spent nine frustrating hours, most over enemy territory. I recall that at the time I thought there must be an easier way of earning a bacon and egg breakfast!

Larry Donnelly, 10 Squadron Whitley

Of the four Whitleys on the Italian targets one hit the Caproni works in Milan causing explosions and fires. Another aircraft, unable to locate the primary target, attacked an unidentified factory south-west of Turin. Bomb bursts were observed and a strong glow was seen as the aircraft left the area. The Fiat works at Turin were also attacked, but no results observed. One of the Whitleys was attacked by a single-engine fighter shortly after leaving Milan. The Whitley tail gunner returned fire claiming to have hit the enemy aircraft which was then lost in cloud.

OPERATIONAL LOSSES

There were no losses

CLOUDY OVER THE WHOLE COUNTRY WITH SCATTERED SHOWERS.

Monday 19th August

A Hudson of 206 Squadron engaged a He111 and left it with one engine put out of action in a combat 23 miles from Lowestoft.

ENEMY AIR ACTIVITY

Cloudy conditions limited air operations, however some small scale raids by the Luftwaffe achieved some results. A large fire was started when an oil farm at Llanreith, Pembroke was hit. Other 'hit and run' raids were made on Bibury, Chelmsford, Dover Castle, Shoeburyness, Canterbury and Deal. After dusk He111s bombed Liverpool and Birkenhead. KGr100 (the Luftwaffe pathfinder unit) attempted a beam-guided attack on Derby. Three of their aircraft crashed on return because of fuel shortage. Other enemy aircraft carried out a low level night strike on RAF Driffield where a hangar and two Whitleys were damaged. Bombing at Hull, Leicester, Nottingham and Sheffield caused twenty-four deaths and seventy-four injured. During the day's air fighting the Luftwaffe lost four aircraft destroyed and RAF Fighter Command lost four fighters.

COASTAL COMMAND OPERATIONS

Before dawn adverse weather conditions affected all routine patrols but throughout the day eighty-two aircraft carried out forty-eight anti invasion, anti submarine and special reconnaissance sorties. Air escort was provided for twenty-three convoys.

1. Two Blenheims on patrol off Norway took photographs of shipping off Stadtlandet. One of the ships was attacked but there was no positive result.

2. A Hudson of 206 Squadron on convoy escort engaged an He111 twenty-three miles from Lowestoft. One of the Heinkel's engines was put out of action and further damage was inflicted, making it unlikely for it to get back to its base. The Hudson sustained some slight damage but there were no casualties.

Night operations

1. Six Swordfish successfully carried out mining operations in the Ems River and Hubert Gat.

2. Six Blenheims of 53 Squadron were detailed to carry out a night attack on the airfield at St. Omer. Four bombed successfully, starting a number of fires. One crew failed to find the primary target so dropped bombs on Cap Gris Nez, extinguishing some searchlights and causing fires.

3. Six Blenheims of 59 Squadron were despatched to attack the airfield at Caen; only one bombed but because of bad visibility was unable to observe the results. Four crews were unable to locate the target and one failed to return.

4. Seven Fairey Battles were detailed to carry out a night strike on enemy surface vessels in Boulogne Harbour. Because of the haze and the glare from searchlights four were unable to locate the target, one returned with engine trouble and another because of a bomb-rack snag. One aircraft failed to return.

BOMBER COMMAND OPERATIONS

1. Seventeen Blenheims of 2 Group were despatched during the day. Twelve crews were detailed to attack oil plants and aircraft depots in Germany, but had to abandon because of lack of suitable cloud cover. Of the remainder, one crew attacked a Flak battery at Amsterdam while another bombed the airfield at Flushing. One crew despatched to Bremen failed to return.

2. Six additional Blenheims carried out an uneventful sweep over the North Sea.

Night operations

1. Thirty-seven Blenheims were detailed to carry out night attacks on airfields in France, Holland and Belgium. Thirty-six got off and twenty-one airfields were bombed. Fires were started at Lisieux, Lintec, Guipavas, Rennes, Montebourg, Flushing, St. Inglevert and Leeuwarden. No results were observed at Evere, Valenciennes, Haamstede, Zandvoort, Soesterberg, Villacoublay, Châteauroux, Bourges, Orleans-Bricy and Chateaudun. Two aircraft failed to return.

2. Forty-eight Wellington crews were detailed; twenty-four were targeted to attack the *Gneisenau* in dock at Kiel and twelve to attack an oil refinery at Hannover. The remainders' targets were the Dortmund-Ems Aqueduct and rail communications at Hamm, Soest and Osnabrük. Because of low cloud and bad visibility the *Gneisenau* was not located, but thirteen aircraft bombed the harbour area and claimed hits on installations. The others bombed the marshalling yards at Hamm, Soest and Osnabrük, starting fires. One crew bombing the Dortmund Aqueduct claimed a direct hit on a nearby bridge. The oil refineries at Hannover, Salzbergen and Ostermoor were hit causing fires. The naval base at Wilhelmshaven, as well as aerodromes were also bombed. The lock gates two miles south of Meppen suffered a direct hit.

A series of photographs depicting the little known fate of Blenheim L9419 SR-X of 101 Squadron, West Raynham. Sergeant A. G. Chelmick, Sergeant J. Carbine and Sergeant H. Martyn were detailed to attack airfields and failed to return, subsequently reported as being prisoners of war.

The photographs show that the Blenheim was brought down whilst attacking Stormede airfield. It would appear that the pilot made a pretty good forced landing with both engines idling before impact. The daily attacks certainly seem to have had an effect in the above photo as half of the personnel scan the sky to identify a distant aircraft noise.

Monday 19th August

Fairey Battles of 12 Squadron. The nearest machine is P6597 lost on this day during a raid on Boulogne.

3. Seventeen Whitleys were detailed to attack the electric power station at Schornewitz (south of Dessau). Eight crews bombed claiming that a large explosion was followed by many fires. Also, successful attacks were claimed on airfields at Bernburg, Magdeburg and Habern. At Bernburg fires were observed at a nearby rail junction.
4. Fourteen Hampdens were detailed to attack the oil targets at Ambés (Bordeaux), thirteen claimed to have attacked successfully. A fire started by the first aircraft was stoked up by others following and the whole area became a mass of flames which reached 2,000 feet. Five other Hampdens successfully carried out minelaying in the Aalborg area.

OPERATIONAL LOSSES

Blenheim L9457 'S' of 248 (F) Squadron, failed to return from a Norwegian sortie after being intercepted by four Bf109s. Sergeant J. H. Round, Sergeant W. H. Want and Sergeant M. P. Digby-Worsley were posted as missing in action and their names are on the Runnymede Memorial.
This aircraft was intercepted by Bf109Es from 4./JG 77 and was shot down by Oberleutnant Wilhelm Moritz.

Blenheim R2795 'A' of 59 Squadron, Thorney Island, target the airfield at Caen, failed to return. Pilot Officer B. Reynolds, Sergeant W. G. F. Whiting and Sergeant W. G. J. Wilkinson were killed and lie in the Bayeux War Cemetery.

Fairey Battle P2331 of 12 Squadron was destroyed during a Luftwaffe air raid on RAF Binbrook.

Blenheim R3892 of 114 Squadron, Oulton, target Bremen, is believed to have crashed in the sea. Sergeant A. Stevenson was subsequently reported as being prisoner, but the bodies of Sergeant K. H. Dobb and Sergeant A.M. Pillans were not recovered. Their names are inscribed on the Runnymede Memorial.
It is likely that this was the Blenheim claimed Unteroffizier Richard Woick of 8./JG 54 at 08.05 hours.

Fairey Battle P6597 of 12 Squadron, Binbrook, target shipping in Boulogne Harbour, failed to return. Pilot Officer P. W. Cook, Sergeant J. Stewart and Sergeant S. I. Harrison were taken prisoner.

Blenheim N3574 of 101 Squadron, West Raynham, attacking airfields, ditched off Lowestoft. Pilot Officer N. H. Bicknell and Sergeant Gingell were rescued, but Sergeant J. H. George drowned and his body was not recovered.

Blenheim L9419 of 101 Squadron, West Raynham, detailed to attack airfields, failed to return. Sergeant A. G. Chelmick, Sergeant J. Carbine and Sergeant H. Martyn were all subsequently reported as being prisoners.

Hampden P2089 of 61 Squadron, Hemswell, target Ambés, force landed near Lyme Regis, Dorset, after running out of fuel. Pilot Officer P. M. de Mestre, Pilot Officer I. H. Stewart, Sergeant J. I. Doyle and Sergeant L. Hodgson escaped unhurt.

Whitley P4968 of 51 Squadron, Dishforth, target Schornewitz, failed to return. Pilot Officer P. G. Brodie, Pilot Officer T. F. S. Johnson, Sergeant R. Entwistle, Sergeant G. P. White and Sergeant W. A. Kelham were subsequently reported as prisoners.

ENEMY AIR ACTIVITY

The Luftwaffe began the day by attempting to 'stoke up' the fire caused at Llanreith oil farm the previous day and also attacked a convoy off Aldeburgh. In the early afternoon twenty-seven Do17s escorted by Bf109s headed for targets in the Thames Estuary, but they were intercepted by our fighters. That night there were sixty raids plotted including a repeat attack on the Rolls-Royce factory at Derby. The night raids caused a total of forty-six civilian fatalities and 108 injured. During the air fighting the Luftwaffe lost six aircraft destroyed including a Ju88 shot down by the newly formed 302 Polish Squadron - its first victory. The RAF lost two fighters.

COASTAL COMMAND OPERATIONS

Once again the weather seriously affected routine patrols, but fifty-three anti invasion, anti sub and special reconnaissance sorties were carried out. Air escort was provided for eighteen convoys. A total of sixty-two aircraft were involved in the operations.

1. A Hudson on routine patrol sighted two destroyers and one U-Boat seventy miles off Horns Reef.

2. A photographic reconnaissance along the coastline between the Loire, Vilaine, Lannion and St. Nazaire revealed no change in activity.

BOMBER COMMAND OPERATIONS

1. Adverse weather conditions restricted activity by 2 Group Blenheims throughout the day and only three aircraft were despatched to attack airfields; Ostend and Schipol aerodromes were attacked by one aircraft each, the third one abandoned because of lack of cloud cover.

2. An additional six Blenheims carried out a daylight sweep over the North Sea. Nothing of interest was observed.

Night operations

All night operations were cancelled due to adverse weather conditions.

OPERATIONAL LOSSES

There were no losses

Despite the weather, Hudsons were still out on patrol. The ZS codes identify these aircraft to be from 233 Squadron.

Wednesday 21st August

CLOUDY OVER THE WHOLE COUNTRY WITH SCATTERED SHOWERS.

A Swordfish displays its pale undersides, soon to give way to black as their night operations intensified.

ENEMY AIR ACTIVITY

Luftwaffe raids were widespread during which three Do17s were destroyed. RAF Bircham Newton was one of the targets where damage to installations and twenty-two casualties resulted. Trains at Guildford were strafed. Three trawlers were damaged at Falmouth. Balloons were shot down at Southampton and four Blenheims of 236 Squadron were damaged and two destroyed when RAF St. Eval was attacked. A convoy running the Dover Straits was shelled by the heavy guns at Cap Gris Nez and sixteen enemy aircraft attempted to bomb it. The Luftwaffe lost thirteen aircraft destroyed and the RAF lost four fighters.

COASTAL COMMAND OPERATIONS

Ninety-two crews carried out forty-seven anti invasion, anti submarine and special reconnaissance sorties. Air escort was provided for twenty-five convoys.

1. Six Blenheims detailed to escort a Sunderland flying boat sighted an enemy aircraft, Ju88, attacking RAF St. Eval. The leader of the Blenheim fighters managed to get a burst of machine-gun fire into the Ju88 before it escaped.
2. Hudsons on a strike against German naval units in the North Sea scored near misses on two motor vessels. Another Hudson dive-bombed two other enemy ships but without success. The Hudsons were attacked by seven Bf109s for thirty minutes but managed to escape. One aircraft was severely damaged which forced the pilot to carry out a belly landing on return to base. There were no casualties.
3. A reconnaissance of Lorient was carried out by a Hudson. Photos were taken of the estuary and the shipping. The crew reported on return that there were three cruisers of an estimated 12,000 thousand tons in the port.
4. A Fairey Battle of 142 Squadron carried out an evening sortie from Detling to Boulogne.

Night operations

1. Six Blenheims of 53 Squadron were detailed to carry out a night attack on Caen airfield. Three bombed causing a heavy explosion which started fires in hangars.
2. Six Blenheims of 59 Squadron were despatched on a night raid on Abbeville airfield. Four bombed scoring hits on the runway and hangars. A hit on a petrol dump resulted in a large fire.
3. Five Swordfish were despatched to sow mines off Schouwen Island, three carried out their task successfully. There were no losses.

BOMBER COMMAND OPERATIONS

1. Twenty Blenheims of 2 Group were despatched during the day to attack enemy airfields, aircraft storage units and oil targets in Germany. Most of their operations were abortive but six aircraft attacked the airfields at De Kooy, Jersey and Rennes, where hits on hangars were observed. The airfield at Bruges and a railway bridge near Paderborn were also bombed.
2. An additional six Blenheims also from 2 Group carried out a sweep over the North Sea. There were no losses.

Night operations

1. Because of unfavourable weather conditions all night operations by Wellingtons and Whitleys were cancelled.
2. Two Blenheims were despatched on a weather reconnaissance. On receipt of an adverse report, Blenheim night operations were also cancelled.
3. Despite the weather, forty-four Hampdens were despatched to carry out a night attack on an oil target at Magdeburg and the ship lifting plants on the Mitterland Canal at Rothensee and Hohenwart. Twelve located and bombed the oil target and claimed that hits were made. Other aircraft attacked the synthetic oil plants at Hannover and Eddinitz, but results were not observed. Successful attacks on the ship lifting plants were also claimed - a direct hit in salvo on the lift under construction at Hohenwart was observed and near misses were also observed on the lift gates at Rothensee and the Neigripp Lock. The remaining crews who were unable to locate primary targets attacked the marshalling yard at Osnabrük , the seaplane base at Texel and the aerodrome at Quackenbruk, where hits were observed.

OPERATIONAL LOSSES

Hampden P4360 of 144 Squadron, Hemswell, target Mitteland Kanal, failed to return. Pilot Officer A. Robson DFC, Pilot Officer D. L. Wingate, Sergeant A. A. Wilmot and Sergeant H. Chambers were lost without trace. All are commemorated on the Runnymede Memorial.

Thursday 22nd August

As darkness fell, Blenheims were out once again to carry out night harassment of enemy airfields. This example is from 40 Squadron.

ENEMY AIR ACTIVITY

A force of thirty Bf110s (in the bombing role) escorted by twenty Bf109s attempting attacks on our southern airfields were driven off by fighters. Another attack by Ju88s on a convoy off the north-east coast was also driven off by escort vessels and fighter aircraft. A convoy in the Straits of Dover suffered air attack and also shelling by the German guns mounted near Calais, but no ships were hit. The RAF airfield at St. Eval was attacked and some damage was caused. Night attacks included the aero-engine works at Filton, the towns of Aberdeen, Middlesbrough, Bradford, Swindon and Harrow plus a convoy off Kinnaird's Head. During the day's air fighting the Luftwaffe lost four aircraft destroyed. RAF Fighter Command lost five.

COASTAL COMMAND OPERATIONS

Forty-eight anti invasion, anti submarine patrols and special reconnaissance flights were carried out as well as escort for twenty-five convoys. Sixty-three aircraft were involved.

1. A Blenheim on a routine patrol off Norway attacked a motor vessel twenty miles from Alsboen without any positive result. The crew also reported seeing sixty small coastal vessels in a harbour north of Stadtlandet.
2. Two of four Blenheims on a reconnaissance of Le Havre attacked and shot down an enemy two-seat bi-plane. Photographs were taken of Le Havre.
3. Another Blenheim crew reported seeing several small derelict ships in the harbour at Boulogne. Photographs were taken of Le Treport, Le Touquet, Calais, Boulogne and Dunkirk.
4. Hudson 'F' of 233 Squadron on convoy escort observed and attacked a U-Boat forty-six miles from Bloody Foreland without any visible result.
5. Three PRU Spitfires took photographs of Abbeville, Boulogne, Haugesund, Bergen and Egersund. It was also reported that there were three large barges and fifteen sea-planes moored in Boulogne Harbour. There were no losses.

Night operations

1. Six Blenheims of 53 Squadron carried out a night attack on St. Omer aerodrome claiming hits on the airfield buildings causing extensive fires. The attack took place as enemy aircraft were landing.
2. Six Blenheims of 59 Squadron carried out an attack in the early hours of the morning (03.10 - 03.50 hours) on the airfield at Dinard, four out of the six claimed successful attacks.
3. Six Fairey battles of 142 Squadron (attached to Coastal Command from Bomber) were despatched to carry out attacks on E-Boats and sea-planes at Boulogne. Two bombed and two failed to return.

BOMBER COMMAND OPERATIONS

1. Poor weather adversely affected Blenheim daylight operations. Thirteen were despatched to attack enemy airfields and a gun battery at Cap Gris Nez, but eleven abandoned. Of the remaining two, one managed to take photographs of the gun battery at Cap Gris Nez, the other attacked the airfield at Merville, but results were not observed.
2. A further six Blenheims carried out an uneventful North Sea search.

Night operations

1. Thirty-three Blenheims carried out harassing night attacks on enemy occupied airfields. Success was claimed at Lisieux, Vannes, Lanvéoc, Deauville, St. Brieuc, Lannion, Rennes and Caen, where fires were started. Other attacks were carried out on the airfields at Audembert, St. Inglevert, Bourges, Chateaux Roux, Angers, Tours, Abbeville, Orleans, Amiens and Dunkirk, but results were not observed. A gun emplacement at Cap Gris Nez was also attacked. From these attacks one aircraft failed to return.
2. Sixteen Wellingtons were despatched to attack the synthetic oil plant at Boltrope and the marshalling yards at Hamm, Soest, Koblenz and Mannheim. The attack on Boltrope caused fires and the raids on the marshalling yards were claimed as successful. One aircraft attempting to bomb the power station at Duisburg overshot and hit the docks. Also the airfield at De Mok and a rail target near Rheine were bombed. One aircraft crashed on return.

Twenty-four Hampdens were detailed to attack an air component factory at Frankfurt, but only four bombed it and the results were not observed. As alternatives, an explosives factory at Griesheim, the inland port of Duisburg-Ruhrort, the power station at Köln and the aerodromes at Erbenheim, Sieburg and Lingen were attacked.

In addition, eleven out of the twelve Hampdens detailed for minelaying successfully laid mines in the Lorient area. One of the minelaying crews also attacked a U-Boat five miles south of Lorient. A 250lb bomb, which burst ten yards astern of the submarine, caused a great disturbance in the water and the enemy vessel was not seen again.

OPERATIONAL LOSSES

Fairey Battle L5503 of 142 Squadron, Eastchurch, detailed to bomb E-Boats at Boulogne, failed to return. Midshipman Taylor RN and Pilot Officer A. G. Middleton were taken prisoner. Sergeant L. M. Lowry has no known grave and appears on the Runnymede Memorial.

Fairey Battle, L5582 of 142 Squadron, Eastchurch, attacking E-Boats at Boulogne is presumed to have come down in the sea. Sergeant G. Thompson survived to become a prisoner. Sergeant E. A. Pearce and Sergeant T. S. Duncan's names are commemorated on the Runnymede Memorial.

In total no less than four Battles were claimed, by Oberfeldwebel Reuter and Unteroffizier Hopp of 6./JG 3, and by Obergefreiter Ernst Jäckel and Unteroffizier Gottfried Haferkorn of 2./JG 26, all between 20.10 and 20.20 hours in the area of Boulogne. Oberleutnants Kurt Ebersberger and Hans Krug of 4./JG 26 claimed Defiants at exactly the same place and time and it is likely that they too were engaged.

Blenheim T1990 of 218 Squadron, Oakington, target Bruges, crashed 10 Km south of Calais. Squadron Leader C. C. House is buried at Guines, and Sergeant P. T. Lefevre is buried St. Tricat. Sergeant J. D. Howard was taken prisoner.

Wellington R3276 'B' of 115 Squadron, Marham, attacked Mannheim, but crashed on return fifteen miles NNW of Norwich. Sergeant N. C. Cook, Sergeant R. Edwards, Sergeant A. Overall, Sergeant Nathan, Sergeant H. V. Watts and Pilot Officer P. G. Waterer were all seriously injured and Sergeant Watts died of his injuries in hospital.

Sgt. Bob Pearce poses for the photographer in the rear cockpit of a Fairey Battle. When asked to 'look aggresive', the lower photo was the best he could offer. It is unlikely to have caused any sleepless nights for the Bf109 pilots!
A fine illustration of a Battle gunner defending his aircraft, apart form the fact that Bob forgot to plug his intercom jack in, (seen hanging over the side).

Friday 23rd August

All types of aircraft were employed on coastal patrols including the Tiger Moth. This example is part of No.5 Coastal Patrol Flight attached to 217 Sqn at Carew Cheriton. The MW codes were also carried by the squadron's Ansons and Beauforts.

ENEMY ACTIVITY

Poor weather affected Luftwaffe operations, but RAF airfields at Manston, Thorney Island and Tangmere were again bombed as were the towns of Cromer, Harwich, Maidstone and Portsmouth. Night attacks took place on Cardiff, Pembroke Dock, the Dunlop factory at Birmingham and other towns in the south-west.

During the day's operations the Luftwaffe lost two aircraft destroyed in combat and three others in non-combat incidents. RAF fighter Command lost one aircraft destroyed in a non-combat incident.

COASTAL COMMAND OPERATIONS

Thirty-nine anti invasion, anti submarine patrols and reconnaissance flights were carried out. Air escort was also provided for twenty-four convoys. Seventy-four aircraft were involved.

1. A Blenheim attacked Dieppe claiming hits on a quayside warehouse.
2. A Sunderland made a reconnaissance of Narvik and neighbouring fjords reporting on the shipping activity. Heavy Flak was encountered over Narvik.
3. A Blenheim fighter patrol of 235 Squadron intercepted and drove off an He111 about to attack Thorney Island.
4. PR aircraft took photographs of the coast from Zeebrugge to Boulogne, oil targets in the Paullic and Gironde area as well as towns and airfields in France including La Ferté, Chateaux Roux and Velencay.

BOMBER COMMAND OPERATIONS

1. Twenty Blenheims from 2 Group were despatched in daylight to carry out attacks against enemy airfields in north-west France, oil targets and aircraft depots in Germany. Twelve crews abandoned their tasks because of adverse weather conditions. One aircraft returned to base U/S. The other crews bombed the airfields at De Kooy, Waalhaven and Schellingwoude. At Schellingwoude three bombs were seen to fall fifty yards from three He59s. A dock at Flushing was claimed to have been hit and a railway bridge over the Dortmund-Ems Canal north of Munster was claimed to have been demolished.
2. A further six Blenheims carried out a routine sweep over the North Sea.

Night operations

1. Thirty-five Blenheims were despatched on harassing night raids on fifteen enemy occupied airfields. As a result of their attacks, fires and explosions were claimed. The airfields targeted were at Amiens, Caen-Carpiquet, St. Omer, Eindhoven, Merville, Rennes, Lisieux, Rouen-Boos, St. Brieuc, Dinard, Beauvais, Villacoublay, Orleans and Vannes. One aircraft bombed Dieppe harbour causing vivid explosions and large fires. Others attacked searchlight, Flak defences and gun emplacements at Cap Gris Nez.
2. Ten Wellingtons were despatched on night operations, four of whom attacked the oil plant at Sterkrade-Holton. While no bursts were observed it is believed that the bombs from one aircraft hit the Schmidhorst pumping station causing fires. The marshalling yards at Mannheim were at attacked where fires were started. At Dinslaken the AA defences were bombed.
3. Forty Hampdens were detailed for minelaying operations. Thirty-one were successful laying mines in the Lorient area. At Brest three small naval vessels were attacked as well as five barges moored at the seaplane base. The nearby aerodromes at Lanveoc-Poulmic and Guipas were also bombed.

OPERATIONAL LOSSES

There were no losses over enemy territory, however **Hampden P2117 of 144 Squadron** crashed while at attempting no to land at RAF Boscombe Down. There were no casualties.

Saturday 24th August

SUNNY IN THE SOUTH WITH RAIN AND HEAVY CLOUD IN THE NORTH.

ENEMY ACTIVITY

A huge anti-cyclone (high pressure area) in the Atlantic improved the weather over Britain. The Luftwaffe took the opportunity to commence the second phase of the German plan to destroy Fighter Command by launching mass daylight raids on RAF airfields and important industrial targets. To further exhaust the defences they carried out widespread raids at night. Their first raid took place during the morning on RAF Manston using forty Ju88s and Do17s escorted by nearly seventy Bf109s. This was followed in the afternoon by another mass raid. 264 Defiant Squadron scrambled from Manston and intercepted them but, being completely out numbered, they were unable to prevent the attackers from bombing and causing considerable damage and lost five aircraft in the process. After this second raid Manston was completely closed until 26th August and afterwards was used as a forward refuelling field only.

Four large formations of Ju88s and He111s attacked RAF Hornchurch and RAF North Weald, but not all of the raiders achieved their objective, being prevented by fighters. Portsmouth was attacked during the late afternoon and casualties were heavy - 118 civilians were killed and 230 injured. Naval casualties totalled another fifty. The final daylight raid was carried out by one hundred fighters over Kent. The night raids were widespread and the first bombs were dropped on the City of London, apparently by a crew who overshot their briefed target. The repercussion occurred on the night of 25th/26th August when RAF Bomber Command, on the order of Mr Churchill, carried out the first of many raids on Berlin. The other night raid by the Luftwaffe was on RAF Driffield, which caused damage to hangars and aircraft. The outcome was that 77 and 102 Whitley Squadrons were evacuated two days later. During this epic day's fighting the Luftwaffe lost thirty-four aircraft destroyed. RAF fighter Command lost twenty-five. This was probably when the Luftwaffe came closest to achieving air superiority over Fighter Command.

COASTAL COMMAND OPERATIONS

Fifty-seven aircraft carried out thirty-seven anti invasion, anti submarine patrols and reconnaissance sorties. Air escort was provided for eighteen convoys.

1. Five Fairey Battles of 142 Squadron were despatched to bomb barges and seaplanes at Boulogne, two managed to bomb in spite of intense Flak opposition.
2. A Blenheim on reconnaissance of the Norwegian Coast was attacked by three Bf109s off Stavanger, but it escaped into cloud.
3. A Hudson attacked a U-Boat sixty-two miles from St. Kilda on a bearing of 275 degrees, but obtained no positive result.

Night operations

1. Fourteen Blenheims of 53 and 59 Squadrons were detailed to attack the airfields at Flushing, Lannion and Dinard. One Blenheim attacking Flushing caused fires while another attacked the docks claiming a direct hit on the main jetty. Dinard airfield was successfully attacked by seven aircraft. Two hangars were set on fire and fires were also started in a nearby wood which was believed to conceal a petrol store.

One of the less common types operating during the Battle of Britain was the Blackburn Botha. 608 Squadron had the unfortunate task of of flying this unpopular aircraft on patrol and escort duties. They lost one of them today when L6209 suffered an engine failure and crashed.

2. Fuel tanks at Vlaadingen were attacked by four of the Albacores of 826 Squadron. Returning crews reported the Flak opposition was intense.
3. Of six Swordfish detailed to carry out minelaying operations off Schouwen Island, three were successful and another laid aid mines south of the Hook of Holland.
4. Crotoy airfield was attacked by three Fairey Battles. One crew reported a hit on the airfield buildings.

BOMBER COMMAND OPERATIONS

1. Nine Blenheims of 2 Group were despatched in daylight to carry out harassing on enemy occupied airfields, four abandoned because of unsuitable weather conditions. The other five attacked the airfields at Schipol, Hingene and Schellingwoude, also a seaplane base and a ship at Zeebrugge. Results were unobserved.
2. In addition six Blenheims of 2 Group carried out a routine sweep over the North Sea.

Night operations

1. Twenty-five Blenheims were despatched on night operations to harass enemy airfields in France, Holland and Belgium. Among those attacked were Dinard, Lannion, Brest, Rennes and Lisieux, where fires were started. At

Bourges bomb bursts were observed on the hangars. In addition attacks were carried out on gun emplacements at Cap Gris Nez and ships at Zeebrugge.

2. Forty Wellingtons were despatched to attack oil tanks at Frankfurt/Main, an electric power station at Köln, the old aqueduct at the Dortmund-Ems Canal and marshalling yards at Hamm and Soest. Adverse weather prevented targets from being located and identified however seven crews managed to attack primary targets at Köln and Frankfurt causing fires and an explosion. One crew claimed a successful attack on the marshalling yards at Hamm, but those against the Dortmund-Ems aqueduct and the marshalling yards at Soest were unsuccessful. Alternative targets such as the aerodromes at Schipol, Köln, Bonn, an explosives factory at Griesheim, road and railway junctions were also attacked, but in most cases the results were not observed.

3. Thirty Hampdens were detailed for minelaying operations; two collided on take-off but there were no casualties. Eleven crews successfully laid mines off St. Nazaire, while twelve sowed theirs off La Pallice. Bombs were dropped on the aerodromes at Dinard, Gael, Vannes, Rennes and Coetquidan as well as an oil store at St. Nazaire and gun positions at Paimboeuf and St. Mare. Another aircraft attacked a motor vessel at the entrance to the Brest Canal.

4. Twenty-nine Whitleys were despatched; ten to bomb the Messerschmitt works at Augsburg where seven claimed successful attacks, nine to attack the Daimler-Benz works at Stuttgart where all nine claimed successful attacks and one failed to return. Another ten crews were detailed to attack a magneto factory at Milan. Four crews returned early because of technical snags.

OPERATIONAL LOSSES

Blenheim T1804 'E' of 235 Squadron, attempting to defend is base of Thorney Island, was shot down by a Hurricane from No.1 (RCAF) Squadron and crashed into Bracklesham Bay. The body of Pilot Officer D. N. Woodger was never found and he is remembered on the Runnymede Memorial. Sergeant D. L. Wright's body was found and returned to his home town of Chasetown, Staffordshire.

Botha L6209 'O' of 608 Squadron, Thornaby, crashed after engine failure for a convoy escort at Ormesby, Co. Durham. Pilot Officer D. H. F. Horner was injured and Pilot Officer Reid escaped injury.

Blenheim T2035 'P' of 53 Squadron, Detling, crashed on return into houses at Dover and burst into flames. Flying Officer S. C. Rochford, Sergeant W. Briggs and Sergeant D. Brook all perished.

Whitley N1473 of 77 Squadron, Driffield, target Augsburg, crashed south-west of Haarlem (Holland). Pilot Officer C. J. D. Montagu DFC, Sergeant J. W. Ward, Sergeant R. T. Penny, Sergeant A. F. Webber and Sergeant E. J. Clarke were all killed and are now buried in Amsterdam (New Eastern) General Cemetery.

The Italian Job

Our crew was one of those detailed for Milan and after briefing we flew from Leeming to Abingdon which was being used as an advanced base for raids on Italy. The weather was fine and after our aircraft had been topped up with fuel we spent the time before take-off lying on the grass enjoying the evening sun. Laying there it all seemed so nice and peaceful until you remembered what we were there for. While we enjoyed the sun our skipper, Flying Officer Henry* DFC, reminded me that this would be our third attempt to get to Italy (the other two had been unsuccessful) and this time we were going to make it if we had to get out and push! Earlier in the day he had been informed that this was to be his last trip of his first tour and he was being posted to 35 Squadron (the first Halifax squadron). He was determined to end his tour on a 'high note'.

Take-off time arrived and we got airborne from Abingdon at 20.00 hours and set course climbing steadily to cross France. We reached the Alps unmolested and as we crossed them we could see the lights of Geneva (in neutral Switzerland) to the north. The weather and visibility continued to be good and the sight of the mountains in the moonlight was a 'never to be forgotten' sight. When we had crossed the Alps south of Lake Maggiore we descended to 8,000 feet and altered course for our target at Milan. As we approached it the defences opened up as we prepared for our run-in. Because of the light no flares were necessary and the bomb-aimer was able to pin-point the target in the moonlight. The skipper had decided we would drop our load in two runs. As we commenced our first run I was able to prepare to drop the loose incendiaries we carried in the fuselage down the flare-chute, my personal contribution to the war effort. We started our vulnerable straight and level run and the bomb-aimer commenced his litany, 'Left, left. Steady. Right, steady. Bombs gone'. We immediately turned away to avoid the Flak and stood off to prepare for the second run. When everything was set up we went in and our luck was in, as we were able to drop the rest of our load and avoid the Flak. We were all quite elated as we set course for home because the bomb-aimer was pretty certain all our bombs had dropped in the target area. This was confirmed by the tail gunner who reported that although it was slightly hazy there was quite a 'glow' indicating that it was likely we'd started a fire. Our good fortune continued, we got away unscathed and had an uneventful return flight landing back at base at 04.50 hours, a bit of a flog, but compared with some of our previous trips, an easy ride.

** Tragically he was killed in 35 Squadron's first Halifax fatal accident on 11th January 1941. We had flown together on operations since the beginning of the war in 1939.*

Larry Donnelly, 10 Squadron Whitley

Sunday 25th August

Some sun in the morning, becoming progressively more cloudy.

Six Blenheims attacked oil tanks at Cherbourg today. The port had been under regular attack since before the start of the Battle, this photo being taken after a raid on 16th June.

ENEMY ACTIVITY

The morning was relatively quiet and there were no large raids by the Luftwaffe until late afternoon when a force of more than three hundred bombers and fighters split up and raided Portsmouth, Weymouth and RAF Warmwell. They were intercepted by Hurricanes of 17 Squadron who saved Warmwell from extensive damage - one Hurricane pilot shot down three of the raiders. The other notable raid took place just after 18.00 hours when a huge force approached Dover heading for targets in Kent, but they were driven off by six fighter squadrons who had been scrambled to deal with them. Night raids continued to be widespread with attacks by single aircraft. Their targets were Stockton on Tees, RAF Cottesmore, Birmingham, Erdington and Croydon. Throughout the period twenty German aircraft were destroyed for the loss of sixteen RAF fighters.

COASTAL COMMAND OPERATIONS

A total of 129 aircraft carried out sixty-seven anti invasion, anti submarine patrols and reconnaissance sorties. Air escort was provided for twenty-two convoys.

1. Six out of seven Blenheims despatched, bombed oil tanks at Cherbourg.
2. Blenheim 'S' of 59 Squadron engaged two Hs126s. The engagement was inconclusive.
3. Hudson 'X' of 233 Squadron attacked a U-Boat at 57 degrees 57'N/11 degrees 30'W, without positive results.
4. Fairey Battle 'C' of 12 Squadron carried out an early morning bombing attack on E-Boats at Boulogne. No results were observed.
5. Anson K8703 (Sergeant Sawyer) of 48 Squadron attacked a U-Boat without success.
6. Anson 'J' of 502 Squadron attacked a U-Boat with bombs at 55 degrees 04'N/06 degrees 36'W. An oil patch was observed, but there was no positive result.

BOMBER COMMAND OPERATIONS

1. Eighteen Blenheims of 114 and 139 Squadrons were despatched to carry out daylight attacks on enemy airfields. Because of unsuitable cloud cover eleven abandoned their task, however the remainder attacked the following; De Kooy, Evere, Wunstorf, Bergen and Texel where a low-level attack was carried out resulting in direct hits being claimed on the hangars and admin buildings. The seaplane base at De Mok was bombed and hits claimed on the slip-way. The hangars appeared to have been demolished.
2. Six Blenheims of 21 Squadron carried out a North Sea sweep from Lossiemouth.

Night operations

A total of 102 aircraft were detailed for night operations including the first bombing raid on Berlin in retaliation for the bombing of the City of London and other cities by the Luftwaffe on the previous night.

1. Twelve Blenheims were detailed to attack enemy occupied airfields at Lisieux, Plouescat, Le Treport, Fécamp, Boulogne and St. Inglevert. Successful attacks were claimed against Lisieux, Le Treport and Plouescat causing fires and explosions. Another crew bombed and extinguished searchlights at Hardelot. Three crews failed to return.
2. Twenty-one Wellingtons were despatched to attack the Siemens factory in Berlin and marshalling yards at Hamm, Scherte and Köln. Because of the heavy cloud only one crew attacked the Berlin target but claimed to have caused fires. Five crews claimed successful attacks on the marshalling yards and other targets attacked included a gas works at Texel and a concentration of Flak and searchlights.
3. Despite the weather conditions, ten Hampdens out of the forty-six despatched to Berlin claimed to have attacked

their target, the Klingenberg power station. Another target in the vicinity of the power station was also attacked. One crew bombed the Henschel airframe factory claiming direct hits on buildings. Templehof airfield was bombed, but the results were not observed. A direct bit was claimed on a viaduct ten miles south-east of Berlin and other attacks were made on Pangsdorf aerodrome (fifteen miles south of Berlin) and marshalling yards in the outskirts of the city. Five aircraft failed to return, but three of the crews were rescued from the sea.

4. The adverse weather over Berlin which made target identification very difficult also affected the twenty-two Whitleys detailed to attack the Siemens works and only two claimed success. A single aircraft bombed a concentration of part of the defences of western Berlin. As an alternative another crew carried out a low-level attack on the dockyards at Bremen. Although this first attack on Berlin caused little damage, it did have a significant effect on the course of the battle. The Luftwaffe was suffering unsustainable losses in its attempts to knock out Fighter Command by mass daylight raids so, to reduce their losses and take revenge for the first raid on Berlin, Hitler switched the Luftwaffe from daylight attacks on airfields to night attacks against British cities. Fighter Command was given a chance to get its 'second wind'.

OPERATIONAL LOSSES

Blenheim R3011 of 40 Squadron, Wyton, detailed to bomb the airfield at Querqueville, was lost without trace. Squadron Leader F. G. R. Thomas, Pilot Officer G. L. Bayliss and Sergeant G. M. Dickson, are commemorated on the Runnymede Memorial.

Blenheim T1927 or 40 Squadron, Wyton, was lost without trace. Sergeant P. C. Riley, Sergeant F. H. Newson and Sergeant J. S. Smith are commemorated on the Runnymede Memorial.

Blenheim P6928 of 57 Squadron, Elgin, target enemy airfields, was lost without trace. Sergeant E. A. H. Riley, Sergeant A. Gibson and Sergeant R. C. E. Stiles are commemorated on the Runnymede Memorial.

Blenheim L8870 of 101 Squadron, West Raynham, target St. Malo, crashed after hitting a barrage balloon cable one mile south-east of Eastleigh, Hants. Sergeant J. H. Balmer, Sergeant W. J. C. Corker and Sergeant T. G. J. Cranston were all killed.

Hampden P4416 of 49 Squadron, Scampton, target Berlin, lost without trace. Pilot Officer N. B. Fawcett, Sergeant J. C. Clarke, Sergeant J. Baker and AC1 G. Reay are commemorated on the Runnymede Memorial.

Hampden P2070 of 50 Squadron, Lindholme, target Berlin, believed to have forced landed near Lautersheim, Germany. Pilot Officer R. D. Wawn, Sergeant J. Schofield, Sergeant R. H. L. Smith, and Sergeant H. J. Bushell were taken prisoner.

It was a bad night for the Hampden squadrons with six being lost after being sent to Berlin at the limit of their range. Here, the remains of a 49 Squadron Hampden and one of its crew members lie in a hedgerow.

Hampden P2124 of 50 Squadron, Lindholme, target Berlin, ditched of Scarborough Pier. Pilot Officer G. A. C. Potts, Pilot Officer R. S. Hook, Sergeant Wood and Sergeant Ashmore were rescued by a trawler which tried, unsuccessfully, to salvage the aircraft.

Hampden P1354 of 83 Squadron, Scampton, target Berlin, ditched in the Wash. Flying Officer N. H. Svendsen DFC, Sergeant J. C. Threfall, Sergeant S. R. Gear and Sergeant S. Dale were rescued unhurt.

Hampden P4380 of 83 Squadron, Scampton, target Berlin, ditched in the North Sea off Grimsby. Pilot Officer A. J. G. Mills, Pilot Officer J. A. Mundy, Sergeant E. Groves and Sergeant T. Highton were rescued after spending seven hours in their dinghy.

Hampden X2895 of 83 Squadron, Scampton, target Berlin, crashed at Boldon, Co.Durham, trying to land at RAF Usworth. Pilot Officer R. H. Bunker DFC and Sergeant G. T. Thomas were seriously injured. Sergeant Vivian and Sergeant H. S. Haste were uninjured.

Monday 26th August

SOME SUN IN THE SOUTH WITH CLOUDS IN THE NORTH.

This Spitfire P9385 of the PRU went to Dieppe and Calais on this day to photograph the build up of invasion barges.

ENEMY ACTIVITY

Early reconnaissance flights by the Luftwaffe preceded three major raids during the day. The raid first took place during the late morning involving fifty bombers and escorting fighters heading for southern fighter aerodromes. They were intercepted by Fighter Command's 11 Group Squadrons (616 Spitfires, 264 Defiants and 1 (Canadian) Hurricanes) between Canterbury and Maidstone. During a bitter battle there were losses on both sides, but the raiders were turned away from Biggin Hill. The next raid comprising forty Do17s escorted by 120 Bf109s and Bf110s was making for Debden, Hornchurch and North Weald when the raiders were intercepted by all the 11 Group squadrons available. Only three of the raiders got through to bomb Debden where they caused some damage. The remainder of the force jettisoned their bombs and turned to get back to France, but they suffered heavy casualties when their fighter escort, running short of fuel, left them unprotected. The third major attack was mounted during the late afternoon when fifty He111s escorted by over one hundred Bf109s and Bf110s attempted to bomb Southampton and Portsmouth. They were intercepted by 11 Group squadrons who inflicted heavy losses and prevented them from bombing Southampton, some of the raiders did get through and bombed Portsmouth, but they missed the dockyards. That night approximately 200 bombers, mainly operating singly, carried out widespread raids during which, Tottenham, Wood Green, Southgate and Wormwood Scrubs were hit, in some cases causing major damage. Other towns hit were, Plymouth, Dartford, Tilbury, Bournemouth, Coventry, Newcastle and RAF Cottesmore - one of six RAF stations attacked. By dawn on the 27th thirty-seven civilians had been killed and 102 injured. During the day's fighting the Luftwaffe lost thirty-four aircraft destroyed and the RAF twenty-seven.

COASTAL COMMAND OPERATIONS

Ninety-seven aircraft carried out sixty-six anti invasion, anti submarine patrols and reconnaissance sorties. Air escort was provided for seventeen convoys.

1. Anson, R3308 of 48 Squadron on patrol from St. Eval attacked a U-Boat unsuccessfully, because their two Mk.III anti submarine bombs failed to explode.
2. A Blenheim on a patrol twenty miles south-west of Portland found a German seaplane tender carrying an He59. It was being escorted by another He59, but before the Blenheim could take offensive action it was driven off by two Bf109s obviously called up for additional protection.
3. Six Blenheims of 59 Squadron carried out an attack on fuel tanks at Cherbourg during the late evening.
4. Sunderland 'C' of 204 Squadron, Sullom Voe, on patrol

off Tromsoy (Norway) attacked eight moored He115s and claimed to have destroyed three and damaged others.
5. Three Fairey Battles of 142 Squadron were detailed to attack the airfield at Crotoy - two bombed.
6. Nine PR sorties were carried out; Spitfire P9310 on Ushant and Brest, Spitfire P9382 on Bergen-Stavanger, P9384 to Kristiansund, P9385 to Dieppe and Calais, R6804 to Terschelling and Den Helder, and R6894 to Rotterdam.

BOMBER COMMAND OPERATIONS

Sixteen Blenheims of 2 Group were despatched to carry out daylight harassing attacks against enemy occupied airfields. Because of adverse weather conditions fourteen abandoned, the remaining two pressed on claiming successful attacks on Hoya and De Kooy airfields.
2. A further six Blenheims carried out a sweep over the North Sea.

Night operations

1. Eighteen Blenheims were despatched to carry out night raids on enemy occupied airfields. All except one claimed successful attacks. At St. Omer, Fécamp, De Kooy, Le Treport and Plouescat fires were started. At Texel hits were claimed on hangars and a big explosion was reported. Deauville, Brest-Lannion, Flushing, Haamstede, Brest-Poulmic, Morlaix, Caen, Dinard and Forêt de Guines were also attacked, but results unobserved.
2. Forty-nine Wellingtons were despatched to attack targets at Frankfurt, Köln, Hamm, Duisburg, Scherte, Griesheim and airfields at Evere and Antwerp. Nineteen crews bombed primary targets, nine alternatives, twelve targets of opportunity, eight brought their bombs back and one jettisoned.
At Frankfurt large fires were reported at the component factory and also at the oil storage tanks. The marshalling yards at Hamm and Scherte were successfully attacked and explosions were reported at the factories at Griesheim and Hochst.
In addition, successful attacks were claimed on the airfields at Evere, Rhein-Main, Waalhaven, Flushing, Arnhem and Arras. A crew of 115 Squadron shot down a twin-engined enemy aircraft near Nivelles aerodrome.
3. Fourteen Whitleys were detailed to attack a magneto works at Milan and the Fiat aircraft works at Turin. Three aircraft failed to take off because of engine snags. Ten crews bombed the primary targets and those attacking the Fiat works at Turin claimed hits which left the target on fire at the conclusion of the raid. The crews attacking the magneto factory at Milan also claimed success reporting fires and smoke up to a height of 6,000 feet. One aircraft failed to return.
4. Thirty-two Hampdens were detailed to attack an oil target at Leuna (Merseburg), six to attack the aerodrome at Leipzig-Mockau and the Leipzig gas works and two more to bomb the Dortmund-Ems old aqueduct. Seven crews attacked the oil plant at Leuna claiming hits which started fires. Those who bombed the gas works also claimed success. Adverse weather frustrated the attempts to bomb the old aqueduct on the Dortmund Canal. One aircraft failed to return and another crashed on return.

OPERATIONAL LOSSES

Anson N9898 'Y' of 500 Squadron, Detling, crashed on take-off for a patrol at 01.15 hours. Pilot Officer P. W. Peters and crew safe.

Anson N5317 of 500 Squadron, Detling, crashed on take-off for a patrol at 01.20 hours. Pilot Officer P.W. Peters and crew safe. (Peters was pilot of both crashed aircraft).

Anson N5229 of 500 Squadron, Detling, crashed on take-off for a patrol and caught fire. Crew safe.

Hampden P4324 of 61 Squadron, Hemswell, target Merseburg, ran out of fuel and force landed on the Dutch Island of Vlieland. The aircraft was found intact and flown to Germany for inspection. Flying Officer P. D. Tunstall, Sergeant A. E. Murdock, Sergeant M. J. Joyce and Sergeant W. J. Brook were taken prisoner.

Two views of Peter Tunstall's P4324 after it force landed on the Dutch island of Vlieland.

Hampden, P1317 of 50 Squadron, Lindholme, was hit by Flak and crashed on return attempting to land at Hemswell. Sergeant Abbott, Sergeant Bryce, AC1 Green and Sergeant Harney were all uninjured.

Whitley P4990 'T' of 10 Squadron, Harwell, target Milan, believed to have been shot down at Valera 45 Km. NNW of Milan. Sergeant H. G. H. Howard, Pilot Officer J. H. K. Parvin, Sergeant N. R. Johnston, Sergeant J. W. Stephenson and Sergeant H.W. Carter were all killed and are buried in the Milan War Cemetery.

Tuesday 27th August SOLID CLOUD COVER OVER SOUTHERN ENGLAND WITH HEAVY RAIN IN PLACES.

A 210 Squadron Sunderland on patrol in 1940. The early wartime camouflage was soon worn away by the sea and spray, especially around the waterline.

ENEMY ACTIVITY

With the weather improving early, the Luftwaffe carried out reconnaissance flights over the Portsmouth and Southampton areas. Later in the day small enemy formations operated over Kent and single aircraft attacked airfields, without success. During the night of the 27th/28th Birmingham was bombed and in the early hours of the 28th Gillingham suffered three dive-bombing attacks. During the day's fighting the Luftwaffe lost five aircraft destroyed in combat and the RAF lost one.

COASTAL COMMAND OPERATIONS

Ninety-one aircraft carried out sixty anti invasion, anti submarine patrols and reconnaissance sorties during the period. Twenty convoys were provided with air escort.

1. A Hudson on routine patrol reported seeing thirty Danish fishing smacks fifty-two miles from Horns Reef. The Hudson carried out strafing attacks but no results were observed.
2. Blenheim 'F' of 59 Squadron attacked five E-Boats twenty miles off Cherbourg. There were no positive results.
3. A Hudson on an Air Sea Rescue search for another Hudson missing from a reconnaissance over Cuxhaven reported that the crew had been picked up by a drifter, but one man was missing.
4. During the early morning three Fairey Battles of 12 Squadron and one of 142 Squadron carried out an attack on E-Boats at Calais. The results were not observed.
5. A Sunderland of 201 Squadron, Sullom Voe, carried out a search for a U-Boat reported south-east of Yell, Shetlands.
6. Sunderland 'B' of 210 Squadron attacked a U-Boat with two DCs at 56 degrees 24'N/90 degrees 24'W with no obvious result.
7. A photo reconnaissance of Oslo showed a seaplane base at Horton and considerable shipping in Oslo Harbour. Also at Oslo aerodrome there were twelve aircraft dispersed near the runways. Six seaplanes and one destroyer were photographed in the large inland fjord south of Stavanger.

Night operations

1. Two Blenheims of 53 Squadron were detailed to carry out a night attack on the Schellingwoude seaplane base at Amsterdam. One crew dropped bombs on the floating jetties in the target area.
2. Six Blenheims of 59 Squadron were detailed to attack fuel installations at Cherbourg; four of the crews claimed direct hits.

There were no losses.

BOMBER COMMAND OPERATIONS

1. The harassing operations against enemy airfields in daylight continued but the weather conditions again affected plans. Of the thirteen Blenheims despatched, twelve abandoned their task. The one remaining bombed a ship fifteen miles from Den Helder. No result was observed and there were no losses

Night operations

1. Eighteen Wellingtons were detailed to carry out night operations; twelve were to attack the docks at Kiel with the German warship *Gneisenau* as their prime target. Their other target was an explosives factory at Köln. Despite intense Flak and searchlight opposition the attack on the dock yards was pressed home, but the *Gneisenau* was not located. However, the crews claimed that they scored hits on the mole and that fires were started in many parts of the dockyard area. A successful attack was carried out against the transformer station at Kelsterbach near Frankfurt. The crew reported that their salvo from 2,000 feet hit the centre of the target and the whole station seemed to have been demolished in the ensuing explosion. The docks at Wilhelmshaven, an aerodrome at Husam and two unidentified airfields were also attacked. One aircraft failed to return.

2. Sixteen Whitleys were detailed to attack the Fiat airframe factory at Torino and three to the magneto factory at Sesto San Giovani. Another four aircraft were to attack the airframe factory at Augsburg - a long flog.

The targets for the other six were marshalling yards and oil stores at Frankfurt and the marshalling yards at Mannheim. The aircraft on the Italian targets encountered severe icing crossing the Alps, but two crews claimed success when their incendiaries caused extensive fires at the airframe factory at Turin. The attack on Sesto San Giovani was deemed to be successful, but the results were not confirmed. The aircraft attacking Augsburg airframe factory caused fires and an explosion occurred. The oil stocks at Frankfurt and the marshalling yards at Mannheim were also attacked, but the results were unobserved. Crews unable to locate their primary targets bombed an airfield (probably Rastel) and searchlights near Koblenz.

3. Seventeen Hampdens were detailed - nine to attack oil targets at Ambes and eight to carry out minelaying in the Lorient (Brittany) area. The first crews attacking the oil targets at Ambes and Poullac started fires which were 'stoked up' by the aircraft attacking later. Minelaying was successfully carried out in the designated area and attacks were made on an E-Boat and a barge in the vicinity. A railway siding was bombed and one crew machine-gunned a Do17 which was last seen to be at a very low altitude with flames issuing from its starboard engine.

OPERATIONAL LOSSES

Blenheim (F) L9449 'U' of 248 Squadron, Sumburgh, failed to return from a Norway patrol after being intercepted west of Egersund by Leutnant Heinrich Setz of 6./JG77. Pilot Officer C. J. Arthur and Sergeant E. A. Ringwood were posted as missing in action. The body of Sergeant R. C. R. Cox was washed ashore at Stromstad and is now buried at Kviberg Cemetery, Sweden.

Hudson N7321 of the PRU, Coltishall, damaged by Flak over Cuxhaven and ditched fifteen miles north of Sheringham, Norfolk. Flying Officer Bamber, Sergeant Rowland, Sergeant Walker and LAC Hatfield were rescued by boats, but Sergeant F. C. Sawyer was lost and his name appears on the Runnymede Memorial.

Wellington P9272 'A' of 149 Squadron, Mildenhall, target Kiel, failed to return. Flight Lieutenant P. F. R. Vaillant, Sergeant R. W. Saywood, Sergeant D. H. G. Connolly and Pilot Officer M. G. Butt, Sergeant L. F. Mabey (RNZAF) Sergeant J. Fender were taken prisoner.

Blenheim fighter pilots of 248 Squadron pose for a photo early in 1940.

Wednesday 28th August

MOSTLY SUNNY OVER CLOUD, BUT CLOUD OVER THE SEA.

A 210 Squadron Sunderland on patrol

ENEMY ACTIVITY

Luftwaffe reconnaissance flights at dawn over the south-east coast were followed by a build up of He111s and Do17s escorted by Bf109s over France. Fighters preceded their progress northwards towards the airfields. Although defending fighter squadrons fought valiantly they were unable to prevent the raiders from reaching and bombing Eastchurch and Rochford. During the afternoon a battle, mainly between fighters, developed over the Canterbury - Dungeness - Margate area.

That night (28th/29th) the beam-riding He111s of *KGr.100* (the Luftwaffe's pathfinders) were used to bomb Merseyside, but the bombing went astray hitting and setting houses on fire in Liverpool instead of military targets. Bombing also took place at Birmingham, Bourne, Derby, Manchester and Sheffield. At Altringham a 50,000 gallon oil tank was set on fire. By the end of the day the Luftwaffe had lost twenty-six aircraft destroyed and the RAF seventeen. The RAF had no success at night.

COASTAL COMMAND OPERATIONS

Anti invasion, anti submarine patrols, reconnaissance sorties and air escort for convoys were carried out throughout the period.

1. The search for a U-Boat off Yell continued and a sighting was reported twelve miles from Sumburgh Head. A Sunderland from Oban was ordered to carry out a search off Barra Head for another U-Boat.

2. Sunderland P9606 of 201 Squadron located the motor vessel Staresby, unmanned and burning off Cape Wrath.

3. Sunderland 'H' of 210 Squadron attacked a U-Boat at 56 degrees 40'N/10 degrees 41'W. The RN destroyer Mackay joined the attack and claimed that the enemy vessel had been sunk.

4. The ALO, Dover reported that eight E-Boats and two barges were operating off the French coast. HQ Coastal Command reported one E-Boat and a seaplane were picking up bodies. Six Blenheims of 59 Squadron and three Blenheim fighters of 235 Squadron were sent to attack.

Night operations

1. Two Blenheims of 53 Squadron carried out a night strike against the sea-plane base at Schellingwoude.

2. Six Blenheims of 59 Squadron who were detailed to attack Caen airfield bombed, scoring hits on hangars which caused fires.

3. Six Swordfish successfully carried out minelaying at Zeebrugge.

BOMBER COMMAND OPERATIONS

Six Blenheims carried out an uneventful routine reconnaissance over the North Sea. Two other Blenheims were detailed to attack the enemy held airfields at Querqueville and Dinard, but because of unfavourable weather conditions they were abandoned.

Night operations

Seventy-nine aircraft were despatched to carry out night operations; Blenheims to harass enemy airfields,

Wellingtons to attack targets in Berlin; Whitleys to attack the Junkers aircraft factory at Dessau and oil and power targets at Dortmund and Reisholtz and Hampdens to targets in Berlin, Kiel, Hamburg and Dortmund.

1. Fifteen Blenheims carried out their attacks against, Caen, Châteauneuf, Haamstede, Abbeville, Leeuwarden, Octeville, Le Touquet, Hingene and Schipol. Results were mostly unobserved, but several fires and explosions were seen at Schipol.

2. Twenty Wellingtons claimed good results on the Berlin and other targets. Seven aircraft attacked the power station at Klingenberg, causing fires and explosions which damaged buildings. Another five aircraft claimed hits on an adjacent marshalling yard and fires were started at Templehof aerodrome by three more. An airframe factory at Leipzig was attacked and, in addition to the bombing, leaflets were dropped over Berlin, Leipzig, Osnabrük, Brandenburg and Halle.

4. Berlin was the primary target of the Hampdens, the Siemens and Halske factory being attacked by fourteen aircraft, the majority of the crews reporting fires and explosions. Other targets in the Berlin area; an oil reservoir at Nordenham and also railway sidings north of Berlin were attacked, but results were not observed. The remainder of the force attacked a number of enemy aerodromes where, in some instances, hits were claimed on aerodrome buildings.

A large vessel on the canal near Rathenow suffered a direct hit which caused it to explode. The objectives at Kiel, Hamburg and Dortmund-Ems aqueduct were not located because of the local weather conditions. One aircraft ditched on return from Berlin.

OPERATIONAL LOSSES

Blenheim T2046 'J' of 53 Squadron, Detling, failed to return from a patrol to the Hook of Holland. Pilot Officer W. E. Fitzpatrick, Sergeant J. Bann and Sergeant H. Dunnington were posted as missing in action and their names are on the Runnymede Memorial.

Blenheim R2794 'F' of 59 Squadron, Thorney Island, flew into the ground near Littlehampton, Sussex, when returning from Caen at 20.15 hours. Pilot Officer J. Dellow, Sergeant K. A. Edwards and Sergeant L. E. Bettis were killed

Hampden X2897 of 83 Squadron, Scampton, target Berlin, ditched on return alongside a trawler off Skegness, Lincs. The crew; Flight Lieutenant J. A. Pitcairn-Hill DSO, DFC, Flying Officer Watson, Sergeant T. P. Byrne and Flying Officer R. Stannion were rescued unharmed.

The crew of X2897 safely on board a trawler after ditching in the North Sea off Skegness. They had been in the air for nine hours after the raid on Berlin and simply ran out of fuel upon their return. The pilot, Jamie Pitcairn-Hill had previously led the Dortmund-Ems raid which resulted in Rod Learoyd being awarded the VC. He was awarded the DSO for the same operation.

L-R; Flying Officer Watson, Flying Officer Stannion, Flight Lieutenant Pitcairn-Hill and Sergeant Byrne.

Wednesday 28th August

The First Raids on Berlin

Squadron Leader Andrew Jackson. DFC, AE, MID. completed two operational tours, including the first raids on Berlin, events which Hitler and Goering had boasted would never be allowed to happen. Andrew Jackson is convinced that these raids had a direct bearing on the change in German tactics. The following account of those first raids on Berlin is followed by evidence confirming Andrew's views, in the form of a transcript of a speech made by Hermann Goering at that particular time:

"On the 28th August, 1940, we took off from Norwich airfield, as an advanced base from Marham to attack Berlin, on the first operation by Wellington bombers. An earlier raid by Hampden aircraft was made on the 25th August, 1940. The target was considered to be at the extreme range of the Wimpey, hence the use of Norwich airfield. To further conserve fuel, we began a very gentle climb over the North Sea, which was covered by low cloud. Without warning we were under attack from anti-aircraft fire coming from our own ships below, presumably protecting an Allied convoy. Having escaped serious damage, we continued on our long flight to the German capital.

Searchlights and heavy flak were encountered on our flight, but over the actual target very little opposition - not what we had expected. We had a clear view of the city of Berlin, the marshalling yards were identified and attacked. Two nights later we returned to be met by numerous searchlights and well directed and intensive flak. The target this time Templehof airfield. Our numbers were small, and there is no claim that much damage resulted from our bombing, but it is very likely that these raids had a consequential effect, triggering off a profound change in direction by the enemy. The raids must have destroyed the myth of German invincibility, thus causing considerable anger to Hitler and Goering who had boasted that such raids would never happen. It is believed that the attacks on the German capital so infuriated Hitler, that he radically changed tactics. In future, the Luftwaffe would concentrate their bombing on the cities in a renewed effort to achieve a quick victory.

Fighter Command was at that time in dire straits, Biggin Hill, Tangmere, Manson and other airfields were being subjected to a terrible pasting. In some attacks, 100 bombs would be dropped on one airfield and their viability as operational units was at grave risk. The change of target by Goering's Luftwaffe gave Fighter Command the respite it so desperately needed. A.C.M. Lord Dowding described it as a miracle!

The daylight attacks on our cities were undertaken at high level, giving our C.H.L.s the opportunity to detect the approach of enemy aircraft at an early stage, and giving our fighters time to reach optimum height. London was at the extreme range of the deadly Bf109s, and this contributed to higher enemy losses. Historians may view these early raids in August 1940 on the German capital as of immense consequential importance, in the part they played in changing the enemy's tactics from a winning formula - to one that denied them victory. Fighter Command recovered from its onslaught of airfields and aircraft, and went on to defeat the Luftwaffe thus carving its name in history which it so richly deserves.

For the first time, Hitler's rampage through Europe had been halted, his patience was being tested; the time of year required an early decision to be made on the date for the invasion of UK. This no doubt, also had a bearing on Hitler's change of tactics. Hitler's objective however was unaltered - to carry out his invasion plans; and from beginning to end this was what the Battle of Britain was all about! It is evident that the general public's perception of this historic battle requires correction, as somehow it has become skewed, and reference should be made to the part played by the RAF. In particular, any reference to air losses should be those of the RAF in our fight for our national survival. The total is correctly recorded in the Roll of Honour in the Battle of Britain Memorial Chapel in Westminster Abbey."

Andrew Jackson, DFC,AE MID.

Hermann Goering on a German Wireless Broadcast on 7th September, 1940. (Note: this speech was made only two weeks after the first raids on Berlin).

"I now want to take this opportunity of speaking to you, to say this moment is an historic one. As a result of the provocative British attacks on Berlin on recent nights the Fuhrer has decided to order a mighty blow to be struck in revenge against the capital of the British Empire. I personally have assumed the leadership of this attack and today I have heard above me the roaring of the victorious German squadrons which now, for the first time, are driving toward the heart of the enemy in full daylight, accompanied by countless fighter squadrons. Enemy defences were as we expected beaten down and the target reached, and I am certain that our successes have been as massive as the boldness of our plan of attack and the fighting spirit of our crews deserve. In any event this is an historic hour in which for the first time the German Luftwaffe has struck at the heart of the enemy."

ENEMY ACTIVITY

The increased number of night raids must have affected the Luftwaffe daylight effort, because it was afternoon before Do17s and He111s were flown on a Channel sweep between Beachy Head and Hastings. This was followed at 18.00 hours by a battle mainly between Hurricanes and Bf109s over Hawkinge. With the approach of dusk single Luftwaffe bombers struck at Debden, Duxford and East Anglian aerodromes. Widespread raids continued during the night when Merseyside, south Wales, the Midlands, Manchester, Carlisle, the Tees and Tyne areas and Scotland were attacked. The main attack was by 200 bombers which dropped 130 tons of bombs on Merseyside - a small consolation was that only fifty tons were on industrial targets. During the day's fighting twelve enemy fighters were destroyed for the loss of nine RAF fighters.

An unexploded bomb is detonated at Hemswell after the was attacked by a lone German bomber on this day.

COASTAL COMMAND OPERATIONS

The usual daily anti invasion, anti submarine patrols and reconnaissance sorties took place throughout the period - fifty-three flights being carried out by eighty-two aircraft. Air escort was provided for twenty convoys.

1. A Blenheim on a routine patrol attacked an enemy submarine fifty-six miles from Bergen on a bearing of 276 degrees. No hits with bombs were obtained, but the enemy vessel was machine-gunned.
2. A Sunderland on convoy duty co-operated with a Royal Naval unit to attack a U-Boat, fifty-six miles from Barra Head on a hearing of 262 degrees. The RN unit claimed the submarine had been sunk.
3. PRU photographs of Boulogne showed six E-Boats and one torpedo boat at Quay Chanzy. Three He59s and three Arado Ar96s were in the outer harbour with another three He59s on the beach. Other photographs were taken of Bordeaux, Lorient and Brest which revealed shipping including a U-Boat, a cruiser, three E-Boats and a concentration of small craft. At Lanveoc there were six seaplanes.
4. Fairey Battle L5398 of 12 Squadron, detailed to bomb Mardy, abandoned its task because of adverse weather conditions.

BOMBER COMMAND OPERATIONS

1. Twenty Blenheims were despatched in daylight to attack the enemy held airfields at De Kooy, Bergen/Alkmaar, and shipping off Den Helder, but weather conditions were unsuitable and in many cases the tasks were abandoned. However, seven crews pressed home their attacks at De Kooy and Alkmaar. One aircraft suffered severe Flak damage.

Five other aircraft attacked a large concentration of shipping including motor vessels and minelayers between Texel Island and Den Helder. Other attacks were made on shipping north of Borkum and trawlers north of the Frisian Islands.

In addition, six Blenheims carried out a routine reconnaissance over the North Sea. There were no losses.

Night operations

The following were detailed for night operations; eighteen Blenheims to attack enemy occupied Airfields, twenty-nine Wellingtons to oil targets at St. Nazaire, Boltrope and marshalling yards at Hamm and Mannheim. Twelve Whitleys to the synthetic oil plant at Köln and oil stocks at Ludwigshaven. Twenty Hampdens to a synthetic oil plant at Gelsenkirchen.

1. The Blenheims carried out their attacks as briefed against Lannion, Le Treport, Berck, Authie, Evere, Ockenburg, Waalhaven, Dunkirk, Fécamp, Dinard and St. Malo. In most cases results were unobserved, but large fires were claimed to have been started at Dinard and Le Treport. One aircraft failed to return.
2. The Wellingtons' primary target was the oil at St. Nazaire, where fires and explosions were reported. The synthetic oil plant at Boltrope was also successfully attacked. Other objectives attacked were the Krupps works at Essen, a blast furnace near Essen, a factory north of Hamm, railway targets near Boltrope and enemy airfields.
3. The Whitley crews were hampered in their operations by the low cloud and haze, but it was claimed that the oil stocks at Ludwigshaven and the synthetic oil plant at Köln were attacked. In addition attacks were made on a blast furnace near Bonn and what was thought to be a power station at Reisholtz.
4. Despite unfavourable weather conditions, the Hampden crews claimed successful attacks against the synthetic oil plant at Gelsenkirchen and the power station at Duisburg, where hits were claimed in the target area. Rolling stock at Hamm marshalling yards was also hit. One aircraft failed to return.

OPERATIONAL LOSSES

Blenheim N3620 of 107 Squadron, Wattisham, target enemy airfields. Shot down by Flak north-east of De Kooy airfield. Flying Officer E. R. Berry, Sergeant A. P. Sully and Sergeant H. Bentham were killed and are buried in Bergen Op Zoom War Cemetery.

Hampden P4372 of 44 Squadron, Waddington, target Gelsenkirchen, failed to return. Pilot Officer T. G. Hynes, Sergeant L. H. Wainwright, Sergeant R. M. Wicker were taken prisoner, Pilot Officer C. O. Dunkels was killed and is buried in the Rheinberg War Cemetery.

Hampden P1334 of 83 Squadron, Scampton, target Gelsenkirchen. Returned early and crash-landed at Scampton - no serious injuries reported.

Friday 30th August

A Wellington of 214 Squadron takes off heading for Germany. If the target is Berlin then the crew have several tense hours of flying ahead of them. If they are lucky...

ENEMY ACTIVITY

Taking advantage of the good weather, Luftwaffe raids started early. Do17s escorted by Bf109s attempted to attack a convoy sailing from the Thames. During the morning, three Gruppen of Bf109s came in over Kent to pave the way for forty He111s, thirty Do17s and another ninety escorting Messerschmitts. RAF fighters intercepted them and a big battle took place which lasted until the early afternoon. From 13.00 hours small groups of bombers escorted by many fighters crossed the Kent coast and for two hours roamed over south-east England. By 16.00 hours another force of 300 enemy aircraft had crossed the Kent Coast heading for inland targets. This was the biggest operation so far, which resulted in the bombing of Biggin Hill, North Weald and Kenley, where damage and casualties were suffered. Despite the efforts of fighters the Vauxhall motor factory at Luton was also bombed, causing damage and casualties. The Luftwaffe lost twenty-four aircraft destroyed, the RAF lost twenty.

COASTAL COMMAND OPERATIONS

Fifty-four aircraft carried out thirty-five anti invasion, anti submarine patrols and reconnaissance sorties. Air escort was provided for twenty-two convoys. At 17.30 hours RAF Detling was bombed and the 500 (Anson) Squadron area suffered damage.

1. A Blenheim on a routine patrol attacked a U-Boat which was eighty miles from Sumburgh Head on a bearing of 064 degrees. Fragmentation and incendiary bombs were dropped ahead of the diving submarine, but results were inconclusive.

2. Three Blenheims successfully bombed a jetty and shipping at Den Helder despite accurate anti-aircraft opposition. Three other Blenheims were unable to locate the target due to adverse weather conditions.

3. PR photographs were taken of Den Helder, Ijmuiden, Emden, Bremen, part of Hamburg, the Kiel Canal from Rendsburg to Brunsbuttel, Cuxhaven and Wilhelmshaven. A sortie over France resulted in photographs of La Boule, St. Nazaire, Lorient, Boulogne Calais and St. Omer. Photos of Nantes revealed an extension to the airfield.

Night operations

1. Six Blenheims bombed oil storage tanks at Cherbourg.

2.Five Albacores attacked shipping at Boulogne.

BOMBER COMMAND OPERATIONS

The daylight raids for twelve Blenheims on enemy held airfields were abandoned because of adverse weather conditions. Six other Blenheims carried out an uneventful reconnaissance over the North Sea. There were no losses.

Night operations

1. Eighteen Blenheims were despatched on night operations; fifteen to attack shipping at Emden and three to attack gun emplacements at Cap Gris Nez. Eight claimed successful attacks at Emden. The others achieved success at Cap Gris Nez and airfields at De Kooy and Papenburg.

2. In this, the third consecutive night that Berlin was the prime target, twenty-nine Wellingtons were detailed to attack the Siemens Halske factory and the Henschel airframe factory in Berlin and marshalling yards/rail facilities at Hamm and Soest. Nine crews carried out successful attacks on the Siemens factory, four the Henschel factory, one the power station at Klingenberg and others a gasworks and marshalling yards in the Berlin area. Attacks were carried out on Olbrek airfield and Schellingwoude seaplane base. One aircraft of 214 Squadron was shot down over Emmerich by Oberleutnant Streib.

...if not. German soldiers inspect the grim remains of a Wellington, shot down over Germany in 1940.

3. Twelve Whitleys were despatched to attack industrial targets in Berlin, docks at Hamburg and enemy occupied airfields. Eight crews claimed to have attacked their Berlin targets successfully, four the docks at Hamburg and enemy airfields. One aircraft was ditched off Hornsea on return.
4. Twenty-five Hampdens successfully attacked oil targets at Magdeburg and Gelsenkirchen as well as rail facilities at the Dortmund-Ems Canal and Krefeld. One aircraft failed to return.

OPERATIONAL LOSSES

Blenheim L9378 of 18 Squadron, West Raynham, target shipping at Emden, crashed in bad visibility near Weasenham, fourteen miles east of Kings Lynn. Sergeant L. A. Williams, Sergeant A. E. Owles and Sergeant R. H. G. Jones were all killed.

Blenheim L9326 of 40 Squadron, Wyton, target Emden, crashed on take off and burst into flames. Pilot Officer W. R. Evans, Sergeant Little and Sergeant J. A. Watt were all killed.

Blenheim R3773 of 110 Squadron, Wattisham, target Emden, crashed on return seven miles north-west of Ipswich. Pilot Officer J. S. F. P. Price and Sergeant H. A. Tune were killed. Sergeant Macdonald was injured.

Wellington T2559 of 214 Squadron, Stradishall, target Berlin, shot down over Emmerich and crashed near Halle. Flying Officer L. M. Craigie-Halkett, Pilot Officer W. B. S. Cunynghame, Sergeant G. E. Merryweather, Sergeant G. H. Bainbridge, Sergeant S. J. Haldane, and Sergeant A. B. Puzey were all killed and are buried in the Protestant Cemetery Zelhem (Halle).
This fell to Oberleutnant Werner Streib of 2/NJG 1 at 22.34 hours.

Hampden L4079 of 50 Squadron, Lindholme, target Munchengladbach, crashed 14 Km east of Arnhem, shot down at 00.32 hours by Oberleutnant Werner Streib who reported it as a Whitley and his second victory of the night. Pilot Officer K. R. K. Smettem, Sergeant A. A. Horsfall, Sergeant H. H. Best and Sergeant E. W. J. Skinner were all killed and are buried in the Groesbeek Canadian War Cemetery at Nijmegen.

Wellington P2530 of 214 Squadron, Stradishall, target Berlin, low on fuel on return, undershot the runway and ran into a ditch losing its undercarriage. Flying Officer R. R. O'Connor and crew were uninjured.

Whitley P5002 'T' of 58 Squadron, Linton-on-Ouse, target Berlin, ran out of fuel on return and was abandoned in the vicinity of Hornsea. Pilot Officer N. O. Clements, Pilot Officer T. H. Hadley, Sergeant I. A. Zamek and Pilot Officer R. F. Williams baled out and landed successfully, but Sergeant M. Hill drifted out to sea and he was presumed drowned. His name is recorded on the Runnymede Memorial.

Saturday 31st August

MOSTLY SUNNY WITH HIGH CLOUD IN PLACES.

ENEMY ACTIVITY
The weather was good and the first indication of attacks was when an enemy force was detected forming up over the French coast early in the morning. A big battle commenced when fighters intercepted the first of the raiders heading for Debden, Eastchurch and Bircham Newton. The battle continued during the afternoon with attacks on Biggin Hill, Hornchurch and radar stations in Kent and Sussex. There was no let up and the raids continued during the night when 100 bombers carried out attacks on the Merseyside and the Midlands. By the end of the day the Luftwaffe had lost nine bombers and twenty-nine fighters. RAF losses were nine Spitfires and twenty-five Hurricanes.

COASTAL COMMAND OPERATIONS
The month of August drew to a close with Coastal Command squadrons continuing their anti invasion, anti submarine patrols, reconnaissance sorties and convoy escorts. RAF Detling, home of 500 (Anson) Squadron and 53 (Blenheim) Squadron was dive-bombed and strafed. Casualties and damage to buildings and aircraft was caused.
1. Six Blenheims of 53 Squadron carried out an evening attack on Vlaadingen (Amsterdam) where they bombed fuel storage tanks. One aircraft failed to return.
2. Two Swordfish of 812 Squadron carried out an attack against barges at Amsterdam. One came down in the sea.
Night operations
1. Six Blenheims of 59 Squadron carried out a night attack against oil tanks at Cherbourg. Five bombed successfully, one failed to return.

BOMBER COMMAND OPERATIONS
1. Over the North Sea and Germany the weather was far from suitable and a daylight sortie planned for a Blenheim of 114 Squadron to Paderborn was abandoned, as was a North Sea sweep by six other Blenheims.
Night operations
The Wellingtons of 3 Group and the Hampdens of 5 Group kept up the night raids on Berlin.
1. Twenty-four Wellingtons were despatched to attack the Henschel aircraft works and a gas works in Berlin as well as marshalling yards at Hamm, Soest, Osnabrük and Scherte. Berlin was mostly obscured by cloud but six managed to bomb the primary targets. Twelve crews bombed alternatives, three brought their bombs back, two jettisoned and one aborted.
2. Twenty Hampdens were despatched to attack the BMW factory and Templehof aerodrome at Berlin and an oil refinery at Magdeburg with airfields as alternatives. The weather affected the attacks on Berlin, but fifteen crews managed to bomb the oil refinery at Magdeburg and alternative airfield targets. One aircraft failed to return.
3. Nine Whitleys were detailed to attack the synthetic oil plant at Köln (Wesseling) and a chemical works at Leverkusen. Three crews claimed successful attacks at Köln and three at Leverkusen.
4. Twenty Blenheims were despatched to attack guns at Cap Gris Nez, docks and shipping at Emden and airfields at Ypenburg and Bremerhaven. Despite the weather conditions most crews claimed successful attacks.

OPERATIONAL LOSSES

Blenheim T1940 'D' of 53 Squadron, target Vlaadingen, failed to return after being shot down by Flak at Welplaat, Holland. Wing Commander E. C. T. Edwards, Sergeant L. L. Benjamin and Sergeant J. T. Beesley were killed and buried at Crooswijk, near Rotterdam.

Swordfish L9716 'P' of 812 Squadron came down in the sea. One crew member was rescued. Lieutenant G. Villiers-Tuthill was killed and lies buried at Rozenburg Cemetery, west of Rotterdam, Holland.

Blenheim R3880 'S' of 59 Squadron, Thorney Island, target Cherbourg, failed to return. Pilot Officer J. J. Finlay and Sergeant F. J. Leonhardt were posted as missing in action and are on the Runnymede Memorial. Sergeant A. L. Peddie lies in the Quiberville Churchyard, France.

Above: Sgt. Leonhardt 59 Sqn – missing
Below: Sgt. Peddie 59 Sqn – killed in action

Hampden P2123 of 44 Squadron, Waddington, target Berlin, ditched on return off the beach at Cromer. Pilot Officer D. Romans DFC, Pilot Officer D. E. Stewart, Sergeant H. Logan and Sergeant Mandale were unhurt and came ashore in their dinghy.

September 1940

The Climax. A Close Run Thing

September - The Climax. A Close Run Thing

The eternal symbol of the Battle of Britain, vapour trails over the south-coast of England.

The crucial battles of the airfields which had commenced in August continued as the Luftwaffe persisted in its attempts to put RAF Fighter Command out of action and gain air superiority, the prerequisite for the German invasion of Britain. This had originally been planned to commence on 3rd September and Goering assumed temporary direct command of Luftwaffe operations. He affirmed that the RAF could be shattered in four to five days, but he under the impression that the battle of the airfields was all but won and ordered the Luftwaffe to switch their attacks to the London docks.

On 7th September a force of 300 bombers escorted by fighters attacked. During eleven hours of continuous operations substantial damage was inflicted on the docks and casualties caused among civilian workers, but the cost to the Luftwaffe was thirty-eight aircraft destroyed and eleven damaged. RAF losses were twenty-eight fighters destroyed and eleven damaged. The Air Officer Commanding 11 Group, Air Vice Marshal Keith Park, while expressing his dismay at the damage and casualties caused on the London docks, was relieved that the Luftwaffe had switched its attacks from his airfields thus giving a respite to enable Fighter Command to get its 'second wind' and replace losses. This became evident on 15th September when the Luftwaffe attempted to deliver its 'knock-out blow' and suffered its most serious losses since the start of the battle; fifty-six aircraft being destroyed against the loss of twenty-six fighters by Fighter Command. 15th September is looked upon as the climax of the battle, revered and remembered annually.

In the meantime, the 'Battle of the Barges' was being waged by Bomber and Coastal Command squadrons who carried out successful day and night attacks on the shipping and barges of the invasion fleet assembled in the Channel ports. Twenty percent of the barges were claimed as having been sunk or destroyed, crews reporting that the fires raging in the Channel ports resembled 'Blackpool illuminations'.

During the night of 15th/16th September, Bomber Command's second Victoria Cross of World War II was awarded to Sergeant John Hannah, the eighteen year old WOp/AG of 83 (Hampden) Squadron, for his supreme heroism during an attack on the barges at Antwerp.

On 17th September, the German Naval Staff stated, 'The enemy air force is by no means defeated, on the contrary it shows increasing activity. The weather situation over England is unfavourable, therefore the Fuhrer has decided to postpone *Operation Sealion* indefinitely'. This was confirmed on 19th September when a secret German signal was intercepted ordering the dismantling of invasion facilities in Holland.

On 24th September, remnants of the invasion fleet were observed to be dispersing from the Channel ports, giving an indication that the threat of invasion was diminishing. The enemy air raids, however, continued by both day and by night but large scale escorted bomber raids were over, the last one taking place on 30th September. From then on the daylight raids were carried out mainly by single or small groups of fighter bombers. Bomber and Coastal Commands continued their day and night raids on the Channel ports, Berlin and a variety of relevant targets throughout September and October. The last raid during the threatened invasion period took place on 12th/13th October.

Title Page: A weary Hampden crew return from a sortie.

A Wellington of 37 Squadron that raided Hannover on this night.

ENEMY ACTIVITY

Although enemy activity was on a reduced scale there was no let-up in air raids. Bombers escorted by fighters concentrated on putting RAF airfields out of action; Detling, Eastchurch and Biggin Hill were hit by low flying Dorniers. Biggin Hill in particular was badly hit - its Sector Operations room was badly damaged - two WAAFs who remained at posts throughout the raids and carnage were subsequently awarded Military Medals. At night raids, compared to the previous nights, were also on a reduced scale. Isolated raids were carried out on the industrial Midlands, but the main attacks were made on Kent, Bristol Channel, south Wales and Tyne and Tees. It was reported that RAF Detling had been attacked again. Minelaying was suspected as having taken place in the Bristol Channel, the Humber, Thames Estuary, Dungeness and Poole. During the day's fighting the Luftwaffe lost five aircraft destroyed. RAF Fighter Command had a bad day losing twenty-five fighters.

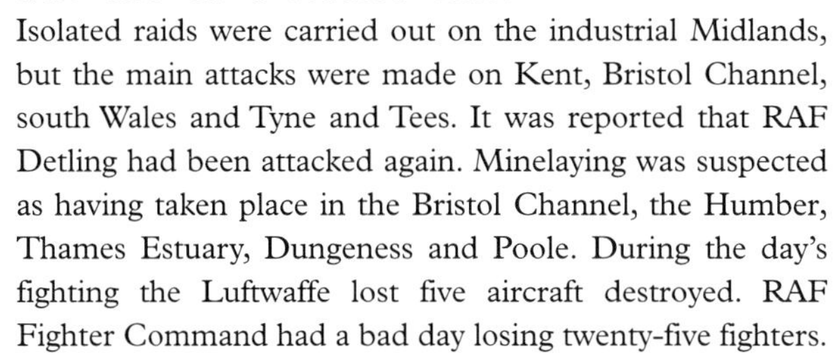

COASTAL COMMAND OPERATIONS

108 aircraft carried out the usual anti invasion, anti submarine patrols and reconnaissance sorties. Twenty-five convoys were provided with air escort and, in addition, Blenheims escorted Royal Navy units throughout the day from Terschelling to the east coast.

1. The 500 (Anson) Squadron area at RAF Detling was bombed and machine-gunned in the late afternoon.
2. Anson 'D' of 500 Squadron on patrol attacked a U-Boat 54 degrees 14'N/06 degrees W, but there were no positive results.
3. Three out of six 59 Squadron Blenheims bombed Lorient.
4. A Photo reconnaissance of the Beveland Canal by the PRU, revealed 160 barges - twenty heading suspiciously south.

Night operations

1. Three Blenheims carried out a night attack on the shipyard at Lorient causing fires and explosions.
2. A single Fairey Battle attacked shipping at Calais, but results were not observed.

BOMBER COMMAND OPERATIONS

1. Eighteen Blenheims were detailed to carry out daylight harassing attacks on occupied airfields, but because of lack of cloud cover only three managed to bomb airfields in Belgium. Six Blenheims carried out a routine reconnaissance over the North Sea

Night operations

A total of seventy-one aircraft were detailed for night raids on Germany and Italy. Blenheims were detailed to attack a petrol dump at Nordenham and shipping at Emden. Despite adverse weather most crews claimed to have attacked their primary or alternative targets with success.

Hampdens attacked the Bosch factory at Stuttgart, oil stocks at Ludwigshaven and marshalling yards at Mannheim. Whitleys attacked the Fiat works at Turin, the magneto factory at Milan, the bridge over the River Po at Alessandria and the BMW works and marshalling yards at Munich. Wellingtons attacked the aircraft works at Leipzig, the aluminium works at Bittefeld, the power station at Kassel, the marshalling yards at Soest and the airfields at Soesterberg and Antwerp.

OPERATIONAL LOSSES

Blenheim T1880 of 59 Squadron, Thorney Island crashed in flames near Thorney Island returning from Lorient. Fortunately Pilot Officer Short, Sergeant Hewitt and Sergeant Burney escaped unhurt.

Hudson N7367 of 206 Squadron, Bircham Newton, swung on take-off and caught fire after the undercarriage collapsed. Pilot Officer Blackett and his crew escaped before the bomb load exploded.

Blenheim R3663 of 18 Squadron, West Raynham, target north west Germany, crashed on return while trying to land at Great Massingham. Flight Lieutenant Howden and crew escaped unhurt.

Blenheim L8796 of 40 Squadron, Wyton, target north west Germany, crashed on return at West Raynham airfield. Pilot Officer Whitehead and crew escaped unhurt.

Wellington N2992 of 37 Squadron, Feltwell, target Hannover, flew into the North Sea on return. Pilot Officer M. S. Burberry was the sole survivor, rescued two days later by *HMS Niger*. Pilot Officer G. H. Jackson, Pilot Officer H. Philippe, Sergeant C. J. Hooper, Sergeant T. C. M. Browne (RNZAF) and Sergeant P. W. Barber were all presumed drowned.

Wellington R3159 of 75 Squadron, Mildenhall, target Hannover, crashed on return while approaching East Wretham airfield. Pilot Officer R. N. Peel and the five members of his crew were injured.

Monday 2nd September SUNNY WITH CLEAR SKIES AFTER ANY EARLY FOG DISPERSED IN THE SOUTH.

The wreck of Sunderland P9602 at Oban after Flt Lt. Cohen's landing accident on 2nd September.

ENEMY ACTIVITY

The pattern employed by the Luftwaffe was the same as for previous days - escorted bombers attempting to attack RAF stations and put them out of action. A fierce battle took place and continued all day, reaching its climax when ninety RAF fighters opposed 160 Bf109s. By then six airfields had been bombed, Eastchurch (where the bomb dump was hit), Detling, Kenley, Biggin Hill, Hornchurch and Brooklands where the Hawker and Vickers aircraft factories were sited. Night attacks were widespread, carried out by single aircraft. The raids started at dusk and continued until 01.30 hours on the 3rd, the targets being mostly industrial areas in the south. Minelaying was suspected to have taken place chiefly in the Wash and the Tyne although it was reported that Scapa Flow was also included. A rare occurrence took place when a Westland Lysander of the Special Flight at Christchurch shot down a Do17 which crashed into the sea. During the day's fighting the Luftwaffe lost twenty-six aircraft destroyed. RAF Fighter Command lost twenty-three fighters.

COASTAL COMMAND OPERATIONS

Eighty-four aircraft were involved in the usual anti invasion, anti submarine patrols and sorties as well as providing escort for twenty-two convoys.

1. At the beginning of September the Bristol Beauforts of 22, 42 and 217 Squadrons were committed to operations despite engine troubles being experienced, the first sortie by 22 Squadron taking place during the late evening when three aircraft bombed Flushing docks.

2. Five Blenheims of 53 Squadron and four out of eight from 59 Squadron carried out a bombing strike on shipping at Ostend.

3. A Hudson attacked a U-Boat forty miles west of Texel, but no result was observed.

4. Ansons attacked two U-Boats; one ten miles east of Malin Head and the other forty-four miles north of St. Kilda. Again no results were observed.

5. Sunderlands attacked a U-Boat seven miles west-north-west of Cape Wrath. There were no positive results.

6. Photographs were taken of the Dutch, Belgian and north-east French coasts.

Night operations

Seven aircraft carried out a night attack on oil tanks at Flushing while five more attacked shipping at Ostend.

2. A reconnaissance was made of the Norwegian Coast, Texel and Terschelling and attacks made on motor vessels. There were no losses.

BOMBER COMMAND OPERATIONS

1. Four Blenheims detailed to carry out a North Sea sweep abandoned because of adverse weather conditions. There were no losses.

Night operations

Eighty four aircraft were detailed for night operations.

1. Hampdens attacked an oil target at Ludwigshaven, mar-

shalling yards at Hamm, communications at Dortmund-Ems, the Bosch factory at Stuttgart and the U-Boat base at Lorient. One aircraft failed to return.
2. Blenheims attacked targets in north-west Germany. One aircraft failed to return.
3. Wellingtons carried out fire attacks on military stores in the Black Forest.
4. Whitleys attacked the power station at Genoa and oil stocks at Frankfurt. Two aircraft ditched on return.

OPERATIONAL LOSSES

Beaufort L9879 of 22 Squadron, Bircham Newton, undershot on a night landing at North Coates. Wing Commander Braithwaite and his crew escaped injury.

Sunderland T9043 'F' of 210 Squadron, Oban, failed to return from a convoy patrol. Flight Lieutenant P. D. Parry-Jones, Flying Officer B. L. A Pusey, Pilot Officer I. W. Phillips, Pilot Officer M. H. Dalzell-McKean, Sergeant R. G. Fitzgerald, Sergeant M. A. F. Drewitt, LAC W. T. James, AC1 L. E. Stokes, AC1 L. J. Caunter, AC1 W. H. Blackmore and AC1 D. H. Jones were posted as missing in action and recorded on the Runnymede Memorial.

Sunderland P9602 of 10 (RAAF) Squadron, Oban, ran aground after a landing accident and was wrecked. Flight Lieutenant J. A. Cohen (RAAF) and his crew were safe.

Blenheim L8757 of 40 Squadron, Wyton, target north west Germany, crashed in the North Sea. Flight Sergeant R. B. Broadhurst is buried at Den Burg (Texel). Sergeant A. Marsden and Sergeant A. J. Burns are commemorated on the Runnymede Memorial.

Hampden P4370 of 144 Squadron, Hemswell, target Ludwigshaven, shot down by a night-fighter and crashed 15km north-east of Maastricht. Pilot Officer R. S. A. Churchill and Pilot Officer I. C. Kirk were taken prisoner. Sergeant A. E. Walker and Sergeant A. C. H. Edmeads were killed during the fighter attack and are buried in Maastricht General Cemetery.
This fell to Feldwebel Paul Gildner of 3./NJG 1, who claimed it as a "Whitley" at 00.45 hours.

Whitley. N1427 of 58 Squadron, Honington, target Genoa, ditched successfully on return just off Margate. Squadron Leader J. S. Bartlett, Sergeant F. M. Kerr, Sergeant Coubrough and Sergeant M. C. Caryll de Tilkin paddled ashore in their dinghy.

Whitley N1459 'A' of 58 Squadron, Honington, target Genoa, ditched successfully on return fifteen miles north-east of Harwich. The crew; Flight Sergeant D. H. A. Moore, Pilot Officer P. C. Elliott, Sergeant Craig, Sergeant Harvey and Sergeant Conner took to their dinghy and were rescued by *HMS Pintail.*

A Beaufort returns home after a sortie. Note the black undersurfaces for night operations.

Tuesday 3rd September

RAIN IN THE NORTH, MAINLY SUNNY IN THE SOUTH.

ENEMY ACTIVITY

Again RAF airfields were the Luftwaffe's main target. North Weald was carpet-bombed by fifty Do17s preceded by fighters. Before fighters could intervene two hangars, the operations block and other buildings were badly damaged. Other attacks were attempted on Debden and Hornchurch, but the raiders were unable to press home their attacks. Luftwaffe reconnaissance aircraft flew over the Midlands. Three Blenheim fighters were scrambled but they were mistakenly attacked by Hurricanes, unfortunately one was shot down and another forced to crash-land. That night a steady stream of single aircraft attacked the Midlands, the Wash area and Merseyside. Two of the raiders were shot down by Blenheim night fighters. Extensive minelaying was suspected from the Forth of Firth to Poole Harbour, the Bristol Channel and Liverpool Bay. During the air fighting the Luftwaffe lost twelve aircraft and RAF Fighter Command lost fifteen fighters.

COASTAL COMMAND OPERATIONS

Anti invasion, anti submarine patrols, reconnaissance and offensive sorties were carried out. Seventeen convoys were provided with air escort. Eighty-three aircraft were involved in the day's operations.
1. An Anson of 612 Squadron attacked a U-Boat. No result was observed.
2. Five Blenheims of 53 Squadron attacked shipping and docks at Ostend.
3. Three Beauforts of 22 Squadron bombed barges in the South Beveland Canal.
4. Photographs were taken of the Norwegian, Dutch and French ports, aerodromes and water 'dromes. There were no losses, but a Hudson of 206 Squadron hit trees on take-off from Bircham Newton and crash landed without injury to the crew.

Night operations

1. Night strikes were carried out on shipping and the docks at Ostend and hits were claimed in the target area.
2. Terneuzen was bombed and hits obtained on barges in the canal basin. Explosions and fires followed.
4. Barges in the Beveland Canal were set on fire. There were no losses.

BOMBER COMMAND OPERATIONS

1. Because of unsuitable conditions all daylight tasks were abandoned except a North Sea patrol by six Blenheims. There were no losses.

Night operations

Sixty-eight aircraft were tasked for night operations; Blenheims to carry out harassing raids on northern France and Dunkirk, Wellingtons to carry out fire raids on military stores in the Hartz Mountains and Grunewald Forest and to bomb railway targets at Scherte and Hamm, Whitleys to bomb a transformer station and gasworks in Berlin, Hampdens to bomb the Berlin West power station and an oil target at Magdeburg.
1. Successful harassing attacks on the aerodromes at St. Omer and Le Touquet were made by the Blenheims.

A 15 Squadron Blenheim starts up with the ever faithful groundcrew in attendance.

2. The Wellington attacks on the Hartz Mountains target resulted in fires and two explosions were caused the result of the attack on the Grunewald Forest (near Berlin).
3. The Whitley attacks on the Berlin targets were claimed as being successful. The attack on the gasworks resulted in a large fire. In addition hits on a 'self illuminating' target at Osterburg were observed.
4. Although the Hampdens were hampered by heavy cloud which made observation of results difficult, the crews were able to observe hits in the target areas of the west power station and armament factory at Berlin, and also at the oil works at Magdeburg.

In addition aerodromes in Holland and Germany were attacked, as were railway targets at Hannover and Magdeburg.

OPERATIONAL LOSSES

Blenheim R3769 of 15 Squadron, Wyton, target St. Omer, crashed three miles south-east of Kettering and caught fire. Pilot Officer D. E. C. Myland DFC, Sergeant H. A. Powys-Jones and Sergeant P. J. Petrie were all killed.

Blenheim L9188 of 18 Squadron, West Raynham, target north-west Germany, crashed while attempting to land at Great Massingham airfield. The only details available are that it comprised Sergeant J. W. K. Allen and Sergeant E. E. R. Walsh who were killed. A third crew member escaped injury.

Whitley P4967 of 10 Squadron, Leeming, target Berlin, crash-landed five miles east-north-east of Northallerton on return. Flight Lieutenant D. G. Tomlinson, Pilot Officer Brant, Sergeant Walters, Sergeant Hughes and Sergeant McIntosh escaped uninjured.

Coastal Command Blenheims were in action again today.

ENEMY ACTIVITY

Throughout the day it was estimated that the Luftwaffe employed a total of 650 aircraft. Their main attacks took place in east Kent and Thames Estuary area. They also carried out reconnaissance around the north-east and Welsh coasts. During the morning heavily protected Bf110s and He111s attacked the Hurricane and Wellington aircraft factories causing damage and casualties. By now some Spitfire squadrons were being re-equipped with Mk.IIs which they used to good effect destroying the Luftwaffe fighter escorts. One of their most notable victims being the escort's Gruppenkommandeur. The surviving bombers had to make their way back to their bases mainly unprotected. Luftwaffe losses were twenty-one aircraft destroyed. RAF Fighter Command lost fifteen.

COASTAL COMMAND OPERATIONS

Anti invasion, anti submarine patrols, reconnaissance sorties and escorts for twenty convoys were carried out. Eighty-five aircraft took part in the day's operations.

1. Near Terschelling a Hudson engaged an He115. The enemy aircraft was damaged but managed to escape.
2. Another He115 received the attentions of a Hudson east of Flamborough Head and was also damaged, but the engagement was inconclusive.
3. PRU photographs revealed fifty motor boats off Cap Gris Nez. These were subsequently reported to be in Boulogne Harbour. Pictures were also taken of Terneuzen and Ostend revealing the presence of one hundred barges at each location.
4. In the Kiel Canal area ten ships were photographed entering the canal from the Baltic.
5. Photographs of the submarine base at Lorient showed considerable U-Boat activity, six submarines being photographed.

Night operations

1. Five Blenheims of 53 Squadron carried out a night strike on stores at Flushing, where fires were started.
2. 59 Squadron attacked the oil tanks at Cherbourg with eight aircraft causing a very large fire.
3. Six Swordfish attacked the barges at Terneuzen, the crews claiming that a large explosion occurred.

BOMBER COMMAND OPERATIONS

Because of unsuitable weather conditions the only daylight operation was a reconnaissance by six Blenheims over the North Sea. It was uneventful and there were no losses.

Night operations

The pattern of night operations followed the previous nights – harassing attacks on airfields in France and Belgium, fire raids on military targets in the Grunewald Forest, attacks on military targets in Berlin and attacks on oil targets at Magdeburg and Stettin.

1. Eighteen Blenheims carried out successful attacks on the airfields at Forêt de Guines, St. Omer, Dunkirk, Mardiek, Abbeville and Twente as well as on the marshalling yards at Hamm and a Flak ship west of Alkmaar.
2. Thirty-two Wellingtons carried out fire raids on the targets in the Grunewald Forest area causing fires. Attacks were also carried out on the airfields at Chartres and Deurne (Antwerp).
3. Five of the six Whitleys successfully bombed their primary target in Berlin, but one failed to return. Five of the other six successfully bombed the oil target at Magdeburg, the sixth bombed Bremen.
4. Twenty out of the twenty-four crews detailed to bomb the oil target at Stettin claimed a very successful attack. One aircraft failed to return.

Wednesday 4th September

Hampdens of 49 Squadron being bombed up at Scampton. EA-D in the background is P1347, one of today's casualties.

OPERATIONAL LOSSES

Blenheim R3824 of 107 Squadron, Wattisham, target Mardiek, on return to base collided with a parked aircraft. Pilot Officer F. J. Otterway and Sergeant S. Bews were killed. Sergeant A. Brand escaped uninjured.

Hampden P1347 'D' of 49 Squadron, Scampton, target Stettin, strayed off track on return and forced landed in a field near St. Brieuc after being fired on by light Flak. Flying Officer L. M. Hodges, Sergeant S. J. Hitchings, Sergeant J. H. Wyatt and Sergeant L. C. Turnbull were all taken prisoner.*

**Flying Officer Hodges and Sergeant Wyatt eventually escaped and got back home via Gibraltar. Flying Officer Hodges resumed what was to turn out to be an illustrious wartime and post-war flying career in the RAF. He was highly decorated and retired from the RAF with the rank of Air Chief Marshal.*

Whitley P4973 of 51 Squadron, Dishforth, target Berlin (Charlottenberg power station), ditched off the Dutch coast on return. Sergeant M. H. Jones was trapped in the aircraft and was drowned, his name is on the Runnymede Memorial. Flying Officer J. M. Taylor, Sergeant V. B. Housego, Sergeant H. Maylin and Sergeant M. F. Johnson were rescued by a Luftwaffe He59 float plane of the German Air Sea Rescue Service and subsequently incarcerated as PoWs.

Loading bombs into a Wellington's bomb bay.

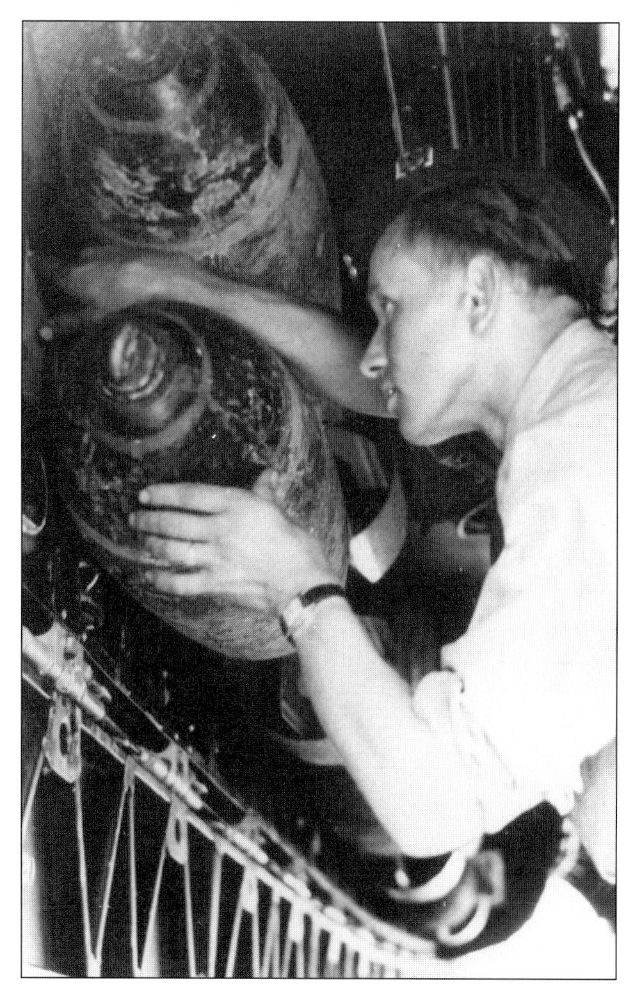

Thursday 5th September

ENEMY ACTIVITY

The Luftwaffe carried out two main raids; the first in the late morning with approximately 150 aircraft against targets in the Thames Estuary and to the north of it, but most of the fighting took place over Kent. Heston airfield was slightly damaged. The second raid comprising some 250 aircraft took place between 3 and 4 o'clock in the afternoon on RAF Detling and Thameshaven, where five fuel tanks were set on fire. At night the raids were widespread and the London districts Hammersmith, Woolwich and Leyton suffered damage. The other targets at Bristol, Liverpool and the Lancashire area were mostly by single aircraft. Damage was caused mostly to residential areas rather than industrial areas. Losses during the period were even, both the Luftwaffe and RAF Fighter Command losing twenty-one aircraft destroyed.

COASTAL COMMAND OPERATIONS

The usual patrols and sorties were carried out by eighty-three aircraft and escort was provided for twenty-three convoys.

1. A Hudson of 233 Squadron attacked a U-Boat 122 miles west-north-west of Barra Head, but no results were observed.
2. Two Beauforts, 'G' and 'Q' of 22 Squadron bombed shipping in Boulogne Harbour.
3. Photo reconnaissance pictures show the *Gneisenau* and *Scharnhorst* in a floating dock at Kiel. The *Tirpitz* and a cruiser berthed at Wilhelmshaven. Also eleven U-Boats are shown in the Kiel Canal and another at Wilhelmshaven.

BOMBER COMMAND OPERATIONS

1. Again unsuitable weather conditions precluded daylight operations apart from a North Sea sweep carried out by six Blenheims.

Night operations

The principal targets for the night operations were the Fiat aircraft works at Turin, oil targets at Regensburg, Stettin, Hamburg and Kiel and military stores in forest areas. In addition one aircraft was detailed to attack the *Tirpitz* at Wilhelmshaven. Other targets were E-Boats at Boulogne, guns at Cap Gris Nez and searchlights at Calais.

1. Seventeen Blenheims were dispatched and eleven of them claimed successful attacks on the Boulogne, Calais and Cap Gris Nez targets.
2. Twenty-nine Wellingtons successfully attacked military stores in the forest areas, oil depots at Kiel and marshalling yards at Hamm and Soest.
3. Fifteen Whitleys were dispatched to Turin and Regensburg. Five out of nine bombed the primary oil target at Regensburg the crews claiming good results. The other four bombed alternative targets and carried out '*Razzling*' (incendiary attacks) on the military stores in forest areas. Five crews out of the six bombed the Fiat aircraft works at Turin reporting that the raid caused an explosion sending smoke up to five thousand feet.
4. Hampdens bombed the oil targets at Stettin and Hamburg and communications on the Dortmund-Ems Canal claiming success. The raid by the single aircraft on the *Gneisenau* was affected by weather conditions.

The Battleship Scharnhorst which was photographed in Kiel today by the PRU. The men of Bomber Command would soon get to know her well as she became a high priority target for the British High Command.

Thursday 5th September

One of the increasing problems facing the Hampden crews was the little margin for error in fuel consumption on their sorties to ever distant targets. Targets such as Berlin and Stettin were at the very limit of the Hampden's range and a change in wind or a mistake in navigation could easily result in a ditching off the coast or forced landing, as in the case of this 50 Squadron machine.

OPERATIONAL LOSSES

Blenheim R3755 of 21 Squadron, Lossiemouth, lost without trace on an anti-shipping sortie. Sergeant J. E. Moss, Sergeant K. L. Daly and Sergeant C. Mein are all remembered on the Runnymede Memorial.

Hampden P4290 'B' of 44 Squadron, Waddington, ditched out of fuel off Lowestoft when returning from Stettin. P/O D. Romans DFC, P/O A. R. Kerr, Sergeant H. Logan, Sergeant Simons were all rescued by a passing ship. Hampden P4350 of 49 Squadron, Scampton, target Stettin, ditched on return off Calais. Flight Lieutenant J. D. Haskins, Sergeant W. L. Evans, Sergeant R. Cartwright and Pilot Officer J. V. Silverston all survived, but were taken prisoner.

Hampden X2894 of 61 Squadron, Hemswell, target Stettin, crashed on return after running out of fuel ten miles west-south-west of Swaffham. Flight Lieutenant D. J. How DFC, Sergeant A. A. Brooker and Sergeant R. C. Dickinson DFM escaped unharmed, but Sergeant C. J. Knight was fatally injured.

Hampden P1172 of 144 Squadron, Hemswell, target Hamburg, lost without trace. Pilot Officer J. E. Newton-Clare, Sergeant C. O. Clarke, Sergeant W. Thomson and Sergeant W. L. Powell are all commemorated on the Runnymede Memorial.

Hampden P4378 of 144 Squadron, Hemswell, target Hamburg, overshot landing at base on return, stalled and crashed. Sergeant J. W. Carter, Sergeant W. I. Mackay DFM, and Sergeant F. J. Drake-Carnell were killed. Squadron Leader G. F. Lerwill survived injured.

Wellington R3163 'G' of 149 Squadron, Mildenhall, target military stores in the Black Forest, failed to return. Flying Officer H. Burton*, Pilot Officer G. M. R. Smith, Sergeant A. R. Peacock, Sergeant H. G. Barnes, Sergeant J. Bailey and Pilot Officer D. A. McFarlane were all taken prisoner.
**Flying Officer Burton was the first RAF prisoner to escape from a PoW camp in Germany and carry out a successful 'Home Run'.*

Friday 6th September

ENEMY ACTIVITY

The three main attacks which took place during the day were aimed at targets in south-east England and the Thames Estuary. The raids were intercepted and in most cases failed to reach their targets. Single enemy aircraft carried out reconnaissance over the Midlands. It is estimated that 720 aircraft were involved in the enemy's operations during the day. During the night enemy activity was on a reduced scale, raids taking place over the Thames Estuary, south Wales and the Midlands. Minelaying was suspected to have taken place on the east coast as far north as the Humber. Luftwaffe losses were thirty-four aircraft destroyed and two Bf110s which landed undamaged at Manston and Hawkinge. They were immediately taken away for examination and evaluation. RAF losses were twenty fighters.

COASTAL COMMAND OPERATIONS

Eighty-three aircraft carried out forty-eight anti invasion, anti submarine patrols and offensive reconnaissance sorties. Escort for twenty convoys was also provided.

Flight Lieutenant Mike Henry DFC
Blenheim gunner 110 Squadron

TARGET - INVASION BARGES, No. 3 BASIN, DUNKIRK HARBOUR
F/Lt Powell, Sgt Richmond, Sgt Henry
Blenheim R3772

The six aircraft of 'A' Flight, were split - one section (including us) would attack Dunkirk before midnight, while the second section would take-off to attack Boulogne in the early hours. During the Battle of Britain, invasion barges were being massed in the Channel ports - Ostend, Dunkirk, Calais and Boulogne (and to a smaller extent, Antwerp). Blenheims of No 2 Group were beginning a blitz on those ports. We were absolutely astounded when, before crossing the coast a little to the south of Dunkirk, we saw the reception that other aircraft over the target before us were getting. It was an inverted rainstorm of light flak. We had been briefed to attack at between 6,000 and 8,000 feet - both dangerous heights for light flak. It was an awesome sight - this was really war between the ground and the air! The searchlights were dazzling, especially the purplish master light which outshone the rest. As we ran up on the target, the flak came up in what seemed to be our direction; masses of it in a variety of colour, the light from it all revealing the dark blodges of the heavy flak, not normally seen on a dark night. It was a frightening scene, and how we flew through it all and survived remains a mystery to this day. As soon as our bomb load had been discarded in the appropriate direction we headed for the coast and the peace of the North Sea.

1. Hudson 'B' of 206 Squadron carried out an inconclusive engagement with an He115, forty miles off Cromer. Later Hudson 'W' of 206 Squadron engaged what was presumably the same He115 and forced it to ditch in the North Sea with its engines stopped.

Night operations

1. A Beaufort of 22 Squadron and six FAA Swordfish carried out a night attack on barges at Ostend. The crews claimed hits on the on barges and the dock gates.
2. Blenheims of 53 and 59 Squadrons and FAA Albacores attacked shipping at Boulogne. Bombs fell in the harbour area and nearby railway sidings and an explosion was observed as a result. There were no losses.

BOMBER COMMAND OPERATIONS

1. All Blenheim daylight tasks were abandoned because of unsuitable weather conditions, except for an uneventful North Sea offensive sweep by six aircraft. There were no losses.

Night operations

1. Eighteen Blenheims carried out successful night attacks on gun emplacements at Cap Gris Nez and on enemy airfields in France. Most crews claimed to have hit their targets.
2. Twenty-four Wellingtons continued successful fire raids on objectives in the Black Forest area and also on the West Berlin power station, where hits were claimed in the target area.
3. Five Whitleys attacked oil targets in Berlin, the crews reporting that the target was burning furiously when they left. The marshalling yard at Spandau also received a direct hit.
4. Due to adverse weather over the Ruhr the main Hampden attack was curtailed, only three crews managing to bomb the synthetic oil plant at Dortmund. However, successful mining was carried out off Laes Island.

OPERATIONAL LOSSES

Anson 'M' of 612 Squadron, Stornoway, returning from convoy patrol was unable to get back to base and ditched off The Minches, Lewis. Pilot Officer W. J. R. Redman, Sergeant Strain, Sergeant Abercrombie and LAC Fraser were rescued unharmed by the trawler Sophy.

Hampden P2087 'M' of 44 Squadron, Waddington, target Krefeld, crashed near Munster after being hit by Flak. Pilot Officer S. R. Taunton and Pilot Officer H. J. Vollmer were taken prisoner, but Sergeant W. Bell and Sergeant J. Bracegirdle (New Zealander) were killed and are buried in the Reichswald Forest War Cemetery.

Whitley, P4935 of 10 Squadron, Leeming, target the Salzhot oil depot in Berlin, was lost without trace over the North Sea. After an extensive search, Flying Officer R. H. Thomas, Pilot Officer D. J. A. Stevens, Sergeant R. Hilton, Sergeant H. V. Seed and Sergeant B. W. Neville were presumed lost and appear on the Runnymede Memorial.

Saturday 7th September

MOSTLY SUNNY WITH LIGHT CLOUD IN PLACES.

And so begins the Blitz, Dornier Do17s photographed on the evening of 7th September over West Ham, London.

ENEMY ACTIVITY

Activity by the Luftwaffe started in mid-morning when some thirty aircraft attacked Dover and Hawkinge. Further north the bomber station at RAF Waddington was machine-gunned. The main attack, the beginning of the 'Blitz' on London, began at about 16.30 hours when 350 enemy aircraft made for the Thames Estuary, East London and airfields to the north and south of London. The numbers increased and during daylight as many as 700 aircraft were involved. Despite the valiant efforts of Fighter Command heavy damage and casualties were caused and fires could be seen fifty miles away. The raids continued throughout the night, commencing at 20.10 hours. The targets were the Northolt, Biggin Hill and Kenley areas. A steady stream of bombers penetrated into Greater London. Also isolated raids were carried out on Liverpool, Birmingham and south Wales. It was suspected that minelaying had taken place off the Norfolk Coast. It was 05.00 hours on the 8th before the country was clear of enemy raids. The Luftwaffe lost thirty-eight aircraft destroyed while RAF Fighter Command lost twenty-eight.

COASTAL COMMAND OPERATIONS

The usual patrols and reconnaissance sorties were carried out by eighty-one aircraft and escort was provided for eighteen convoys.

1. A search for unidentified enemy units believed sighted thirty miles south of the Isle of Wight was carried out by four aircraft, but no enemy vessels were sighted.

2. Photographic reconnaissance was carried out over the Belgian and French Coasts from Zeebrugge to Cherbourg. One hundred barges were observed at Dunkirk with fifteen large black conning-towers in diamond formation at their

Flt Lt. Colin Rawlins DFC

Hampden pilot 144 Squadron

With my new crew, I did my first op on 7th September; it was a comparatively easy one to Ostend to attack the collection of barges being assembled by the Germans as part of the transport fleet for their planned invasion of England. We were in the middle of the Battle of Britain and the nation was on alert for a possible invasion. Leave for RAF personnel had been cancelled and Bomber Command was on permanent standby, theoretically ready to go out and stop the Germans by bombing them in their assembly ports, in their transport craft in the Channel and, if it came to it, on the British beaches where they landed. Historically, it was a time of great danger but, looking back, we in Bomber Command did not seem to be taking it very seriously and somehow, I think, the true gravity of the situation was not impressed upon us. We were young and probably thus irresponsible and far too self-centred to take a broad view; perhaps this was paradoxically a good thing as our morale was certainly not affected. As always, we could not imagine the prospect of the Germans conquering us. We thought we were winning the Battle of Britain and indeed we were, but it was much more of a close run thing that we optimistically believed at the time.

Nevertheless, the situation was considered serious enough to put a large part of Bomber Command's effort into attacks on the Channel ports where the Germans were gathering craft of all kinds, in particular barges from the extended system of inland waterways in North-Western Europe covering the great rivers of the Rhine and the Meuse and the canals of the Low Countries. Our trip to Ostend was part of a Bomber Command operation of nearly 100 aircraft, a major effort with the aircraft and crews then available, on all the suspect Channel ports.

head. At Ostend many barges were seen in the docks and at Cherbourg four destroyers were sighted.
There were no losses, but Hudson T2976 crashed without casualties when taking avoiding action at Bircham Newton.
Night operations
Eleven aircraft carried out a night attack on shipping in Boulogne Harbour. All the crews claimed to have dropped their bombs in the target area, but positive results were prevented because of the very thick mist. There were no losses.

BOMBER COMMAND OPERATIONS
1. Six Blenheims were despatched to attack enemy airfields but were obliged to abandon their tasks due to unsuitable weather conditions.
2. Six additional Blenheims carried out an uneventful offensive sweep over the North Sea.
Night operations
Seventy-two aircraft; thirteen Blenheims, twenty-six Wellingtons, twenty-six Hampdens and seven Whitleys were despatched to carry out night attacks on barges and shipping in Belgium and France, the docks and harbour at Emden, marshalling yards in Germany and to carry out incendiary raids on military stores in the Black Forest. The chief targets of barges and shipping were successfully attacked despite heavy opposition. The marshalling yards in the Ruhr, an oil plant at Gelsenkirchen and the Krupps works at Essen were also attacked. The incendiary attacks on the targets in the Black Forest caused fires and an explosion. Three aircraft of 6 Group dropped leaflets over Northern France.

OPERATIONAL LOSSES

'Tirpitz' Tait photographed later in his career, with 617 Sqn.

Whitley N1414 of 51 Squadron, carrying out an operational reconnaissance of the French/Belgian coastline, suffered an engine failure. The crew got their aircraft back across the North Sea, but had to carry out a crash-landing near Wells in Suffolk. Squadron Leader J. B. Tait* and his crew escaped unhurt.
* *Squadron Leader Tait, eventually known as 'Tirpitz' Tait latterly was to have an illustrious wartime career, reaching the rank of Group Captain and highly decorated with the DSO with three Bars and the DFC and Bar.*

Flying Officer H. Lynch-Blosse
Blenheim pilot 110 Squadron

Hugh Lynch-Blosse started his career in the RAF as a cadet at the RAF College, Cranwell, where he trained as a pilot. In his book '*Wings and Other Things*' published in 1990, he describes his involvement in the Battle of Britain.

"I was posted to 110 Blenheim Squadron at Wattisham in September 1940 and carried out my first operational 'trip' on the night of the 7th/8th September to bomb the invasion barges at Boulogne. We were driven out to our aircraft, clambered in and settled ourselves down. For some reason I cannot recall I strapped myself in more tightly than usual. Presumably I thought I'd feel more secure, which may or may not have been true - I know I was quite uncomfortable.

"We arrived over the target area at about 12,000 feet and Sgt. Richmond, our observer, directed me towards the docks, There was a half moon and not much cloud. Suddenly I saw red and white tracer curving up towards the aircraft. It seemed slightly ridiculous that such a display of lights could be lethal if any struck us. Then I saw black shapes all around us. For a fleeting moment I thought they were balloons, part of a barrage, and I panicked momentarily at the thought of flying into the cables. Then I realised it was flak bursting.

"Feeling that I was more or less on probation I resisted the temptation to weave and held the aircraft steady during the bomb run and release. I gave Richmond a minute or two to plot the bomb bursts which he said were in the dock area, then I dived away to get the hell out of the flak. In a minute or two all was peaceful and we were on our way back to Wattisham with myself on a high at the thought of having broken my duck. When we got back there was a noisy party in full swing in the Mess and after debriefing and our aircrew meal I felt qualified to join in, which I did wholeheartedly!

"Other sorties followed, Calais (twice) Boulogne again and Dunkirk so that in ten days I'd completed five 'Ops' - the last four with a new crew, Sgt. Davies and Sgt. Watkins."

On the 18th September Flying Officer Lynch-Blosse was promoted Flight Lieutenant and posted to No. 40 Squadron at Wyton with which he flew Blenheims until the 26th October. He then converted onto Wellingtons with No. 40 Squadron in November 1940 and resumed operations in the latter part of December. He continued on 'Ops' until the night of the 12th/13th/March, 1941, when he and his crew were shot down during a raid on Berlin. They baled out successfully but were taken prisoner. He survived his incarceration in the 'bag' being repatriated after four years and subsequently resumed his RAF career. He retired with the rank of Group Captain in 1967.

 STARTING BRIGHT, BUT BECOMING CLOUDY WITH SCATTERED SHOWERS.

ENEMY ACTIVITY

Because of the low cloud there was little activity during the morning apart from reconnaissance of coastal areas, however come midday there was a raid by one hundred enemy aircraft over Kent, some of which penetrated to the London area. Another small raid took place on London at about 17.30 hours. The night attack on London started before dark and continued until after 05.00 hours on the 9th, resulting in fires and casualties. Luftwaffe losses for the period were thirteen aircraft destroyed. RAF losses were four fighters.

COASTAL COMMAND OPERATIONS

There were offensive sweeps, reconnaissance and cover was provided for seventeen convoys, eighty-one aircraft were involved.

1. At 10.35 hours a Blenheim crew reported sighting fifteen to twenty enemy ships off Cap Gris Nez.
2. This enemy convoy was attacked by five Blenheims of 53 Squadron and a similar number of 59 Squadron. Bombs were dropped, especially near the leading ship, but results were not observed because of attacks by the strong fighter escort that shot down two 53 Squadron Blenheims.
3. Hudsons 'L' and 'V' of 253 Squadron attacked submarines ninety miles west of Bloody Foreland - one attack was claimed as successful.
4. Photo reconnaissance of Trondheim Fjord and the Channel ports was carried out.

BOMBER COMMAND OPERATIONS

Good cloud cover allowed the despatch in daylight of thirty-four Blenheims to attack Dutch and Belgian airfields and to carry out offensive patrols and reconnaissance over the Channel ports. Bombs were dropped on targets at Dunkirk and Boulogne and one aircraft bombed a convoy of six destroyers north-west of Terschelling. The results were not observed, two aircraft failed to return.

Night operations

130 aircraft took part in night raids on barges and shipping at Ostend and Boulogne, shipping at Bremen and Hamburg and marshalling yards in Germany.

1. Twenty-five Blenheims attacked barges at Ostend and Boulogne where fourteen claimed success.
2. Thirty Wellingtons were despatched to attack shipping at Boulogne and Emden. Half of the force successfully attacked the primary targets, but thirteen of them brought their bombs back. One of the 140 Squadron aircraft was badly shot up but made it back to base. An aircraft of 149 Squadron was forced to ditch on return.
3. Forty-nine Hampdens were given the task of attacking shipping in Hamburg, but the adverse weather frustrated their attacks. Some 'pressed on' and fires were caused near the Elbe Tunnel and Hansau Haven.
4. Twenty-six Whitleys were despatched to attack the dockyards at Bremen and the invasion fleet at Ostend. The weather at Ostend was atrocious and only one out of eleven managed to bomb. The conditions at Bremen were better, eleven out of fifteen bombed the primary, one bombed an alternative, two returned early and one failed to bomb.

> On this day we of 10 Squadron were honoured with a visit by the 'Father' of the Royal Air Force, Marshal of the RAF, Lord Hugh '*Boom*' Trenchard. He gave us a 'pep' talk emphasising the morale boosting effect our raids over Germany were having on our British civilians. I could verify this having just come back from leave during which everyone I talked with exhorted me in no uncertain terms to 'Give those Nazi so-and-so's a taste of their own medicine'. It was not only British morale which was affected by our raids. The Dutch aviation historian, Gerrie Zwanenberg MBE, was a teenager in occupied Holland during the war and observed, 'Although we knew our friends were just across the North Sea and that one day they would liberate us, it was the sound of the British bombers going to Germany night after night that gave us the courage to keep going. We will never forget them'.
>
> ***Larry Donnelly, 10 Squadron Whitley***

OPERATIONAL LOSSES

Blenheim R3779 'Z' of 53 Squadron, Detling, attacking an enemy convoy off Calais, was shot down by Bf109s. Flight Lieutenant I. H. Bartlett, Sergeant R. E Aldridge and Sergeant E. D. Sheldrick were posted missing in action and their names appear on the Runnymede Memorial.

Blenheim T2042 'H' of 53 Squadron, Detling, also attacking the enemy convoy off Calais, was shot down into the Channel by Bf109s. Pilot Officer R. G. Hall, Sergeant J. D. Randall and Sergeant M. B. Conacher were posted missing in action and their names appear on the Runnymede Memorial.

The above two Blenheims were claimed destroyed off Calais by Gefreiter Erhardt Scheidt of 1./JG 26 and Oberleutnant Ludwig Franzisket of 7./JG 27.

Hudson N7268 'D' of 224 Squadron, Leuchars, failed to return from a North Sea patrol. Pilot Officer R. G. Cuthbert, Pilot Officer I. H. Dolman, Sergeant E. Duffield and Sergeant M. Rees were posted missing in action and their names appear on the Runnymede Memorial.

Bf109 pilots from 4./JG 77 claimed two Hudsons during the day, Oberleutnant Helmut Henz at 12.10 hours and Feldwebel Erwin Sawallisch at 19.45.

Flying Officer D. Wykeham-Martin and his crew sit on their 53 Squadron Blenheim at Detling. The squadron lost two crews on this day, shot down by Bf109s, the single Vickers gun in the turret proving ineffective against the heavily armed fighters.

Blenheim R3730 of 82 Squadron, Watton, on reconnaissance of the Dutch/Belgian coasts, was lost without trace. Pilot Officer J. M. McCausland, Sergeant J. B. Philpott (RNZAF), and Sergeant R. S. Fletcher are commemorated on the Runnymede Memorial.

Blenheim R3195 of 82 Squadron, Watton, also on reconnaissance of the Dutch/Belgian coasts, was lost without trace. Flying Officer A. W. L. Cobbe, Pilot Officer H. M. Christopher and Sergeant H. Casswells are commemorated on the Runnymede Memorial.
It is probable that the two aircraft above fell to Bf109s. One was credited to Oberleutnant Rudolf Busch of 3./JG 51, while Leutnant Heinz Altendorf of 7./JG 53 claimed another.

Blenheim R3612 of 40 Squadron, Wyton, target Ostend, lost without trace. The names of Sergeant W. I. S. Patrick, Sergeant T. G. S. Jarman and Sergeant V. W. Pegler are recorded on the Runnymede Memorial.

Blenheim P6955 of 101 Squadron, West Raynham, target Boulogne, lost over the sea. Sergeant J. McKee's body was recovered and buried at his home town of South Shields. The names of the other crew members, Flight Lieutenant E. J. Palmer and Sergeant S. K. Booth appear on the Runnymede Memorial.

Our crew was one of the 10 Squadron crews selected to bomb the barges at Ostend. This flight was to be a 'check ride' for our newly formed crew. I was the only remaining member of our original crew, the others having been 'screened'. Our crew comprised 'new boys' apart from myself as WOp/AG and George Dove, filling in as tail-gunner until he took over as WOp with another new crew. Our 'check pilot' for this ride was Flying Officer 'Pinpoint' Prior, one of the squadron's most experienced pilots.
We took off from Leeming shortly after midnight and set course. The weather deteriorated as we flew over the North Sea and when we reached the Ostend area the cloud was down to the deck, completely obscuring the target. We flew around searching for a gap through which to descend but we were out of luck. So we were eventually forced to give it up as a bad job and return to base. We landed there, fed up and frustrated, at 05.50 hours.

Larry Donnelly, 10 Squadron Whitley

Sunday 8th September

Blenheim R2788 of 101 Squadron, West Raynham, target Boulogne, lost without trace. Sergeant C. W. Cooke, Sergeant C. J. Day and Sergeant R. N. Spencer are commemorated on the Runnymede Memorial.

Blenheim T1831 of 107 Squadron, Wattisham, target Ostend. The aircraft crashed at Wambercourt (Pas de Calais). The crew; Pilot Officer C. de V. Halkett, Sergeant A. V. Jacobs and Sergeant J. H. Easton are buried in Wambercourt Churchyard.

Blenheim T1851 of 107 Squadron, target Ostend, lost without trace. Flying Officer A. B. T. Cazalet, Sergeant L. Charnock and Sergeant E. F. Thompson are all commemorated on the Runnymede Memorial.

Blenheim L2188 of 218 Squadron, on reconnaissance, crashed in the North Sea. Sergeant G. L. Clayton and Sergeant F. C. Coish have no known graves. Sergeant G. Taylor is buried in the Bergen op Zoom War Cemetery.

Hampden P4287 of 50 Squadron, Lindholme, target Hamburg, reported at 23.59 hours that the crew was baling out. Squadron Leader F. A. Willan, Sergeant K. W. Wright, Sergeant A. B. Cox, Sergeant F. G. Brook all taken prisoner.

Wellington P9425 'W' of 149 Squadron, Mildenhall, target Boulogne, crashed into the sea off Clacton. Pilot Officer C. W. Parish managed to swim ashore, but the other members of the crew, Sergeant N. J. Bull, Squadron Leader L. V. Andrews, Sergeant J. L. Brown, Sergeant D. M. Payne and Pilot Officer W. G. Searles are commemorated on the Runnymede Memorial.

Wellington R3175 'V' of 149 Squadron, Mildenhall, target Boulogne, presumed lost over the sea. The crew; Pilot Officer J. L. Leeds, Sergeant R. A. Jerritt, Sergeant S. C. Grant, Sergeant H. G. Gledhill, Sergeant W. W. Crooks and Sergeant A. C. Martin are commemorated on the Runnymede Memorial.

Whitley P5094 of 10 Squadron, Leeming, target Ostend, crash landed at base on return. The pilot, Flying Officer J. C. Cairns, sustained a fractured leg. He was pulled from the aircraft by the WOP/AG Sergeant R. E. Nicholson just before the aircraft went on fire. Sergeant Nicholson received a verbal 'pat on the back' from the CO, but little else. He was shot down over Berlin on the 30th September/1st October 1940, and taken prisoner.

The crews of 149 Squadron pose for a photo after their first raid on Berlin. It is likely that some of the eleven squadron members killed on this night are amongst them.

RAIN AND SHOWERS, HEAVY IN THE EAST WITH SOME THUNDER.

Monday 9th September

ENEMY ACTIVITY

Only one or two reconnaissance flights were carried out by the Luftwaffe during the morning. The main attack in daylight took place during the afternoon when 300 enemy aircraft attacked targets in the Thames Estuary and south London area and Biggin Hill airfield. Some of the raiders penetrated as far west as Salisbury. During the raids the enemy maintained defensive patrols over Calais and Boulogne. An intercepted message from the Luftwaffe Gruppe HQ, read, 'Break off task if fighter opposition too strong'. The enemy also carried out reconnaissance flights over our convoys near the east coast. The night attacks started as darkness fell and a continuous stream of raiders headed for London where raids were maintained throughout the night. Some bombs fell in the City causing fires in the vicinity of St. Paul's Cathedral and the Guildhall. Dwellings in the East End and other residential districts in West and North London were hit and damaged causing casualties. The 'All Clear' was sounded at 04.55 hours. Minelaying was believed to have taken place between Newcastle and Middlesbrough. During the period the Luftwaffe lost twenty-five aircraft destroyed. The RAF lost twenty-one fighters.

The bomb-aimer's position in a Fairey Battle, not the safest place to be in 1940!

COASTAL COMMAND OPERATIONS

The usual patrols and reconnaissance sorties were carried out and escort provided for seventeen convoys. 115 aircraft were involved.

1. Attacks were made on enemy troop carriers, motor vessels and barges at sea, mainly off the coast near Ostend. Near misses and a hit on the stern of an auxiliary vessel were claimed.
2. Large concentrations of shipping and barges were reported -200 barges off Ostend, fourteen ships heading for Dunkirk and sixty to seventy ships were anchored south-east of Flushing. Two E-Boats off Cherbourg and St. Malo were sighted flying Red Cross flags.
3. Photo reconnaissance was carried out of German, French, Belgian and Dutch harbours. In the German harbour of Bremen the *SS Bremen* and *SS Europa* were photographed as was the battleship *Tirpitz* at Wilhelmshaven.

Night operations

1. Nine Blenheims of 53 and 59 Squadrons claimed successful attacks on barges at Boulogne.
2. Five Beauforts of 22 Squadron carried out a night attack on shipping at Boulogne and Calais. One aircraft failed to return.

BOMBER COMMAND OPERATIONS

1. Seven Blenheims were detailed to carry out a reconnaissance of the Dutch/Belgian ports but had to abandon because of unsuitable weather conditions. One aircraft failed to return.

Night operations

Fairey Battle squadrons, having resumed operations with 1 Group Bomber Command, were part of the force detailed to carry out night raids.

1. Six Fairey Battles of 103 and 150 Squadrons successfully bombed barges at Calais.
2. Twenty-one Blenheims carried out successful attacks on barges at Ostend.
3. Eighteen Wellingtons detailed to raid marshalling yards at Brussels and Krefeld, the docks at Wilhelmshaven and enemy airfields at Schipol and Bucken. Crews claimed successful attacks.
4. Twenty Whitleys were despatched to carry out raids on Berlin, Wesermunde, Wisburg and Hamburg. Three attacked the Neuköln gas works in Berlin and one crew reported a heavy explosion. Another attacked the BMW works at Spandau, but no results were observed. Bremen was attacked by seven crews who reported that fires were caused in the dock area. The other targets detailed were also attacked but results were not observed.
5. Of the twenty-one Hampdens despatched, eighteen attacked Hamburg, but cloud made observation of results difficult. One aircraft attacked Kiel and an additional three successfully laid mines off the Verdonne/Gironde area. Propaganda leaflets were dropped along the coast from the Lille area to St. Malo.

Monday 9th September

The crew of a Fleet Air Arm Blackburn Skua prepare for a sortie.

OPERATIONAL LOSSES

Skua L2889 of 801 Squadron Fleet Air Arm lost on operations. Petty Officer A. G. Clayton is remembered on the Lee-on-Solent Memorial. Petty Officer H. C. Kimber lies in the Trondheim Cemetery.

Beaufort N1146 'R' of 22 Squadron, Bircham Newton, target Calais/Boulogne. Sergeant R. D. Gunn's body was washed ashore in Britain. Sergeant C. S. F. Beer was found at Texel. The bodies of Sergeant S. G. Twitchin and Sergeant J. Murray and were never found and their names appear on the Runnymede Memorial.

Blenheim. T1894 of 105 Squadron, Watton, on reconnaissance of invasion ports, was lost without trace. The names of Sergeant D. D. R. Hodson, Sergeant E. B. Palmer and Sergeant R. Green are commemorated on the Runnymede Memorial.
This aircraft fell to Leutnant Waldemar Wübke of 9./JG 54 at 18.24 hours

Fairey Battle L5010 of 103 Squadron, Newton, target Calais, lost without trace. Sergeant F. Drinkwater, Pilot Officer W. A. Cooper and Squadron Leader Sub Lieutenant RN) R. A. de Sandoval-Siervier are commemorated on the Runnymede Memorial.

Whitley P5021 of 51 Squadron, Dishforth, target Berlin, hit by Flak and ditched on return 120 miles east of the Firth of Forth. Sergeant W. G. McAlister drowned, but Pilot Officer Millson, Sergeant H. C. G. Brook, Sergeant E. A. Young and Flying Officer D. Careless were rescued by a Royal Navy launch.

Flight Lieutenant Mike Henry DFC
Blenheim gunner 110 Squadron

TARGET - INVASION BARGES IN BOULOGNE HARBOUR
F/O Lynch-Blosse, Sgt. Richmond, Sgt. Henry
Blenheim R3772

Just like the preceding operation, we received a similar reception from the ground defences (one thing about the mass of flak, it kept the night fighters away!). Boulogne was just as well defended as Dunkirk, If anything, more so. The only relief we had on these Channel port sorties was the fact they were on the coast and we only had to survive the brief period over the target while we bombed before turning round and headed out to sea. It was then that the gunner had to be vigilant, as night fighters could be waiting over the sea. Back at base there could be night intruders waiting to pounce on any aircraft thinking that it was completely safe from enemy action. We had also to watch the friendly defences, it wasn't unknown for our own aircraft to be fired upon by enthusiastic, British gunners. The Navy, also, had itchy fingers. We always had the appropriate colour of the period fixed firmly in the breech of our Verey pistol. I too could send the letters of the period on the downward recognition light.

ENEMY ACTIVITY

Luftwaffe aircraft carried out early morning reconnaissance of the Humber, Digby, Yarmouth and convoys along the East Coast. Later Tangmere, Hastings and Shoreham were visited. One aircraft got over Central London but low cloud prevented interception. In the evening there were three small raids on Poling, Tangmere and Portsmouth. Six other raids headed for London but they were intercepted, two aircraft were shot down and the remainder turned tail. That night the raids started early and penetrated the London defences, but they were dispersed by 22.00 hours. Between 21.00 hours and 01.00 hours six raids comprising 130 aircraft approached the Thames Estuary. The 'all clear' in the area was sounded at 04.30 hours. Other targets during the night were south Wales, the Midlands and Liverpool and minelaying was also carried out. During the period the Luftwaffe lost four aircraft destroyed. The only RAF casualty was one aircraft in a non-combat incident.

COASTAL COMMAND OPERATIONS

Ninety-three aircraft carried out sixty-two anti invasion, anti submarine patrols and reconnaissance sorties. Air escort was provided for eighteen convoys.

1. Three Blenheims of 53 Squadron and five of 59 Squadron attacked enemy shipping off Calais.
2. PRU photographs showed thirty small ships at the entrance to Boulogne Harbour; fourteen large motor vessels eight miles off Flushing heading south; twelve small boats off Ostend; fourteen small vessels and 140 barges at Calais; eleven large vessels heading around Cap Gris Nez towards Boulogne. There were no losses.

Night operations

1. Three Beauforts of 22 Squadron were despatched to lay mines in the Cuxhaven area.
2. Five Blenheims and four FAA Swordfish were detailed to attack Barges off Calais and E-Boats and destroyers off Le Havre. They met with little success, their attempts being hampered by adverse weather conditions.
3. One Hudson attacked twenty-eight motor vessels ten miles north of Terschelling, claiming to have scored a hit on one vessel with a 250lb bomb. There were no losses.

BOMBER COMMAND OPERATIONS

1. Two Blenheims attempted a reconnaissance of the Dutch Coast in daylight but they were frustrated by adverse weather conditions.
2. Six other Blenheims carried out a reconnaissance over the North Sea. There were no losses.

Night operations

The Battle of the Barges was 'hotting' up and the German invasion fleet in the Channel ports was the main target for night strikes. All the bomber groups were involved.

1. Six Fairey Battles of 1 Group (103 and 150 Squadrons) attacked barges and shipping in Boulogne Harbour.
2. Thirty-three Blenheims of 2 Group attacked invasion fleet concentrations at Flushing and Ostend Harbours. Gun emplacements at Cap Gris Nez were also attacked.
3. Twenty-six Wellingtons of 3 Group also attacked barges and shipping in Ostend and Flushing Harbours as well as railway targets at Brussels and the airfields at Evere and Deurne.
4. Seventeen Whitleys of 4 Group attacked the dockyards at Bremen and what was claimed by the crews a very successful attack on the Potsdammer railway station in Berlin. Two aircraft failed to return.
5. Twenty-one Hampdens of 5 Group attacked barges, shipping and port installations at Calais and Ostend Harbours. Another three laid mines.

OPERATIONAL LOSSES

Hampden P4371 of 44 Squadron, Waddington, target Calais, crashed into the sea. Flight Lieutenant D. J. Rogers, Sergeant R. J. Brading and Sergeant H. G. Lacey have no known graves, but Sergeant B. N. Westhorp is buried in the Communal Cemetery Oye-Plage.

Hampden L4097 of 50 Squadron, Lindholme, target Ostend, shot down into the sea off Ostend. Flight Lieutenant R. J. Reed (Australian) and Pilot Officer P. W. Roylance were buried at Ostend. Sergeant R. Halls and Sergeant W. A. Johnson are commemorated on the Runnymede Memorial.

Whitley T4134 'T' of 58 Squadron, Linton-on-Ouse, target Bremen, failed to return. Pilot Officer J. E. Thompson, Pilot Officer T. H. Hadley, Sergeant K. D. Hall, Sergeant W. Hughes and Sergeant W. Bull were all taken prisoner.

Whitley T4134 GE-T of 58 Squadron which appears to have force landed on a beach, (before the tide came in!)

Whitley P5042 of 77 Squadron, Linton-on-Ouse, target Bremen, crashed east-north-east of Zwolle. Sergeant J. A. G. Deans*, Sergeant G. B. Clarke, Sergeant H. J. Agnew, Sergeant H. Parkes and Sergeant F. A. Hill were all taken prisoner.

* *Sergeant Deans achieved fame for his leadership in PoW camps Stalag Luft. III and IV. He was subsequently awarded the MBE for his sterling work.*

Wednesday 11th September

SUNNY AT TIMES WITH ISOLATED SHOWERS.

ENEMY ACTIVITY

Activity during the day was following a pattern. In the morning reconnaissance sorties were carried out followed by bombing raids later. Today at 15.30 hours a force of 200 aircraft crossed the Kent coast and fifty penetrated the London area. Shortly afterwards seventy-five aircraft attacked Southampton. Night activity was on a reduced scale. The early raid which started at 20.20 hours was repulsed by the AA Barrage. This was followed from 23.45 hours by raids by single aircraft which approached London from different directions the main damage being caused to Poplar, Shoreditch, Camberwell and London Docks. The all clear was sounded at 05.00 hours. A number of other raids took place over Lancashire and the Midlands, but no serious damage was reported. During the period the Luftwaffe lost twenty-two aircraft destroyed. The RAF lost thirty-one aircraft destroyed.

COASTAL COMMAND OPERATIONS

One hundred and one aircraft carried out the usual reconnaissance patrols, sweeps, and also provided cover for twenty-five convoys.

1. A Blenheim sighted a convoy of eight motor vessels four smaller vessels and six E-Boats between Dunkirk and Nieuport.
2. Five Beauforts failed to locate the convoy but claimed a hit on a ship in the Ostend Roads. Five other ships were machine-gunned.
3. Five Blenheims of 53 squadron and six of 59 Squadron, with FAA Albacores escorted by twelve Blenheim IV (Fs) attacked the convoy off Calais. Intense opposition from a coastal AA battery and thirty-six Bf109s was encountered. Three Bf109s were brought down and a Do18 was damaged. Two Blenheims were lost.

The Germans claimed four Albacores and four Blenheims in this encounter, Albacores by Oberleutnants Oskar Strack and Günther Büsgen of 1./JG 52 and by Oberleutnant Walter Fiel and Siegfried Stronck of 8./JG 53 and Blenheims by Büsgen and Leutnant Franz Essl of 1./JG 52, Fiel of 8./JG 53 and Oberleutnant Jakob Stoll of 9./JG 53.

4. A Blenheim on routine patrol scored a 'near miss' on five destroyers south-west of Calais.
5. Photographic reconnaissance of enemy harbours showed the battleship *Bismarck* at Hamburg, the *SS Bremen* and *SS. Europa* at Bremerhaven together with three destroyers and five torpedo boats.
6. Hudson 'M' of 220 Squadron attacked a U-Boat seventy-one miles from Horns Reef. There was no positive result.

Night operations

Successful minelaying was carried out by five aircraft at Le Havre. There no losses.

BOMBER COMMAND OPERATIONS

1. Three Blenheims were detailed to carry out a reconnaissance of the French/Dutch Coasts. The weather was unsuitable for reconnaissance but one aircraft dropped bombs on an enemy convoy off the Belgian coast. No result was observed.
2. Six other Blenheims carried out a routine sweep over the North Sea. There were no losses.

Night operations

The night attacks were concentrated on the invasion fleet in the German and occupied Channel ports, as well as marshalling yards in Germany. Berlin was also a target.

1. Six Fairey Battles of 103 and 150 Squadrons again attacked shipping at Boulogne. Five claimed successful attacks.
2. Thirty-six Blenheims attacked barges and shipping at Calais, Flushing and Ostend and the guns at Cap Gris Nez.
3. Forty-one Wellingtons were detailed to attack the marshalling yards at Hamm, Ehrang, Mannheim, Köln and Koblenz as well as the docks at Ostend. Thirty-six attacked their primary targets claiming success. One aircraft failed to return.
4. The twenty-seven Hampdens concentrated their attacks on shipping and installations at Bremerhaven, Hamburg and Wilhelmshaven. Bombs were observed bursting near the *SS Bremen*. Three aircraft carried out mine-laying off Verdonne while five more mined the Elbe Estuary.
5. The twenty Whitleys detailed had shipyards and fuel stocks at Bremen and the Anhalter railway station and the aerodrome at Templehof as their targets. 51 Squadron sent four crews to Berlin who bombed their primary target. One aircraft suffered Flak damage. Another four aircraft sent to Bremen also claimed to have bombed the primary target.

Our crew was one of the seven sent to Bremen. We were again on a 'check ride' with '*Pin Point*' Prior because of our abortive trip on the eighth. We took off from Leeming at 19.35 hours and the outbound flight proceeded without incident. As we approached Bremen we could see the defences were already in action, searchlights probing the darkness while the light and heavy Flak hosed upwards. I'd had a healthy respect for the Bremen defences after we received a clobbering from them during a trip in May. As we got closer there were fires burning in the target area. There was no need to drop flares so I stayed up front to watch the proceedings. We ran through the usual gauntlet of Flak on our first run and dropped the first stick. Our new skipper had decided we would carry out three runs - I think he was trying to impress '*Pin Point*'. Beginner's luck must have been with him because we got through without a scratch and George Dove in the tail reported we had stoked-up the fires and when we were well on our way back to base he could still see them.

We got back safely having passed our 'check ride' with flying colours, however, I recall hoping that on future trips our skipper be more economical with the bomb runs - thee times round Bremen is pushing it!

Larry Donnelly, 10 Squadron Whitley

Flight Lieutenant Mike Henry DFC

Blenheim gunner 110 Squadron

TARGET - INVASION BARGES IN CALAIS
F/Lt. Powell, Sgt. Richmond, Sgt. Henry
Blenheim T1993

Back with my own crew. This time we attacked the third Channel port on our list - Calais. Much the same awe-inspiring sight met our eyes. Searchlights In great profusion, light and heavy flak; 'flaming onions' which came up in a string, just like enlarged Christmas decorations, then levelling out at approximately our height to burst one after the other! One's heart sometimes did a loop when out of the corner of one's eye the frightening moment when the heavy flak bursts looked like a balloon barrage. Nowadays, living in Kent, I took the ferry to Calais every month to purchase my 'medicine' (whisky) and my wife's - some good Californian red wine! And I may say I am lucky to be able to do that when I think back to those vivid and frightening days.

78 Squadron despatched five crews to Berlin, one returned early, two bombed the primary and the other two bombed alternatives. 10 Squadron despatched seven aircraft to attack the shipping and fuel stores at Bremen, all bombed the primary.

OPERATIONAL LOSSES

Blenheim IV(F) Z5725 'G' of 235 Squadron, Thorney Island, lost escorting an Albacore strike off Calais. Flight Lieutenant F. W. Flood, Pilot Officer N. B. Shorrocks and Sergeant B. R. Sharp were presumed killed and recorded on the Runnymede Memorial.

Blenheim IV(F) L9396 'F' of 235 Squadron, Thorney Island, shot down when escorting Albacores on a shipping strike off Calais. Pilot Officer P. C. Wickings-Smith, Pilot Officer A. W. V. Green and Sergeant R. D. H. Watts were presumed killed and recorded on the Runnymede Memorial.

Hampden P1338 of 44 Squadron, Waddington, target Bremerhaven. Flight Lieutenant T. L. S. Smythe DFC, Pilot Officer S. C. Wise, Sergeant W. H. Jones and Flying Officer W. F. E. Coombes are all buried in Becklingen War Cemetery at Saltau.

Hampden X2913 of 44 Squadron, Waddington, target. Bremerhaven, crashed into the sea after being hit by Flak. Pilot Officer D. E. Stewart, Sergeant W. Goodwill and Sergeant G. J. Hobson are buried in Becklingen War Cemetery at Saltau. The name of Sergeant D. A. Joyce is on the Runnymede Memorial.

Wellington 'R' of 38 Squadron, Marham, target Ostend, shot down by Flak and crashed near the central railway station at Ostend. Flying Officer R. G. Allen, Pilot Officer C. T. Dufton, Sergeant E. James, Sergeant J. W. Johnstone, Sergeant C. E Matthews and Sergeant F. W. Noakes are all buried in the New Communal Cemetery Ostend.

Blenheim fighters of 235 Squadron at Manston prior to the Battle of Britain.

Thursday 12th September

SUNNY AT TIMES, BUT WIDESPREAD SHOWERS.

ENEMY ACTIVITY

Although enemy bombing activity was on a reduced scale there was an increase in reconnaissance flights over southern England. The isolated bombing raids were widespread; the Majestic Hotel at Harrogate, commandeered by the RAF, was bombed and the main GWR rail services were interrupted at Reading. During the afternoon incendiaries fell on Tunbridge Wells, causing fires. During the night the raids were also reduced, but wide-spread over south Wales and the Midlands, however raids over London lasted for seven hours. Luftwaffe losses during the period were three aircraft destroyed. The RAF lost two aircraft destroyed.

COASTAL COMMAND OPERATIONS

Anti invasion, anti submarine and reconnaissance patrols were carried out and escort provided for seventeen convoys.
1. Four Blenheims of 59 Squadron escorted by three Blenheim IV(F)s attacked fifteen motor vessels off Cap de la Hague. A tanker was hit.
2. Hudson 'V' of 206 Squadron attacked a motor vessel five miles from Maas Light.
3. PRU reported two medium size ships leaving Boulogne; 'E'/Torpedo motor boats in two lines of three abreast thirty-four miles from Cherbourg; six medium size ships (four of which were thought to be light cruisers) anchored off Le Verdonne; seventy-five coastal craft, some of them towing barges from Dunkirk and a similar number anchored off Dunkirk.

BOMBER COMMAND OPERATIONS

1. Routine reconnaissance was carried out by Blenheims over the North Sea. Other planned daylight operations sere abandoned because of lack of suitable cloud cover.

Night operations

The very bad weather over the most of Germany and the occupied countries resulted in most of the night raids being cancelled. However, nineteen Wellington crews claimed successful attacks on marshalling yards at Emden and Flushing, despite the weather.

OPERATIONAL LOSSES

There were no losses

Sergeant Roy Richards

Wellington Gunner 38 Squadron

Roy Richards joined No. 38 Squadron on 12th September 1940 and he writes describing his first 'trip' during the Battle of Britain..

"Our first operation was to bomb the landing barges at Calais. The other 38 Squadron crews were attacking Berlin, but because we were a 'fresher' crew we were given a shorter trip. Take-off was at 22.30 hours and after an uneventful flight we arrived over the target area and carried out our bomb run, however our New Zealander observer missed the target with his first stick. After a crew 'confab' it was agreed we would go round again and carry out another attack from a shallow dive. I cannot remember at what height we were when we were caught in a searchlight from which we couldn't escape and we were hit by flak. The observer was badly hit in the groin so he was helped back to the bed in the fuselage and injected with morphine. We set course for home but the WOP then reported that his W/T was U/S, however between them the captain and second pilot managed to navigate us back across the Channel and from there map read us back to Marham. I was flying in the front turret and I was able to guide us to our identification beacon. As we prepared to land the captain informed us that our hydraulics had been damaged by flak and a belly-landing would be necessary.
Our W/T worked so we were able to inform ground control of our intentions. I left the front turret to take up my landing position and I'm glad to say the skipper carried out a first-class wheels-up landing. Fortunately there was no fire and we were able to get out of the aircraft and into the waiting ambulance without delay. Incidentally Marham was still a grass airfield.
I seem to remember the next morning being told that a 500lb bomb was found hung-up in the bomb bay! The flight had amounted to three and a half hours.
I was selected to fly with another crew two days later to attack shipping at Ostend - no problem!"

Roy Richards continued and survived his 'tour' and the war. He now lives in Somerset not far from Yeovilton and spends his time 'Bird watching' - Naval Harriers from Yeovilton.

Friday 13th September

The Channel Ports were becoming a very dangerous place, as illustrated by the damage inflicted upon this 83 Squadron Hampden in September 1940.

ENEMY ACTIVITY

During daytime the enemy carried out continuous small raids. Bombs fell on Buckingham Palace and incendiaries fell in Downing Street and on the House of Lords. Later, bombs fell on Central London, Kent, Surrey and Northern Ireland. It was estimated that ninety enemy aircraft were involved. That night raids commenced at 20.45 hours and raiders flew over London at ten minute intervals. Enemy activity was also reported over East Anglia, south Wales, Bristol and as far north as the Firth of Forth. The Luftwaffe losses were six aircraft destroyed. The RAF lost two aircraft destroyed.

COASTAL COMMAND OPERATIONS

Anti invasion, anti submarine and reconnaissance patrols were carried out and air escort provided for twenty-one convoys.

1. During the afternoon an enemy convoy comprising ten transport barges, two E-Boats and ten motor vessels were sighted off Boulogne. Five motor vessels towing barges were also sighted off Cap Gris Nez. Three Blenheims of 53 Squadron and five of 59 Squadron attacked the enemy convoy at twenty minute intervals and claimed success.
2. PRU sorties revealed concentrations of barges at Ostend, Blankenberge, Dunkirk and Calais.

Night operations

A night mining sortie was successfully carried out by six aircraft off Le Havre.

BOMBER COMMAND OPERATIONS

1. Sixteen Blenheims were despatched to carry out reconnaissance over The Hague and Boulogne, but most sorties had to be abandoned because of unsuitable weather. A successful reconnaissance was made over the Ostend and Haamstede area and attacks were made on Zeebrugge and Calais. There were no losses.

Night operations

The Battle of the Barges continued and successful night attacks were carried out on concentrations of barges and shipping at Antwerp, Ostend, Dunkirk, Calais and also on gun emplacements at Cap Gris Nez.

1. Thirty-four Blenheims were despatched, twenty claimed successful attacks on barges at Calais and Dunkirk. Other aircraft attacked Ostend.
2. Fifteen out of the eighteen Wellingtons despatched to Antwerp carried out successful attacks.
3. All nineteen Whitleys sent to attack the barges at Dunkirk and Calais claimed success.
4. Successful attacks were carried out on the shipping in Boulogne and Ostend by twenty Hampdens. Eighty barges were sunk in Ostend harbour.

OPERATIONAL LOSSES

Skua L2912 of 801 Squadron Fleet Air Arm, lost on operations off Norway. Petty Officer E. G. R. Harwin and Naval Airman J. R. Maunder are buried at Haugesund, near Bergen, Norway.

Blenheim L9451 'V' of 248 Squadron, Sumburgh, failed to return from a patrol to Norway. The body of Sergeant W. J. Garfield was found and buried at Bergen. Sergeant B. W. Mesner and Sergeant A. Kay were posted as missing in action and recorded on the Runnymede Memorial.

Blenheim R2786 of 15 Squadron, Wyton, target invasion ports, was lost without trace. The names of Sergeant O. M. Yeomans, Sergeant R. E. Hollingshead and Pilot Officer P. L. N. Hughes have no known graves and are inscribed on the Runnymede Memorial

Hampden X2922 of 61 Squadron, Hemswell, target Boulogne, crashed in the sea off the French coast. Flight Lieutenant D. J. How DFC and Sergeant R. C. Dickinson DFM are buried in the Eastern Cemetery at Boulogne. Sergeant A. A. Brooker rests in the Wimeroux Communal Cemetery. Pilot Officer T. H. N. Lane, who has no known grave, is commemorated on the Runnymede Memorial.

Saturday 14th September

Heavy cloud bringing showers and thunder in places.

Feldwebel Kurt Goltsch of 8/JG2 who shot down the PRU Spitfire P9453 on this day.

ENEMY ACTIVITY

Until late in the afternoon enemy activity was confined to raids by single aircraft and reconnaissance sorties. The first raid of any size was by 150 aircraft, some of which penetrated to London. It was followed by another raid on the London area by one hundred aircraft, some of these also reached London. Although the weather conditions were favourable for night raids they were on a reduced scale. There were only small raids and single aircraft got as far as London. A certain amount of activity also took place over the Humber to the Wash as well as over Lincolnshire. The 'all clear' sounded at 04.00 hours when enemy activity ceased. Luftwaffe losses were seven aircraft destroyed. RAF losses were thirteen aircraft destroyed.

COASTAL COMMAND OPERATIONS

Sixty-three aircraft carried out the usual offensive sweeps and reconnaissance as well as providing escort for twenty-one convoys.

1. Two Sunderlands escorted nine Fairey Battles from Wick to Iceland.
2. A Hudson fought off and damaged two He115s eighty miles from Terschelling.
3. Three Beauforts of 22 Squadron operating from Bircham Newton attempted what turned out to be an unsuccessful torpedo strike during the evening in the Flushing Roads.
4. PRU aircraft took pictures of Zeebrugge and Flushing.

BOMBER COMMAND OPERATIONS

One of six Blenheims on a North Sea sweep bombed a suspected U-Boat fifty-five miles north-east of Peterhead. There were no positive results.

2. Eight other Blenheims despatched on a daylight reconnaissance of the occupied ports. All abandoned because of lack of cloud cover except one which bombed Haamstede aerodrome.

Night operations

The principal targets for the night raids were shipping and barges in the Channel ports and marshalling yards in Germany and Belgium.

1. Of the eighteen Blenheims despatched, four bombed barges at Ostend, five bombed barges at Calais and three bombed barges at Dunkirk. Two did not complete operations because of adverse weather. Five successfully bombed the gun emplacements at Cap Gris Nez.
2. Fifty-five Wellingtons were despatched and successfully attacked marshalling yards at Hamm, Krefeld, Brussels, Ehrang, Soest and shipping at Antwerp. Six attacked an enemy headquarters at Chateau Argento.
3. Twelve Fairey Battles bombed shipping in Boulogne.
4. Thirty-eight Hampdens carried out successful attacks on marshalling yards at Mannheim and Osnabrük as well as shipping at Ostend, Calais and Dunkirk.
5. Of the eleven Whitleys sent to bomb shipping, ten bombed successfully at Antwerp. The other bombed at Flushing.

Our crew was on the Antwerp target. I flew as tail gunner to give George Dove the opportunity to keep his hand in operating the W/T as he was soon joining another crew as first WOp/AG. It also appealed to me to get my hands on the four Brownings for a change! The weather wasn't too good as we flew over the North Sea, but it improved as we got near to Antwerp. Fires were already burning in the target area and the bomb-aimer identified it and set us up for our attack. Despite the opposition from the defences he took us in for two runs at 12,000 feet. After our second run I was able to report a big explosion and fires in the target area. We lost no time getting away from the defences and setting course for base. We got a bit of a jolt when I spotted a Bf110 night fighter flying above us. I kept him in my sights but thankfully he flew off without spotting us. We landed safely back at Leeming at 01.50 hours. It was subsequently reported that severe damage had been inflicted at Antwerp."

Larry Donnelly, 10 Squadron Whitley

Flight Lieutenant Mike Henry DFC

Blenheim gunner 110 Squadron

TARGET - INVASION BARGES IN CALAIS HARBOUR

F/Lt. Powell, Sgt. Richmond, Sgt. Henry

Blenheim T1993

The day before the official climax of the Battle of Britain, our crew was one of five detailed to attack Calais. Once again we approached the target, feeling that we were pushing our luck, to meet the same sort of greeting - the pretty-looking but bloody dangerous flak. Once again we returned without any holes for the ground crews to patch. One never stopped wondering how on earth an aircraft can fly through such a barrage and not get a scratch. Mark you, some did. I expect that other squadrons engaged in similar operations lost someone.

It was about this time when night attacks started on London. I distinctly remember looking west from my turret when returning from the Channel port area, and seeing a glow on the horizon. Mistaking it for a full moon about to appear, I wasn't aware that my home town was being blitzed until hearing the BBC news the following morning. Naturally, I was mad and didn't hold any more feelings of guilt being party to dropping bombs on those below. When the East End and dockland got the worst of the enemy attacks — the incendiaries starting conflagrations right across the capital - I was thinking that my parents, at least, might be safer living on the south west side of London. However, it was a shock to see one's own town being ravaged, and it made us even more determined to press on with our attacks.

OPERATIONAL LOSSES

Spitfire P9453 of the PRU, Heston, on a photographic reconnaissance over Boulogne/Le Havre in the morning, failed to return. Flying Officer A. E. Hyde-Parker was posted as missing in action and his name appears on the Runnymede Memorial.
This would appear to have been shot down by a Bf109 of 8./JG 2, credited to Feldwebel Kurt Goltsch.

Spitfire R6879 of the PRU Heston, on a low level photographic reconnaissance over the Belgian Coast, was hit by Flak. Flying Officer P. L. Dakeyne baled out, landed among German troops, and was captured.

Whitley P4966 of 10 Squadron, Leeming, suffered an engine failure outbound and was forced to ditch twenty miles off Spurn Head. Despite the rough sea they carried out a successful ditching and boarded their dinghy safely. After a couple of hours they were picked up by the RN mine sweeper *Kurd* which had just laid the mine-field into which the Whitley had alighted! Squadron Leader K. F. Ferguson and his crew were entertained by the Navy for two days before being put ashore at Grimsby.

Mark Niman was the rear gunner of Whitley P4966 which ditched in the North Sea with engine trouble. Less than a month later, the same crew were forced to bale out of another Whitley returning from Stettin.

Whitley N1478 of 78 Squadron, Dishforth, target Vlissingen, lost without trace. Flying Officer C. S. Robson, Sergeant L. J. Furze, Sergeant R. M. Heyworth, Sergeant J. Kelly and Sergeant J. C. Greig are all commemorated on the Runnymede Memorial.

Sunday 15th September SUNNY WITH SOME HIGH CLOUD IN PLACES, BECOMING CLEARER AT NIGHT.

The wreck of a Dornier Do17 of 8./KG76 shot down on 15th September at Castle Hill, Shoreham.

ENEMY ACTIVITY

The reduction in the number of Luftwaffe raiders on the previous day was a portent of today's activity. The 15th of September was the day agreed by the Germans in August for the start of '*Sealion*' (the invasion of Britain). However, instead it turned out to be the climax of the Battle of Britain. Fighter Command squadrons had been strengthened enormously by the Germans switching their attacks from fighter airfields to London, so fighter sorties were correspondingly reduced. This, together with Bomber Command and Coastal Command attacks against the German invasion fleet and raids on Berlin, were influential in Hitler's postponement and eventual cancellation of *Operation Sealion*. The first raid of the day was by one hundred Do17s escorted by fighters on London, but it was broken up before the raiders reached the Capital. Their bombs were dropped at random across south-east England. Two bombs fell on Buckingham Palace, but failed to explode, providing propaganda peddlers with something to shout about. Another huge formation of bombers headed for London soon after 14.00 hours, but fighters, having been re-armed after the first raid, intercepted them and inflicted decisive losses. The Luftwaffe fighter escort failed to protect the bombers from destruction. Minor raids which took place over south-west England failed to cause any damage of consequence. London was the main object for raids throughout the night. Other raids penetrated to the Midlands and the Bristol Channel areas. A Boulton-Paul Defiant night fighter pilot destroyed one He111 and claimed another as probable. The total Luftwaffe loss during the period was fifty-six aircraft destroyed. RAF losses were twenty-six aircraft destroyed.

A day to remember forever!

COASTAL COMMAND OPERATIONS

106 aircraft continued the daily anti invasion, anti submarine patrols, reconnaissance, defensive sorties and minelaying operations. Air escort was also provided for twenty convoys.

1. Anson R3369 of 48 Squadron found an 8,000 ton motor vessel burning at the stern, but it was not sinking and four armed trawlers were standing by.
2. Anson 'J' of 500 Squadron on convoy escort was attacked by enemy aircraft. The Anson gunner was wounded.

Feldwebel Hermann Neuhoff of 7./JG 53 claimed a Blenheim some 20 kilometres from Etaples at 19.00, possibly this aircraft.

3. Five Blenheims of 53 Squadron carried out a daylight strike on shipping at Sangatte.
4. Sunderland 'F' of 204 squadron attacked a U-Boat at position, 56 degrees 08'N/08 degrees 09'W. No positive result was observed.
5. PRU photographs showed several enemy naval units in Cherbourg Harbour and concentrations of barges at Flushing and Boulogne.

Night operations

1. Two Beauforts of 22 Squadron, 'P' and 'K' carried out a night torpedo strike on shipping off Ijmuiden. Flight Lieutenant Francis carried out the first successful night torpedo attack on a 3,000 ton motor vessel.
2. Five Blenheims of 53 Squadron and eight of 59 Squadron carried out a successful night strike on shipping at Le Havre.
3. Six FAA Swordfish laid mines off Flushing.

Sergeant John Hannah, VC

Hampden WOp/AG 83 Squadron

On the night of the 15th/16th September 1940, Sergeant Hannah was the wireless operator in a Hampden aircraft attacking a large concentration of invasion barges at Antwerp during the Battle of Britain. During the attack the aircraft was subjected to intense anti-aircraft fire and received a direct hit which burst inside the bomb compartment, starting a fire in the wireless operator's and rear gunner's areas. Both the port and starboard petrol tanks had been holed and there was grave risk of the fire spreading. In the meantime both the rear gunner and the navigator had been forced to bale out to save themselves from the fire. Sergeant Hannah could havc acted likewise, but he fought his way through the fire to obtain two extinguishers with which he fought the fire. When they were empty he beat out the flames with his W/T log book and his gloved hands. During this time ammunition was exploding in all directions and he was almost blinded by the fumes and the intense heat. Despite suffering burns to his face and eyes he continued until he succeeded in extinguishing the fire. He then crawled forward and passed the navigator's maps to his pilot enabling him to bring the damaged aircraft back to base.

Sergeant Hannah, who was only eighteen years of age, was subsequently awarded the Victoria Cross in recognition for his conspicuous bravery. This was the second VC to be awarded to Bomber Command in World War II.

BOMBER COMMAND OPERATIONS

1. The only daylight operation carried out was an uneventful North Sea sweep by six Blenheims. All other daylight tasks were abandoned because of lack of cloud cover.

Night operations

The Bomber Command squadrons kept up the pressure with night strikes on the invasion ports and German targets. 'Maximum Effort' was the order of the day and night.

1. Forty-eight Blenheims successfully attacked the barges at Boulogne, Dunkirk, Flushing and the Guns at Cap Gris Nez.
2. Twenty-four Whitleys attacked a variety of targets, Berlin, Hamburg, Wesermunde, Wilhelmshaven, Cuxhaven, Dunkirk and Wangerooge. Most crews claimed successful attacks.
3. Thirty-six Wellingtons successfully attacked the marshalling yards at Soest, Krefeld and Brussels as well as shipping at Calais.
4. Twelve Fairey Battles (some of them from Polish squadrons) bombed Boulogne.
5. Thirty-nine Hampdens bombed the marshalling yards at Hamm, Osnabrük and shipping at Antwerp. Another six mined the Elbe Estuary.

There were no losses but Hampden P1355 of 83 Squadron, while attacking shipping in Antwerp from low level, (2,000 feet) received a direct hit by Flak in the bomb-bay, setting it on fire. Within seconds the bottom gun turret was disintegrating with the heat. The gunner was forced to bale out to save himself. Believing the aircraft to be doomed, the navigator also baled out. Sergeant John Hannah, the wireless operator, could have done the same but instead he fought the flames and managed to quell them using his hands and his W/T log book. He was badly burned in the process. He then gave assistance to his pilot and enabled him to fly the crippled aircraft back to base. For his valour Sergeant Hannah was subsequently awarded the Victoria Cross, becoming only the second and the youngest Bomber Command recipient in World War II. His pilot, Pilot Officer C. A. Connor was awarded the DFC at the same time, but unfortunately he lost his life when his aircraft crashed into the Humber returning from a raid on Kiel on the 2nd/3rd November 1940.

OPERATIONAL LOSSES

There were no losses

Monday 16th September

The Sunderlands of Coastal Command kept up their patrols throughout the Battle of Britain, providing some form of air cover for the many convoys passing through the British coastal waters and beyond.

ENEMY ACTIVITY

The weather changed dramatically with low cloud, but Goering persisted in sending his bombers in force over Kent to attack London during the morning. However, they were met by reinforced fighter defences which prevented the main force from pressing home their attacks. The adverse weather limited other raids to reconnaissance off and over the coasts. It was estimated that some 350 enemy aircraft flew over the UK during daylight hours. That night raids were of greater intensity, carried out in two phases - from 19.40 hours to 02.40 hours and 03.30 hours to 05.30 hours. The first phase penetrated to London, north Wales, East Anglia and Liverpool. During the second phase the enemy attacked London and other aircraft were over the east coast probably minelaying. During the whole period the Luftwaffe lost nine aircraft destroyed. The RAF lost two aircraft destroyed.

COASTAL COMMAND OPERATIONS

Forty-six aircraft carried out thirty-five anti invasion, anti submarine and reconnaissance patrols. An escort was also provided for sixteen convoys.

1. Shipping was observed off the Dutch coast by a Hudson which sank a motor vessel in a convoy off Amelang (Holland).
2. Two large motor vessels of 5,000 tons and 7,000 tons were observed in the Trondheim (Norway) area.
3. A Sunderland dropped depth charges on an oil patch near Cape Wrath and later an enemy U-Boat was sighted by a Hudson crew.
4. A convoy with some of the vessels being towed was sighted by a PRU Spitfire between Ostend and Dunkirk.

There were no losses.

Night operations

Minelaying was successfully carried out at Le Havre.

BOMBER COMMAND OPERATIONS

1. Ten Blenheims carried out offensive reconnaissance patrols in daylight and bombed the ports of Calais, Dunkirk, Ostend, Zeebrugge and the airfield at Haamstede. Attacks were also made on two convoys, but no result was observed. There were no losses.

Night operations

Because of adverse weather there were no night operations.

OPERATIONAL LOSSES

There were no losses

Pilot Officer Richard Muspratt poses for a photo with his crew, Sgt. Doug Smart (left) and Sgt. Reg Cole (right) in September 1940. Behind them is their 53 Squadron Blenheim with black undersides, reflecting the squadron's nocturnal activities of that period.

ENEMY ACTIVITY

Presumably because of the adverse weather only reconnaissance sorties by single aircraft took place during the morning, but a big formation, mainly of Bf109s, attacked targets in the east Kent area at about 15.30 hours. A series of formations crossed the coast at Lympne, Dover and Deal. Single aircraft penetrated as far as the Midlands. The enemy night activity was concentrated mainly on London and the south-east counties, but a few penetrated to the Midlands. Land mines were dropped for the first time causing devastation and casualties. The laying of sea mines was probably carried out in the Thames Estuary and off the east coast. Luftwaffe losses for the period were eight aircraft destroyed. RAF losses were six aircraft destroyed.

COASTAL COMMAND OPERATIONS

Sixty-six aircraft carried out anti invasion, anti submarine, reconnaissance and offensive sorties. Twenty-one convoys were escorted.

1. A Sunderland reported a ship, possibly the *Crown Arran*, had been torpedoed in a convoy 182 miles from St. Kilda. Another ship was sunk twenty miles from the Butt of Lewis.
2. PRU aircraft carried out reconnaissance over the French, Belgian and Dutch harbours.

Night operations

1. Night attacks were successfully carried out on shipping in Cherbourg by six Blenheims of 53 Squadron, eight of 59 Squadron and FAA Albacores of 826 Squadron.
2. Six Beauforts of 22 Squadron, 'A', 'I', 'G', 'K', 'Q' and 'X' also attacked shipping in Cherbourg. Four torpedoes were released but no results observed. 'Q' crash-landed on return and 'K' failed to return.
3. FAA Swordfish successfully laid mines off Schouwen Islands and in the mouth of the Scheldt.

BOMBER COMMAND OPERATIONS

1. Fifteen Blenheims were detailed to attack shipping in the Channel ports in daylight. Most of them abandoned their task because of lack of cloud cover, but nine 'pressed on' and bombed barges. There were no losses.

Night operations

The greatest number of bombers despatched at night to date concentrated on attacking the invasion barges in the Channel ports and shipping in the German ports.

1. Twenty Fairey Battles successfully bombed barges at Boulogne.
2. Forty out of forty-six Blenheims successfully bombed barges at Boulogne (13) and Dunkirk (27).
3. Thirty-nine Hampdens successfully bombed shipping at Flushing, Terneuzen and Antwerp. Eight other aircraft laid mines off Lorient.

4. Forty-two Wellingtons claimed successful attacks on shipping at Calais, Ostend and targets at Ehrang, Mannheim, Krefeld, Osnabrük, Brussels and Soest.
5. Twenty-nine Whitleys were despatched; Two returned early, nine whose target was Battleship '*Bismarck*' berthed in Hamburg, bombed despite fierce opposition, nine attacked shipping at Zeebrugge successfully and of the remaining seven bombed primary targets and one an alternative. One aircraft as damaged by Flak and a crewman wounded.

OPERATIONAL LOSSES

Beaufort L4508 'K' of 22 Squadron, Thorney Island, failed to return from a night torpedo attack on shipping at Cherbourg and crashed at Tourlaville. Pilot Officer T. Atherton, Pilot Officer R. A. MacFarlane, Sergeant J. L. Feather and Sergeant C. J. Harvey are all buried at Bayeux.

Hampden P2121 of 44 Squadron, Waddington, target Antwerp, shot down by Flak in the target area. Sergeant T. V. Henderson, Pilot Officer R. G. Goode, Sergeant J. H. Angus and Sergeant J. Sugden are buried in Schoonselhof Cemetery.

Put that light out!

Sgt. Joe Taylor , 61 Squadron Hampden

It was during this period of activity over the channel ports that I saw my first enemy aircraft close to. We had bombed barges at Ostend, and were heading out from the coast feeling rather pleased with our efforts. Barges were so thickly concentrated that it was well nigh impossible to miss.

Suddenly to our starboard there was a flash as a cigarette lighter sprang into flame and illuminated the helmeted head and face of the pilot of a German Bf110 as he carelessly lit a cigarette. Up to this time we hadn't seen him although he was flying a parallel course and not more than 50ft away. More importantly he had not, it would appear, seen us. I called the skipper and shouted "throttle back!" The skipper and the rest of us held our breath while he eased the throttles back to allow speed to decay and the 110 to draw away ahead. We all breathed a sigh of relief and were somewhat shaken to see how easily we could have been stalked to death by him.

Squadron Leader N. Hearn-Phillips AFC, DFM

Beaufort pilot 22 Squadron

Norman Hearn-Phillips joined the RAF in 1936 as a Direct Entry Sergeant Pilot. He trained on Hawker Harts and Audax gaining his wings and the rank of Sergeant. He was then posted to RAF Gosport where he was trained on Fairey Swordfish and initiated into the difficult art of dropping torpedoes, after which he joined No. 22 Squadron equipped with Vildebeestes. His next training was in General Reconnaissance Navigation. On the outbreak of war he flew anti-submarine patrols from Thorney Island. When No. 22 Squadron was re-equipped with Beauforts he converted, flying bombing and mining operations from North Coates. He survived many sorties and became one of the most competent and knowledgeable pilots on the squadron.

During the late summer of 1940, the squadron commenced torpedo attacks on enemy shipping in the North Sea, off the Belgian and Dutch Coasts. On the 17th September, six of the No. 22 Squadron Beauforts were detached from North Coates to Thorney Island and detailed to attack shipping in Cherbourg Harbour. He and his crew were among those detailed, but although he had completed twenty operations in Beauforts he had only dropped torpedoes in practice. The attack was to be a combined attack with eight Blenheims of No. 59 Squadron, who were to drop bombs and flares to light the way for the Beauforts.

By the time the Beauforts got to Cherbourg the No. 59 Squadron Blenheims had started fires in the docks and installations. The defences were alerted, searchlights probing the night sky while the Flak batteries kept up a continuous barrage over the target. Hearn-Phillips brought his Beaufort down to sea level and headed for the target, flying at eighty feet and 140 knots. As he released the torpedo the Flak was intense and the aircraft was hit as he turned away. The port elevator had been shot away and the rudder and hydraulics damaged. Despite this Hearn-Phillips nursed his crippled aircraft back to Thorney Island, where he carried out a successful belly landing. There were no casualties.

The raid was highly successful, shipping sunk, oil tanks and dock installations severely damaged. Hearn-Phillips was awarded the DFM in November and he continued on operations until December, when he was posted to instruct at the Beaufort OTU at Chivenor after completing his tour of operations. While at Chivenor he was recognised as one of the best and most knowledgeable instructors. He was commissioned in April 1941 and returned to Beaufort operations in July 1942 in the Middle East, and later on Beaufighters operating from Ceylon. He was awarded the AFC in June 1944. After the war he stayed in the RAF having reached the rank of Squadron Leader. Later he became an Air Traffic Controller. He retired in 1965.

ENEMY ACTIVITY

Daylight activity was concentrated on the London area on which three major attacks were launched. The first attack comprised mainly fighters (four fighters to every bomber). Their targets were Gillingham, Chatham, Gravesend and Maidstone, where damage and casualties were caused. By 19.55 hours eight 'red' warnings had been received by Central London and it was estimated that 800 enemy aircraft operated over the UK during daylight hours. By night a large formation of 200 raiders was plotted before 20.00 hours and from 21.00 hours a steady stream concentrated on the London area. The Liverpool, north-east coast and Bristol areas were also targeted. The Plessey main works were damaged and set on fire. The north coast to the Wash and Spurn Head to St. Abbs was suspected as having been mined. Luftwaffe losses during the period were eighteen aircraft destroyed. The RAF lost eleven aircraft destroyed.

The SS Europa was the 'target for tonight' for five Beauforts of 22 Squadron.

COASTAL COMMAND OPERATIONS

Seventy-seven aircraft carried out the usual patrols. Air escort was provided for twenty-three convoys and an extra escort was provided for an Empire civilian flying-boat.

1. Blenheim 'M' of 53 Squadron bombed Le Touquet in daylight from 10,000 feet. There were no losses.

Night operations

1. Six Blenheims of 59 Squadron attacked shipping at Cherbourg while another six of 53 Squadron attacked shipping at Den Helder.
2. Five Beauforts were detailed to torpedo the *SS Europa* berthed in Wilhelmshaven. One located the ship but was unable to attack because of the intense searchlight glare. Three others of the 22 Squadron strike force released their torpedoes at smaller ships at sea without success.

BOMBER COMMAND OPERATIONS

1. One Blenheim detailed to reconnoitre and attack Ostend in daylight had to abandon due to lack of cloud cover.
2. Six other Blenheims carried out an uneventful North Sea sweep.

Night operations

Again a large force was despatched on night raids mainly against the invasion fleet in the Channel ports and communications targets in Germany.

1. Of the fifty-three Blenheims despatched, forty-six carried out successful attacks on barges at Calais, Dunkirk, Ostend and the guns at Cap Gris Nez.
2. Twelve Fairey Battles were sent to attack Boulogne; eleven claimed to have attacked successfully.
3. Forty Wellingtons carried out successful attacks on shipping at Flushing and Le Havre and communications targets at Osnabrük, Ehrang and Brussels.
4. Thirty-nine Hampdens also claimed success with their attacks on shipping at Le Havre. An additional eight aircraft laid mines in the Elbe Estuary.
5. Twenty-eight Whitleys carried out successful attacks on shipping and barges at Le Havre, Zeebrugge and Antwerp. Railway targets at Hamm, Krefeld, Mannheim and Neubeckum were also attacked.
6. Leaflets were dropped by three 6 Group aircraft on Amiens, Rouen and Brest.

OPERATIONAL LOSSES

Blenheim T1852 of 107 Squadron, target Calais, lost without trace. Pilot Officer C. Preston, Sergeant T. D. W. Ross and Sergeant W. H. Kilgour are all commemorated on the Runnymede Memorial.

Blenheim L9339 of 105 Squadron, Watton, target Ostend, lost without trace. Sergeant C. Bowles, Sergeant A. Lackenby and Sergeant V. Radford are commemorated on the Runnymede Memorial.

Hampden P1183 of 83 Squadron, Scampton, target Le Havre, shot down into the Seine Estuary, Le Havre. Squadron Leader J. A. Pitcairn-Hill DSO, DFC, Pilot Officer A. P. Linsdell and Pilot Officer V. A. Rendell are buried in local cemeteries. Sergeant C. G. McCarthy is commemorated on the Runnymede Memorial.

Hampden P1259 of 106 Squadron, Finningley, minelaying, shot down over the Elbe Estuary. Pilot Officer E. T. Watkin, Sergeant C. Kenmure, Sergeant J. McL Fraser and Sergeant S. B. Keats are all commemorated on the Runnymede Memorial.

Wednesday 18th September

Wellington P9242 of 99 Squadron, Newmarket, target north-west Germany, Pilot Officer M. C. A. Linden, Sergeant M. E. L. Wood, Sergeant H. E. Smart, Sergeant T. Watson, Sergeant D. T. Heard and Sergeant V. Beverley are all buried in the Rheinberg War Cemetery.

Wellington R3160 of 149 Squadron, Mildenhall, target Le Havre, presumed lost over the Channel. Pilot Officer J. S. Pay, Pilot Officer D. R. Tuppen, Pilot Officer D. S. Cox, Sergeant W. R. Pope, Sergeant H. H. Harrison and Pilot Officer G. R. M. Ford. Four of the names are on the Runnymede Memorial, but the body of Sergeant Pope was found and he lies in the Houlgate (Beuzeval) Cemetery on the Normandy coast.

Whitley P5008 of 58 Squadron, Linton-on-Ouse, target Hamm, shot down by a night-fighter and crashed 11 Km north west of Winterswijk (Holland). Sergeant A. A. E. Crossland, Pilot Officer E. Ford, Sergeant C. F. Marshall, Sergeant R. E. Salisbury and Sergeant D. W. Austen were all killed and buried at Winterswijk Cemetery.

Whitley N1425 of 77 Squadron, Linton-on-Ouse, target Soest, shot down by a night-fighter and crashed 12 Km south of Ruurlo (Holland). Pilot Officer P. E. Eldridge, Sergeant V. C. Cowley, Sergeant F. Crawford and Sergeant R. C. Dawson are buried in Ruurlo RC Churchyard while Acting Squadron Leader P. O. Williams (RN) rests in Winterswijk General Cemetery.
Both the above aircraft appear to have fallen to Feldwebel Paul Gildner of 3./NJG 1, who claimed "Hampdens" at 22.30 and 00.28 hours.

Whitley P4992 of 77 Squadron, Linton-on-Ouse, target Antwerp, presumed crashed in the sea off the Belgian coast. Pilot Officer W. M. Douglas and Sergeant D. V. Hughes are buried in the Schoonselhof Cemetery at Antwerp. Pilot Officer R. P. Brayne, Sergeant J. A. Raper and Sergeant J. Baguley have no known graves.

* *This was the most costly night yet for the Bomber Command squadrons - not a single one of the forty-one aircrew involved, which included one RN member on detachment, survived.*

Squadron Leader J Pitcairn-Hill DSO DFC

Hampden pilot 83 Squadron

Sqn Ldr. Jamie Pitcairn-Hill was one of the 83 Squadron stalwarts who took part in most of the early war raids with great enthusiasm and gallantry. The son of a Scottish minister, he excelled at sport and played rugby for the RAF. On 12th August 1940, Pitcairn-Hill led the successful raid on the Dortmund-Ems Canal in which Rod Learoyd won the VC and for which he was awarded the DSO. He served alongside Guy Gibson in 83 Squadron and would undoubtedly have gone on to achieve similar public recognition had he survived his tour.

However, at this point of the Battle of Britain, Bomber Command was throwing everything it had into the attacks on the Channel ports as the invasion seemed imminent. Crews were going there night after night and the flak defences were starting to take a fearful toll. The night of 18th September saw Bomber Command suffer its highest losses to date when 41 men lost their lives on operations. One of them was the brave and fearless Pitcairn-Hill whose Hampden was literally shot to pieces over the target area during an attack on Le Havre.

Thursday 19th September

The object of Bomber Command's attention during September 1940. Invasion barges stockpiled and waiting for the order to sail. This photo was taken by an 83 Squadron Blenheim on this day, 19th September, and shows some of the barges at Dunkirk. There is considerable evidence of damage to the dock facilities with craters on many of the road and rail links. Despite this, most of the barges remain afloat and this fact alone would see the bomber crews being sent back to Dunkirk many times over the coming weeks.

Thursday 19th September

ENEMY ACTIVITY

The activity during the day was less than it had been. Fighter Command's success in depriving the Luftwaffe air superiority and Bomber and Coastal Commands incessant attacks on the German invasion fleet was having its effect. However, the night attacks were increasing in intensity. At 19.50 hours the usual heavy stream of bombers started to head for London. Parts of the City were attacked with land-mines causing heavy damage and numerous casualties. It was estimated that these raids were the worst experienced to date. Although the Capital was the main target, objectives in the West Country, southern England and East Anglia were targeted. RAF Lyneham was attacked where a hangar was hit. During the period the Luftwaffe lost eight aircraft destroyed plus a Ju88 which was captured complete with crew and bombs at Oakington. RAF Fighter Command suffered no casualties!

COASTAL COMMAND OPERATIONS

Thirty-five anti invasion, anti submarine patrols and offensive reconnaissance sorties were carried out by fifty-three aircraft. Twenty three convoys were escorted.

PRU photographs were taken of Bruges, Zeebrugge, Ostend, Dunkirk, Calais and Le Havre. The Le Havre photographs revealed five to ten ships of 5,000 tons in the harbour.

Night operations

1. Three FAA Swordfish carried out a night strike on shipping at Cherbourg.
2. Five Beauforts were detailed to carry out night torpedo attacks on shipping off the Dutch and German coasts but were unsuccessful.

BOMBER COMMAND OPERATIONS

1. Twelve Blenheims were despatched in daylight to reconnoitre and attack Channel ports, but because lack of cloud cover only one bombed Dunkirk - results were not observed.
2. Six other Blenheims carried out a reconnaissance over the North Sea.

Night operations

Because of adverse weather conditions over the Continent, only Hampdens of 5 Group and Whitleys of 4 Group carried out night operations.

1. Thirty-seven Hampdens attacked the Dortmund-Ems canal, and shipping at Flushing and Ostend. The attacks were pressed home but results were un-observed. An additional eight Hampdens mined the River Gironde Estuary.
2. Eight Whitleys carried out attacks on the marshalling yards at Mannheim. Five crews bombed the primary target and three alternatives.

Flight Lieutenant J. E. Mackinlay

Wellington Observer 99 Squadron

'Mac' Mackinlay flew as an observer with No. 99 (Wellington) Squadron. He writes describing his recall of operating with a bomber squadron during the epic days and nights of the Battle of Britain.

" My first operation during the battle was on the 11th. September 1940, to bomb the German invasion fleet at Ostend. We continued throughout the whole of September and October bombing the barges and shipping in the Channel ports. I vividly recall all our night take-offs from Newmarket for France and on the way seeing practically the whole of London on fire. As we crossed the Channel and the Channel ports the same sight greeted us, they were also on fire, we were replying in kind! We were also involved in bombing Berlin where we were always subjected to intense anti-aircraft fire. I left Newmarket on the 20th November for Malta to continue my tour, which I fortunately survived."

OPERATIONAL LOSSES

Blenheim T4025 of 53 Squadron, Detling, failed to return from daylight patrol 'Dundee 2'. Crashed off Berck-sur-Mer. Pilot Officer C. F. Tibbitts (New Zealander), Sergeant R. W. Grace and Sergeant E. Harrold were posted as missing in action and appear on the Runnymede Memorial.

This crew seems to have fallen victim to Oberfeldwebel Franz Kaiser of 2./JG 53, who shot the Blenheim down south of Hastings at 17.25 hours.

Messerschmitt Bf109s of JG53. One of its pilots was responsible for the only loss of the day, detailed above.

Friday 20th September

Sunderland L5802 which attempted to bomb oil storage tanks at Narvik today. She is seen here in her pre-war RF codes of 204 Squadron.

ENEMY ACTIVITY

Reconnaissance flights took place during the day over the south-east coast, the West Country and the Midlands. The main bombing raid was carried out by a force of one hundred aircraft, mostly fighter-bombers, starting at 11.00 hours. It was heading for London, but was intercepted before it got there. The night activity was on a smaller scale, again carried out by single aircraft, and London was the target. Minelaying took place off the north-east coast and in the Humber as far as Cromer. During the period the Luftwaffe lost three aircraft destroyed. RAF Fighter Command lost seven aircraft (Spitfires) destroyed. One crumb of consolation was that photo-reconnaissance revealed that units of the German invasion fleet appeared to be dispersing from the Channel ports.

COASTAL COMMAND OPERATIONS

Twelve aircraft patrolled, reconnoitred and escorted convoys.

1. Six Ansons of 217 Squadron escorted by three fighter Blenheims attempted a daylight strike on shipping west of Brest, but were unsuccessful.
2. Five Blenheims of 53 Squadron carried out a dawn attack on Willemsoord Harbour.
3. Attacks by single aircraft of 59 Squadron were carried out in daylight on the airfields at Le Treport, St. Aubyn, Bos Robort and Abbeville.

Night operations

1. Six Blenheims of 59 Squadron carried out a night attack on shipping at Cherbourg.
2. Five Beauforts of 22 Squadron were detailed to carry out night torpedo attacks on shipping off Den Helder, but no ships were located.
3. Sunderland L5802 of 201 Squadron on a night reconnaissance over Norway attempted to bomb oil storage tanks at Narvik. No results observed

BOMBER COMMAND OPERATIONS

1. Three Fairey Battles carried out a dawn strike on Cap Gris Nez.
2. Six Blenheims carried out a routine reconnaissance over the North Sea in daylight. Other daylight tasks were abandoned due to adverse weather. There were no losses.

Night operations

Another strong force carried out night attacks on the invasion fleet in the Channel ports, marshalling yards in Germany and communications targets at Dunkirk, Antwerp and Dortmund plus minelaying off St. Nazaire.

Flight Lieutenant Colin Rawlins DFC
Hampden pilot 144 Squadron

Another slavishly followed tactic in the early part of the bomber war was to de-synchronise the engines which, it was believed, made it more difficult for the flak guns to locate the aircraft accurately. This practice gradually ceased as it became clear that the guns were radar –rather than sound– controlled. It had also probably had some negative effect on aircraft speed and fuel consumption, not to mention the slightly irritating effect on the crews of listening to the discordant engine sounds.

Friday 20th September

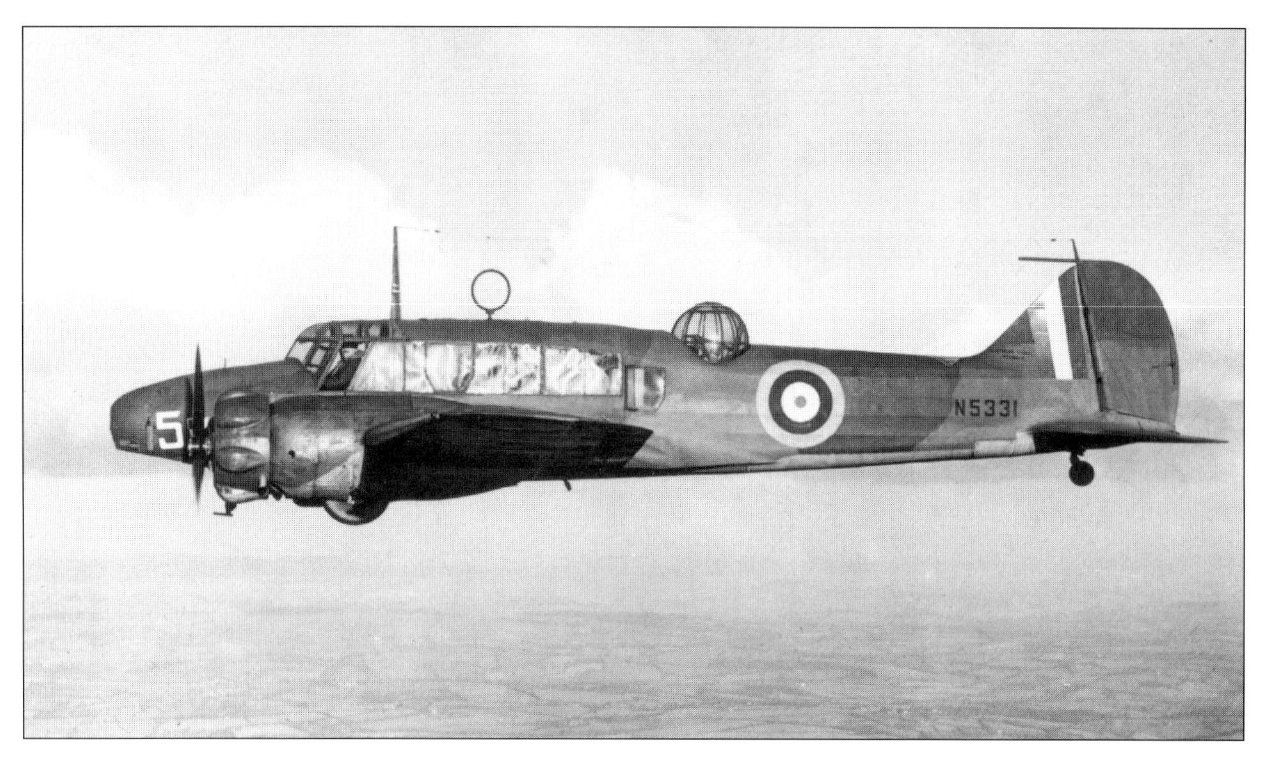

Six Ansons of 217 Squadron were sent to bomb shipping off Brest on this day, an indication of the maximum effort made by all during this critical phase of the Battle.

Sergeant D. A. Walters

Blenheim gunner, 59 Squadron

Douglas Allen Walters joined the RAF in 1938 and trained as a Wireless Operator and Air Gunner. During the Battle of Britain he was flying in that capacity with No. 59 (Blenheim) Squadron participating in raids on the German invasion fleet in the Channel ports. On the night of the 20th/21st September, operating from RAF Thorney Island, his aircraft was shot down while attacking shipping at Cherbourg, by a German night fighter. It crashed in flames in a field near the village of La Vast. The crew, Pilot Officer N. V. Palmer, Sergeant L. B. Wright and Sergeant D. A. Walters all perished.

The crash was witnessed by a number of the villagers of La Vast including Jean and Alexander Alix, the two young sons of the farmer in whose field the Blenheim had crashed. The two boys went to the scene early next morning and managed, despite the wreckage being under German guard, to obtain two small bits of the Blenheim, which they subsequently gave to his brother. The German authorities instructed that the three crew members were to be buried at the scene of the crash, but the Mayor of the village, a Monsieur Thin, insisted they receive a Christian burial in the local Roman Catholic Church grounds. During the service the Union Flag of Great Britain was flown inside the church and the church bells were rung in direct contravention of German regulations.

Gerry Walters. and his family made a special visit to the grave at La Vast on the 15th August 1988. The villagers made them very welcome and they were introduced to the brothers Jean and Alexander Alix who took them to the crash site. The Church at La Vast is an old stone building in a lovely rural setting. One couldn't wish for a better resting place for the three brave men whose sacrifice for the liberty of the free world was so much appreciated by the local French community that they were prepared to defy the German authorities and ensure the crew had a decent Christian burial.

"Our village La Vast sincerely remembers the drama which happened on that September night with the crash of the RAF bomber and the three young victims. At the time the French people were still suffering the shock of defeat and German occupation and desperately down-hearted. Only the appearances of British 'planes were able to start a hope of Liberation. Believe me we felt very thankful and were so sad when friendly planes were shot down by the hated Germans. May it be a consolation for you to know that the crew were treated in death with sorrow and respect. The fact that they were foreigners probably belonging to another religion did not change our behaviour. Throughout the past fifty years we have cared for the crew's grave and their memory will be cherished forever."

A 44 Squadron Hampden back home after a run in with a night fighter, note the cannon shell holes in the rear cockpit.

1. Forty-five Blenheims carried out successful attacks on the invasion shipping at Dunkirk and Ostend.
2. Twelve Fairey Battles claimed that their attacks on shipping at Boulogne were also successful.
3. Twenty-five Hampdens attacked the invasion shipping at Antwerp, Boulogne, Dunkirk and the Dortmund-Ems Canal. Also eight were detailed for minelaying.
4. The force of forty-five Wellingtons carried out successful attacks on invasion shipping at Calais, Flushing and Ostend.
5. Twenty-three Whitleys were despatched to attack marshalling yards, docks and industrial targets. Ten bombed the marshalling yards at Hamm successfully, but four suffered Flak damage. Three claimed success at Osnabrük, two at Mannheim, one at Flushing and seven at Krefeld.

OPERATIONAL LOSSES

Blenheim R3635 'V' of 59 Squadron, Thorney Island, targets Le Treport and Abbeville, failed to return and crashed at La Vast, Manche, France. Pilot Officer K. V. Palmer, Sergeant E. E. Wright and Sergeant D. A. Walters are buried in the cemetery.

Wellington T2463 of 75 Squadron, Mildenhall, target invasion ports, failed to return. Sergeant A. J. Green, Sergeant J. E. McCormick, Sergeant N. MacDonald, Sergeant L. D. Anderson (RNZAF) and Sergeant L. A. White DFM, are buried in the Adegem Canadian Cemetery. Pilot Officer M. R. Braun is buried in the New Communal Cemetery, Ostend.

Our crew had been selected for the Hamm target and we got off from Leeming at 21.25 hours. The weather wasn't too bad and we had a relatively smooth outward flight. As we crossed the enemy coast we could see that the boys were already stirring things up in the invasion ports. Crossing over into Germany we proceeded to Hamm. The visibility was fairly good (for a change) and Tubby Dickenson, our new navigator, was able to set us for our run-in after identifying the target. Hamm was always a 'hot one' and by now the searchlights and Flak was having a go at the early birds. I went to my usual position in the fuselage by the flare chute to drop flares and the loose incendiaries. The bomb-run started and during the final stages the Flak was bursting uncomfortably close. I could smell the acrid smoke as we flew through the heavy bursts. I was pleased when the bomb-aimer called 'Bombs Gone' over the intercom and I was able to crawl back through the tunnel leading to the cockpit to join the others at the 'sharp end'. As I put my hand on the table in front of the W/T set to raise myself back into my seat I felt a sharp stab of pain in the fleshy part of my thumb, near my wrist. At this time my hand was on my open W/T log book and as I lifted it I saw blood on the pages. 'Tubby' also saw the blood and his eyes popped. This was only his fourth trip and obviously, believing the hair-raising tales the old hands had been feeding him, he thought I'd been grievously hit. I reassured him that I hadn't been and removed my leather gauntlet. As I did so I saw that my white silk inner glove was now red and protruding from my hand was a sliver of metal which I was able to remove. I wrapped a handkerchief around my wound to staunch the blood and I was able to resume my key-bashing without much discomfort. On reflection I realised that the Flak had got much closer than I'd thought! We escaped from the unwelcome attentions of the defences and set course for home. Our return flight was uneventful and we landed back at Leeming at 04.30 hours. During de-briefing and our after-flight bacon and eggs I had to put up with some leg-pulling concerning my wound!

Larry Donnelly, 10 Squadron Whitley

Saturday 21st September

MOSTLY SUNNY WITH THE OCCASIONAL CLOUD.

Naval Officers were often taken up on the Hudson coastal patrols to help co-ordinate operations. These two officers are wearing Irvin 'Harnessuits' onto which a parachute could be quickly fastened in an emergency.

ENEMY ACTIVITY

During the day Bf109s roamed high above south-east England and small numbers of Ju88s carried out nuisance raids. It was not until 18.00 hours that a major raid took place involving two hundred enemy aircraft. A parachute mine dropped on Ipswich was impossible to diffuse and was exploded on site demolishing seventy houses and damaging more. The night raids started at 20.00 hours on the London docks where land-mines were also used. Other areas, East Anglia, Liverpool and Wales were targeted and minelaying took place off the north-east coast, the Tyne area, the Firth of Forth and the entrance to Stranraer. During the period the Luftwaffe lost nine aircraft in combat. RAF losses were nil.

COASTAL COMMAND OPERATIONS

Eighty-seven aircraft were used on anti invasion, anti submarine and reconnaissance patrols. Escort was provided for fifteen convoys.

1. Six Blenheims of 53 Squadron carried out a strike on enemy motor vessels off Cap Gris Nez.
2. Thee Blenheims of 59 Squadron detailed to attack enemy occupied airfields, lacked cloud cover so bombed barges in the Dieppe area.
3. Four Hudsons and six Blenheims detailed to attack two destroyers and a U-Boat sixty miles south-west of Horns Reef were unable to locate them.
4. Six Hudsons of 206 Squadron attacked two motor vessels fifty three miles south-west of Horns Reef and claimed a direct hit on one of them. A 6,000 to 8,000 ton motor vessel two miles south of Borkum was attacked and hit with incendiaries.
5. Hudson P5137 reported sighting three enemy cruisers at Lorient.

Night operations

Three Blenheims were detailed to attack shipping at Rotterdam.

BOMBER COMMAND OPERATIONS

1. Eighteen Blenheims were despatched in daylight to reconnoitre and attack enemy occupied ports and shipping on the French, Belgian and Dutch coasts. Seven carried out their tasks as briefed, five abandoned because of lack of cloud cover. Six others carried out a North Sea sweep without incident.

Night operations

Shipping and barges at Calais, Ostend and Boulogne were the targets of the night strike force.

1. Thirty Wellingtons were despatched to attack the barges at Dunkirk and bombed Calais. Twenty-nine crews bombed the primary target successfully while the other bombed an alternative. The crews reported fires and explosions.
2. Twenty-six Blenheims carried out successful attacks on barges and shipping at Dunkirk and Ostend.
3. Three Fairey Battles of 142 Squadron were despatched. One bombed barges at Boulogne, one the guns at Cap Gris Nez and one aborted.
4. Eight Hampdens successfully bombed shipping at Ostend.
5. Despite severe opposition twenty-two Whitleys successfully bombed the invasion shipping at Boulogne.

OPERATIONAL LOSSES

There were no losses.

ENEMY ACTIVITY

Only a small number of nuisance raids took place during daylight hours, carried out mainly by fighters and single bombers crossing the coast between Portsmouth and Harwich. The night raids started early, raiders coming in over Rye at 19.30 hours. From 20.30 to 02.30 hours there was a steady stream heading for London, but East Anglia, Hampshire, Wiltshire, Bristol, south Wales, Liverpool and the Humber areas were also visited. There was a short lull in the London raids between 02.30 and 03.30 hours. During the assault on London a parachute mine exploded in Ilford demolishing one hundred houses, Poplar and Lambeth suffered fifty fatalities when air-raid shelters were hit. During the period the Luftwaffe lost two aircraft destroyed in combat. RAF losses were nil.

COASTAL COMMAND OPERATIONS

Forty-two anti invasion, anti submarine, offensive patrols and reconnaissance sorties were carried out and thirteen convoys given escort. Fifty-nine aircraft were involved.

1. Blenheim 'S' of 59 Squadron carried out an early (07.00 hours take off) daylight bombing raid on Lorient.
2. Aircraft on patrol during the day reported that a large number of ships and barges were sighted along the Belgian and French Coasts.

Night operations

During night operations, five aircraft were despatched to lay mines off The Hook of Holland; four to attack shipping at Zeebrugge; eleven to attack shipping and installations at Brest and six to carry out a strike on shipping at Den Helder.

BOMBER COMMAND OPERATIONS

1. Fourteen Blenheims were detailed to reconnoitre and attack Dutch, Belgian and French Ports as well as Waalhaven airfield. The operation was abandoned because of lack of cloud cover.
2. Six other Blenheims carried out an uneventful North Sea sweep.
3. Three Fairey Battles attacked shipping at Boulogne.

Night operations

Again the main night force concentrated on attacking the invasion fleet in the occupied ports. However, nine Whitleys were also despatched to attack the aluminium works at Lauta (near Dresden) and another five to bomb industrial targets in Berlin.

1. Thirty four Wellingtons were despatched. Six bombed shipping at Boulogne; eight bombed shipping and barges at Calais; twelve attacked shipping and installations at Le Havre and eight bombed shipping at Ostend. The overall results were good.
2. Thirty three Blenheims were also despatched. Twelve bombed shipping and barges at Calais; five bombed targets at Dunkirk, ten shipping at Ostend and six shipping at Zeebrugge.
3. Twenty-nine Hampdens claimed successful attacks on shipping at Le Havre, Boulogne, Ostend Antwerp and Flushing.
4. Fourteen Whitleys were detailed to attack Lauta and Berlin. Eight crews claimed successful attacks on the aluminium works. One failed to bomb due to adverse weather obscuring the target. Of the five crews sent to Berlin, three bombed primary targets, one returned early and one bombed an alternative.

Ten and a half hours!

Ours was one of the crews selected to go to Lauta. George Dove, our tail gunner, had been upgraded to first WOp/AG and had joined another crew and had been replaced by Sergeant '*Slim*' Summerville - he had picked a long flog for his first trip with us. We got airborne from Leeming at 19.10 hours and set course climbing away from the airfield. We crossed the English coast and as we flew over the North Sea the weather deteriorated. There were numerous heavy clouds and electrical storms. However, we managed to weave our way through and on ETA we calculated we were getting near to Lauta. We spent some time searching, but eventually identified the target and began our bomb-runs. This was the first time Lauta had been attacked (euphemistically in aircrew jargon, a 'Virgin' target) so we were hoping that the opposition would be inexperienced - how wrong can you get. Despite this we carried out two runs and got through unscathed and high-tailed it for home. As we left the target area '*Slim*' in the tail reported there were fires burning. The electrical storms hadn't abated and I found it difficult to read the Morse through the crackling interference, but I managed to pass my 'bombs gone' signal to Group and get a couple of W/T fixes from the long-range D/F at Butser Hill. It wasn't my night. Shortly afterwards we were struck by lightning which burnt off the trailing aerial and damaged my transmitter/receiver. Then to pile on the agony our engine-driven generator packed-in, but somebody must have been looking after us because we managed to scramble back and get into our diversion airfield of Linton-on-Ouse. We had been airborne for ten and a half hours. As we turned off the flare-path one of our engines cut - we had run out of gravy! This time we had really earned our after flight bacon and eggs."

Larry Donnelly, 10 Squadron Whitley

OPERATIONAL LOSSES

There were no losses

Monday 23rd September

MAINLY SUNNY.

ENEMY ACTIVITY

An early attack developed over east Kent and the Thames Estuary at 09.30 hours involving 200 enemy aircraft. They were intercepted by fighters and the raiders failed to penetrate the London area. A second London attack with 100 aircraft started at 17.30 hours. There was also activity which was widespread from East Anglia to south Cornwall. The night raids which again headed for London started at 19.45 hours. There were also isolated raids over the Midlands and south Wales and minelaying took place from the Humber to the Firth of Forth. It is estimated that 200 enemy aircraft were used during the night operations. During the period the Luftwaffe lost thirteen aircraft destroyed. The RAF lost ten aircraft destroyed.

COASTAL COMMAND OPERATIONS

Ninety-one aircraft carried out anti invasion, anti submarine and reconnaissance patrols. Thirteen convoys were escorted. During reconnaissance of the French, Belgian, Dutch and Norwegian coasts enemy convoys were sighted.

1. Six Ansons of 217 Squadron carried out an early (01.15 to 04.15 hours) raid and bombed Brest Harbour. Subsequent PR photographs showed oil floating in the harbour. The Royal Navy suggested a Blenheim raid to ignite the oil!

2. Two Beauforts 'A' and 'G' of 22 Squadron carried out a torpedo attack on an enemy convoy north of Schiermonnikoog and claimed two hits.

3. Between 04.00 and 08.40 hours four Blenheims of 53 Squadron bombed Lorient.

4. Three Blenheims of 53 Squadron carried out a strike on a large motor launch E-Boat south-east of Dungeness.

5. Sunderland P9645 of 10 (RAAF) Squadron carried out a search for a Do24 after a shipping attack.

Night operations

1. Seven Blenheims of 53 Squadron carried out a night strike on shipping at Flushing and Zeebrugge.

BOMBER COMMAND OPERATIONS

1. Six Blenheims were despatched in daylight to attack targets on the French, Belgian and Dutch Coasts, but the task was abandoned because there was no cloud cover.

2. Six other Blenheims carried out a successful North Sea sweep.

Night operations

The main concentration of the night force of Wellingtons, Hampdens and Whitleys was centred on Berlin. They were detailed to attack eighteen separate targets, railway yards, electric power stations, gasworks and aero engine and aircraft component factories. The raid lasted three hours, during which the 112 aircraft bombed their targets from between 4,500 and 16,000 feet. Other aircraft were despatched to attack the Channel ports so the total involved was over 200, the first time this figure had been exceeded. Good results were reported on the attacks on the Berlin and the Channel ports targets.

Bombing Brest...in an Anson!

Wg Cdr Frank Tams OBE
Anson pilot 217 Squadron

Of all the bombing operations proposed by the British High Command during that hectic summer of 1940, there was probably none more bizarre than the order to send a squadron of Ansons to bomb the heavily defended port of Brest, in broad daylight! The Avro Anson was a somewhat flimsy twin-engined patrol and communications aircraft which had a cruising speed of only 150 mph and at best could only carry 360lbs of bombs, all externally. Nevertheless, an order came through to the C/O of 217 Squadron for him to prepare a squadron strength raid on Brest, to be carried out in daylight. Quite rightly, the C/O queried this order and when it was confirmed he simply refused to send his men to almost certain annihalation. Frank Tams, who was one of those who would have been sent, remembers what happened next. *"The C/O refused to send us and as a consequence was removed from his duties, having saved the lives of 40 or 50 highly trained aircrew."*

A 217 Squadron Anson.

The squadron did subsequently send Ansons to bomb Brest at night on three occasions, one of which was the 23rd September. Frank Tams remembers it well!

"We suffered no losses on these raids, there were no night fighters to worry about and all the flak seemed to burst in front of us. Obviously a total disbelief in our speed! It was scary nevertheless".

A sequence of photos showing the demise of L7788 'E' of 311 Squadron, East Wretham which failed to return from a raid on Berlin. Flight Lieutenant K. Trojacek force landed the Wellington owing to engine trouble at Leidschendam in the Den Haag area of Holland. The crew were all captured except Sergeant K. Kunka who tragically shot himself with his Verey pistol when German troops attempted to capture him the following day.

This was the Czech manned 311 Squadron's first operational loss, coming just two weeks after they commenced operations.

Monday 23rd September

1. Fairey Battle Squadrons of 1 Group bombed targets at Calais and Ostend and also carried out a security patrol over Calais.
2. The Blenheims of 2 Group were also busy and attacked the shipping at Calais and Ostend.
3. The Wellingtons which were despatched to Berlin attacked the Neukôln gasworks and the Wilmersdorf electric power station. Others bombed the barges at Le Havre. 6 Group Wellingtons dropped leaflets on Lille, Amiens, Rouen and Brest.
4. The Hampden force which went to Berlin bombed the electric power stations at Klingenberg and Charlottenberg and claimed success. Hampdens of 14 and 16 OTUs dropped leaflets on Jersey and Guernsey.
5. Of the Whitleys despatched one returned early, twelve claimed to have bombed the Berlin targets successfully. Another twelve bombed alternatives which included Wismar and Hamburg. Three more bombed the docks at Calais. One ditched on return.

OPERATIONAL LOSSES

Swordfish L7635 of 821 Squadron Fleet Air Arm, lost on operations off Orkney. Sub Lieutenant D. J. T. Marais, and Naval Airman 1 G. H. Gaynon killed. Sub Lieutenant F. C. Saunders was posted missing and his name appears on the Lee-on-Solent Memorial.

Hampden L4049 'L' of 83 Squadron, Scampton, target Berlin, hit by Flak and crashed near Bethen, Germany. Sergeant A. F. Blatch (RNZAF) Sergeant J. E. Gorwood DFM and Pilot Officer F. J. Watson DFC, at buried in the Becklingen War Cemetery at Saltau. Squadron Leader O. A. Ridgway DFC was taken prisoner.

Whitley P5046 'O' of 77 Squadron, Linton-on-Ouse, target Berlin, hit by Flak over Berlin and ditched on the return flight eighty miles off the English coast. Four days later two survivors were picked up from the dinghy by the Royal Navy, but one man died within hours of being rescued. Pilot Officer A. W. Dunn DFC, Sergeant D. A. Gibbons and Sergeant B. L. Saville DFM are missing. Sergeant D. B. Allen died after rescue. Sergeant G. H. Riley was rescued, injured. Pilot Officer Dunn had been involved in four previous operational incidents which had merited him the award of the DFC for his fortitude and courage. Sergeant Riley, the sole survivor, subsequently recorded an account of the crew's suffering in the book, '*So Few*' by David Masters.

Wellington L7788 'E' of 311 Squadron, East Wretham, target Berlin, failed to return. Force landed owing to engine trouble at Leidschendam in the Den Haag area of Holland. Flight Lieutenant K. Trojacek, Sergeant A. Zabry, Flight Lieutenant Z. Prochazka, Sergeant F. Knotek and Flight Lieutenant V. Kilian were subsequently reported as PoWs. Sergeant K. Kunka shot himself with his Verey pistol when German troops attempted to capture him the following day.

Members of the crew of L7788, 311 Squadron's first operation loss.

Left: Sgt. Karel Kunka of 311 Sqn who killed himself rather than face capture by the Germans.
Centre: Sgt. Zabry (right), co-pilot of L7788, with his lofty 9 Squadron friend Rupert 'Tiny' Cooling.
Right: Flt Lt. Karel Trojacek, the pilot of L7788, in captivity.

Tuesday 24th September

A 139 Squadron Blenheim similar to the one shot down into the Channel on this day.

ENEMY ACTIVITY

Two major battles were carried out over Kent and the Thames Estuary during the morning. The first, involving 200 aircraft, attacked Tilbury and Gravesend. The second attack was in two waves, both of which were intercepted by fighters. Other fighters escorted Blenheims carrying out a daylight attack on enemy shipping in the Channel. During the night London was the main target, but there were other widespread raids encompassing East Anglia, the Midlands, Liverpool and Scotland. The RAF aerodromes at Hemswell and Feltwell were bombed and machine-gunned. Luftwaffe losses during the period were seven aircraft destroyed. Fighter Command lost a similar number.

COASTAL COMMAND OPERATIONS

A total of eighty-four aircraft carried out the usual patrol tasks. Twenty-one convoys were given air escort.

1. An Anson despatched to attack E-Boats in the Channel was engaged in combat with two enemy aircraft. The Anson crew silenced the rear-gunner of one of them and scored hits on the other. During the fight the Anson pilot and navigator were wounded, but the pilot brought his aircraft safely back to base.
2. Six Beauforts of 22 Squadron were despatched on an anti shipping patrol off Den Helder and Cuxhaven, but no attacks were carried out.
3. Three Blenheims of 53 Squadron sent on an anti shipping patrol off Rotterdam abandoned because of adverse weather conditions.

Night operations

1. Six FAA Swordfish were detailed to lay mines off Texel Island.
2. Ansons were detailed to attack shipping and oil tanks at Brest.
3. Four Blenheims were sent to attack shipping at Cherbourg and carry out a roving patrol between Den Helder and Boulogne.

BOMBER COMMAND OPERATIONS

1. Twelve Blenheims of 114 and 139 Squadrons attacked enemy E-Boats off Dover. Five of the boats were bombed and two direct hits and near misses were claimed. The Blenheims were attacked by three Bf109s. In the ensuing battle one Bf109 was shot down. One Blenheim was also shot down and another damaged.
2. Six other Blenheims carried out a routine North Sea sweep.

Night operations

The night bombing operations were carried out by:-

1. Thirty-two Blenheims were despatched to attack barges and shipping at Calais, Le Havre and Ostend, twenty-nine claimed successful attacks.
2. Twelve Fairey Battles of 1 Group attacked shipping at Boulogne.
3. Thirty-five Wellingtons carried out successful attacks on the invasion shipping at Calais, Boulogne and Le Havre.
4. Twenty-one Hampdens successfully attacked the shipping at Calais, Le Havre and Ostend.
5. Twenty Whitleys given the task of attacking a transformer works at Berlin and an electrical power station at Finkenheerd. The weather was bad and only two claimed to have bombed the Berlin primary successfully. The crews on the Finkenheerd target also had weather problems but all bombed alternatives claiming good results.

OPERATIONAL LOSSES

Blenheim T1794 of 139 Squadron, Horsham St. Faith, shot down into the Channel during the strike on E-Boats. Squadron Leader M. F. Hendry, Sergeant P. M. Davidson and Sergeant V. Arrowsmith were killed. They are commemorated on the Runnymede Memorial.

The bomber fell to Feldwebel Eberhard v.Boremski of 9./JG 3.

Tuesday 24th September

Fairey Battle L5351 of 301 (Polish) Squadron, Swinderby, target invasion ports, failed to return. Pilot Officer J. Kulinski, Sergeant J. Waronski and Sergeant K. Paliwoda were all killed.

Blenheim T1883 of 107 Squadron, Wattisham, target Calais, crashed near Guemps, Pas de Calais. Pilot Officer W. S. Shann, Pilot Officer A. F. Etherington and Sergeant W. H. Powell are buried in the Churchyard at Guemps.

Hampden X2911 of 61 Squadron, Hemswell, target Calais, took off at 23.03 hours and collided with Hampden P4397, also of 61 Squadron. Sergeant J. E. Hills was killed. Sergeants Mills, Keet and Fenwick were injured.

Whitley N1470 'J' of 58 Squadron, Linton-on-Ouse, target Berlin, crashed just after take-off. Sergeant H. Cornish, Pilot Officer A. I. Watterson and Sergeant L. H. Taylor were killed. Sergeant Fowlie and Sergeant Chamberlain were injured.

In August 1940 an order was made to extend the black undersurfaces up the sides of the fuselage of all RAF 'heavy' bombers to help concealment at night. This Whitley also appears to have had her roundels toned down, another common feature of this period.

"We were one of the crews briefed to attack the electrical works at Finkenheerd, near Frankfurt on Oder, sixty miles east of Berlin, another long flog. We took off from Leeming at 18.40 hours and after an uneventful flight over the North Sea we crossed the German coast. The cloud was building up as we got deeper into Germany and as we got near to our ETA Finkenheerd we were in solid cloud, but we ploughed on. On ETA we stooged around attempting to find a break through which we could descend. We were unable to find a hole so the skipper decided we would go to our alternative target which was Templehof airfield, Berlin.

As we got near to Berlin the cloud started to break up so we pressed on. We got lucky and were able to see the ground through the breaks. The bomb aimer was down in the front map reading and he confirmed we were now over the 'Big City'. This was verified by the amount of Flak and the number of searchlights active in our vicinity. We were unable to pinpoint Templehof, but the bomb aimer spotted what he identified as a large railway station, a worthwhile target, so we started to run up on it. It was possible that we were one of the few aircraft over Berlin at this time so we were getting a lot of attention from the defences.

During our bomb-run the bomb aimer complained that cloud was partially obscuring the target. An anonymous voice over the intercom advised him that if he couldn't see railway lines, tram lines would do. The advice improved the bomb aimer's eyesight because his next announcement was, 'Bombs Gone'. At this time I was in the fuselage dumping my loose incendiaries and although I couldn't see the Flak I was well aware of it by the bumps and grinds from the bursts nearby.

We left the area fast, heading into what we believed was obscurity of the clouds. Our luck held and we got away unscathed and had the good fortune to cross Germany unhindered and get back safely to land at West Raynham, our diversion airfield. This time we had been airborne for ten hours and forty minutes, even loner than our last trip, but at least this time the fans kept turning until we got back to dispersal."

Larry Donnelly, 10 Squadron Whitley

SUNNY WITH SOME HIGH CLOUD IN PLACES.

Wednesday 25th September

ENEMY ACTIVITY

Except for three attacks; one on the Bristol aircraft works at Filton, one on Portland and the other on Plymouth, action was confined to south-east England. The attack on the Bristol works at Filton by twenty-seven escorted bombers caused considerable damage and casualties. The attacks on Portland and Plymouth, also by small numbers of escorted bombers, were unsuccessful. The night activity was mostly wide spread over the London area and maintained throughout the night concentrating on rail communications targets. There were other raids which penetrated to the Midlands, the West Country and south Wales. The Luftwaffe lost thirteen aircraft destroyed, the RAF lost three.

COASTAL COMMAND OPERATIONS

Ninety-six aircraft carried out sixty anti invasion, anti submarine patrols, reconnaissance, offensive and PRU sorties. Escort was also provided for twenty-two convoys.

1. Two Beauforts of 217 Squadron carried out a dawn bombing raid on Brest.
2. Six Blenheims of 59 Squadron attacked Brest and one claimed to have shot down a Do18.
3. A Hudson on offensive patrol attacked three motor vessels off Terschelling, claiming direct hits on the leading vessel which was subsequently seen sinking by the stern.
4. A patrolling Hudson of 233 Squadron escaped the unwelcome attentions of a Bf110 off Lister Light.
5. Sunderland 'B' of 10 (RAAF) Squadron spotted a lifeboat from the torpedoed *City of Benares* and guided Sunderland 'E' of 210 Squadron and a Royal Navy boat to the scene which affected a rescue.
6. Sunderland 'E' of 10 (RAAF) Squadron engaged a Do18 at 49 degrees 29'N/08 degrees 58'W.
7. Sunderland 'H' of 10 (RAAF) Squadron engaged a FW200 at 56 degrees 28'N/11 degrees 40'W.

Night operations

Aircraft were detailed for night operations over Brest

BOMBER COMMAND OPERATIONS

1. Six Blenheims carried out an uneventful sweep over the North Sea.
2. Another seven Blenheims carried out an offensive sweep looking for shipping off the Dutch coast. One aircraft failed to return.

Night operations

The main night attacks continued to concentrate on the Channel ports, but other targets in Germany were attacked, emphasising that the RAF still had the ability to strike back.

1. Twenty-seven Blenheims successfully attacked shipping in Boulogne, Calais, Antwerp and Brussels. Six aircraft flew security patrols over Calais/Marck.
2. Fourteen Fairey Battles of 103, 150 and 300 (Polish) Squadrons successfully attacked shipping at Ostend.
3. A total of thirty-three Wellingtons operated, twenty-seven joining the Blenheims in successful attacks on shipping at Calais and Boulogne. The other six attacked marshalling yards at Hamm, Mannheim, Scherte and the airfield at Benheim.

Pilot Officer Alec McCurdy of 59 Squadron is a study of concentration as he heads for Brest in his Blenheim.

4. Twenty-one Hampdens had power stations at Berlin and marshalling yards at Ehrang and Osnabrük as their targets; they claimed success.
5. Nineteen Whitleys were allocated and carried out attacks on German naval and shipping targets; the *Gneisenau*, *Scharnhorst* and *Lutzow* in Kiel and shipping at Antwerp.

OPERATIONAL LOSSES

Blenheim L8793 of 59 Squadron, Thorney Island, crashed in the entrance to Chichester Harbour, Sussex, on return from Brest. Pilot Officer R. F. W. Johnson was killed. Sergeants Abell and Andrews were injured and rescued by boat.

Anson N9890 'J' of 217 Squadron, St. Eval, crash landed on Rhossili beach, Glamorganshire after returning from Cherbourg with Flak damage. Flight Lieutenant Arnold and his crew were unhurt.

Blenheim P6905 of 101 Squadron, West Raynham, failed to return from a North Sea sweep and crashed in England. Sergeant F. R. Lorrimar, Sergeant P. W. Booth and Sergeant D. B. Simms were all killed and buried near their home towns.

Wellington L7868 of 99 Squadron, Newmarket, target Calais, crashed shortly after take-off from at 02.30 hours. The bomb load exploded but no serious injuries were reported to Pilot Officer Vivian's crew.

Thursday 26th September

OVERCAST AND CLOUDS COVERING MOST OF EUROPE.

A fighter's view of the Beaufort's blind spot.

ENEMY ACTIVITY

Until the afternoon, enemy activity was confined to reconnaissance. An attack by one hundred aircraft was mounted in the late afternoon against the Isle of Wight and Southampton area, during which the Vickers Supermarine works was severely damaged and heavy casualties were suffered. At night the main attacks were centred on London, but other targets on a line from Liverpool to the Humber were attacked and damaged. Luftwaffe losses were eight aircraft destroyed. RAF Fighter Command lost seven aircraft destroyed.

COASTAL COMMAND OPERATIONS

The usual patrols and other tasks were carried out by ninety-two aircraft. Seventeen convoys were escorted.

1. A Blenheim sent on an ASR detail found a dinghy seventy-eight miles north-east of Flamborough Head. A Royal Navy vessel was contacted which picked up the survivors.
2. Two Beauforts, 'H' and 'C' of 217 Squadron carried out a dawn bombing attack on Brest and dropped two 250lb bombs in the dockyard.
3. Hudson 'L' of 220 Squadron was engaged by two He115s seventy-two miles from Flamborough Head. The Hudson was damaged by an explosive bullet which entered the cockpit, but was rescued by 'X' and 'P' also of 220 Squadron who fought off the enemy aircraft.
4. A Blenheim on patrol bombed a motor vessel thirty-two miles north-east of Utyoer, but only managed near misses.
5. Photographs were taken by the PRU of most of the Channel ports, but attempts to photograph Lorient and St. Nazaire were unsuccessful.

Night operations

1. Six Ansons attacked shipping in Den Helder.
2. Six Beauforts laid mines in the rivers, Elbe, Jade and Weser.
3. Blenheim T2221 of 53 Squadron hit a tree during a night take-off from Detling, but there were no fatalities.

BOMBER COMMAND OPERATIONS

1. Six Blenheims carried out the usual routine daylight North Sea sweeps.
2. Six other Blenheims of 114 Squadron were sent to reconnoitre the French, Belgian and Dutch coasts in daylight. Because of unsuitable weather conditions four abandoned. One bombed Calais without results and one aircraft failed to return.

Night operations

The principal targets for the night force were again the Channel ports, but in addition German warships in Kiel were included. Mines were also laid in the La Pallice area.

1. Of the sixteen Blenheims detailed to attack the invasion fleet, fifteen were successful, five bombing the shipping at Boulogne, five bombing the barges at Calais and five shipping at Ostend.
2. Sixteen Wellingtons successfully attacked shipping at Le Havre.
3. Twenty-one Hampdens carried out attacks on warships at Kiel, communications on the Dortmund-Ems Canal and barges at Calais. Three other aircraft laid mines at La Pallice.
4. Fifteen Whitleys carried out attacks on the invasion craft at Le Havre.

OPERATIONAL LOSSES

Fokker T-VIIIW AV963 of 320 Squadron, Carew Cheriton, lost over the St George's Channel whilst on a convoy patrol. Officer Schevenhoven, Sergeant Akkers and Seinersmaat Scholman, all of the RNNAS, were lost.

Blenheim R3809 of 114 Squadron, Oulton, on an offensive reconnaissance to Boulogne, presumed crashed in the English Channel. Sergeant F. A. R. Wheeler's body was recovered from the sea off the Isle of Wight. Sergeant T. K. Johnson and Sergeant D. Hooker are commemorated on the Runnymede Memorial.

This aircraft was claimed as a "Hampden" by Feldwebel Herbert Schramm of 7./JG 53 at 13.16 hours.

Hampden. L4062 of 50 Squadron, Lindholme, target Calais, crashed into a tree at when attempting to land in fog. Pilot Officer R. T. Mulligan and Pilot Officer G. O. R. Kilner were injured. Sergeant C. J. Smith and Pilot Officer C. W Leonard escaped unhurt.

Hampden P2090 of 61 Squadron, Hemswell, target warships in Kiel. Hit by Flak and destroyed in a crash near Oresund, Sweden. Pilot Officer R. P. Earl (an Australian) is buried at Kviberg. Pilot Officer W. D. Hermon, Sergeant J. C. Williams and Sergeant D. Sinclair are buried at Halsingborg (Palsjo) Municipal Cemetery.

Hampden X2914 of 106 Squadron, Finningley, mining at La Pallice. After running out of fuel on return the aircraft was abandoned and crashed at West House Farm, Chilton Polden. Sergeant W. Huggins escaped safely. Sergeants E. H. W. Shelfer, J. J. A. Bogue and B. Harvey were killed.

Cloud and rain in the north, sunny spells in the south.

Friday 27th September

ENEMY ACTION

During the day there were three major attacks on London, south-east England and a smaller attack on Filton. The first comprised 180 aircraft in six formations, the second 300 aircraft, also in six formations, and the third 160 aircraft (fifty of which were bombers). The smaller attack on Filton was carried out by two formations of twenty-five bombers escorted by fifty fighters. This attack was intercepted before reaching the Filton works, but Filton railway station was hit. During the hours of daylight it was estimated that a total of 850 enemy aircraft operated over this country. During the night, although the raids were chiefly directed towards London, Edinburgh was also targeted. There were also scattered raids in the Liverpool, Birmingham and Nottingham districts up till midnight, but in the early hours of the morning London activity was renewed. During the day's fighting the Luftwaffe lost forty-nine aircraft destroyed, RAF fighter command lost twenty-eight destroyed.

Hampden crews of 83 Squadron brief for the night's raid.

COASTAL COMMAND OPERATIONS

Eighty-three aircraft carried out the usual patrol and reconnaissance tasks and fourteen convoys were escorted.

1. Three Blenheims of 53 Squadron carried out and evening attack on torpedo works at Den Helder.
2. Five Beauforts of 22 Squadron were detailed to carry out mining off Cuxhaven, but due to adverse weather only one mine was dropped.

Night operations

Fifteen aircraft were detailed to carry out night attacks; three to attack the torpedo works at Den Helder, six to attack shipping at Le Havre and six to drop mines in the Elbe, the Jade and the Weser Rivers.

BOMBER COMMAND OPERATIONS

1. Nine Blenheims were despatched to reconnoitre and attack targets on the French, Belgian and Dutch coasts. Six abandoned their task because of unsuitable weather, but three carried out individual attacks on small ships off the Dutch coast. Results were not observed.
2. Six additional Blenheims carried out a successful reconnaissance over the North Sea.

Night operations

The night force continued to inflict heavy damage on Hitler's invasion fleet in the occupied ports and the marshalling yard targets in Germany.

1. Six Blenheims carried out successful attacks on invasion shipping at Ostend. Two crews successfully attacked shipping at Boulogne, seven attacked shipping and barges in Calais, four attacked relevant alternative targets, one crew did not attack.
2. Twenty-two Hampdens carried out attacks on shipping at Lorient and St. Brieuc.
3. Thirty Wellingtons attacked shipping at Le Havre, Ostend and marshalling yards at Hamm, Mannheim, Ehrang, Köln, Gremberg and Soest.
4. Twelve Whitleys were detailed and eleven attacked shipping and installations at Lorient. The other crew attacked invasion craft at Le Havre.

OPERATIONAL LOSSES

Hampden P4392 'P' of 83 Squadron, Scampton, became lost on return from Lorient and abandoned by the crew over Lincolnshire. Pilot Officer D. D. Snooke was killed when his parachute failed. Pilot Officer C. L. Turner, Sergeant K. McKenzie and Pilot Officer E. C. Brighouse landed safely. The aircraft went on to crash on St. Matthias Church in Lincoln.

Wellington L7843 of 214 Squadron, Stradishall, target Mannheim, last heard on W/T at 04.33 hours sending distress signals. Sergeant J. R. Hall and Pilot Officer J. Rea are buried in the Haverlee War Cemetery. Sergeant H. E. Sambrook rests in the Belgrade Cemetery, Namur, Belgium. Sergeant T. F. Williams and Sergeant K. S, Thompson were reported later as PoW. The sixth crew member, Sergeant A. C. Peck, is believed to have also survived.

We were one of the Whitley crews detailed to bomb Lorient. We took off at 19.45 hours and it was a pleasant change not having to fly over the North Sea and then spend nail-biting hours over the heavily defended German mainland as we had been doing, sometimes over 600 miles from our base. We flew down to the south coast along the defence organisation corridor, then across the Channel to the north-west corner of France. For a change the weather was good and we followed the French coast to Lorient. Coastal targets or those having recognisable geographic features were better to pinpoint than inland targets. We bombed against slight opposition and as we left the area Slim (in the tail) reported fires. We had an uneventful return flight landing at 04.35 hours. I suppose if any bombing operation could be classed as easy this was it.

Larry Donnelly, 10 Squadron Whitley

Saturday 28th September

CLOUDY WITH OCCASIONAL BRIGHT SPELLS.

Sunderland P9600 of 10 RAAF Squadron which had an inconclusive engagement with a Do17 today. This huge and well armed flying boat was by no means an easy kill and dozens of Luftwaffe aircraft fell to its guns during the war.

ENEMY ACTIVITY

The Luftwaffe launched two attacks on London during the morning using Bf110s and Ju88s as bombers protected by Bf109s, however, only a small number managed to penetrate the defences. In the afternoon forty bombers escorted by 120 fighters heading for London were engaged by fighters and fifty Bf110s were intercepted off Portland. After dark 120 bombers attacked the western suburbs and rail centres in London. Other raids were plotted over Lincolnshire, Norfolk, the Bristol Channel and Middle Wallop areas. Minelaying was suspected off North Foreland and the Thames Estuary. The enemy night activity over the UK lasted for nine hours. Luftwaffe losses during the period were eight aircraft destroyed. RAF Fighter Command lost fifteen aircraft destroyed.

COASTAL COMMAND OPERATIONS

The daily anti invasion, anti submarine, reconnaissance and offensive sorties were carried out by seventy-two aircraft. Twenty-two convoys were escorted.

1. During the early morning (06.30) four Beauforts of 22 Squadron, 'G', 'I', 'J' and 'M' mined the River Elbe. Two more, 'U' and 'K', detailed to mine the Rivers Jade and Weser did not drop their mines.
2. Sunderland P9600 of 10 (RAAF) Squadron, flown by Squadron Leader Cohen and crew, had an inconclusive engagement with a Do17 ninety miles from Bishop's Rock.
3. Hudson 'F' of 220 Squadron found a dinghy eighty miles from Spurn Point. The two occupants were rescued later.

Night operations

1. Four Beauforts of 42 Squadron were detailed for night mining off Lorient. 'R' and 'G' mined the river mouth, 'P' abandoned with engine trouble and one aircraft failed to return.
2. Three Blenheims of 53 Squadron acted as a flare force for the Beaufort operation at Lorient.

BOMBER COMMAND OPERATIONS

1. Seven Blenheims were detailed to carry our offensive reconnaissance of the Channel ports. Five crews abandoned because of lack of cloud and two carried out individual attacks on barges at Ostend.
2. Six Blenheims carried out a routine North Sea sweep.

Night operations

Again the target for night bombing was the Channel ports, but some targets in Germany were attacked; power stations and gas works in Berlin, marshalling yards and industrial targets in the Ruhr.

1. Thirty-four of the forty-seven Blenheims despatched successfully attacked the barges and shipping in Boulogne, Calais and Dunkirk, also the guns at Cap Gris Nez.
2. Successful attacks were carried out by twenty Hampdens on the Dortmund-Ems Canal, marshalling yards at Hamm and Mannheim and shipping at Le Havre.
3. Thirty Wellingtons carried out attacks on the nickel works at Hanau, marshalling yards, airfields and the invasion ports.
4. Among the Whitley targets were the Berlin west and Waldeck power stations, Charlottenberg and Neuköln gasworks, the Fokker aircraft factory at Amsterdam and shipping and installations at Wilhelmshaven and Hamburg. Most of the crews on Berlin attacked the primaries or alternatives as did those on Hamburg and Wilhelmshaven, but because of adverse weather conditions crews were unable to locate the Fokker target in Amsterdam.

OPERATIONAL LOSSES

Hudson P5129 'E' of 269 Squadron, Wick, failed to return from a patrol to Norway. Shot down by JG77 off Herdla. Pilot Officer L. B. Emeno, Sergeant J. W. C. Heath, Sergeant J. N. McDonald and Sergeant P. S. Brown were presumed missing and are recorded on the Runnymede Memorial.

The Hudson was intercepted and shot down northwest of Bergen at 19.43 hours by Unteroffizier Otto Niemeyer of 4 Staffel.

Beaufort N1149 'V' of 42 Squadron, Thorney Island, failed to return from the mining sortie at Lorient, crashed in the sea off Finisterre. The bodies Flying Officer J. R. Bendell, Sergeant C. K. Woolnough, Sergeant C. F. Masson and Sergeant J. MacNaughton were all found along the Finisterre coast and buried locally.

Saturday 28th September

Wellington T2505 'W' of 9 Squadron, Honington, target Köln, crashed near Antwerp. Sergeant C. W. Oliver survived and was taken prisoner but his crew, Sergeant K. B. Gladwin, Sergeant L. W. Hardy, Sergeant J. Woods, Sergeant E. J. Milsom and Sergeant S. G. Brooker perished and are buried in the Schoonselhof Cemetery at Antwerp.

Wellington T2472 of 9 Squadron, Honington, target Hanau, crashed on return. Flying Officer A. H. C. Cox was killed.

Wellington R3164 'B' of 149 Squadron, Mildenhall, target Hanau, failed to return. Sergeant W. T. Hallam was killed and is buried in Durnbach War Cemetery. Pilot Officer H. R. Peterson, Sergeant K. Holden, Sergeant A. Botten, Sergeant C. McK. Laird (RNZAF) and Sergeant A. B. Witton (RNZAF) survived and were taken prisoners of war.

It wasn't just the efforts of the aircrews that helped win the Battle of Britain, it was also achieved with the hard work and dedication of the groundcrews. These men toiled around the clock in all weathers to keep the aircraft serviceable. Here, a group of 9 Squadron groundcrew pose for a photo with Wellington WS-Z.

Sunday 29th September

Mostly sunny, some cloud during the day, becoming clear later.

A 75 Squadron Wellington is prepared for the coming night's operations.

ENEMY ACTIVITY

Until the afternoon activity was limited to reconnaissance and a few attacks on shipping convoys. Shortly after 16.00 hours a sweep over London and Kent was carried out by one hundred enemy aircraft (mostly fighters) which flew at great altitudes. Night activity started early in the evening and continued until 06.00 hours on the 30th. The raids were widespread. London was again the main target and many fires were started. In the south west of London and in the Home Counties raids were heavy and damage was inflicted on a hospital and a nurses home. Liverpool was a target and fires were started on Merseyside. The Midlands, south Wales, Hampshire and East Anglia were also visited. During the period the Luftwaffe lost eight aircraft destroyed, RAF Fighter Command lost five.

COASTAL COMMAND OPERATIONS

Although the weather was far from good, patrols and other tasks were carried out.

1. Hudson 'O' of 224 Squadron attacked a surfaced U-Boat at 56 degrees 08'N/ O9 degrees 40'W. No positive result was observed.
2. Sunderland 'E' of 210 Squadron attacked a U-Boat at 58 degrees 37'N/16 degrees 54W. No result observed.
3. Six Blenheims of 59 Squadron carried out an evening strike (17.35 hours) on Lorient. Six Blenheims of 53 Squadron carried out an evening (18.25 hours) strike on Rotterdam.
4. Four Beauforts carried out late evening (18.45-23.30 hours) mining sortie to the Jade and Weser estuaries.
5. PRU aircraft photographed the French and Belgian Coasts, but adverse weather prevented photography over Norway.

BOMBER COMMAND OPERATIONS

1. Six Blenheims carried out an uneventful North Sea sweep.
2. Three other Blenheims were despatched to reconnoitre Channel ports, but abandoned because of no cloud cover.

Night operations

Night raids were despatched to attack the invasion fleet in the Channel ports and industrial targets in Germany.

1. Twenty-one Blenheims attacked the invasion fleet at Calais, Boulogne, Flushing, Le Touquet and Ostend.
2. Eighteen Hampdens carried out successful attacks on the Bosch factory at Stuttgart and marshalling yards at Hamm, Gremberg, Soest and Eifeltor.
3. Twenty-two Wellingtons attacked the aluminium works at Bittefeld and the marshalling yards at Mannheim, Ehrang and Osnabrük.
4. The Whitley targets were Magdeburg and Hannover. One crew returned early. The conditions were not good and most bombed alternatives. One aircraft returned from Amsterdam on one engine.

The reality of an operational loss statistic. A Wellington rear gunner lies with his parachute as his shroud in the wreckage of his rear turret.

OPERATIONAL LOSSES

Hampden X2902 of 50 Squadron, Lindholme, target Stuttgart, lost without trace. Squadron Leader J. C. Taylor, Sergeant K. W. Watchous, Sergeant A. G. Hobson and Sergeant P. A. Merrick are all commemorated on the Runnymede Memorial.

Wellington R3150 of 37 Squadron, Feltwell, target Bittefeld, shot down near Osnabrük. Pilot Officer A. C. Dingle, Pilot Officer G. P. Turner, Sergeant G. H. Taylor, Sergeant P. A. Young, and Pilot Officer J. Littlejohn are buried in the Reichswald Forest War Cemetery. Pilot Officer D. K. Hayes was made a PoW.
This was brought down by Oberleutnant Heinrich Greise of I./NJG 1 at 00.34 hours.

Wellington R3168 of 75 Squadron, Mildenhall, target Leipzig, ran out of fuel and crashed on return on Exmoor near Lynton. Pilot Officer F. H. Denton, Sergeant White, Sergeant Orrock, Sergeant Hayter and Sergeant Farquhar escaped with injuries, but Pilot Officer E. A. Jelley was killed.

Right: The rear turret of a Wellington. Statistically, the gunner was the most vulnerable member of a bomber crew.

Monday 30th September

CLOUDY, SOME SHOWERS, WITH OCCASIONAL BRIGHT SPELLS.

Torpedoes are brought out to waiting Albacores in a staged press photo. Quite how the groundcrew will load the tin fish with the rotating propellers is not clear!

ENEMY ACTIVITY

This was the day when the Luftwaffe carried out its last major daylight raids on the United Kingdom during World War II. Six raids developed during the day, four over east Kent and two in the Portland area. They started early when two waves of 200 aircraft approached London just after 09.00 hours. The majority were turned back by fighters; the few who got through dropped bombs in the west London area. At 10.00 hours a sweep by Bf109s heading for Weymouth retreated when engaged by fighters. During the afternoon 100 bombers escorted by 200 hundred fighters attempted to reach London. A Gruppe of Ju88s with their Bf109 escort broke through to the southern suburbs but lost heavily when engaged by fighters. Forty He111s escorted by Bf110s were driven back when they attempted to get through to the Westland aircraft factory at Yeovil. The night raids were wide-spread. Although Central London and the suburbs were the main targets, Merseyside was also attacked where fires were started. Minelaying is thought to have taken place in the Thames Estuary, Harwich and as far north as the Firth of Forth. During the hectic days fighting the Luftwaffe lost forty-one aircraft destroyed. RAF Fighter Command lost fifteen aircraft destroyed.

COASTAL COMMAND OPERATIONS

109 aircraft carried out anti invasion, anti submarine patrols, reconnaissance and offensive sorties. Nineteen convoys were given escort.

1. Four Blenheims of 59 Squadron were despatched to carry out an early dawn attack on Lorient. Two bombed successfully.
2. Two Beauforts of 42 Squadron carried out a dawn mining sortie at Lorient and four Beauforts of 22 Squadron mined the Jade and Weser estuaries.
3. Photographic reconnaissance of enemy ports was also carried out.

Night operations

Fourteen aircraft were detailed to carry out a night raid on Rotterdam and another four minelaying in the Jade and Weser estuaries.

BOMBER COMMAND OPERATIONS

Bomber Command Headquarters was informed on this day that the imminent danger of German invasion had passed.

1. Three Blenheims were despatched to carry out a daylight reconnaissance of the Channel ports. The task was abandoned due to lack of cloud cover.
2. Six Blenheims carried out an uneventful North Sea sweep. There were no losses.

Night operations

The night force was detailed to attack ports and shipping, the German Air Ministry in Berlin, an oil plant at Leuna, marshalling yards in the Ruhr and also to carry out minelaying in the Elbe Estuary.

1. Thirty-four Blenheims successfully attacked the barges and shipping at Boulogne, Calais, Dunkirk and Ostend.

2. Forty-two Hampdens, Wellingtons and Whitleys were given the German Air Ministry in Berlin as their target. Seventeen crews claimed to have pinpointed and bombed it.
3. Twelve Wellingtons attacked the synthetic oil plant at Leuna and Merseburg, while nine attacked the marshalling yards at Mannheim and Osnabrük.
4. As well as attacking the Air Ministry in Berlin, Hampdens attacked shipping at Antwerp and another five mined the Elbe Estuary.
5. Six Whitley crews claimed to have bombed the German Air Ministry in Berlin and reported the opposition as severe. One crew bombed shipping at Le Havre and Verden.

OPERATIONAL LOSSES

Albacore L7100 of 826 Squadron Fleet Air Arm, lost on operations. Lieutenant C. S. H. Kennaway, Midshipman R. J. Lane were posted as missing and their names appear on the Lee-on-Solent Memorial. The body of Naval Airman 1 G. F. K. Howe was recovered and buried at Sage War Cemetery, Germany.

Blenheim T2044 'G' of 53 Squadron, Detling, target Rotterdam, crashed in the sea off Sheerness. The bodies of Pilot Officer S. R. Bevan-John and Sergeant S. Macquire were recovered and buried at their home towns. Sergeant H. A. Shaw was posted missing and is recorded on the Runnymede Memorial.

Hudson T9326 'V' of 224 Squadron, Aldergrove, crashed shortly after take-off for a patrol. Sergeant K. Posgate, Sergeant A. J. Gibbs, Sergeant R. C. Cox, Sergeant S. Swann, Sergeant J. P. O'Connor were all killed.

Blenheim N6191 of 107 Squadron, Wattisham, target invasion ports, crashed on take off and burst into flames. One member of the crew was pulled from the blazing wreckage by Wing Commander L. F. Sinclair who was later awarded the George Cross. The other members of the crew, Sergeant J. E. Merrett and Sergeant S. Walters were killed.

Hampden P4411 of 50 Squadron, Bircham Newton, target Berlin, hit an earth bank on return when landing at Docking, Norfolk. Pilot Officer Powell and his crew escaped injury.

Wellington R3219 'Q' of 38 Squadron, Marham, target Leipzig, failed to return. Pilot Officer D. Maclean was killed and is buried in the Reichswald Forest Cemetery. Sergeant A. S. Williams, Sergeant J. Tipping, Sergeant V. F. Gammon, Sergeant J. Hamilton and Pilot Officer W. T. Mathieson were taken prisoner.

Wellington R3292 'F' of 115 Squadron, Marham, target Osnabrük, failed to return. The crew of Sergeant C. Wessels, Sergeant N. W. G. Thompson and Sergeant A. D. Cameron are buried in the Reichswald Forest Cemetery.

German flak batteries open up on the incoming RAF bombers.

Monday 30th September

Sergeant A. J. Pennington, Sergeant J. G. C. MacNair and Sergeant H. W. Pritchard have no known grave and are recorded on the Runnymede Memorial.

Whitley T4130 of 10 Squadron, Leeming, target Berlin, shot down over Bad-Bergen by Oberleutnant Werner Streib of 2./NJG1 at 23.19 hours. Sergeant V. Snell and Sergeant G. L. Ismay were killed and are buried in the Reichswald Forest War Cemetery. Sergeant W. D. Chamberlain, Sergeant A. S. Shand and Sergeant R. E. Nicholson were taken PoW.

Whitley N1483 of 10 Squadron, Leeming, target Berlin, ditched in the Irish Sea on return. Flying Officer Wood and his crew were rescued unhurt, but embarrassed!

Wellington T2549 'K' of 115 Squadron, Marham, target Osnabrük , Pilot Officer A. J. J. Steel and Sergeant R. P. Mogg were taken prisoner. Sergeant C. Dowsett is commemorated on the Runnymede Memorial. Sergeant L. G. Goldie, Sergeant J. Le B. R.Walter and Sergeant D. E. Westwood are buried in the Reichswald Forest War Cemetery.

Apart from Streib's victory noted previously (claimed as a "Hampden", he also claimed a Wellington at Bersenbrück at 22.49 hours and another Wellington at Menslage at 23.35 hours, the first Luftwaffe nightfighter pilot to gain a 'triple'. Additionally, a third Wellington was claimed at Loningen at 00.38 hours by Oberleutnant Heinrich Greise of I./NJG 1.

The night of 30th September/1st October was a memorable time for me. During the day the group signals officer paid a visit to our squadron W/T section. While he had a chat with the WOp/AGs he asked us in turn how many operations we had carried out. When I gave him my total he did a double-take, telling me I was overdue for 'screening'. Some short time after he had left us I was called to see our squadron commander who informed me it had been brought to his attention that I should have been screened, and that he was rectifying the oversight. I was to be screened forth-with. His actual statement was a well-worn cliché, 'I've got some good news and some bad news for you. You're screened, but you are going to have to fly tonight because Group have called for a 'maximum effort'.

Looking back I suppose my reaction was first relief, knowing that my luck could not last forever. I had been on operations since the beginning of the war. Second came apprehension that I was going to have to go through Flak Alley once again that night. When I gave the news to my 'oppos' in the section I got the predictable commiserations. 'You shouldn't have joined if you can't take a joke' and 'what's one more to an Ace like you?'

My morale got another jolt at briefing when our target was revealed as the German Air Ministry in Berlin and also that our usual skipper and tail gunner had been replaced, but to compensate the skipper was one of the squadron's most experienced pilots and the group gunnery leader was our tail-gunner. At least I was doing my last 'dice' with the higher paid help!

I took a little longer than usual with my pre-flight preparations, missing nothing from my superstitious ritual, lucky coins etc. We took off from Leeming at 18.03 hours and by the time we reached the enemy coast I had regained some of my composure. However, as we passed to the south of Wilhelmshaven my composure was disturbed when somebody remarked over the intercom, 'They're knocking Hell out of some poor so-and-so over there'. I looked through my side window to see the aircraft in question held at the apex of a cone of searchlights into which the Flak batteries were firing everything they could. As I watched I was sure I saw the stricken aircraft fall away in flames. My reaction was to turn up the volume of my W/T receiver and concentrate on my listening watch. Eventually we weaved our way to the 'Big City'. From the searchlight and Flak activity it was evident the reception committee was having a go at the early arrivals. By this time the bomb-aimer was map reading us to the target and I was down the fuselage preparing to drop parachute flares. As we started our bomb-run I dropped a couple of flares and the surplus drift incendiaries for my own satisfaction.

I heaved a sigh of relief when the bomb-aimer called 'Bombs Gone'. By now the defences were having a real go at us, evident from the way the tail-gunner's voice rose in pitch as he reported the close proximity of the bursts. However, my lucky charms and pre-flight superstitious ritual worked because we got away from the target area without a scratch. Back at the W/T set I sent my 'Bombs Gone' signal and listened for my fellow squadron W/Ops who were flying with us to do the same. I was pleased to hear one of them send his signal, but dismayed to learn later that just after he had transmitted his aircraft was shot down - luckily he survived as a prisoner of war.

Our return flight seemed to me, for obvious reasons, interminable but we got back across the North Sea without incident and landed safely at Watton, our diversion airfield. After de-briefing, a meal and a lapse of a few hours we flew back to Leeming where we learned that in addition to our aircraft shot down over Berlin, we had lost another which had ditched in the Irish, yes Irish, Sea. Fortunately they were rescued, shaken but unhurt, and landed at Holyhead. Two days later I was posted to be a W/T instructor at the Whitley OTU at Kinloss, Having completed forty-one operations, seventeen of them during the Battle of Britain.

Larry Donnelly, 10 Squadron Whitley

October 1940

'Sealion' Invasion Tamed!

October - 'Sealion' Invasion Tamed!

The interception of the secret German signal on 17th September, containing the information that Hitler was postponing '*Sealion*' indefinitely, and the follow up signal ordering the dispersal of the invasion fleet, was confirmation that the invasion of Britain was no longer imminent. Despite this the Luftwaffe continued its air attacks, but with changed tactics. During daylight the Dornier and Heinkel bombers almost disappeared from the scene, being reserved for the nightly 'Blitz'. They were replaced by fighter bombers carrying out 'hit and run' raids. Although the cessation of mass daylight raids substantially reduced Fighter Command's losses, October proved to be one of the most severe tests of the battle. Dealing with the fighter bomber raids was a different 'kettle of fish', but the command coped even though, as John Terraine states in his book, '*The Right of the Line*', 'It was stretched like the strings of a violin.

Throughout October the weather continued to deteriorate and the tasks of Bomber and Coastal Command crews became more difficult, but they kept plugging away, the heavy bombers attacking more strategic targets as the risk of invasion diminished.

The Coastal Command squadrons continued their sterling work carrying out anti invasion, anti submarine patrols, reconnaissance and offensive sorties plus convoy escorts. They were, however, able to devote more time to attacking coastal land targets as well as shipping in the North Sea from Norway down to the French/Spanish border.

The Photographic Reconnaissance Unit also continued to fly sorties, obtaining vital photographic information concerning the enemy's shipping strength and disposition.

The Battle of Britain proved that the fighter reigned supreme in daylight. As autumn approached the bombers of both sides were forced to seek the cover of darkness.

Previous page: A 149 Squadron Wellington taxies out under the moonlight.

Tuesday 1st October

Sunderland P9600 was in action again, this time scrapping with 3 Bf110s off Lands End.

ENEMY ACTIVITY

Although three attacks were made in the Kent area and another towards Poole and the Isle of Wight, they were on a reduced scale. Two Ansons were destroyed in an attack on Carew Cheriton. Interceptions were carried out by fighters that prevented all but a few raiders penetrating the London defences. Reconnaissance flights were also on a reduced scale. Night activity was less than usual. London was the main objective, but other raids were scattered over a wide area during the early part of the night. Some of the raiders penetrated to the Midlands and south Wales. During the period the Luftwaffe lost six aircraft destroyed. RAF Fighter Command lost a similar number.

COASTAL COMMAND OPERATIONS

The usual routine tasks were carried out by seventy-six aircraft and twenty convoys were given protection.

1. Two Beauforts of 42 Squadron carried out a dawn mining sortie in the harbour at Lorient.

2. Throughout daylight hours Blenheims gave cover to naval units operating off Texel. Other Blenheims attacked Cherbourg.

2. Ansons and Swordfish of 812 FAA Squadron carried out a sea sweep between Hastings and Gt. Yarmouth.

4. Three Beauforts searched for U-Boats off the east coast and Hudsons looked for enemy shipping between Karma and Lister.

5. Sunderland P9600 of 10 RAAF Squadron fought an indecisive engagement with three Bf110s fifty-eight miles from Land's End.

BOMBER COMMAND OPERATIONS

1. An uneventful daylight sweep was carried out by seven Blenheims over the North Sea. Other tasks were abandoned because of adverse weather.

Night operations

The night force comprising Blenheims, Wellingtons, Hampdens and Whitleys were detailed to attack a variety of objectives; munitions, power stations, oil plants, marshalling yards, canal docks, enemy aerodromes, shipping and gun positions. A mining sortie was also detailed. A total of eighty-eight aircraft were involved.

1. Blenheims attacked invasion shipping at Boulogne, Calais and Dunkirk. They also attacked marshalling yards at Mannheim, Ehrang, Köln/Eifeltor, Gremberg and Koblenz. The majority of crews claimed success.

2. The Hampdens' targets were a power station at Cologne and marshalling yards in the Ruhr. An additional six aircraft mined the Verdonne - Gironde area, Squadron Leader Broad of 44 Squadron had the undercarriage of P1324 collapse on his return.

3. Some of the Wellingtons went to Berlin where a munitions factory and the Elgemeine power station were successfully attacked. Others attacked the marshalling yards at Soest and Gelsenkirchen and shipping at Le Havre.

4. The synthetic oil plant at Sterkrade-Holten and shipping at Rotterdam was successfully attacked by the Whitley force.

OPERATIONAL LOSSES

Blenheim R3626 of 248 (F) Squadron, Sumburgh, failed to return from a Norwegian coastal patrol. Pilot Officer C. C. Bennett (Australian), Sergeant G. S. Clarke and Sergeant G. B. Brash were posted as missing in action and their names appear on the Runnymede Memorial.

Hampden X2965 of 44 Squadron, Waddington, target Köln, crashed into the sea. The bodies of Sergeant H. Day and Sergeant G. J. Devlin were washed ashore. The other two members of the crew, Sergeant J. Tomlinson and Sergeant E. R. Sillett are commemorated on the Runnymede Memorial.

Wellington R3282 'G' of 9 Squadron, Honington, target Berlin, came down in the sea off Lowestoft on return. None of the crew survived. Flight Lieutenant C. D. Fox, Sergeant R. E. Thompson, Sergeant D. B. Fleming, Sergeant J. D. Robertson, Sergeant R. P. Sweet and Sergeant C. M. Le B. Newbery (RNZAF), are commemorated on the Runnymede Memorial.

Whitley P4964 of 78 Squadron, Dishforth, target Sterkrade Holten, believed to have been shot down by a night-fighter working in conjunction with radar controlled searchlights, 21 km east of Arnhem. Pilot Officer N. H. Andrew, Pilot Officer H. W. Morgan, Sergeant G. E. Matson, Sergeant P. H. Richmond and Sergeant A. Roscoe all perished. They are buried in a communal grave at the commune of Hummelo-en-Keppel, close to the crash site. *Their opponent was Leutnant Hans-Georg Mangelsdorf of 2./NJG 1, credited with a victory at 00.10 hours.*

Wednesday 2nd October

Sunny in most parts, but cloud developing at night

Blackburn Skua L2929 of 801 Squadron Fleet Air Arm which was lost on operations today off Norway.

ENEMY ACTIVITY

During the day there were six attempted raids on London, but bombers participated in only one, dropping a few bombs on south London and various places in Kent and Sussex. A number of reconnaissance flights took place over other areas and two enemy aircraft were shot down, one over Dulwich and the other one over Skegness. A Ju88 which left Amsterdam at 00.30 hours got lost and landed at 06.30 hours at Brightlingsea, intact and with crew! In the late evening (20.15 hours) a convoy was attacked off Peterborough, but the raiders were intercepted and an He115 was shot down. Night raids were widespread over Scotland, north-west England and south-east England, including London, where bombs were dropped indiscriminately causing damage and casualties. The raids continued until 06.30 hours. Luftwaffe losses were fourteen aircraft destroyed. RAF Fighter Command lost three aircraft destroyed.

COASTAL COMMAND OPERATIONS

The usual routine patrols and other tasks were carried out and escort provided for eighteen convoys. During the patrols some motor vessels and barges were attacked in various locations but results were not observed.

1. Five Ansons of 217 Squadron carried out a strike at dawn on barges in the Isle de Bas - Ushant - Brest area.
2. Anson N9741 of 612 Squadron on convoy patrol drove off an attacking Bf110.
3. PR photographs were taken of Ports in France, Belgium, Holland and Norway.
4. Four Beauforts of 22 Squadron mined the Ems Estuary during the evening.

Night operations

Ten aircraft were detailed to carry out a night strike on Rotterdam and four others to mine the Ems Estuary.

BOMBER COMMAND OPERATIONS

1. Six Blenheims carried out a routine North Sea sweep.

Night operations

1. Seventy-four Blenheims, Wellingtons, Hampdens and Whitleys attacked shipping at Amsterdam, Rotterdam, Antwerp, Flushing and the Channel ports as well as oil plants at Stettin, Hamburg and Boltrope. The Krupps works at Essen, aerodromes, docks at Hamburg and Wilhelmshaven and a power station at Finkenheerd were also attacked. Six additional Hampdens laid mines in the entrance to the Langelands Belt. All the operations were seriously hampered by the adverse weather conditions.

OPERATIONAL LOSSES

Skua L2929 of 801 Squadron Fleet Air Arm, lost on operations off Norway. Sub Lieutenant A. Hartoch lies buried at Bergen, Norway. The name of Naval Airman 1 E. J. Adlam appears on the Lee-on-Solent Memorial.

Blenheim T1896 of 105 Squadron, Watton, target Calais, crashed 10km south-west of Calais. Sergeant K. Lord. Sergeant F. V. Bundock and Sergeant H. Dunbar all perished and are buried at Pihen-les-Guines.

Hampden X2896 of 50 Squadron, Lindholme, target Hamburg, crashed on return attempting to land at a dummy flare-path four miles south-east of Dunbar. Only one member of the crew was injured, Sergeant E. Smith, the others were unhurt,

Whitley N1434 of 58 Squadron, Linton-on-Ouse, target Finkenheerd, failed to return. Flying Officer W. C. Espley, Pilot Officer P. S. Dally, Sergeant I. A. Zamek, Sergeant A. J. Cheesman and Sergeant A. E. Chetter are all buried in the Berlin 1939-1945 War Cemetery.

Thursday 3rd October

ENEMY ACTIVITY

The weather conditions were a deciding factor. Poor visibility resulted in the Luftwaffe resorting to single aircraft to carry out attacks on targets in various parts of the country, London in particular. Bombs were dropped at random causing some damage and a train was machine-gunned. An attack by two enemy aircraft on RAF St. Eval caused a small amount of damage to hangars and Anson K8783 of 217 Squadron was destroyed in a hangar fire. Hatfield aerodrome was also attacked causing damage and heavy casualties, seventy-seven killed and twenty-four injured. Poor weather conditions precluded interception by fighters. Enemy night activity was also on a reduced scale, London again being the main objective. Single raiders visited Norfolk, Debden and Bedford. Luftwaffe losses were eight aircraft destroyed. RAF Fighter Command suffered no losses.

COASTAL COMMAND OPERATIONS

Thirty-seven patrols and offensive sorties were carried out and thirteen convoys provided with escort. Fifty-five aircraft were involved.

1. A Hudson on patrol fifty-two miles from Gt. Yarmouth fought an inconclusive engagement with two He115s.
2. A Blenheim crew attacked a Do215 off Sumburgh, but broke off when the pilot and observer were wounded.
3. Five aircraft attacked targets in the Cherbourg area.

BOMBER COMMAND OPERATIONS

1. Six Blenheims carried out a routine reconnaissance of the North Sea.
2. Five Blenheims were despatched on a reconnaissance of Dutch, Belgian and French Coasts. Three crews abandoned because of adverse weather and, of the two remaining, one bombed a coastal steamer and the other attacked twelve ships off Dunkirk. No results were observed.
3. Four other Blenheims were sent to attack oil targets. They failed their primary task, but dropped bombs on Rotterdam Harbour, barges at Heusen and an iron works near Wesel.

Night operations

All night operations were cancelled because of unfavourable weather.

OPERATIONAL LOSSES

There were no losses

A Heinkel 115 being prepared for a mission. These large floatplanes were frequently encountered during Coastal Command patrols, as today when a Hudson ran in to a pair of them off Great Yarmouth.

Friday 4th October

Mist, rain and poor visibility throughout the day. Fog at night.

Above: Beauforts of 42 Squadron. One of their number was shot down on this day by Oberleutnant Ulrich Steinhilper of 3./JG 52 (pictured left).

ENEMY ACTION

Adverse weather again affected operations. Throughout the day enemy action was confined to raids by single aircraft or small formations, their main objectives being south-east England and London. A few reconnaissance aircraft penetrated to the Liverpool area. The weather precluded any interception. The enemy might activity increased slightly but was still on a restricted scale with London again as the main target except for a few aircraft which penetrated to the Bristol and Liverpool areas. Minelaying was suspected in the Thames Estuary and the Orfordness and Lowestoft areas. During the day the Luftwaffe lost nine aircraft destroyed. Fighter Command lost one aircraft destroyed.

COASTAL COMMAND OPERATIONS

Despite the weather conditions thirty-five aircraft carried out patrols and escort was provided for twelve convoys.

1. Anson 'V' of 500 Squadron on convoy escort twelve miles east of Southwold drove off an attacking Ju88, claiming hits on the enemy aircraft.
2. Two Beauforts of 42 Squadron were despatched on a search and torpedo strike sortie in the Ijmuiden/Ostend area. They were intercepted by four Bf109s. During the engagement Beaufort L4505 was damaged but managed to escape and carry out a crash-landing at RAF Thorney Island after jettisoning its torpedo in Thorney Creek. The other Beaufort, L4488, was shot down by the enemy aircraft.
3. Sunderland 'F' of 10 RAAF Squadron attacked a U-Boat at 49 degrees 04'N/12 degrees 31'W without any positive result.
4. Four aircraft attacked enemy airfields in occupied France.

BOMBER COMMAND OPERATIONS

1. Thirty Blenheims were sent in daylight to attack targets in Germany despite the adverse weather. Most aircraft experienced severe icing and fourteen of them abandoned their tasks altogether. One managed to bomb its primary target and the remainder bombed alternatives.
2. Six other Blenheims carried out a North Sea sweep.

Night operations

Operations were cancelled because of adverse weather.

OPERATIONAL LOSSES

Beaufort L4488 of 42 Squadron, Thorney Island, was shot down by Bf109s while attempting a torpedo strike on shipping in the Ijmuiden/Ostend area. Pilot Officer F. D. Flinn, Sergeant F. W. Shirley, Sergeant F. A. O'Malley and Sergeant A. M. B. Robertson were taken prisoner. *This was credited to Oberleutnant Ulrich Steinhilper of 3./JG 52.*

ENEMY ACTION

There were reconnaissance flights during the early morning but they decreased later. During the day six bombing raids took place, four on London causing fires and two against Portsmouth and Southampton. Air battles took place over the Kent and Sussex coasts. It was estimated that five hundred and forty enemy aircraft operated over the UK during the day. At night the activity was directed mainly against London and adjacent areas in the eastern counties and south-east England bombs were dropped causing fires. Luftwaffe losses during the period were fourteen aircraft destroyed. RAF Fighter Command lost seven aircraft destroyed.

COASTAL COMMAND OPERATIONS

Seventy-two aircraft carried out forty-five patrols and offensive sorties during the day but after 23.00 hours all patrols were cancelled because of adverse weather conditions. Air escort was provided for seventeen convoys.

1. During offensive patrols off the Norwegian coast Hudsons carried out a dive-bombing attack on two motor vessels scoring near misses. Another motor vessel was attacked off Sola (Stavanger) with bombs and machine-guns.
2. An Anson searching for the stricken motor vessel *Ottoland*, located it and guided two mine-sweepers to the scene that picked up two life boats of survivors.

Night operations

Six aircraft were detailed to carry out a night strike on shipping at Brest and another six to attack barges and motor transport concentrations at Gravelines.

A 206 Squadron Hudson returns to base after a patrol.

Saturday 5th October

A Hampden takes off in the gathering gloom, heading for a long night over Germany. The aircraft is carrying two bombs under the wing racks as well as up to 2000lbs of bombs internally.

Evasive Action

Flight Lieutenant Colin Rawlins DFC
Hampden pilot 144 Sqn

We got used to carrying out the gyrations popularly supposed to make the flak-gunners' task more difficult. Depending upon the intervals of flak fire, one got used to flinging the aeroplane about in an abandoned "split arse", (as the crude term then was), way which, if repeated in daylight over friendly territory, would have the pilot and crew terrified almost to the point of baling out. But the sight and sound of shells exploding nearby would rapidly overcome any fears about stalling speeds and other aerodynamic limits and, in any case, the darkness of night covered up such excesses. Of course, the pilot watched the airspeed but might indulge in turns, climbs and dives of a violence which, were he still under instruction, would probably end his flying career there and then.

BOMBER COMMAND OPERATIONS

1. Six Blenheims carried out a daylight reconnaissance over the North Sea from Lossiemouth Two enemy naval vessels were sighted south of Utsire Island. A stick of bombs was dropped on two escort vessels in the island harbour scoring near misses and a hit on the jetty.
2. Another seven Blenheims were sent in daylight to attack oil and aluminium targets in Germany, but all tasks were abandoned because of lack of cloud cover.

Night operations

1. Adverse weather conditions curtailed night operations, but four Wellingtons attacked shipping at Rotterdam. Two crews claimed success reporting that bomb bursts were observed between Maashaven and Waalhaven and that a building was set on fire near Merewhaven. Flushing was also bombed and explosions observed on the south-west side of Verbredd.
2. Thirty Hampdens were despatched, eight to attack marshalling yards and twelve to attack the oil plant at Gelsenkirchen.
3. Another ten Hampdens were sent to lay mines in the Elbe Estuary.

50 Squadron line up for a photo in July 1940.

OPERATIONAL LOSSES

Hudson P5117 of 233 Squadron, Leuchars, failed to return from patrol. Flying Officer G. K. Brackenridge, Pilot Officer J. McIntosh, Sergeant D. Bruce and Sergeant A. Russell and crew were posted as missing in action. An investigation revealed that the crew returned to the coast in appalling weather, but were unable to fix their location. The crew baled out, but landed in the North Sea and were lost and are remembered on the Runnymede Memorial. The abandoned aircraft flew on to eventually crash at the hamlet of Oxford, Northumberland.

Blenheim R2771 of 53 Squadron, Detling, flew into the ground near Manston on return from a patrol to the Hook of Holland. Pilot Officer K. A. Faulkner and Sergeant G. B. Fielder were injured. Sergeant A. R. S. Hall was killed.

Hampden P4417 of 50 Squadron, Lindholme, target Köln, lost without trace. Sergeant F. J. Brooker, Pilot Officer A. S. Boak, Sergeant J. D. Marshall and Sergeant C. H. Wise are all commemorated on the Runnymede Memorial.

Hampden X2920 of 61 Squadron, Hemswell, mining Elbe Estuary, crashed on the Yorkshire Moors near Leeming on return. Pilot Officer G. D'Arcy-Wright, Sergeant W. A. Cannon, Sergeant W. B. Rayment and Sergeant A. Algar all perished in the crash.

Hampden X2977 of 83 Squadron, Scampton, iced up on the way to Gelsenkirchen and crashed near base on an early return. Sergeant Hawkes, Sergeant Gilmour and Sergeant E. S. Phillips were injured. Sergeant C. A. Sherwood was killed.

Hampden P4362 of 144 Squadron, Hemswell, mining Elbe Estuary, lost without trace. Sergeant R. J. Neale, Sergeant H. Bennett, Sergeant G. Wood and Flight Sergeant P. H. Yorath are all commemorated on the Runnymede Memorial.

Hampden X2963 of 144 Squadron, Hemswell, undershot on landing in strong winds returning from a Gardening sortie. Squadron Leader Lerwill and his crew escaped injury.

Friendly Fire

Sgt. Joe Taylor
Hampden WOp/AG 61 Squadron

One time during shuttle bombing of the channel ports when Hitler was massing barges for the threatened '*Operation SeaLion*', aircraft were being flown over the targets, returning to base for re-bombing up and flown straight off again. I had to go to change the accumulators for the radio on one of the Hampdens which had just landed. To get to the accumulator rack which was up above the under turret in the tail boom, a certain amount of scrambling had to be done. This aircraft was still warm, still smelly of hot oil, cordite fumes and petrol, the engines were crackling as heat subsided and cylinders contracted. Whoever it was that had just vacated the lower gun position had of need, left his pair of Vickers 'K' guns mounted ready for the next crew. Normally each gunner or wireless operator gunner had his own pair of matched and 'coned' machine guns which he moved from aircraft to aircraft. I suppose I was as much to blame as he for what happened next, but as I climbed up over the mounted guns to reach the wet batteries, I grasped the trigger block of one of them to help me climb. Unfortunately, the ammo pans were in place and the guns cocked with safety catches off. Are you ahead of me? - yes, there was a burst of fire and about a dozen rounds of mixed A.P. incendiary tracer and ball screamed out at the grass under the tail, up again through the tail boom and tail plane and away towards the hangars half a mile away. I was in a state of panic stricken shock. Suppose I've killed or injured someone. Suppose the aircraft has been put out of commission and cannot be used again? With the usual rough good humour found with long suffering ground crews, the flight rigger came over to inspect the damage. "Its all right Sarge." He said with a broad grin, "I'll dope a few patches on, there's only one or two pinholes in her." I said to wait until I had reported the mishap at the flight offices and left him. Fortunately for me the Flight Commander wasn't unduly disturbed but warned me about the need for more care in the future. The Hampden was patched up with linen and dope and all was well.

Sunday 6th October

HEAVY RAIN THROUGHOUT THE COUNTRY.

The intense activity around this 110 Squadron Blenheim at Wattisham is probably staged for the camera. Then again, would the erks really lift a 250lb bomb for the sake of the press?!

ENEMY ACTIVITY

Adverse weather restricted Luftwaffe daytime activity to raids by single aircraft over land. Two raids in strength were made on a convoy off the east coast. Machine-gun attacks were made on a number of towns and villages. Several RAF stations, including Northolt, were bombed and machine-gunned, causing damage to hangars and offices. The bad weather restricted enemy activity during the night. Towards daybreak several single aircraft were reported over southern England where activity was still in progress at 06.00 hours. The Luftwaffe lost six aircraft destroyed. RAF fighter Command suffered no losses.

COASTAL COMMAND OPERATIONS

Bad weather restricted operations but, despite this, thirty aircraft carried out patrols and escort was provided for fourteen convoys.

1. During the morning three Hudsons of 220 Squadron attacked two armed motor vessels off Horns Reef. No results were observed. One of the Hudsons was hit by AA from the ships and crashed into the sea in flames.

2. Two Beauforts of 42 Squadron were despatched in the afternoon to attack shipping in the Cherbourg - Le Havre area, but were unable to carry out their task.

BOMBER COMMAND OPERATIONS

1. Twenty-one Blenheims were despatched in daylight to attack targets in Germany. Owing to adverse weather ten abandoned, alternatives including shipping and barges at various locations were attacked by the remainder. One crew attacked Diepholtz aerodrome and reported bomb bursts on the tarmac in front of the hangar. A crew attacking Calais shot a Bf109 down in flames.

Night operations

All night operations were again cancelled because of the adverse weather.

OPERATIONAL LOSSES

Hudson T9323 of 220 Squadron, Thornaby, on North Sea patrol. Shot down when attacking an armed motor vessel near Horn's Reef. Pilot Officer H. Parkinson, Sergeant P. H. Fletcher, Sergeant L. Dudley and Sergeant J. C. Murray were posted as missing in action and remembered on the Runnymede Memorial.

Monday 7th October

A 149 Squadron Wellington taxies out of a night operation. The main target for tonight for the Wellington crews was Berlin, one failed to return.

ENEMY ACTIVITY

During the day four main attacks were attempted against targets in the London area, but only a few bombs fell on south-east London. Other attacks were wide-spread over south east England and in the west over Dorset and Yeovil. Night attacks commenced as soon as it got dark, they were also wide-spread and encompassed London, the West Country and north-west England, the Midlands, Wales and south-east Scotland. During the attacks HE and incendiary bombs fell on Central London.

During the period the Luftwaffe lost nineteen aircraft destroyed. RAF Fighter Command lost thirteen.

COASTAL COMMAND OPERATIONS

The usual daily tasks were carried out by eighty-six aircraft. Twenty-seven convoys were also protected.

1. Le Havre was attacked by five aircraft and Trouville by a single aircraft.
2. Three Hudsons attacked a 3,000 ton motor vessel ten miles north west of Lister Light, and reported near misses. Another Hudson attacked a fishing vessel one hundred and forty miles south-west of Lister Light.
3. A Blenheim on reconnaissance over the English Channel was attacked by three Bf109s and shot one of them down in flames. This aircraft, T1874 of 53 Squadron flown by Pilot Officer Wellon, was badly damaged. He was unhurt, but his crew, Sergeants Neale and Wood, were both wounded. *Oberleutnant Siegfried Bethke and Unteroffizier Wolfgang Liedig of 2./JG 2 were both credited with victories, Bethke for a flying-boat!*
4. Projected sorties by Beauforts to carry out torpedo attacks in the late afternoon and early night on shipping at Den Helder, Cherbourg and Le Havre failed to materialise.
5. The PRU was able to photograph ports on the Belgian and French coasts, but because of unsuitable weather conditions wasn't able to photograph Bergen, Bordeaux and the Gironde.

Night Operations

1. Six aircraft were sent to attack barges and shipping at Rotterdam.
2. Three crews were detailed to attack shipping at Le Havre and Cherbourg.
3. Six more crews were detailed to lay mines in the Maas Estuary.

BOMBER COMMAND OPERATIONS

1. Twelve Blenheims were despatched in daylight to attack targets in Germany and the occupied countries. Ten crews abandoned because of lack of cloud cover, one attacked barges near Goes and the other attacked barges at Sommelsdijk. Another six crews carried out a North Sea sweep.

Night operations

The night bomber force of Blenheims, Wellingtons, Whitleys and Hampdens attacked a variety of targets in the occupied countries and Germany. Berlin was the main target for the Wellingtons and Whitleys whose objectives included three main electrical power stations.

Hampdens attacked marshalling yards and the Fokker aircraft works at Amsterdam.

Blenheims weighed in attacking aerodromes, harbour installations and shipping at Lorient and the Channel ports as well as gun positions at Cap Gris Nez.

Monday 7th October

OPERATIONAL LOSSES

Blenheim L9310 of 110 Squadron, Wattisham, target invasion ports, crashed on return. Flight Lieutenant H. J. Lyon, Sergeant Hardwick and Sergeant Henry were all injured.

Wellington P9287 of 38 Squadron, Marham, target Berlin, failed to return. Squadron Leader R. O. O. Taylor, Sergeant H. F. Green, Sergeant F. P. O'Regan, Sergeant G. Holliday, Sergeant R. Stephens and Sergeant H. Whelpton are all buried in the Berlin 1939/1945 War Cemetery.

Wellington L7896 'G' of 99 Squadron, Mildenhall, damaged by a night fighter and made an emergency landing at Honington. Pilot Officer Topham and his crew escaped before the aircraft was destroyed by fire.

Whitley P4995 'P' of 102 Squadron, Linton on Ouse, suffered engine failure during a convoy patrol and ditched in the Atlantic. Fg Off H. M. Young and crew rescued after 22 hours in dinghy by *HMS St Mary*.

Flying Officer H. M. Young who ditched in the Atlantic today and earned the nickname 'Dinghy'. He was killed in 1943 taking part in the famous Dambuster raid.

Flight Lieutenant Mike Henry DFC

Blenheim gunner 110 Squadron

TARGET - INVASION BARGES - BOULOGNE
F/Lt. Lyon, Sgt. Hardwick, Sgt. Henry
Blenheim IV L9310

I was now flying with my third operational pilot. He should have been an experienced one as his rank indicated an early start in his RAF career. However, he tried his best, maybe unintentionally, to kill us when we arrived back at Wattisham. Approaching the airfield at just before two in the morning, I was looking forward and noticed that the angle of glide indicator was showing red and we still had about a mile to go before crossing the boundary! We did arrive at the airfield without hitting the trees on approach, but he was no longer in line with the goose-neck flarepath. Opening up to go round again, and switching on his wing landing lamp, we roared across the all-grass airfield without gaining any height. I could have almost touched a goose-neck flare as we crossed the flarepath (at the wrong angle), but my big worry was whether he would gain height before retracting the flaps because that procedure courted disaster. Thank the Lord he didn't. We carried on at nought feet until I felt the port wing drop. I immediately sensed a major accident. It was! With a rending crash, I saw stars (not the astral kind).

When silence came, I was standing in my turret cupola. There were flames roaring about in the fuselage. I was trapped. The hatch ladder was across my back, blocking any exit through the camera hatch. I turned round and noticed a jagged hole in the fuselage side, big enough for my head to go through. So through I went and with my feet against the fuselage side I pushed with the desperation of a trapped animal. The side opened up after exerting my utmost strength which would have matched the effect of a gallon of Guinness! My shoulders were protected by my parachute harness and my thick Irvin jacket, but I tore my thigh when getting out. I suppose I must have fallen on my head (that explains a lot!) because of the angle at which I struggled out. Anyway, the ambulance and fire crews were on the spot, right by the burning aircraft, as usual risking their own lives as the tanks were due to explode any minute; the oxygen bottles were getting airborne, and my ammunition was popping off. One of the rescue lads and the duty MO walked me to the waiting ambulance. On the way I looked round to see whether the pilot and observer were alive. They were on their feet but faces covered with blood. How they survived being up front, I'll never know.

Back in sick quarters I learned that they had been taken to Ipswich Hospital. Both were concussed - not surprisingly - and the pilot suffered a broken jaw. I was attended to by the medics who dressed the wound on the back of my head (I had wondered what was dripping down my neck!), and thigh. They gave me the usual anti-tetanus jab and a nice hot, sweet cup of tea. The CO and duty officer visited me and asked what had happened. All I could tell them was what really happened and left it at that. Congratulating me on my lucky escape, they left me to rest with certain thoughts buzzing through my head: What if I hadn't instinctively ducked when the Blenheim hit the ground? I might have been decapitated. What if the bang on the back of my head had knocked me unconscious? Would those outside have had time to cut me free before I fried?

And so ended my tenth operation. I never saw Flight Lieutenant Lyon again. I did hear that he was found dead in the middle of an airfield, other than that I know not the details.

Tuesday 8th October

ENEMY ACTIVITY

Four main Luftwaffe attacks took place during the morning, two of which penetrated to London and two to the Kent area. Damage and fatalities were caused in Central London and bombs were dropped indiscriminately on coastal towns in Kent and Sussex. Because of adverse weather during the afternoon only two fighter airfields were able to operate. Following reconnaissance flights by the Luftwaffe in the early evening, night raids commenced early and continued throughout the night. The raids were wide-spread and included London, the Portsmouth/Southampton and Liverpool areas. From 03.00 to 06.00 hours enemy aircraft penetrated to East Anglia and the Midlands. Minelaying took place off the north-east coast between Hartlepool and St. Abbs Head and Flamborough Head and the Humber. During the period the Luftwaffe lost ten aircraft to RAF Fighter Command's two.

COASTAL COMMAND OPERATIONS

Anti invasion, anti submarine patrols and reconnaissance sorties were carried out by eighty-five aircraft. Air escort was given to twenty-three convoys.

1. Two He60s were shot down by Blenheims, one off St. Catherine's Point and the other near Portland Bill.
2. Two enemy Flak ships were attacked our aircraft on a search/strike patrol off the Danish Coast. Damage to one of the ships was caused by a bomb which exploded on the vessels port side.
3. Beauforts 'K' and 'W' of 22 Squadron were despatched on a search/strike sortie off Ijmuiden and Ems, but no targets were found.
4. Three Beauforts of 42 Squadron were sent on a torpedo search/strike in the Le Havre - Dieppe area. One returned early and one crashed at Chidhampton.
5. PRU suffered casualties. One aircraft failed to return from a sortie over Kiel and another was shot down by two Bf109s when heading out over Kent.

Night operations

1. Three FAA Swordfish were detailed to carry out a night mining sortie in the Ems Estuary.
2. Six Blenheims were despatched to attack shipping and barges at Gravelines.

BOMBER COMMAND OPERATIONS

1. Two Blenheims were despatched to reconnoitre and attack Boulogne and Ostend. One abandoned because of adverse weather, the other attacked shipping in Boulogne where bombs were observed to fall among twenty vessels in the outer harbour.

Night operations

1. Thirty-seven Blenheims carried out successful attacks on the invasion shipping and barges remaining at Calais, Boulogne, Flushing and Le Havre.
2. Thirty-four Wellingtons were sent to attack oil targets, ship building docks at Hamburg and Bremen, and marshalling yards at Mannheim and Gremberg.
3. Fifteen Whitleys attacked an oil target, the metal alloy factory at Hanau and the Fokker aircraft factory at Amsterdam.
4. The nineteen Hampdens' main target was the battleship *Tirpitz* berthed in the naval base at Wilhelmshaven.

A PRU Spitfire down on the continent.

OPERATIONAL LOSSES

Spitfire P9382 of the PRU, Heston, failed to return from a sortie over Kiel. At 33,000 feet over the Friesian Islands the aircraft was hit and the pilot wounded. At 2,000 feet Flight Lieutenant J. R. T. Smalley DFC, baled out and landed near Noordbroek, Holland, where he was taken prisoner.
A PRU Spitfire was claimed by Oberleutnant Adolf Kinzinger of Stab I./JG 54, some 30 kilometres southwest of Emden.

Spitfire R6894 of the PRU, Heston, was shot down in flames at 10.25 hours by two Bf109s when heading out over Kent. Flying Officer W. B. Parker (RNZAF) baled out and survived despite being badly burned. The aircraft crashed at Adisham Court Farm, near Canterbury. *From the time given, it would appear that the attacker was Leutnant Max-Hellmuth Ostermann of 7./JG 54.*

Beaufort L4484 'E' of 42 Squadron, Thorney Island, crashed after engine failure on return from Cherbourg. Flight Lieutenant J. Kerby and his crew escaped before the aircraft was destroyed by fire near Chidham, Sussex.

Blenheim T2036 of 53 Squadron, Detling, target Gravelines, failed to return from Gravelines. Shot down by Flak at Frethun, near Calais. Pilot Officer J. C. Mallon (New Zealander), Sergeant W. P. Whetton DFM and Sergeant A. T. Shackleford were all buried at Guines.

Blenheim T2032 of 82 Squadron, Bodney, crashed at base on return from Calais. Sergeant H. G. Brittain and his crew escaped injury.

Blenheim T2277 of 82 Squadron, Bodney, crashed at base on return from Calais. Sergeant R. L. Smith and his crew escaped injury.

Whitley T4137 'K' of 58 Squadron, Linton-on-Ouse, target Gelsenkirchen, crashed on return at RAF Bircham Newton killing the entire crew: Pilot Officer R. A. Hadley, Sergeant C. A. Wright, Pilot Officer R. A. Phillips, Sergeant J. M. Ramsay and Sergeant G. E. Hall.

Whitley P5091 'Y' of 77 Squadron, target Hanau, crashed into high ground near Snape, Yorkshire. Sergeant G. W. Brown, Midshipman Haddingham (RN), Sergeant W. G. Macmorland, Sergeant J. R. Wardman and Sergeant C. Cottham were killed.

Wednesday 9th October

RAIN IN THE SOUTH, CLOUDY ELSEWHERE.

ENEMY ACTIVITY

The main raids during the day were carried out by fighter bombers against targets in the south of England including London, Kent and Sussex. Minor damage and casualties were inflicted. Enemy patrols were active over the Straits of Dover and reconnaissance was carried out over the Midlands, East Anglia and Portsmouth. Night activity commenced early. London was the main target, having to endure raids for twelve hours during which bombs fell in forty districts. Other raids were wide-spread, carried out by single aircraft aiming for targets in the West Country and the North. Minelaying covering the areas the Wash to St. Abb's Head and later from Montrose to the Thames Estuary was suspected.

Losses for the period were: Luftwaffe eleven aircraft destroyed. RAF Fighter Command three destroyed.

COASTAL COMMAND OPERATIONS

The usual operational tasks were carried out by fifty-five aircraft. Air escort was provided for ten convoys.

1. An Anson on patrol sighted a U-Boat, but it submerged before the aircraft could make an attack.
2. Blenheims attacked Le Havre, but the results were not observed.

BOMBER COMMAND OPERATIONS

Eight Blenheims were despatched on daylight sorties to attack targets in France and Germany. Three abandoned because of adverse weather. One scored a direct hit on an oil target at Homburg and three bombed barges and a bridge at Boulogne.

Night operations

1. Eight Fairey Battles of Polish squadrons successfully bombed barges at Calais.
2. Forty-two Wellington crews claimed success with their attacks on an aluminium works and marshalling yards in Germany.
3. Twenty Hampdens were despatched to attack the Krupps works at Essen, however, because of severe icing conditions only three attacked. Six additional Hampdens successfully laid mines at Lorient.
4. One Whitley carried out a special reconnaissance over Le Havre and leaflets were dropped by four other Whitleys from the OTU.

The 2 and 4 Groups bombing operations were cancelled.

OPERATIONAL LOSSES

Blenheim N3530 'S' of 235 Squadron, Thorney Island, failed to return from the Le Havre operation after an engagement with enemy fighters. Pilot Officer J. C. Kirkpatrick, Pilot Officer R. C. Thomas and Sergeant G. E. Keel were all killed. *Pilots from III./JG 2 were involved in this interception. Hauptmann Otto Bertram of Gruppenstab claimed two Blenheims at 18.35 and 18.37 hours, while Oberfeldwebel Hans Klee of 7 Staffel claimed a "Hereford" at 18.50 hours*

Hudson T9357 of 206 Squadron, Bircham Newton, crashed on landing at Docking. Flight Lieutenant B. O. Dias and his crew escaped injury.

Sunderland P9621 of 201 Squadron, Sullom Voe, force landed in bad weather and ran aground at Scalasaig Bay, Colonsay. Flight Lieutenant E. J. Brooks and his crew were uninjured.

Wellington P9273 'V' of 149 Squadron, Mildenhall, target Herringen, lost without trace. Pilot Officer R. G. Furness, Sergeant P. T. Catto, Sergeant F. G. R. McDonald, Sergeant K. McN. Davidson, Sergeant M. P. Reynolds and Sergeant K. Shimells are all commemorated on the Runnymede Memorial.

149 Squadron Wellington crews walk to their aircraft.

A 42 Squadron Beaufort. Two aircraft from this squadron carried out a torpedo attack off Boulogne today.

ENEMY ACTIVITY

Four major enemy attacks took place during the day, but only a few raiders penetrated the London area. At night the attacks started as soon as it was dark, London being the main objective and most districts of the Capital were bombed. During other raids bombs were dropped in southern England, south Wales and the Tyne area. During the period the Luftwaffe lost two aircraft destroyed. RAF Fighter Command lost five aircraft destroyed.

COASTAL COMMAND OPERATIONS

Ninety-four aircraft were employed on the usual tasks and patrols. Escort was provided for nineteen convoys.

1. There was an early evening torpedo strike by two Beauforts of 42 Squadron on shipping in Boulogne. The crew of one aircraft claimed a hit on the stern of a motor vessel. The other crew released its torpedoes too early and achieved no results. The Beaufort was also attacked by Bf109s and damaged, which caused it to crash-land at base on return.
2. Four Blenheims were detailed to carry out a daylight attack on Boulogne. Because of the lack of cloud cover they failed to carry out their primary task, but two of them dropped bombs near a large ship which was surrounded by twenty to thirty smaller vessels.
3. Hudson 'M' of 220 Squadron attacked two small ships ninety-one miles west-north-west of Heligoland, but results were not observed. The PRU aircraft took photographs of Boulogne and La Rochelle.

Night operations

1.Nineteen aircraft were detailed to carry out night attacks on shipping in various harbours. The force included four Albacores of 819 Squadron that attacked Brest and six others which laid mines.

BOMBER COMMAND OPERATIONS

Night operations

Because of adverse weather no daylight operations were carried out on the 10th, but at night 157 aircraft attacked the Channel ports, marshalling yards and industrial targets in Germany.

OPERATIONAL LOSSES

Beaufort L4491 'R' of 42 Squadron, Thorney Island, crash-landed with wheels up as the result of suffering battle damage from Bf109s during its torpedo attack on shipping in Boulogne harbour. Flying Officer G. S. P. Rooney DFC and Flying Officer Simmonds were wounded. Sergeant R. F. Henry and Sergeant W. R. J. Little escaped unhurt. *The German unit involved was 3./JG 77 and both Oberleutnants Karl-Gottfried Nordmann and Günther Beise were credited with a "Blenheim" shot down south of Folkestone.*

Albacores were busy at night dropping bombs and mines.

Friday 11th October

CLOUD AND RAIN OVER THE COASTS, BECOMING FOGGY AT NIGHT.

ENEMY ACTIVITY

Seven attacks by the Luftwaffe developed against this country during the day. As usual London was the main target but most of the raiders were turned back before reaching the Capital. Some of the raids were carried out by fighters alone and on others there were three fighters to every bomber. The night raids again started early, directed mainly against London, but Liverpool, Manchester and Bristol were also targeted. Activity was heavy until midnight, then it gradually diminished. During the day the Luftwaffe lost five aircraft destroyed. The RAF lost nine aircraft destroyed.

COASTAL COMMAND OPERATIONS

Seventy-two aircraft carried out anti invasion, anti submarine patrols and the other usual tasks. Escort was given to twenty-one convoys.

1. A Hudson attacked an enemy motor vessel sixty-four miles from Alsboen Light no results were observed.
2. A FW200 attacking a convoy was driven off by an Anson of 48 Squadron whose crew claimed hits en the enemy aircraft.
3. PRU aircraft photographed a number of ports in France and Belgium and a number of airfields in northern France, attempts to photograph Kiel, Hamburg and Oslo were unsuccessful.

Night operations

1. Six Blenheims were sent to carry out night attacks on shipping at Rotterdam and six FAA Swordfish to lay mines in the Hubert Gat.

BOMBER COMMAND OPERATIONS

1. Six Blenheims carried out an uneventful sweep over the North Sea in daylight. There were no other operations and no losses.

Night operations

Shipping in the Channel ports and the German ports of Wilhelmshaven, Kiel and Hamburg was the target of the night force. The Channel ports were heavily attacked, but the crews on the German targets were forced, because of poor visibility, to bomb alternative and last resort targets. Twelve Hampdens carried out mining.

OPERATIONAL LOSSES

Anson K8769 'Q' of 217 Squadron, St. Eval, belly-landed at night at Trevose Head, Cornwall. Flying Officer Bursey and crew were safe.

Glide attacks

Flt Lt.Colin Rawlins DFC
Hampden pilot
144 Squadron

On one occasion, in order to be sure of getting our bombs on the target we came down to the unusually low level of 1500ft, after a motorless descent from some 5000ft. Such glide attacks were seen as tactically advantageous, the then prevailing assumption being that German flak depended upon engine sound for accurate direction. But it was about now that flak fire began to be directed by radar (radar impulses received from the aircraft) rather than sound, so the glide technique became academic. Another reason for not using it was the fear that aircraft engines, throttled back for the glide, and in the cold night air, might not pick up again at the bottom of the descent. This was a more realistic fear during winter and at much higher altitudes; on this occasion our engines responded perfectly and we made what we thought was a successful attack.

ENEMY ACTION

Seven raids took place during the day, five penetrating the London area, but no major damage was inflicted. One raid attacked Hatfield and another Biggin Hill. It was now significant that defence against the Luftwaffe was having its effect. Most of the raids were now being carried out by fighter bombers in an obvious attempt to reduce their losses in aircraft and trained aircrew. Bombs fell in Kent, Surrey and the Isle of Wight, but damage was slight.

The main night activity was confined to Bristol, the Midlands and the London areas, with slight activity in East Anglia. The London attacks were intermittent with damage confined to railway systems. An exception was a heavy raid carried out by the Luftwaffe special force on Coventry, which caused heavy damage and numerous casualties. Minelaying is thought to have been carried out from Portland to the Needles, Selsey Bill to Coquet Island and North Foreland to Southwold. During the period the Luftwaffe lost five aircraft destroyed. RAF Fighter Command lost nine aircraft destroyed.

COASTAL COMMAND OPERATIONS

The usual routine and other patrols were carried out and twenty-one convoys received escort.

1. Three Blenheims assisted the successful search for survivors of a trawler.
2. Two Blenheims on a special North Sea patrol off the Norwegian coast sighted and attacked seven motor vessels north-west of Trondheim. One crew claimed success indicated by a large column of grey smoke. Another crew had a near miss and carried out machine-gun attacks.

Night operations

Five aircraft were detailed to carry out night attacks on targets at Lorient. Four bombed the power station causing fires and the fifth bombed Quimper aerodrome, but results were not observed.

BOMBER COMMAND OPERATIONS

1. Six Blenheims carried out a successful reconnaissance over the North Sea in daylight.
2. One Blenheim was despatched to attack the synthetic oil plant at Homburg, but abandoned because of lack of cloud cover.

Night operations

Although 138 aircraft were detailed for night raids only ninety-three operated because of adverse weather conditions.

1. Six Fairey Battles of 301(Polish) Squadron carried out raids on shipping at Calais and Ostend.
2. Twenty-four out of thirty-six Blenheims attacked shipping at Amsterdam, Dunkirk and Le Havre while others attempted to attack industrial targets in Germany.

These raids carried out on the Channel ports by the Battles and Blenheims represented the last major attacks on these targets in the invasion period.

3. Those who operated despite the adverse weather conditions, attempted to attack aluminium works at Heringen, the Krupps works at Essen, the Fokker aircraft works at Amsterdam, oil plants at Cologne and Hannover, the Dortmund-Ems aqueduct and military targets in Berlin.

OPERATIONAL LOSSES

There were no losses.

A 254 Blenheim fighter tucks in tight to the camera aircraft on take off.

Sunday 13th October

SUNNY IN THE MORNING, BUT CLOUD DEVELOPING DURING THE DAY.

The newly formed Polish squadrons were now operational in their Fairey Battles. 300 Squadron crews, pictured here, were sent to Calais on this night and suffered their first loss when L5499 crashed on return with the loss of all three crew.

ENEMY ACTIVITY

There were four main attacks by the Luftwaffe during the day with formations of aircraft comprising fifty plus, the four attacks totalling approximately 300 aircraft. The first formation failed to penetrate to London, but the other three did, causing damage to residential districts. A few reconnaissance flights were also carried out over the east and south east coasts and a convoy was attacked during the afternoon. Out of 180 aircraft operating very few were bombers. The night raids were heaviest between 19.00 and 23.00 hours. The 'All Clear' was sounded at 06.00 hours. The main target was again the London area where thirty-six districts suffered heavy residential damage and casualties. Twenty provincial areas including Liverpool, Bristol, the Midlands, East Anglia, Lincolnshire were also bombed and the north east, where two communal shelters were hit. The Luftwaffe lost two aircraft destroyed. RAF Fighter Command lost three aircraft destroyed.

COASTAL COMMAND OPERATIONS

The usual patrols and tasks were carried out by seventy aircraft. Nineteen convoys were given escort.

1. An Anson of 612 Squadron on a search for a U-Boat dropped two bombs on a moving oil slick, but there were no positive results.
2. Hudson 'S' of 206 Squadron attacked four motor vessels forty-nine miles from Terschelling, but results were not observed.
3. Another Hudson attacked a U-Boat forty miles from Barra Head, but there were no positive results.
4. A successful reconnaissance of Norwegian fjords from Stadtlandet to the south of Kristiansund was carried out.

Night operations

Six Blenheims were detailed attack shipping at Flushing. Fires were started but details were not observed.

BOMBER COMMAND OPERATIONS

Night operations

127 aircraft were despatched to carry out night bombing operations.

1. Twelve Fairey Battles were sent to attack invasion ports, two crashed on return.
2. Twenty-three Blenheims were sent to attack Le Havre and oil plants and marshalling yards in Germany.
3. Forty-seven Wellingtons were sent to attack shipyards at Kiel, an oil plant at Gelsenkirchen and the aerodrome at Eindhoven.
4. Thirty-five Hampdens were sent to attack naval targets at Wilhelmshaven.

OPERATIONAL LOSSES

Fairey Battle L5428 of 142 Squadron, Binbrook, target Calais, abandoned on return after running out of fuel. The aircraft crashed ten miles north-west of Lincoln. Pilot Officer Stevenson and his crew were safe.

Fairey Battle L5499 of 300 (Polish) Squadron, target Calais, crashed on return at Oxton, eight miles north-east of Lincoln. Flying Officer J. Gebicki, Sergeant T Egierski and Sergeant E. Morawa were all killed.

Wellington P9243 of 99 Squadron, Newmarket, target Wilhelmshaven, lost without trace. Flying Officer W. E. N. Keller, Sergeant C. H. Douglas (RNZAF), Sergeant A. R. Mattick, Sergeant R. F. Denning, Sergeant B. Shuttleworth and Sergeant A. Wright, are all commemorated on the Runnymede Memorial.

Whitley T4150 which crash landed near Driffield returning from a long sortie to Stettin on the night of 14th October.

ENEMY ACTIVITY

There were many scattered raids by individual enemy aircraft and an attack on the Portsmouth area by thirty-four bombers. The enemy also flew hostile day patrols and reconnaissance over the English Channel and the straits of Dover. At night the raids were concentrated on London where they caused extensive damage and numerous fires. Coventry was also heavily attacked and enemy planes were active over Liverpool and East Anglia. The Luftwaffe lost two aircraft destroyed. RAF Fighter Command had no losses.

COASTAL COMMAND OPERATIONS

The usual anti submarine patrols reconnaissance and convoy escorts were carried out. The other following operations were executed.

1. Unsuccessful searches were carried out for a Hudson which had failed to return from a North Sea patrol.
2. A Blenheim carried out a successful reconnaissance of the Namsos area and an enemy submarine was sighted in Nansen Fjord, but not attacked.

Night operations

1 Six Blenheims were despatched to carry out a night attack on the shipping and the port of Lorient. There were no losses.

BOMBER COMMAND OPERATIONS

1. Twelve Blenheims were despatched in daylight to attack the Channel ports and German oil targets, aluminium works, ship-building yards and communications. Nine out of the twelve abandoned because of lack of cloud cover.
2. Six Blenheims carried out an uneventful North Sea sweep.

Night operations

Seventy-eight Hampdens, Whitleys and Wellingtons were despatched on night raids concentrating on targets in eastern and western Germany and Le Havre. The specific locations were Berlin, Stettin, Bohlen, Magdeburg and Le Havre.

OPERATIONAL LOSSES

Blenheim Z5741 'X' of 235 Squadron, Thorney Island, crashed on landing after a patrol. Sergeant R. F. Tatnell and his crew were safe.

Hudson N7362 of 206 Squadron, Bircham Newton, failed to return from a North Sea patrol. Flying Officer J. R. H. Lascelles, Pilot Officer J. G. I. Acheson, Sergeant R. E. Garstin and Sergeant J. T. Farlowe were all posted missing and are remembered on the Runnymede Memorial.

Hudson T9343 'Z' of 233 Squadron, Leuchars, failed to return from a reconnaissance of Norway after being intercepted by JG77. Flight Lieutenant L. P. Rowley, Pilot Officer R. A. Hanks, Sergeant J. W. Purt and Sergeant J. J. Wilks were all posted missing and their names recorded on the Runnymede Memorial. *This was claimed by Oberleutnant Horst Carganico of Stab II./JG 77.*

Blenheim R3671 of 139 Squadron, Horsham St faith, on anti-shipping sortie crashed in the sea. Sergeant A. S. Ogilvy, Sergeant B. Walker and Sergeant D. Neill lost. Sergeant Neill's body was washed ashore. His two companions are commemorated on the Runnymede Memorial.

Hampden X2910 of 44 Squadron, Waddington, target Berlin, shot down by a night-fighter north east of Wolfsburg. Germany. Sergeant L. J. Burt, Sergeant J. Baldwin DFM, and Pilot Officer R. M. Carrell are buried in the Berlin 1939/1945 War Cemetery. Sergeant D. Windle DFM was taken prisoner.

Victim to Leutnant Hans-Georg Mangelsdorf of 2./NJG 1 west of Gerdelegen at 03.02 hours.

Hampden X2993 of 50 Squadron, Lindholme, target Berlin, shot down by a night fighter and crashed near Kalbe, Germany. Pilot Officer A. H. Davies and Pilot Officer E. J. Andrews were killed and are buried in the Berlin 1939/1945 War Cemetery. Sergeant H. L. Hurrell and Sergeant Lee were taken prisoner.

Werner Streib, now promoted to Hauptmann and commanding I./NJG 1, destroyed this bomber near Kalbe at 03.05 hours.

Wellington T2464 'K' of 9 Squadron, target Magdeburg, crashed at Salzwedel, north-north-west of Magdeburg. Squadron Leader J. O. Hinks, Pilot Officer G. P. W. Austin, Sergeant A. E. Skidmore, Sergeant C. Hay, Sergeant E. Nield and Pilot Officer J. E. Bartlett all perished and are buried in the Berlin 1939/1945 War Cemetery.

Shot down by Oberfeldwebel Gerhard Herzog of I./NJG 1 at 00.55 hours,

Monday 14th October

Whitley P4993 'V' of 10 Squadron, Leeming, target Le Havre, on return collided with a balloon barrage cable near Weybridge, Surrey. Sergeant D. R. Wright, Pilot Officer K. Cooney, Sergeant J. J. Caswell, Sergeant B. L. Henry and Sergeant E. Davis were all killed.

Whitley P4952 'H' of 10 Squadron, Leeming, target Stettin, on return after flying for eleven hours being short of fuel and unable to break through the cloud they abandoned the aircraft thirteen miles north of Hexham. Squadron Leader K. F. Ferguson and his crew baled out successfully and were unhurt.

Whitley T4143 'J' of 10 Squadron, Leeming, target Stettin, on return unable to break through the cloud, the order was given to abandon near Thirsk. Flight Lieutenant D. G. Tomlinson, Sergeant Byrne and Sergeant Somerville baled out successfully and were unhurt, but Pilot Officer R. J. Dickinson, and Sergeant L. P. Neville's bodies were found in the wreckage.

Whitley T4150 of 58 Squadron, Linton-on-Ouse, target Stettin, the crew crash-landed the aircraft five miles east-north-east of Driffield on return. Flying Officer B. Brooke and his crew escaped injury even though the aircraft was badly damaged.

Whitley T4206 'A' of 77 Squadron, Topcliffe, target Stettin, while attempting to land in poor visibility on return undershot the landing area and crashed into a tree. Squadron Leader G. R. H. Black was fatally injured, but Sergeant T. E. Coogan, Sergeant Garwood, Sergeant Boddington and Sergeant Woodroffe were less seriously injured.

Crash Investigation
Whitley P4993 10 Squadron

Sergeant Wright's crew was one of the three from No.10 Squadron based at Leeming in Yorkshire detailed to attack Le Havre. They took off at 17.31 hours and headed south, on a course that should have taken them to the west of London's anti-aircraft defences, but all was not going according to plan.

On the ground near Weybridge in Surrey observers saw coloured flares fired from an aircraft, then cheered as it fell to the ground in flames. At last the defences of Brooklands had taken revenge for the terrible raid on its aircraft factory that had taken place on 4 September. When the first of the five bodies was found the terrible truth dawned; they had brought down an RAF bomber. The Whitley had flown into a balloon cable flown from Site 21, which had severed a wing. A subsequent investigation determined that incendiaries had ignited in the bomb bay, but whether this occurred before or after hitting the cable was not known. The wing fell at Weybridge Park, the tail unit with the rear turret fell onto a house named Elgin Lodge in Elgin Road, the rest of the aircraft exploded in flames at Hangar Hill near the railway embankment close to Weybridge station.

Eighty-one year old Thomas Dickson was living in Elgin Lodge with his wife and staff and wrote this account which was provided by the family to researcher Stephen Flower for his book Raiders Overhead:

At Elgin Lodge we have so far been fortunate in escaping any injury by the enemy bombers, although every night they make great efforts all round us to get armament works near this. However, on Monday the 14th the house was severely damaged, not by the enemy, but, alas, by one of our own bombers. Mrs Dickson, Miss Niven and I dine at seven pm. The enemy is generally overhead by seven-thirty.

We had finished and were in the drawing-room before a good fire. We usually, when the explosions get dangerously near, shut up and retire to our cellar shelter, where we are safe against anything but a direct hit, and sleep in good cabin bunks with the staff: five in all. We were just deciding to get down to our shelter when there was a fearful crash, with a crescendo of falling glass, and the whole house trembled. We all got down to the shelter in thirty seconds and waited, while bomb after bomb exploded close by. After ten minutes the explosions ceased and the parlour maid, who is fearless, went up to see what had happened. She came back and waved her hand to me, but said nothing.

I went upstairs to the large bedroom, where Mrs Dickson and I sleep in peacetime. The door could only be opened a few inches, but enough to show me the room piled with wreckage, a large hole in the ceiling and floor above, and a larger one in the roof above that, with the moon shining in a clear sky. As there had been no explosion in the house, I concluded that a delayed-action bomb had struck us. I at once went out to get help and luckily found a flight lieutenant and three Army officers and a couple of cars waiting at the end of Elgin Road. They offered their services, and one of the RAF men said he would have a look outside before going upstairs, produced his torch, and in a moment said, 'Well, you have had an escape, your house has been hit by an aeroplane, and only the lightest part of it.'

Next day we learned what had happened. A British Whitley two-engined bomber had evidently left to attack the French coast, but developed engine trouble which forced the pilot to return without dropping his bombs. He was seen in difficulties, flying low round St. George's Hill, evidently seeking a landing place. Unfortunately, he fouled a balloon cable, dropped both wings in different places; engines and bombs fell on the commons, burnt themselves out and exploded the bombs. The tailpiece and turret with four machine guns and full load of cartridges carried on and cut into the Elgin Lodge roof, scraped off the turret guns and cartridges, weighing nearly a ton, leaving it on Mrs Dickson's bed, and landed on the tennis court, carrying the drawing-room verandah with it. The crew of five were all killed. They hadn't a dog's chance; they were too low down to allow their parachutes to open and their dead bodies were found in various directions.

Sentries were put on the wreckage at once. The corporal slept in a chair in the hall. Next morning, from daylight numberless inspectors, officers, wardens and others came to look at the wreckage. It was only then that the machine was identified and it was not until the same evening that the last of the dead was found.

Elgin Lodge was patched up with a tarpaulin over the roof, but the occupants would have had an uncomfortable winter. In June 1941 Thomas Dickson, veteran of the Boer War and First War, heard the air raid sirens sound again. He rose suddenly from his bed, and died of a stroke

ENEMY ACTIVITY

There were five enemy fighter sweeps and air reconnaissance over the Kent coast and the Thames Estuary during the day, some raiders penetrated to Hornchurch and central London. One formation flew over Plymouth. Again the night attacks started early, at 18.30 hours, London, the Midlands and Birmingham being the main targets. The Luftwaffe lost twelve aircraft destroyed. RAF Fighter Command lost fifteen aircraft destroyed.

COASTAL COMMAND OPERATIONS

Anti submarine patrols, reconnaissance and convoy escorts took place.

1. A Sunderland on convoy duty located a lifeboat ninety miles west of St. Kilda containing approximately thirty men and dropped supplies, medical aid, navigation gear and instructions.

Night operations

1. Blenheims were despatched to carry out night attacks on targets at Lorient, Terneuzen, Flushing and Brest.

BOMBER COMMAND OPERATIONS

All daylight tasks were abandoned due to lack of cloud cover.

Night operations

134 aircraft were detailed for night operations. The targets were the Channel ports and German industrial targets such as oil plants and communications as well as naval targets. Seventy-five crews of the force were detailed to attack the naval bases at Kiel and Hamburg, where an oil storage tank was set on fire and damage was caused to dockyards. Calais and Boulogne were heavily bombed. The attacking aircraft included nine Fairey Battles, the last occasion Battles would operate with Bomber Command. Minelaying off Kiel was carried out by three Hampdens. There were two OTU sorties.

The pilot's view from the cockpit of a Hampden. The fuselage was only three feet wide so the pilot was more or less stuck in his seat for the entire flight, sometimes up to 9 hours! The button on the control column shaft is the firing button for the pilot's single machine gun in the nose.

OPERATIONAL LOSSES

Hudson T9303 of 206 Squadron, Bircham Newton, missing from patrol. Pilot Officer D. E. Teden, Pilot Officer J. L. De Keyser (South African), Sergeant W. Kent and Sergeant J. Steel missing in action and remembered on the Runnymede Memorial.

Hampden X2901 'B' of 83 Squadron, Scampton, target Magdeburg, ran out of fuel and landed on Southwold beach, Suffolk. Flight Lieutenant D. W. F. Barker and his crew escaped injury.

Balloons

Colin Rawlins Hampden pilot 144 Sqn

Hamburg was regarded as an unpleasant target with plenty of flak and, so it was thought, barrage balloons. There was a widespread although irrational fear of what seemed to be balloons, generally at the height one was flying over these big targets, which in those days would have been mainly between 10,000 and 15,000ft. As we soon learned, the grey, rugby-ball-shaped object of our concern was not a very high-flying barrage balloon but the remains of an exploded anti-aircraft shell. The fact that these appeared to be hanging on a level with us only confirmed that the German flak had correctly calculated our altitude, if, fortunately, not yet our actual position in the sky!

Wednesday 16th October

Fog covering most of N-W Europe with heavy rain in places at night.

ENEMY ACTIVITY

Enemy day raids were mostly by single aircraft. One attack on RAF Ternhill destroyed a hangar and damaged a number of aircraft. The night raids were heavy until midnight mostly directed against London, but south Wales, the Midlands and Liverpool were also bombed and a communal shelter at Liverpool hit. Luftwaffe losses were ten aircraft destroyed. RAF Fighter Command lost one aircraft destroyed.

COASTAL COMMAND OPERATIONS

Ninety-five sorties, patrols and reconnaissance were carried out and nineteen convoys were escorted.

1. A Blenheim on patrol shot down an He115 twelve miles from Bishop's Rock.
2. A Sunderland of 210 Squadron attacked a U-Boat 59 degrees 56'N / 15 degrees 00'W with no visible results.
3. Anson 'V' of 217 Squadron attacked a U-Boat with two 100lb AS bombs without result. The same crew engaged a He115 in the same area registering hits.
4. Blenheims bombed Cherbourg Harbour.

Night operations

1. Six Blenheims were detailed to carry out a night attack on Brest. No losses were reported.

BOMBER COMMAND OPERATIONS

1. Six Blenheims carried out a routine sweep over the North Sea in daylight.
2. Another six Blenheims were detailed to carry out a daylight attack on the Channel ports, but lack of cloud cover prevented them. One crew attacked an enemy convoy off Gravelines.

Night operations

1. Night raids were carried out by seventy-three Wellingtons and Hampdens that successfully attacked the naval and dockyard targets at Bremen and Kiel where fires were started. An oil target at Merseburg / Leuna was also attacked and incendiary devices were also dropped in the Hartz Forests.
2. Four Hampdens laid mines off Bordeaux and two more dropped leaflets.

OPERATIONAL LOSSES

Hudson T9328 'F' of 224 Squadron, Aldergrove, flew into Slievenanee Mountain, Northern Ireland, after becoming lost on an anti submarine patrol. Flight Lieutenant F. C. Scott, Pilot Officer R. J. Davies, Pilot Officer A. B. Tisdall, Sergeant A. B. Nayler and Sergeant A. F. Thomas were all killed.

Hampden X2997 of 44 Squadron, Waddington, target Merseburg, crashed into a disused hangar at RAF Waddington attempting to land in fog. Squadron Leader H. P. Broad and Sergeant Hammond were injured. Sergeant Logan and AC1 E. Edgar were unhurt.

Hampden L4129 of 49 Squadron, Scampton, minelaying off Bordeaux, shot down by Flak 11 km north east of Bordeaux. Sergeant D. S. Imber, Sergeant R. F. Rose, Sergeant K. C. Friend and Sergeant F. Corbett all perished and are buried near the crash site at Ambares-et-Lagrave.

Hampden L4195 of 49 Squadron, Scampton, minelaying off Bordeaux, crashed on return nine miles north west of Ashford, Kent. Pilot Officer Evans was injured, Sergeant R. Potter killed and LAC Glover unhurt.

Hampden P2143 of 49 Squadron, Scampton, target Bordeaux, crashed on return when probably out of fuel near Andover, Hants. Flying Officer C. D. Pitman, Flying Officer R. C. Parker, Sergeant J. Brown and Sergeant P. Flanagan were all killed.

Hampden X2900 'S' of 49 Squadron, Scampton, overshot landing at Abingdon on return from a Gardening sortie. Sergeant G. M. Bates and his crew escaped injury.

Hampden X2979 of 61 Squadron, Hemswell, target Merseburg, crashed on return at Sporle, Norfolk, attempting to make an emergency landing. Pilot Officer W. H. Clemerson, Pilot Officer E. C. Gardner, Sergeant W. H. Hewitt and Sergeant D. Flanagan all killed

The remains of Hampden X2997 after it hit a hangar on landing.

Hampden X2973 of 144 Squadron, Hemswell, target Merseburg, presumed down in the sea north of Terschelling. Sergeant J. H. Brown, Sergeant R. G. Young, Sergeant J. A. Ferguson and Sergeant E. A. G. Rands all perished. The body of Sergeant Brown was washed ashore at Strandlehen on the 3 December 1940 and he is buried at Haurvig, Denmark. His companions are commemorated on Runnymede Memorial.

Hampden X2988 of 144 Squadron, Hemswell, target Merseburg, abandoned out of fuel eleven miles east-north-east of Kings Lynn. Pilot Officer T. Dawson, Sergeant E. A. Barker, Sergeant R. L. Hayes and Sergeant J. J. Jackson - who was the only fatality.

Wellington P9278 'B' of 9 Squadron, Honington, target Kiel, diverted because of bad weather on return. Crashed en-route to Abingdon six miles north west of Luton. Sergeant F. Bevan, Sergeant W. F. Jones, Sergeant H. Rossiter and Sergeant J. M. McLean, the only crew members named in the ORB, were all injured.

Wellington L7857 of 75 Squadron, Mildenhall, target Kiel, abandoned five miles north of Penrith, Cumberland. Pilot Officer J. E. S. Morton only name listed. One airman reported to have been slightly injured.

Wellington L7844 of 311 Squadron, East Wretham, En-route to Kiel the aircraft was attacked over the Zuider Zee by a night fighter of 6./NJG6 based at Deelen. The Wellington crashed in flames near Oosterwolde, north-north-west of Apeldoorn, Holland. Pilot Officer B. Landa killed, Sergeant E. Novotny captured, Sergeant A. Sestak captured, Pilot Officer H. Jarosek killed, Sergeant K. Klimt killed, Sergeant O. Jirsak killed.
Shot down by Leutnant Ludwig Becker of 4./NJG 1 at 21.25 hours.

Wellington N2773 'K' of 311 Squadron, East Wretham, lost radio contact over the Dutch coast on return from Kiel and was abandoned over Nottinghamshire due to heavy icing and crashed at Blidworth. Flight Lieutenant J. Snajdr's crew landed safely, but the wireless operator, Pilot Officer M. Vejrazka, was shot and killed by over zealous members of the Home Guard.

Above: Flt Lt. Josef Snajdr, pilot of N2773.
Below: Sgt. Leo Anderle, co-pilot of N2773.

Wellington N2771 'H' of 311 Squadron, East Wretham, radio and compass failed on the return from Kiel. The aircraft hit a balloon cable that tore off one wing and crashed near Bentley Priory, Middlesex, close to the HQ of Fighter Command. Five of the crew were killed; Squadron Leader J. Vesely, Sergeant F. Zapletal, Pilot Officer J. Slaby, Pilot Officer J. Matousek and Sergeant J. Albrecht. Sergeant F Truhlar survived, but was seriously burnt.
Frantisek Truhlar was sent to East Grinstead Hospital and placed under the care of Archibald McIndoe. He was a founder member of the Guinea Pig Club. Later in the war he trained as a fighter pilot and flew Spitfires with No. 312 Squadron. When returning to Appledram in thick fog after a patrol over Normandy on 11th June 1944 he hit a hedge bordering the airfield and crashed. The aircraft burst into flames and Frantisek once again suffered serious burns.

Left: This night was a black one for 311 Squadron which lost three out of the four aircraft sent out. Casualties included Pilot Officer Bohumil Landa, a First World War veteran.

Thursday 17th October

SCATTERED CLOUD AND SHOWERS WITH SOME BRIGHT INTERVALS.

The Wellington crews of 75 Squadron had the night off along with the rest of Bomber Command as adverse weather caused the cancellation of all operations.

ENEMY ACTIVITY

The Luftwaffe carried out four sweeps during the day, at 08.20, 13.05, 15.10, and 16.30 hours using a total of approximately 300 fighter aircraft, some carrying bombs. From south-east England some reached the London district and the Thames Estuary. Apart from St. Pancras damage was slight and all the sweeps were intercepted by fighters. The night raid was one of the longest so far, London being the main target with the concentration on rail communications. Westminster and the suburbs were bombed where varying amounts of damage was caused. Birmingham and Liverpool were also attacked but although there was only slight damage there were a number of casualties. The Luftwaffe lost nine aircraft destroyed. RAF Fighter Command lost five aircraft destroyed.

COASTAL COMMAND OPERATIONS

Forty-five sorties comprising a variety of tasks were carried out.

1. Two Beauforts of 22 Squadron attacked a minelaying tender at Cuxhaven and four destroyers near Ushant.
2. Sunderland 'E' of 10 RAAF Squadron picked up twenty-one survivors of the *SS Sangrant* and landed them at Oban.
3. Sunderland P9624 of 210 Squadron attacked a submerging U-Boat at 59 degrees 11'N / 17 degrees 50'W. This was followed by two attacks by naval forces, but the only visible result was rising air bubbles.
4. Sunderland 'P of 210 Squadron attacked a U-Boat with depth charges 150 miles from Rockall.
5. Sunderland 'D' of 10 RAAF Squadron engaged and claimed to have sunk a U-Boat west of Bishop's Rock.

Night operations

All night operations were cancelled.

BOMBER COMMAND OPERATIONS

Adverse weather forced the abandonment of all eight daylight raids despatched to Germany and occupied France, except one which bombed De Kooy aerodrome. No results were observed and there were no losses.

OPERATIONAL LOSSES

Beaufort L9856 'K' of 22 Squadron, North Coates, damaged by ships' Flak off the Dutch coast, but returned to make a crash landing at Sutton Bridge. Flight Lieutenant R. P. M. Gibbs and Sergeant J. Coulson escaped injury, but Sergeant R. E. Cree and Pilot Officer McFadden were injured by the Flak.

Blenheim T2319 'D' of 59 Squadron, St Eval, failed to return from an attack on destroyers Brest. Pilot Officer E. E. Hives is remembered on the Runnymede Memorial. The bodies of Sergeant B. D. Jones and E. Jones were recovered from the sea and buried near their home towns.

Sea mines bein g delicately prepared for loading aboard Hampdens.

Boom

Sgt. Joe Taylor, 61 Sqn Hampden

On one occasion at Hemswell, we were graced by a visit from Lord Trenchard, "The Father of the Royal Air Force". We were at briefing in the operations room when he appeared, a huge figure of a man but beginning to stoop, and hard of hearing. He was introduced to us and took his place on the rostrum with the Station Commander.

After the briefing which was for a mine laying operation, Trenchard stood up to speak. We all took notice for he was really a father figure, our man, and held in great esteem. His voice boomed out as we had come to expect from his nickname of "*boomer*" Trenchard. "*It must not be very satisfying for you men to have to do jobs like this*" he began, "*never seeing any results from your work, and never in the news*". There was a general murmur of approval from the audience for here was someone in authority who was appreciative of the fact that the glamour status enjoyed by the fighter boys was not shared by the lads of Bomber Command. "*The vegetables you will leave behind must make a helluva bang, and I don't suppose any of you have ever seen one explode*", he said.

Had Lord Trenchard been given a button to trigger off the next turn of events, it could not have happened more quickly or more on cue. There was an almighty bang from somewhere on the station followed by a hail of broken glass, curtains streamed inwards as every pane of glass in the briefing room smashed. Almost as quickly, everyone from Group Captain Rice downwards were down on the floor, hands above heads, wondering what in hell's name had happened. All eyes apprehensively looked up to the rostrum where the great man had been standing. He was still standing. Perhaps he was not agile enough to drop to the floor. It could not be that he had failed to hear the bang, but surprisingly enough he was unhurt and we all felt a little sheepish to have prostrated ourselves as we had done.

The briefing session ended somewhat hurriedly, and we all rushed out to learn the worst. A sea mine -one of our vegetables to be laid that night - had exploded as it was being towed away from the bomb dump. Of the tractor driver and the bomb crew there was no trace, they just disappeared. Beyond this there were no other casualities but a fair amount of damage, principally to windows and doors, was evident all over the station. We knew then that they made "one helluva bang"!! and hoped they would never do so when we were in the process of dropping one.

ENEMY ACTION

During the day action was on a reduced scale and consisted mainly of reconnaissance and raids by single aircraft. A few bombs were dropped in Kent, Surrey and London, but damage was minor and casualties few. It is estimated that forty enemy aircraft operated over or near the coasts during the day. During the night from 19.00 to 21.00 hours raids on Liverpool and Birmingham caused considerable damage especially at the latter. From 21.00 to 23.00 hours a continuous stream of raids occurred on London, Kent and Essex with isolated sorties to East Anglia and Buckinghamshire. The Luftwaffe lost eleven aircraft destroyed. RAF Fighter Command had no losses.

COASTAL COMMAND OPERATIONS

Twenty-six aircraft were involved in routine patrols and reconnaissance. Seventeen convoys were escorted.

1. Four Blenheims carried out a successful reconnaissance of the Norwegian coast from Bjornsund to Lister Light. One aircraft was attacked by three Bf109s, but escaped and continued its task. There were no losses.

Night operations

Due to adverse weather all night operations were cancelled.

BOMBER COMMAND OPERATIONS

One Blenheim despatched to bomb the Blohm and Voss yards at Hamburg in daylight abandoned because of lack of cloud cover.

Night operations

Twenty-eight Hampdens and Whitleys were despatched to attack Hamburg docks, Lunen aluminium works, a factory at Dortmund, wharves at Duisburg and marshalling yards at Scherte, Osnabrük and Dortmund.

OPERATIONAL LOSSES

Hampden L4104 of 83 Squadron, Scampton, target Hamburg, the aircraft was abandoned on return and crashed at Coneysthorpe, Yorkshire. Sergeant J. G. Loveluck and his crew landed safely by parachute.

Whitley P4933 'F' of 102 Squadron, Linton-on-Ouse, target Lunen, abandoned out of fuel on return. The aircraft crashed at Maltby, Yorkshire. All of Pilot Officer K. T. Hannah's crew landed by parachute, but two of the crew were slightly injured.

Saturday 19th October

CLOUDY WITH A FEW SUNNY SPELLS IN THE AFTERNOON.

Above: A Sunderland ploughs through the water with the general intention of getting airborne at some point. The two men in the upper gun position are probably wet and deafened at this point!

Below: The view from their position as the flying boat finally becomes airborne.

ENEMY ACTION

Luftwaffe day operations were on a reduced scale limited to an ineffective raid by fighters on London. An attack on Coventry caused damage to industrial property and the by-pass was machine gunned. There was some reconnaissance activity off the south and south-east coasts. It is estimated that 230 enemy aircraft operated over the UK during the day. The night raids commenced at dusk and were very heavy for the first four hours, London rail communications appeared to be one of the main objectives as well as targets at Coventry, Liverpool and Birkenhead. The 'All Clear' was sounded countrywide at 05.50 hours. The Luftwaffe lost one aircraft destroyed. RAF Fighter Command suffered no losses.

COASTAL COMMAND OPERATIONS

Thirty-eight aircraft involved on the usual patrol and reconnaissance tasks were carried out and fourteen convoys were escorted.

1. One aircraft reported sighting a motor vessel of about 1,000 tons foundering north-west of Bloody Foreland.
2. Sunderland 'J' of 210 Squadron dropped depth charges on a suspected U-Boat 185 miles from Bloody Foreland - possibly the sighting in (1). There were no losses.

Night operations

There were no night operations due to adverse weather conditions.

BOMBER COMMAND OPERATIONS

1. Six Blenheims carried out an uneventful sweep over the North Sea.
2. Ten Blenheims were despatched to attack Channel ports and enemy airfields in France, but because of adverse weather all were forced to abandon. There were no losses.

Night operations

Although 151 aircraft were detailed for night operations, because of adverse weather over the UK only three were despatched, two Whitleys and one Hampden to Osnabrük and Berlin. One of them bombed Osnabrük and started a fire in the marshalling yards, the other bombed an aerodrome beacon near The Hague. The third aircraft returned early 'unservicable'.

OPERATIONAL LOSSES

There were no losses

ENEMY ACTION

Fighters and fighter-bombers were used by the Luftwaffe during five main day raids on south-east England. Some of the attacks penetrated to London. Enemy patrols and reconnaissance were also maintained over the Channel and the Straits of Dover. The night raids commenced at 18.30 hours, the main concentrations being over London and the Midlands, especially Birmingham. The raids were maintained until 01.00 hours. Minelaying was active off East Anglia and from the Humber to the Tees. The Luftwaffe lost nine aircraft destroyed. RAF Fighter Command lost four aircraft destroyed.

COASTAL COMMAND OPERATIONS

The usual patrols and other routine tasks were carried out and sixteen convoys were escorted.

1. Blenheims of 248 (F) Squadron on patrol off Utsire Light engaged enemy aircraft. During the fight two enemy aircraft and two Blenheims were shot down.
2. Sunderland 'B' of 210 Squadron convoy escort sighted four full lifeboats from the Swedish motor vessel *Janus*, 112 miles from Rockall.
3. Sunderland 'B' of 210 Squadron, also on convoy escort, sighted a lifeboat with twenty survivors 130 miles from Bloody Foreland and dropped supplies, navigation charts and instructions.

Night operations

1. Swordfish of 812 FAA Squadron were detailed to drop mines off Flushing. There were no losses.

BOMBER COMMAND OPERATIONS

1. Six Blenheims carried out a sweep over the North Sea without incident.
2. One Blenheim sent to reconnoitre and attack Morlaix airfield abandoned the task because of unsuitable weather conditions.

Night operations

135 aircraft out of 192 detailed Blenheims, Hampdens Wellingtons and Whitleys, carried out successful night attacks on targets which included Channel ports, German marshalling yards and naval ports also armament factories in Czechoslovakia and factories in Italy. The largest number on any one target was thirty Hampdens to Berlin. The longest raids were carried out by Whitleys to Pilsen (Czechoslovakia) and Milan (Italy).

OPERATIONAL LOSSES

Blenheim P6952 of 248 Squadron, Sumburgh, shot down off the Norwegian coast when on patrol and landed on the sea. Flight Lieutenant G. M. Baird, Sergeant D. L. Burton (RNZAF) and Sergeant S. V. Wood rowed to the coast on a dinghy the next day. Sergeant R. Copcutt went down with the aircraft when it sank and is remembered on the Runnymede Memorial.
Shot down off Haugesund at 10.23 hours by Leutnant Heinrich Setz of 6./JG 77.

Blenheim L9453 of 248 (F) Squadron, Sumburgh, shot down when on patrol in the Stadtlandet area of Norway. The body of Pilot Officer S. R. Gane was washed ashore and now rests in the Stavne Cemetery, Trondheim. Pilot Officer M. D. Green and Sergeant N. J. Stocks were posted missing in action and are remembered on the Runnymede Memorial.
Shot down west of Stavanger at 10.57 hours by Unteroffizier Fröba of 4./JG 77

Hampden L4154 of 44 Squadron, Waddington, target Berlin, forced landed at Colchester, out of petrol on return. Sergeant A. R. Atkins and his crew were unhurt.

Hampden P2137 of 44 Squadron, Waddington, target Berlin, shot down by Flak near Berlin. Sergeant C. W. Hartop, Sergeant C. V. Stubbs, Sergeant R. G. Bennett and Sergeant R. L. Milbourne are all buried in the Berlin 1939/1945 War Cemetery.

Hampden X2962 of 49 Squadron, Scampton, target Berlin, off track on return and out of fuel, force landed six miles south-east of Truro. Pilot Officer J. H. Green and Sergeant W. Hirst were unhurt. Pilot Officer E. Bingham and Sergeant R. W. Coutts were injured.

Whitley P5095 of 51 Squadron, Wattisham, target Milan, after an arduous return flight of twelve hours broke cloud over water and out of fuel and ditched in shallow water five miles north of the River Mersey. Pilot Officer S. O. Hookway and his crew were later rescued from their dinghy, wet and shaken but unhurt.

Whitley P5058 of 58 Squadron, Linton-on-Ouse, target Pilsen, ditched in the River Humber north of Scunthorpe close to the shore on return. The crew spent three hours in the dinghy before being rescued. For three of the crew this was their second crash in less than a week. Flying Officer B. Brooke and Sergeant Greene were injured. Sergeant C. S. Halley (RAAF), Sergeant Henderson and Sergeant Duncan were unhurt.

Whitley P5089 of 58 Squadron, Linton-on-Ouse, target Pilsen, ditched on return out of fuel off Blakeney Point, north Norfolk. Pilot Officer A. Wilding and crew were all rescued unhurt by the lifeboat *'Foresters Centenary'*.

Whitley T4171 of 58 Squadron, Linton-on-Ouse, target Pilsen, shot down by Hauptman Karl Hulsoff of I/NJG2 flying an intruder mission. The Whitley crashed on fire at Bottom Head, near Ingleby Greenhow, Yorkshire. This is believed to be the first successful enemy intruder sortie of the war. Pilot Officer E. H. Brown, Sergeant L. F. P. Adlam and Sergeant M. C. Caryll-Tilkin were killed. Sergeant R. E. Langfield and Sergeant C. S. G. Green were injured, but Sergeant Green died of his injuries two days later.

Monday 21st October

HEAVY CLOUD, FOG AND RAIN THROUGHOUT EUROPE.

ENEMY ACTIVITY

Day activity by the Luftwaffe was on a small scale, mostly by single aircraft on London, the Midlands and Liverpool areas. Weather conditions made interception difficult. The night activity which was on a considerable scale concentrated on London, the Midlands and Liverpool areas. Other attacks were made on north-east towns and urban and country districts in south-east England. The Luftwaffe lost five aircraft destroyed. Fighter Command lost three aircraft destroyed.

COASTAL COMMAND OPERATIONS

The usual patrols and reconnaissance sorties were carried out and eleven convoys were escorted. No incidents of note were reported and no night operations took place.

BOMBER COMMAND OPERATIONS

1. Twelve Blenheims were despatched during the day to reconnoitre and attack St. Omer airfield. Seven were forced to abandon due to adverse conditions but the remainder attacked shipping and docks at Boulogne and shipping off the French coast.
2. Six Blenheims carried out an uneventful sweep over the North Sea.

Night operations

The Blenheim, Battle and Hampden crews were given the night off - adverse weather helped. However, Wellingtons were despatched to attack the *Bismarck* at Hamburg and the oil refinery at Reisholtz, while Whitleys were sent to attack an oil target at Cologne and an aircraft component factory at Stuttgart. The Wellingtons attempting to bomb the *Bismarck* started eight large fires in the Hamburg dock area.

OPERATIONAL LOSSES

Blenheim R3699 'U' of 53 Squadron, Detling, was damaged in combat during a patrol and was abandoned over Kent by the crew. The aircraft fell at Dernier Road, Tonbridge where it killed one civilian and injured sixteen more. Pilot Officer H. J. W. Meakin and his crew landed safely by parachute.

Wellington R3158 of 75 Squadron, Mildenhall, target Eindhoven, crash-landed on Manston airfield after luckily surviving a collision with a balloon barrage cable. Flying Officer R. P. Elliot and his crew escaped unhurt.

Wellington T2820 of 75 Squadron, Mildenhall, target Hamburg, due to fog at their base on return crashed two miles from Methwold airfield attempting to land. Flight Lieutenant G. L. Gilbert, Pilot Officer Edwards, Sergeant Harris, Sergeant Haigh, Sergeant Broad and Sergeant Read were all injured.

Whitley T4152 'Z' of 10 Squadron, Leeming, target Stuttgart, failed to return. Flight Lieutenant A. S. Phillips DFC, Sergeant D. B. Gordon, Sergeant W. A. Lofthouse, Sergeant C. P. Mapplethorpe and Sergeant I. G. Wills are all buried in the Durnbach War Cemetery. Flight Lieutenant Phillips had only recently returned to operational flying after recovering from severe injuries sustained on 4th June 1940.

A 75 Squadron Wellington was lost when trying to land in fog. All the crew were injured.

Tuesday 22nd October

WIDESPREAD FOG TURNING TO RAIN LATER IN THE DAY.

ENEMY ACTIVITY

Because of adverse weather early in the day enemy activity was limited to coastal reconnaissance, but as the weather improved two fighter sweeps took place, one over Kent and the other over south-east London and the Thames Estuary. Several of the isolated raids were over Devon, Sussex and Surrey. For a change no bombs fell on London. It was estimated that seventy enemy aircraft operated over the coast during the day. The night attacks were on London, the Home Counties, the Midlands, Liverpool and south Wales. The Midlands bore the brunt and considerable damage was inflicted on Coventry. The Luftwaffe lost nine aircraft destroyed. Fighter Command lost five aircraft destroyed.

COASTAL COMMAND OPERATIONS

Thirty patrols and reconnaissance sorties were carried out and fourteen convoys were provided with escort.

1. An aircraft over Brest on reconnaissance reported seven destroyers in the harbour.

Night operations

Six Blenheims were despatched to carry out a night attack on the power station at Lorient with shipping as the alternative.

BOMBER COMMAND OPERATIONS

Due to adverse weather only one Blenheim crew was despatched in daylight to reconnoitre and attack targets at Amsterdam. They attacked a cargo ship three miles north of the Hook of Holland, claimed a direct hit, and got back safely.

Night operations

Due to adverse weather all night operations were cancelled.

OPERATIONAL LOSSES

There were no losses

Above: A Hudson pilot checks a few last details with the groundcrew before a patrol.

Below: The weather was getting worse with fog and low cloud hampering the bomber offensive. Here, an 83 Squadron crew disembark after a landing in marginal weather conditions.

Wednesday 23rd October LOW OVERCAST FOR THE WHOLE COUNTRY, OCCASIONAL DRIZZLE.

ENEMY ACTIVITY

There was no enemy activity until after 12.00 hours and then it was limited to isolated attacks by single aircraft over the south-east and Midlands areas. Night raids were carried out on London and minelaying was thought to have taken place off the Lancashire Coast. The Luftwaffe lost three aircraft destroyed. RAF Fighter Command lost one aircraft.

COASTAL COMMAND OPERATIONS

Routine patrols, reconnaissance and escorts took place.

1. Photo-reconnaissance off Bergen revealed two 10,000 ton ships and the presence of six motor vessels of medium tonnage in the harbour.
2. Another reconnaissance aircraft successfully evaded attacks by three Messerschmitts.
3. Two Flak ships were sighted near Horn's Reef, but low cloud prevented an attack.
4. Two Beauforts, 'A' and 'G' of 22 Squadron attacked an enemy convoy of nine motor vessels and three escorts five miles north of Schiermonnikoog. Each aircraft released torpedoes from fifty feet scoring hits on a 4,000 ton vessel and another of 2,000 tons. Explosions were observed and one ship was seen to be down by the stern and the decks of another were awash. There were no losses.

Night operations

1. Night operations. Five FAA Swordfish were detailed to lay mines off Ijmuiden.
2. Six Blenheims were detailed to attack shipping at Le Havre.

BOMBER COMMAND OPERATIONS

1. Eight Blenheims were detailed for offensive sea sweeps and attacks on French airfields but adverse weather curtailed operations. However, attacks were carried out by single aircraft against shipping off Walcheren and in Ostend harbour. Also a factory at St. Nicholas was attacked and a large explosion was observed.
2. Six Blenheims carried out a routine reconnaissance over the North Sea.

Night operations

Seventy-nine aircraft attacked a variety of targets in Germany and the occupied countries ranging from ports, dockyards, oil plants, marshalling yards, aircraft plants, shipping and airfields. The main attacks were carried out by twelve Wellingtons which bombed Emden and another eleven which reached and bombed Berlin. OTU aircraft were included in the force.

OPERATIONAL LOSSES

Wellington P9292 of 75 Squadron, Mildenhall, target Berlin, believed to have crashed into the sea off the west coast of Jutland. Pilot Officer R. M. Sanderson, Pilot Officer W. J. Finlayson (RNZAF), Sergeant J. Gibbs DFM, Sergeant W. G. Hitchmough and Sergeant R. W. B. White all perished and are remembered on the Runnymede Memorial. The body of Pilot Officer F. B. Cleak was recovered from the sea and buried at Esjberg.

Wellington T2740 'E' of 149 Squadron, Mildenhall, target Emden, crashed on return attempting to make an emergency landing three miles west of Clacton. Flying Officer D. W. Donaldson and his crew escaped injury.

Pilots of 75 Squadron line up in front of ill-fated Wellington P9292 which failed to return on this day with the loss of the entire crew of six.

Thursday 24th October

A 269 Squadron Hudson on patrol over Norway. One of the squadron aircraft was shot down by a Bf109 off the Norwegian coast today.

ENEMY ACTIVITY

Again there was little enemy activity during the morning and what occurred was limited to a few reconnaissance sorties. Later in the day it increased and enemy aircraft penetrated to the Midlands, East Anglia, and the West Country. The night raids were also not on a large scale, London and Birmingham being the main objectives. Fires were started in Birmingham which damaged commercial property. A German report stated that Italian bombers had taken part for the first time. Minelaying was extensive in the Thames Estuary off the Essex Coast and also off the coast between Scarborough and the Tyne. The Luftwaffe lost two aircraft destroyed. Fighter Command had no losses.

COASTAL COMMAND OPERATIONS

The usual patrols and routine tasks were carried out and twenty-two convoys and one Empire Flying Boat were given escort.

1. A Hudson attacked a stationary vessel at Ijmuiden, but no result was observed.
2. Later Hudsons attacked two He115s off St. Abb's Head without a decisive result.
3. Three Hudsons on patrol sighted one hundred fishing smacks near Horn's Reef, but lack of cloud precluded attacks.

Night operations

1. Blenheims were detailed to attack targets at Le Havre and FAA Swordfish to lay mines in the Maas Estuary.

BOMBER COMMAND OPERATIONS

1. Nine Blenheims were despatched to reconnoitre and attack French, Belgian and Dutch Channel ports, Ostend and targets in northern France were attacked.
2. Six Blenheims carried out a successful North Sea reconnaissance.

Night operations

113 aircraft carried out night raids on many targets; oil plants, aluminium works, naval ports and dockyards, communications and a Berlin target.

1. Wellingtons carried out a heavy raid on Hamburg and although cloud conditions made observation difficult thirteen fires, some of them large were left burning.
2. Hampdens bombed Hannover and an additional five laid mines.
3. The Berlin target was attacked by the Whitleys.
4. There were seven sorties by OTU aircraft.

OPERATIONAL LOSSES

Hudson P5132 'F' of 269 Squadron, Wick, failed to return from extended North Sea patrol. Flight Lieutenant N. B. Mole, Sergeant D. A. J. Smith, Sergeant J. E. R. Sharvin and Sergeant A. W. Campbell were posted missing in action and are remembered on the Runnymede Memorial.
Shot down off the Norwegian coast by Leutnant Deuschle of 6./JG 77.

Wellington L7809 'T' of 38 Squadron, Marham, target Hamburg. Flight Lieutenant E. G. F. Chivers, Sergeant F. W. Davis, Sergeant J. B. McConnell, Sergeant W. Cosgrove, Sergeant A. J. Hughes and Sergeant R. W. James are all buried in the Becklingen War Cemetery at Saltau.

Whitley P5073 'D' of 102 Squadron, Linton-on-Ouse, target the German Air Ministry building in Berlin, shot down after taking off by Feldwebel Hans Hahn of 3./NJG2 and crashed four miles north-north-west of base. Pilot Officer T. R. Murfitt, Sergeant I. C. Scoular (RNZAF) and Pilot Officer T. E. Lee were killed. Pilot Officer A. G. Davies and Sergeant A. S. Wilson were injured.
This was the second Whitley to fall victim to an intruder in less than a week.

Friday 25th October

LOW OVERCAST FOR THE WHOLE COUNTRY, BUT ONLY ISOLATED SHOWERS.

Another Hudson was lost today, this time suffered by 224 Squadron operating out of Northern Ireland.

ENEMY ACTIVITY

Luftwaffe operations during the day were on a larger scale than of late and almost continuous, the main objectives being London and the Home Counties. Some raids were intercepted but others got through and caused heavy casualties in London where some bombs hit crowded public transport. Enemy reconnaissance ranged from the Orkneys to the Thames Estuary and thence along the coast to Land's End. Four sweeps were carried out over Kent and a convoy off North Foreland was attacked by twenty enemy aircraft, but they were all off the mark. A total of 440 enemy aircraft operated over the UK during the day. The night activity commenced at approximately 18.30 hours with London and Birmingham as the main objectives, but areas from south Wales and the Midlands up to Liverpool were also targeted. Minelaying extended from North Foreland up to Aberdeen. Aerodromes which were attacked included Montrose where a hangar and buildings were damaged and Arbroath and Cardington where there were some fatal casualties. The Luftwaffe lost nineteen aircraft destroyed. RAF Fighter Command lost ten aircraft destroyed.

COASTAL COMMAND OPERATIONS

The usual routine tasks were carried out by the coastal squadrons during the day.

1. A Blenheim on a special reconnaissance of the Norwegian coast from Trondheim to Stadtlandet sighted approximately forty motor vessels along the coast.

Night operations

1. Six Blenheims were detailed to carry out night attacks on shipping at Antwerp. Three crews observed bombs bursting in the target area, but two were unable to locate the target and the other returned unserviceable.
2. Six other Blenheims were despatched to attack the power station at Brest.

BOMBER COMMAND OPERATIONS

1. Six Blenheims were despatched in daylight to attack shipyards at Wilhelmshaven, Kiel, Bremen and Hamburg but they had to abandon due to adverse weather.
2. An additional six Blenheims carried out a successful reconnaissance over the North Sea.

Night operations

Ninety-two aircraft were despatched on night operations. Targets attacked included dockyards, marshalling yards and oil targets in north and central Germany, airfields in occupied territory and gun emplacements on the Channel coast. Five Hampdens laid mines in Kiel Bay and the Elbe.

OPERATIONAL LOSSES

Hudson N7240 'Q' of 224 Squadron, Aldergrove, failed to return from a convoy escort over the Atlantic. Pilot Officer J. H. H. Gladdis, Pilot Officer A. R. Carrick, Sergeant T. A. Hughes, Sergeant J. D. Dowson and Sergeant J. McGhie are all remembered on the Runnymede Memorial.

Hampden X2971 of 61 Squadron, Hemswell, target Kiel, lost without trace. Sergeant H. C. Loadsman, Sergeant K. R. Humphrey, Sergeant D. I. Pallett and Sergeant F. D. Walter are all commemorated on the Runnymede Memorial.

Hampden X2998 of 144 Squadron, Hemswell, target Kiel, crashed on return three miles south-east of Gainsborough, Lincolnshire. Sergeant R. J. Curtis, Sergeant A. Goulder, Sergeant E. H. Woods and Sergeant W. C. Anderson were all injured.

A Swordfish was lost on operations today. This rare photo shows a black painted Swordfish in a French field in November 1940.

ENEMY ACTIVITY

During the day the Luftwaffe carried out sporadic raids using single or small groups of Bf109s over south-east England, The Straits of Dover and extending as far west as Poole. A larger attack comprising about eighty aircraft developed towards noon and headed inland towards London, but only a few penetrated as far as the Capital. Other enemy aircraft attacked RAF Lossiemouth, one of them was shot down and crashed, exploding on the aerodrome.

The scale of the night attacks was moderately heavy to start with, but they petered out and only London was kept on alert with nuisance raids by single aircraft. Minelaying aircraft crossed the Yorkshire coast to sow their mines off the Lancashire coast. The Luftwaffe lost nine aircraft destroyed. RAF Fighter Command lost five aircraft destroyed.

COASTAL COMMAND OPERATIONS

The usual patrols, reconnaissance and escorts were carried out.

1. An early morning raid by five Blenheims on Brest power station resulted in fires in buildings in the target area.
2. A Hudson bombed and machine-gunned five motor vessels forty-five miles west of Den Helder. Bombs fell just thirty yards in front of the leading vessel.
3. A Sunderland with three Blenheims assisted in the rescue of survivors from the *Empress of Britain* which was on fire eighty-six miles west of Bloody Foreland.
4. Photo-reconnaissance Ostend, Dunkirk, Boulogne and Brest were successful.

BOMBER COMMAND OPERATIONS

1. A routine North Sea sweep was carried out by six Blenheims.
2. Another six Blenheims despatched to attack naval and oil targets in Germany had to abandon because of adverse conditions.

Night operations

Ninety-seven aircraft were detailed for the night operations over Germany and France:

1. Forty-five to attack oil targets.
2. Twenty to attack targets at Berlin.
3. Nine to attack Communications.
4. Nine to attack Channel ports.
5. Nine to attack French airfields.
6. Five to sow mines in the River Gironde.

The heaviest raid was carried by Hampdens on the Berlin targets.

OPERATIONAL LOSSES

Swordfish L2794 of 821 Squadron Fleet Air Arm, lost on operations. Sub Lieutenant P. B. Laycock, Naval Airman I B. F. A Brewster and Midshipman R. T. Chambers missing. Their names appear on the Lee-on-Solent Memorial.

Saturday 26th October

Beaufort L9813 of 42 Squadron, Wick, shot down by Bf109s when attacking shipping in Sogne Fjord, Norway. Squadron Leader F. G. L. Smith DFC, Pilot Officer H. F. Burns and Sergeant E. A. Brown were captured. Sergeant W. R. Perrin was killed and lies in the Stavne Cemetery.

Beaufort L1159 of 42 Squadron, Wick, shot down by Bf109s after attacking shipping in Aspo Fjord, and crashed into Sogne Fjord, Norway. Sergeant G. R. Brocklehurst, Sergeant V. W. Gadson, Sergeant W. H. Bolton and Flying Officer A. MacRury are all remembered on the Runnymede Memorial.

These two Beauforts were intercepted southwest of Bergen by Bf109s from 4./JG 77. Three victories were credited to Leutnant Jakob Arnoldy. Unteroffizier Vogel and Oberleutnant Wilhelm Moritz between 16.50 and 16.52

Blenheims R3760 and T2233 of 21 Squadron were destroyed in an air raid on Lossiemouth when about to take off at night. There were six aircrew casualties; Pilot Officer P. H. Slater, Sergeant H. Jones and Corporal O. H. S. Holland were killed. Sergeant Green, AC1 Windeler and AC1 Bristow were injured.

Hudson N7301 of the PRU, Heston, caught fire near Vlissingen. Flight Lieutenant A. A. Rumsey, Sergeant Williams, Sergeant Phillips and LAC A. J. Dixon landed safely by parachute. Pilot Officer C. G. Broome also baled out, but was found dead and now lies in the Vlissingen Cemetery.

This was credited to Leutnant Hans-Erich Heimbockel of Stab III./JG 54 at 13.26 hours.

Hudson P5130 of 269 Squadron, Wick, was destroyed in an air raid.

Hampden X2990 'Z' of 83 Squadron, Scampton, failed to return from a mining sortie to the Gironde Estuary. Sergeant J. G. Joveluck, Sergeant K. E. Young, Sergeant J. M. Dall and Sergeant G. L. Middleton were all lost and are remembered on the Runnymede Memorial.

Whitley T4136 'H' of 102 Squadron, Linton-on-Ouse, target Politz, hit by Flak over the enemy coast on return. The crew baled out over Yorkshire and the aircraft crashed at Ebberston. Pilot Officer J. S. G. Crawford and his crew landed safely by parachute.

A 21 Squadron Blenheim runs her engines up under the trained eyes and ears of the groundcrew. The squadron lost two aircraft and three aircrew during the night when a German bomber attacked just as they were preparing for take off.

Sunday 27th October

The damage caused at Honington by the 27th October raid.

ENEMY ACTIVITY

Four attacks were made on south-east England by the Luftwaffe during the morning. In the afternoon another took place on Plymouth and Southampton. The formations were almost entirely comprised of fighters. Night activity was similar to previous nights but on a slightly reduced scale. There was a change in target selection when enemy bombers carried out a dusk attack on a large number of RAF airfields - Catfoss, Coltishall, Dishforth, Feltwell, Hawkinge, Heston, Honington, Horsham-St- Faith, Kirton-in-Lindsay, Leconfield, Lindholme, Martlesham Heath, Mildenhall, Newmarket and North Weald. Only slight damage was caused at all the locations. The following aircraft were destroyed by bombing on the ground: Blenheim T2034 of 101 Squadron at Great Massingham; Blenheims R3749 and R3807 of 110 Squadron at Wattisham. Other raids penetrated to the Midlands and the Bristol Channel but the main activity appeared to be over London. Minelaying was active from the Thames Estuary to the Firth of Forth with a concentration in the Hartlepool area. The Luftwaffe lost eleven aircraft destroyed. RAF Fighter Command lost nine aircraft destroyed.

COASTAL COMMAND OPERATIONS

The usual reconnaissance and routine patrols were carried out and twenty convoys were escorted.

1. A Blenheim on routine patrol attacked a ship off Denhelder - result unobserved.
2. Three Blenheims on a special shipping strike off the French coast were driven off by enemy fighters. Another Blenheim successfully attacked the enemy airfield at Querqueville.
3. Beauforts made unsuccessful torpedo attacks while on '*Rover*' patrols off Texel, Borkum, Denhelder and Ameland. Two Beauforts suffered Flak damage.
4. A Hudson on convoy escort sighted an enemy FW200 (Condor) attacking a convoy west of Bloody Foreland but the enemy aircraft made off before the Hudson could attack.

BOMBER COMMAND OPERATIONS

Nine Blenheims were despatched to attack German naval targets, but only one attacked mine sweepers off Terschelling. Blenheims carried out a routine sweep over the North Sea.

Night operations

Eighty-two were detailed for the night operations; Blenheims, Whitleys, Wellingtons and Hampdens. Their many targets in Germany and the occupied countries included the Skoda works at Pilsen (Czechoslovakia) oil Plants at Hamburg Ostermoor, Hanover, Gelsenkirchen and Magdeburg, marshalling yards at Krefeld, Hamm and Mannheim, docks at Wilhelmshaven and Hamburg and the Channel ports of Antwerp, Flushing and Ostend, as well as occupied airfields. Seventy-six crews claimed to have bombed their targets successfully. Five Hampdens carried out minelaying off Lorient. Two sorties were carried out by OTU crews.

OPERATIONAL LOSSES

Blenheim L8789 'E' of 53 Squadron, Detling, shot down by Bf109s off Dover during a shipping strike. Pilot Officer R. L. Buckley, Sergeant C. Henderson and Sergeant P. E. J. Neale were posted as missing in action and are remembered on the Runnymede Memorial.

This aircraft would appear to have been the opponent for Leutnant Ltn. Waldemar Wübke of 9./JG 54, who claimed it shot down into the sea off Den Helder at 10.35 hours

Sunday 27th October

Note a second Blenheim from 53 Squadron PZ-R flown by Pilot Officer Plumtree, crash-landed at Martlesham Heath after a running fight with Bf109s. Plumtree and his crew, Sergeants Wood and Kinsey, were both wounded.
Gefreiter. Werner Heidorn of 2./JG 51 claimed a Blenheim and Feldwebel Georg Pavenzinger claimed two, but it is possible that only Heidorn's was actually credited.

Hudson N7266 'G' of 224 Squadron, Aldergrove, damaged by fire from an FW200 and returned to base, but was written-off later. Sergeant K. B. Files and his crew escaped injury.

Hampden X3027 'A' of 49 Squadron, Scampton, target Hamburg, shot down by an intruder and crashed in the sea off Skegness. Pilot Officer J. R. Bufton, Pilot Officer K. Ballas-Anderson, Sergeant R. F. Robertson and Sergeant F. J. W. Bichard all killed. The body of Pilot Officer Ballas-Anderson was never found and his name is on the Runnymede Memorial.
This aircraft fell to Leutnant Heinz Völker of 2./NJG 2, who correctly claimed a Hampden at Scampton at 00.30 hours.

A Shaky Do

Sgt George Parr, Blenheim Observer 18 Sqn

This sortie, although no enemy action was involved, was by far the nearest we came to complete disaster, and is a good example of the dangers involved in flying in bad weather in 1940. The target was Hamm, where the marshalling yards were frequently bombed, at times on a nightly basis, and just as frequently repaired. The weather was foul. There was a reasonable moon, but the cloud base was too low for us to safely maintain visual contact with the ground. Electricity cables were a particular hazard on dark nights. So we climbed up through turbulent cloud to finally emerge around 20,000 ft, very near the loaded aircraft's ceiling.

We felt very conspicuous, as any fighter flying above our level would be sure to see us against the moonlit cloud tops. However we were again lucky, but I knew it would be difficult to identify the target. Flg Off. Douch kept to the planned speed, height and heading as accurately as possible and at the appropriate time started the descent. I hoped to get an idea of our position from one or other of the industrial cities of the Ruhr. There were usually a lot of furnace fires visible, but there were also a lot of dummies. At 3000 ft we were still in cloud. At 2000 ft we could still see nothing, but shortly after we finally broke cloud at what I estimated to be 1000 ft above the ground, in heavy rain.

I could see nothing, but presumed we were east of our target, so I asked for a westerly heading, which should lead us to a railway running north to Hamm. Bringing a very cold aircraft down into rain produced ideal conditions for the formation of ice, which not only distorted the aerofoil shape of the wing to reduce lift, but added considerably to the aircraft weight. Great lumps flew off the propeller blades and crashed against the perspex of my navigator's compartment in the nose. From time to time I had to put on a light to look at the map, on to which every breath deposited a shower of snow. There was no heating of any kind, but worse still there was no anti-icing boot on the leading edge of the wing. Sgt Barrett in his turret reported half an inch of ice everywhere, then one inch, then one and a half inches. It was obvious that we could not stay airborne much longer at this altitude, but at last I saw, or thought I saw, our railway line, and called 'right'. The pilot responded and I saw and felt the starboard wing dip, and continue to dip to an alarming degree until we suddenly flipped over and fell spinning earthward.

Loose equipment flew about my ears and the pilot announced that he had lost control, which we had already noticed. To me there was absolutely no way that we could avoid making violent contact with the ground within the next few seconds. I managed to grab the bomb release handle and rid us of the four 250 pounders in a futile gesture to reduce the severity of the imminent explosion. It was probably no more than two or three seconds later that I found myself wondering why we were still above ground and suddenly on even keel.

How John Douch managed to regain control was to me nothing less than a miracle. A few years ago he sent me a detailed account of how he had applied the procedures for recovery from unusual positions, in this instance with artificial horizon toppled and direction indicator spinning, although this was not part of pilot training at that time. There is no doubt that his calculated action in the most difficult conditions resulted in the continued existence of all three of us. But for me I think there must have been a measure of divine assistance as well.

All was not yet over. The pilot still had only limited instruments to keep the aircraft under control and these were continually obscured as our breath froze on the glass. I sat by the pilot and continuously rubbed the frost away with a cloth. It was pitch dark outside as he struggled to gain height. The airspeed was very unstable and we proceeded in a series of steep climbs, followed by that empty feeling on a near stall, then finding our stomachs in our boots as we recovered from the subsequent dive. It was a long time before we eventually broke through to see that lovely moon at a height we variously remember as between 12 and 20 thousand feet. The instruments righted themselves and we continued with the rest of our lives.

If I could add a footnote to this account it would be that this was one of a few occasions when we failed to drop our bombs on target, or in the case of a small target like a power station, close to the target, and 'close' would be measured in hundreds of yards rather than in miles. In recent years I have never understood the claims of historians and others that bombing accuracy in the early part of the war was very poor. I admit that bomb aiming was not a precision discipline like firing a rifle or even an artillery piece and we were certainly not the only crew who in difficult conditions may have failed to locate the target. I can only say that under any conditions permitting map reading there was normally no difficulty in identifying a port or an airfield or to find a less prominent target by reference to a town or a water feature. And having identified it, it would be difficult for the bomb aimer to miss by the wide margins quoted. A much quoted figure is that targets were missed by an average of five miles. I don't know how these conclusions were reached and can only comment from my own restricted experience, but I feel that we should speak up for those against whom these accusations are made and are no longer able to speak for themselves. In the account given above, when bombs were jettisoned as an act of self preservation, it is just possible that we 'missed' by 150 miles. Persuing this theory, if every other sortie that we flew resulted in a direct hit then our average 'miss' would indeed have been five miles.

Monday 28th October

A 204 Squadron Sunderland, similar to the one lost today.

BOMBER COMMAND OPERATIONS

1.Seven Blenheims were despatched during the day, one on a roving commission which abandoned its task and the others to attack enemy occupied airfields and barges. A successful attack was carried out on Berck airfield.
Six Blenheims carried out a routine reconnaissance over the North Sea.

Night operations

Ninety-four aircraft were despatched to carry out night attacks on various targets, marshalling yards, oil plants, ports, shipping and shipyards in Germany and occupied airfields in Belgium and Holland. The biggest raid was carried out on Hamburg by Hampdens. Damage and casualties resulted.

ENEMY ACTIVITY

During the day the enemy carried out two mine sweeps and one major attack, but no aircraft penetrated to central London. Reconnaissance was active over the Bristol Channel and the Thames Estuary. It is estimated that 250 enemy aircraft operated over or near the coasts. Fighter Command flew 117 patrols with 603 aircraft. The early night raids were widespread over most of the country and London and its suburbs together with Birmingham received most attention. The enemy dropped incendiary leaves, the equivalent of Bomber Command's 'Razzle' close to RAF Digby, but they extinguished before reaching the ground. At Biggin Hill, approximately 300 hundred incendiary bombs fell on the airfield, but the fires they caused were soon extinguished and there were no casualties. The Luftwaffe lost eight aircraft destroyed. RAF Fighter Command lost one aircraft destroyed.

COASTAL COMMAND OPERATIONS

Routine patrols, reconnaissance and escorts were carried out.
1. Three Blenheims attacked the power station at Lorient. Four direct hits were observed and eight further hits were claimed to be in the target area.
2. A Hudson on routine patrol had a combat with two He115s. Although the Hudson scored hits on the enemy aircraft the engagement was inclusive.
3. Four Beauforts of 22 Squadron carried out attacks on shipping while on 'Rover' Wangerooge - Borkum. One had a near miss on a 2,000 ton tanker six miles north of Terschelling and two more attacked tankers twenty-one miles west of Borkum without success.

Night operations

1. Five FAA Swordfish were detailed to attack barges at Boulogne, but only one bombed dropping a large calibre bomb. Results were not observed. The other four failed to bomb because of adverse weather conditions.
2. Six Blenheims were detailed to bomb the barges at Boulogne, but only one succeeded. The crew claimed that their bombs straddled the target but they were unable to confirm results.

OPERATIONAL LOSSES

Sunderland P9620 'K' of 204 Squadron, Oban, became lost on a convoy patrol when the compass failed in an electrical storm. The aircraft ran out of fuel and landed on the sea 100 miles from St. Kilda. It stayed afloat in a gale for nine hours before breaking up. Nine crew members were rescued by *HMS Australia*, but four were lost. Flight Lieutenant S. R. Gibbs, Pilot Officer Neugebauer, Pilot Officer J. M. Ennis, Sergeant Gough, Sergeant H. W. Taylor, Sergeant Cushworthy, LAC Gay, AC Hicks and A C Bond were rescued. LAC M. E. Towe, Sergeant S. H. MacDonald (RNZAF), AC1 K.W. Beavis and Sergeant M. S. Ross were lost and are remembered on the Runnymede Memorial.

Beaufort L9800 of 22 Squadron, North Coates, crashed in the sea after take-off for a patrol. Sergeant J. P. Rylands, Sergeant D. D. Palmer, Sergeant P. W. Ripley and Sergeant N. H. Jackson killed. The aircraft crashed just a half mile from the shore and all the bodies but Sergeant Rylands' were recovered; he is recorded on the Runnymede Memorial.

Blenheim T1891 of 105 Squadron, Watton, target Homburg, lost without trace. Squadron Leader C. W. Grannum, Pilot Officer N. A. Knight and Sergeant J. E. Greenwood are all commemorated on the Runnymede Memorial.

Blenheim T2229 of 105 Squadron, Watton, target Mannheim, crashed on return two miles north west of Fakenham, Norfolk. Pilot Officer I. Prosser, Sergeant A. F. Dallas (RNZAF), and Sergeant J. Hardcastle were all killed.

Whitley P5082 'L' of 102 Squadron, Linton-on-Ouse, target Bremen, signalled a successful attack, but subsequently crashed in the North Sea twenty miles east of Aberdeen. Flight Lieutenant R. A. Barnwell, Sergeant H. E. Danks, Sergeant F. J. Abrahams, Sergeant T. H. Pegram and Sergeant M. Rose are all commemorated on the Runnymede Memorial.

Tuesday 29th October

COMPLETE HIGH LEVEL CLOUD COVER OVER MOST OF EUROPE.

Beauforts were now cleared for torpedo operations although this 22 Squadron machine would struggle to carry quite the amount of tin fish prepared by the enthusiastic ground crew!

ENEMY ACTIVITY

During the day there were five main attacks in the south-east of England, two attacks in the Plymouth area and dusk attacks against airfields in East Anglia, Lincolnshire and Yorkshire.

Hostile patrols were also maintained over the Straits of Dover and the Channel. The attacks lasted all day and were carried out by formations varying in number. Convoys off Selsey Bill, Dover, the Thames Estuary and Lowestoft also came under attack by the Luftwaffe.

The night raids over London were less than usual, but activity was widespread over the Home Counties. The largest proportion of raids was over Birmingham and Coventry.

Minelaying is suspected as having taken place in the Thames Estuary and between the Firth of Forth and Hartlepool. The 'All Clear' was sounded in the London area at 04.50 hours and at 06.00 hours in the Midlands. The Luftwaffe lost eighteen aircraft destroyed. RAF Fighter Command lost six aircraft destroyed.

COASTAL COMMAND OPERATIONS

Routine patrols, reconnaissance and escorts were carried out.

1. Blenheims bombed the power station at Brest, two crews claiming to have hit the target.

2. Four Beauforts were detailed to carry out torpedo attacks on shipping off the Dutch coast. One aircraft crashed in the sea after take-off.

3. A Whitley on convoy escort attacked a U-Boat one hundred miles north-west of Bloody Foreland dropping four 250lb AS bombs not more than five yards from it, but bad visibility prevented results being observed and contact was lost.

4. A PRU Spitfire detailed to photograph Berlin was prevented from doing so by adverse weather, but on its return flight it photographed Stettin, Cuxhaven and Emden. Other attempts to photograph Calais, Lorient and Brest were unsuccessful due to adverse weather.

There were no night operations.

BOMBER COMMAND OPERATIONS

1. Thirteen Blenheims were despatched during the day. One bombed the docks at Rotterdam, but results were not observed. Six were detailed to carry out dusk attacks on enemy occupied airfields, Giessen, Bercq, Antwerp and Dieppe were bombed. At Antwerp a hangar was demolished and Giessen and Bercq received direct hits.

2. Six other Blenheims completed a reconnaissance over the North Sea

Night operations

Ninety-eight aircraft were detailed for night operations on many targets despite snow storms: Berlin, oil plants at Homburg, Sterkrade, shipyards and docks at Bremen and Wilhelmshaven, shipping at Den Helder, Ijmuiden, Flushing and Ostend, marshalling yards, aerodromes,

searchlight and Flak batteries. The largest number of aircraft were despatched to Berlin, but because of the very bad conditions only four reached and bombed their target. Five additional Hampdens laid mines in the Baltic.
One OTU aircraft dropped leaflets over the Arras area.

OPERATIONAL LOSSES

Sunderland P9622 'W' of 201 Squadron, Sullom Voe, became lost and flew into a hill 28 miles south-west of Wick while on an Air Sea Rescue search. Pilot Officer Field, Pilot Officer Rabou, Pilot Officer Cooper, Sergeant Corbin and Corporal Wells were injured. Sergeant Ault and Sergeant Anderson escaped injury. Sergeant R. Lauder, Sergeant R. W. J. Phelps Sergeant J. L. Carson and AC1 G. A. Nangle were killed.

Sunderland T9045 of 204 Squadron, Sullom Voe, took off to search for P9622, but was forced to land on the sea in darkness. All of Squadron Leader Cumming's crew were rescued by a trawler, but the aircraft sank under tow five miles off Strathie Point, Caithness.

Blenheim T1861 of 144 Squadron, Oulton, target Le Havre, lost without trace. Pilot Officer P. B. Hissey, Sergeant G. E. Ellwood and Sergeant W. Turner are all commemorated on the Runnymede Memorial.

Hampden X3000 of 50 Squadron, Lindholme, target Berlin, iced up on return and the crew baled out, the aircraft crashing near RAF Linton-on-Ouse. Pilot Officer C. J. R. Walker and his crew baled out successfully and were unhurt.

Hampden T2246 of 106 Squadron, Finningley, minelaying in the Baltic, lost without trace. Pilot Officer J. J. Hill, Pilot Officer J. V. F. Gibbs, Sergeant G. L. Howe and Sergeant S. D. Bazeley are all commemorated on the Runnymede Memorial.

Wellington T2546 of 99 Squadron, Newmarket, target Berlin, crashed into a hill near Otterburn, Northumberland. Pilot Officer E. S. I. Hallows was killed, but the rest of Flight Lieutenant E. T. A. Harvey's crew escaped unhurt.

Whitley P4957 'E' of 10 Squadron, Leeming, target Magdeburg, on return flew into a hillside five miles north-north-west of Alston, Cumberland. The cause of their crash was the D/F Station gave them reciprocal instead of homing bearings. Miraculously only one of Pilot Officer W. E. Peers's crew, (Sgt George Dove), was slightly injured.

Whitley P4972 of 51 Squadron, Dishforth, target Merseburg, crashed at base on return attempting to land in a strong crosswind. Sergeant J. R. Brown was killed; Pilot Officer M. E. Sharp and Pilot Officer S. Storey were injured. Sergeant D. H. Crocker and Sergeant A. Brittain were uninjured.

The wreckage of a Sunderland on a remote hillside. This is possibly that of T9045 which crashed on an Air Sea Rescue search on 29th October.

Wednesday 30th October

RAIN AND LOW CLOUD THROUGHOUT THE COUNTRY.

ENEMY ACTIVITY

Two enemy fighter sweeps were made over south-east England, one in the morning and one in the afternoon. A few reconnaissance flights by single aircraft took place over Exeter, Portland, East Anglia and the Firth of Forth. Although bad weather affected night activity, raids were still carried out over London and south-east England during the early evening. There were also a number of raids in the Midlands. The increasingly bad weather brought the Luftwaffe activity to an early close. The 'All Clear' was sounded in all areas by 03.35 hours. The Luftwaffe lost eight aircraft destroyed. RAF Fighter Command lost seven aircraft destroyed.

COASTAL COMMAND OPERATIONS

Despite the adverse weather which curtailed much flying, patrols and escorts were carried out.

Ostend harbour was attacked by Blenheims. No results were observed.

BOMBER COMMAND OPERATIONS

Six Blenheims were despatched during the day to attack French targets. One carried out successful attacks on E-Boats twenty miles north of Cherbourg, one crew bombed three ships off Barfleur and another bombed buildings near the docks at Cherbourg.

Night operations

Most night operations were cancelled because of the adverse weather, however, six Blenheims attacked the industrial port of Duisburg and the Ruhrorthafen marshalling yard.

Four Wellingtons attacked Emden, nine attacked Antwerp and nine Flushing.

OPERATIONAL LOSSES

Blenheim T2246 of 101 Squadron, West Raynham, target north-west Germany, crashed on return six miles north of Scunthorpe. Pilot Officer J. M. Cave, Sergeant J. G. Hitchen and Sergeant C. J. Gooderick all perished.

Sergeant George Dove
Whitley gunner 102 Sqn

George Dove enlisted in the Royal Air Force before the outbreak of WWII and after training as a wireless operator / air gunner he was posted to 10 Whitley Squadron. He commenced his first operational 'tour' in 1940 and flew numerous bombing sorties including raids against the German invasion fleet in the occupied ports and relevant targets in Germany during the Battle of Britain. His tour ended dramatically on the night of the 30th/31st October 1940 when his aircraft crashed in the Pennines returning from a raid on Magdeburg. The Whitley was a 'write-off' but George was the only crew member to sustain injury. After his recovery he was posted to a Whitley OTU as a WOp/AG instructor for a 'rest'.

After being at the OTU for nearly four months, he was awarded the Distinguished Flying Medal, a belated award. Up to April 1941, the only recipients of awards on No. 10 Squadron were pilots. None of the other aircrew categories were decorated, irrespective of merit. The Commanding Officer from the beginning of WWII was a WWI fighter 'Ace' who apparently looked upon aircrew other than pilots as so much ballast! It was fortunate that his successor and other more senior officers were not of his opinion and from then deserving aircrew other than 'drivers airframe' received 'gongs'.

George went back for a second 'tour' of operations in 1943 with No. 101 (Lancaster) Squadron. On the night of the 14th/15th February 1943, he took part in a raid on Milan, flying as mid-upper gunner. After leaving the target their aircraft was attacked by a night-fighter which ignited four 30lb incendiaries still in the bomb bay of the Lancaster. Their rear gunner, although wounded, succeeded in setting the enemy aircraft on fire. In the meantime flames had reached George's turret and he was burned about his face and hands, but despite this he got in a good burst which completed the destruction of the night-fighter. He then left his turret and made his way through the flames and exploding ammunition and succeeded in extricating the wounded rear gunner, staying with him until the fire was subdued and he was relieved by another member of the crew. George made no mention of his injuries until after landing at base. For his determination, courageous action and fearless disregard for danger he was awarded the Conspicuous Gallantry Medal.

Thursday 31st October

With the shadows lengthening and the days getting shorter, the Blenheim crews reflect on a battle won and friends lost. The following year would see these crews suffer horrendous losses once again as they were pitched into a daylight anti-shipping campaign.

ENEMY ACTIVITY

The activity by the Luftwaffe was on a reduced scale during the morning but it increased during the afternoon with reconnaissance and bombing attacks on RAF airfields, Bassingbourne, Lawford Heath, Ingham, Horsham-St-Faith, Newton, Duxford, Gravesend, Kirton-in-Lindsay, Sutton Bridge, Martlesham and Heston, being on the receiving end. Also many towns in the Birmingham district were strafed. Night Activity was in two phases, the first which started at 18.30 hours and was 'All Clear' at 21.00 hours. The second phase started at 00.30 hours when twenty-five to thirty enemy aircraft attacked London and six attacked the Midlands. 'All Clears' were sounded at 06.00 and 07.00 hours. Afterwards some reconnaissance took place over the south-west, east and north coasts. The Luftwaffe lost two aircraft destroyed. RAF Fighter Command lost one aircraft destroyed.

COASTAL COMMAND OPERATIONS

Thirty aircraft were involved in the usual routine and special patrols. Eighteen convoys were given escort.

1. Two of three Hudsons carrying out an offensive reconnaissance of the Norwegian coast bombed a 3,000 ton motor vessel six miles north of Lister, scoring a direct hit amidships. One of the Hudsons was attacked by a Bf109 and damaged. The third Hudson is missing.

There were no night operations because of adverse weather.

BOMBER COMMAND OPERATIONS

1. Five Blenheims were despatched in daylight to attack Duisburg/Ruhort, but abandoned due to adverse weather. In addition three more crews were sent to attack the Channel ports, while three were to attack airfields in France and three were given roving commissions. Of these four abandoned their tasks due to unsuitable conditions. However, railway sidings were attacked at Soesterberg and two E Boats were attacked off the Somme Estuary.

OPERATIONAL LOSSES

Hudson T9377 'R' of 233 Squadron, Leuchars, thought to have been shot down ten miles north of Lister, Norway, by a Bf109. Pilot Officer W. O. Weaber, Pilot Officer B. P. Erskine, and Sergeant J. A. Wallace are buried in the Sola Churchyard. Sergeant H. Dean was lost and is remembered on the Runnymede Memorial.

This aircraft fell to Leutnant Siegfried Freytag of 6./JG 77, who claimed it destroyed west of Lister at 16.00 hours.

In conclusion

During the latter part of September 1940, RAF Photo-reconnaissance of the invasion ports between Flushing and Boulogne revealed that the number of German 'Invasion' barges had declined from 1004 to 691.

On 25th October 1940, 'Ultra' decrypts further revealed that the Luftwaffe had disbanded one of the special units attached to the Invasion force.

As a consequence, on 31st October 1940, the Prime Minister, chairing the Government Defence Committee, agreed that the danger of the German invasion of Britain had become remote and British forces deployed to defend against it were to be stood down from 'Immediate Readiness' for the winter of 1940/41. The Government did not feel entirely safe from invasion until Hitler attacked Russia in June 1941, but this was a firm indication of the belief that the battle fought during July to October 1940 was a victory won by RAF Fighter Command and 'The Other Few' of RAF Bomber and Coastal Commands.

Appendix 1
AIRCRAFT FOR THE 'OTHER FEW'

VICKERS WELLINGTON I

First flew	**December 1937**
Powerplant	**2 x Bristol Pegasus XVIII engines with 1050 hp**
Maximum speed	**235 mph**
Range	**2550 miles**
Service Ceiling	**18,000 feet**
Armament	**8 x .303 machine guns in nose, tail and beam positions**
Bomb Load	**Up to 4500 pounds**
Wing Span	**86 feet 2 inches**
Length	**64 feet 7 inches**
Crew	**5 or 6**

HANDLEY PAGE HAMPDEN

First flew	**May 1938**
Powerplant	**2 x Bristol Pegasus XVIII engines with 1000 hp**
Maximum speed	**254 mph**
Range	**1885 miles**
Service Ceiling	**19,000 feet**
Armament	**Up to 6 x .303 machine guns in nose, and rear positions**
Bomb Load	**Up to 4000 pounds**
Wing Span	**69 feet 2 inches**
Length	**53 feet 7 inches**
Crew	**4**

BRISTOL BLENHEIM IV

First flew	**April 1935**
Powerplant	**2 x Bristol Mercury XV engines with 905 hp**
Maximum speed	**265 mph**
Range	**1460 miles**
Service Ceiling	**27,000 feet**
Armament	**Up to 5 x .303 machine guns in nose and rear turrets**
	(Fighter version carried 4 x .303 Machine guns in a ventral pack)
Bomb Load	**Up to 1320 pounds**
Wing Span	**56 feet 4 inches**
Length	**42 feet 7 inches**
Crew	**3**

ARMSTRONG WHITWORTH WHITLEY V

First flew	**March 1936**
Powerplant	**2 x Rolls-Royce Merlin X engines with 1145 hp**
Maximum speed	**230 mph**
Range	**1500 miles**
Service Ceiling	**26,000 feet**
Armament	**4 x .303 machine guns in rear turret, 1 in the nose turret.**
Bomb Load	**Up to 7000 pounds**
Wing Span	**84 feet**
Length	**70 feet 6 inches**
Crew	**5**

SHORT SUNDERLAND I

First flew	**October 1937**
Powerplant	**4 x Bristol Pegasus XXII engines with 1010 hp**
Maximum speed	**210 mph**
Range	**1780 miles**
Service Ceiling	**17,000 feet**
Armament	**4 x .303 machine guns in rear turret, 3 Vickers K guns in nose and beam positions**
Bomb Load	**Up to 2000 pounds**
Wing Span	**112 feet 8 inches**
Length	**85 feet 8 inches**
Crew	**13**

LOCKHEED HUDSON I

First flew	**December 1938**
Powerplant	**2 x Wright Cyclone engines with 1100 hp**
Maximum speed	**250 mph**
Range	**2160 miles**
Service Ceiling	**24,500 feet**
Armament	**4 x .303 machine guns in nose and rear turret**
Bomb Load	**Up to 750 pounds**
Wing Span	**65 feet 6 inches**
Length	**44 feet 4 inches**
Crew	**4**

FAIREY BATTLE I

First flew **April 1937**

Powerplant **1 x Rolls-Royce Merlin I engine with 1030 hp**

Maximum speed **257 mph**

Range **1000 miles**

Service Ceiling **25,000 feet**

Armament **! x .303 machine gun in starboard wing and 1 Vickers K gun in rear cockpit**

Bomb Load **Up to 1000 pounds**

Wing Span **54 feet**

Length **42 feet 4 inches**

Crew **3**

BRISTOL BEAUFORT

First flew	**October 1938**
Powerplant	**2 x Bristol Taurus engines with 1130 hp**
Maximum speed	**260 mph**
Range	**1035 miles**
Service Ceiling	**16,500 feet**
Armament	**4 x .303 machine guns in nose and rear turret**
Bomb Load	**Up to 1500 pounds or one torpedo**
Wing Span	**57 feet 10 inches**
Length	**44 feet 7 inches**
Crew	**4**

AVRO ANSON I

First flew	**January 1935**
Powerplant	**2 x Armstrong Siddeley Cheetah engines with 350 hp**
Maximum speed	**188 mph**
Range	**790 miles**
Service Ceiling	**19,000 feet**
Armament	**1 x Vickers gun in nose and 1 Lewis gun in dorsal turret**
Bomb Load	**Up to 360 pounds**
Wing Span	**56 feet 5 inches**
Length	**42 feet 3 inches**
Crew	**4**

FAIREY SWORDFISH

First flew	**April 1934**
Powerplant	**1 x Bristol Pegasus IIIM engine with 690 hp**
Maximum speed	**138 mph**
Range	**1030 miles**
Service Ceiling	**10,700 feet**
Armament	**1 x .303 machine gun in nose and 1 hand-held Lewis gun in rear cockpit**
Bomb Load	**Up to 1500 pounds or 1 torpedo**
Wing Span	**45 feet 6 inches**
Length	**35 feet 8 inches**
Crew	**3**

FAIREY ALBACORE

First flew	**December 1938**
Powerplant	**1 x Bristol Taurus XII engine with 1130 hp**
Maximum speed	**160 mph**
Range	**930 miles**
Service Ceiling	**20,700 feet**
Armament	**1 x .303 machine gun in nose and 2 Vickers K guns in the rear cockpit**
Bomb Load	**Up to 2000 pounds or 1 torpedo**
Wing Span	**50 feet**
Length	**39 feet 10 inches**
Crew	**3**

BLACKBURN SKUA

First flew	**February 1937**
Powerplant	**1 x Bristol Perseus XII engine with 890 hp**
Maximum speed	**225 mph**
Range	**760 miles**
Service Ceiling	**20,000 feet**
Armament	**4 x .303 machine guns in wings, 1 Lewis gun in rear cockpit**
Bomb Load	**1 500 pound bomb**
Wing Span	**46 feet 2 inches**
Length	**35 feet 7 inches**
Crew	**2**

SUPERMARINE SPITFIRE PR1

First flew	**March 1936**
Powerplant	**1 x Rolls-Royce Merlin III engine with 1030 hp**
Maximum speed	**365 mph**
Range	**1885 miles**
Service Ceiling	**29,000 feet**
Armament	**None**
Bomb Load	**None**
Wing Span	**36 feet 10 inches**
Length	**29 feet 11 inches**
Crew	**1**

Appendix 2
THEY ALSO SERVED

A Wellington ground crew, happy at their work.

The role played by ground crew in any airborne offensive is often overlooked. Their distinctly unglamorous job would see them out in all weathers, doing their best to keep the aircraft serviceable and safe for the aircrews.

Ron Low was an electrical fitter with 83 Squadron during the Battle of Britain. Here, he recalls some of his memories of the period;

Our duties were to look after fifteen Hampdens on the flights and sign the form 700s daily along with rostering for hangar guard duty and for duty electrician on the flare path etc. On arrival at Scampton, we were promptly advised that we could not leave the station at all, there was a war on!

Electrical Problems

Due to the fact that all the aircraft, except those that were under inspection, would be at dispersal and never under cover, there were a lot of electrical problems. One was the engine rev counter, this was really a voltmeter calibrated in RPM. The engine fitter would run an engine up, a perfect even note, no vibration, but the rev indicator would be erratic and up and down the scale. An obvious electrical problem. The problem would be compounded if the aircraft had a crew aboard ready for flying. The pilot would be forced to shut the engine down and all hell would break loose. no tannoy – no mobiles – nothing to call the electrician so a van had to be sent to find me. Once discovered, I had to go to the section in the hangar and collect the cleaning equipment and torches and hurry to the aircraft. The generator, which was only the size of a small cup was fitted at the rear of the engine. The brush caps were about half an inch in diameter and had to be unscrewed to withdraw the brushes which were of gold wire in a bakelite frame. These then had to be cleaned with spirits and refitted. This often had to be done in darkness by torchlight. To reach the generator at the rear of the engine, I had to stand on the top of the oleo legs and entwine myself around the undercarriage hydraulic rams to reach it at arm's length. The engine was very hot at this time, another hazard! but at the end, to see the pilot run up the engine and give the ground crew the thumbs up was quite rewarding.

Previous page: Ron Lowe about to do a DI on a Hampden at a frosty Scampton, March 1940

The Sunderland ground crews also got wet frequently!

Flare Paths
Scampton was an all grass airfield at that time and consequently a flare path had to be laid out for night flying when required. The flare path was laid out in the form of a letter 'T'. The bar across the top had three flares, each one containing five gallons of paraffin with a clipped lid having a five inch diameter hole containing large wicks. The goose-neck flares on the leg of the 'T' were large watering cans holding several gallons of paraffin with the spout containing a large wick. also at the bottom of the 'T' leg was a *Chance Light,* a large portable floodlight which had two thousand watt tungsten lamps and when adjusted to the flare path, lit the touchdown point.

The system worked satisfactory until we started receiving air-raid warnings with instructions to extinguish all lights. A simple switch was enough for the *Chance Light* but dousing all the paraffin flares was a nightmare because it took a long time, especially if the wind was blowing. We had, on one or two occasions, to seek the help of the station fire brigade because some of the paraffin had spilt and was on fire.

The Station Commander was not satisfied and spent time with us because he wanted the job to be done quicker. The only way that could be achieved was to have an electrical flare path. A sort of makeshift path was consequently laid down in 24 hours. The goose-neck flares were replaced by four-gallon petrol tins with a five inch hole on each side and a 100 watt normal filament lamp fitted inside. We looped these all together and controlled them from the

Chance Light. This was examined by the Station Commander and squadron C/Os and was blessed. Cheers all round, but on the first night when aircraft used the system, a pilot veered off the line and collected the cable and a couple of petrol tins. The lights went out and pandemonium soon followed!

Modifications

Early in 1940, during night flying circuits and bumps, it became apparent that the aircraft electrical system was not satisfactory. The main generator was a 500 watt differential compound with a 12 volt-40 amp accumulator. The Hampdens would be doing a lot of taxiing and not much flying and the accumulator was slowly being drained. As the evening progressed, the brilliance of the landing lights became very dim. Many of the pilots being trained had never flown a Hampden at night before and as there was no room for an instructor to sit beside the pilot, things were getting dangerous.

The aircraft had to be sent back to Handley Page for urgent modifications, these included the fitting of a 750 watt shunt and a carbon pile regulator. this gave the accumulator a boost and solved the problem. At this time also, the fuel tanks were changed to self-sealing types and the defensive armament in the rear positions was doubled. In response to the crew's complaints, 5″ diameter rubber pipes were used to divert some of the engine heat to the interior of the fuselage.

Engine Starting

When the Hampden's Pegasus engines were being started, if the pilot pumped the throttle he flooded the engine and it would not start. Instead it would cough and splutter and grind to a halt, igniting petrol in the induction system. Panic usually followed, the ground crew would first call to the pilot for the ignition switch to be off, waiting for the pilot to reply with the thumbs up sign. Then the ground crew would stuff their Glengarries into the air-intakes in order to shut off the air supply into the induction system. Spin the engine round to draw in the burning fuel – fire out!

The WOp/AG's position in the Hampden. note the rubber pipe in the foreground which supplied a little heat to the frozen crew.

Appendix 3
A FEW OF THE 'OTHER FEW'

A few of the Other Few

FLIGHT LIEUTENANT LARRY DONNELLY DFM
WOP/AG 10 SQUADRON WHITLEY
Flew 41 Whitley Ops between Sept. '39 and Oct. '40 went on to do 3 tours and became a pilot.

FLIGHT LIEUTENANT EDDIE WHEELER DFC
WOP/AG 150 SQN BATTLE & 214 SQN WELLINGTON
Flew 69 Ops in total, 2nd tour on Pathfinders

FLYING OFFICER BOB PEARCE DFM
WOP/AG 142 SQUADRON BATTLE
Flew in the Fairey Battle against the Channel Ports went on to do a tour on Wellingtons.

PILOT OFFICER C A CONNOR DFC
PILOT 83 SQUADRON HAMPDEN
The pilot of the Hampden in which John Hannah won the VC. Killed in Action 3-4 Nov 1940.

Previous page: A Czech Wellington crew walk past a bomb trolley.

FLIGHT LIEUTENANT MARK NIMAN DFM
WOP/AG 10 SQUADRON WHITLEY
Flew a total of 76 Ops on Whitleys, Catalinas and Halifaxes. Survived ditching and bale-out.

FLIGHT LIEUTENANT RUPERT 'TINY' COOLING DFC
PILOT 9 SQUADRON WELLINGTON
Flew throughout the Battle of Britain and later in Italy, still on Wellingtons

WING COMMANDER FRANK TAMS
PILOT 217 SQUADRON ANSON AND BEAUFORT
Was sent to bomb Brest in an Anson and then converted to Beauforts.

SQUADRON LEADER MAX MEYER
PILOT 144 SQUADRON HAMPDEN
Flew Whitleys before the war and a tour on Hampdens during the Battle.

A few of the Other Few

Top: 83 Squadron's survivors in January 1941   Above: 144 squadron airmen lined up at the beginning of the Battle in July 1940.

A few of the Other Few

FLIGHT LIEUTENANT RUPERT 'TINY' COOLING'S CREW
9 SQUADRON WELLINGTON
Jock Gilmour (N), Maclean (RG), Frank Sevan (2P), Curly Jones (WOp), Rositer (FG).

PILOT OFFICER HARKNESS'S CREW
75 SQUADRON WELLINGTON
Sgt Henderson (Obs) P/O Saxelby (2/P) P/O Harkness (Capt) Sgt D Humphries (WOp/AG) Sgt Gosden (RG)
Wellington is R3297 AA-S

ROLL OF HONOUR

Roll of Honour

In May 1947 a Roll of Honour for the Battle of Britain, 10 July to 31 October was published. Uniquely, this small volume listed Bomber Command, Coastal Command and Royal Naval losses alongside the now familiar names of Fighter Command pilots. The above list has been based on this 1947 list, but with the addition of casualties for the first nine days of July, to conform with the main body of this book, and an additional column for the date of the loss which was not included in the original work.

Although no details of the original criteria for inclusion in the listing were published it has been taken that only losses incurred during operations, or due to enemy action, have been included. Thus some entries have been omitted where research has revealed that they were sustained in non-operational accidents, including ferrying and training.

Names prefixed asterix (*) appear in the 1947 list, but details of the casualty have not been established or listed here.

Some men who served with 10 Squadron (Bomber Command) are listed as being attached to Coastal Command and have been left as such. (10 BC)

Those wishing to persue their research into the casualties are directed to the Commonwealth War Graves Commission web site: **http://www.cwgc.org** where further personal details are available on-line.

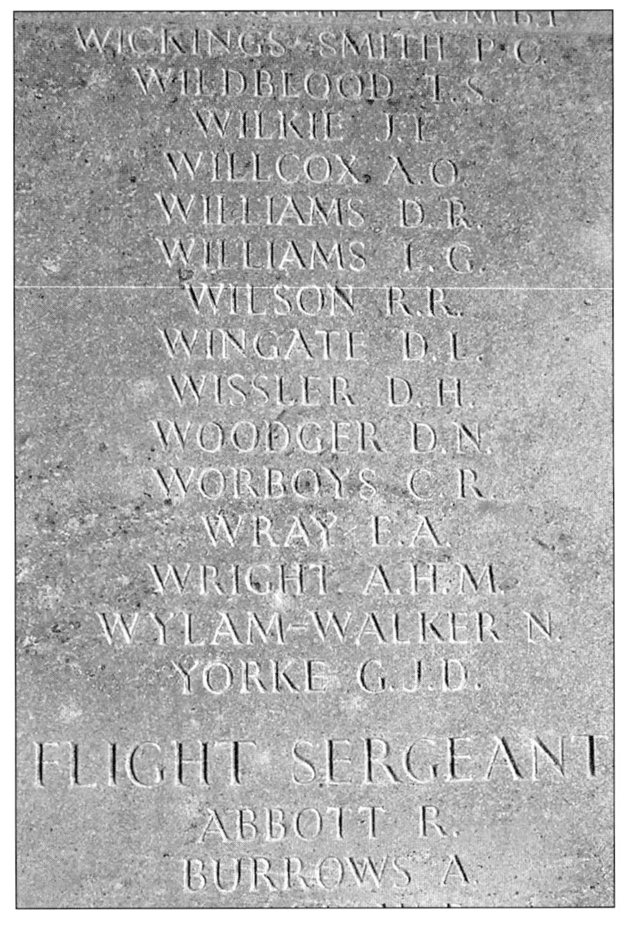

Above: Some of the 20353 names recorded on the Runnymede Memorial.
Below: The approach to the Runnymede Memorial.

THE RUNNYMEDE MEMORIAL

Throughout this work reference has been made to the Runnymede Memorial. The Air Forces Memorial memorial was created after World War Two to honour the 20353 airmen who have no known grave. It is situated on a hill at Englefield Green, four miles from Windsor, overlooking the River Thames. For many of the young men lost during the period covered by this book, this their only memorial.

Roll of Honour

BOMBER COMMAND PILOTS

Number	Rank	Name	Squadron	Date of loss
746662	Sgt	ADLAM, Leonard Frank Percy	68	20 October
740664	Sgt	ALLEN, John Wollaston Keith	18	4 September
70009	F/O	ALLEN, Richard Guy	38	11 September
NZ36262	P/O	ANDREW, Neville Halsey	78	1-2 October
26196	S/L	ANDREWS, Lionel Vincent	149	8-9 September
41360	P/O	ATKIN-BERRY, Harold Leslie	107	10-11 July
SA77130	P/O	AUSTIN, Guy Paul Wentworth	9	14-15 October
42585	P/O	BALL, Ralph Alan Anthony	37	6-7 July
42688	P/O	BALLAS-ANDERSEN, Konstantine	49	27-28 October
745574	Sgt.	BALMER, John Hawes	101	25-26 August
42375	P/O	BAMBER, Hugh Christopher Morris	15	7 July
36163	F/L	BARNWELL, Richard Antony	102	28-29 October
39005	S/L	BATT, Robert Hector, DFC	40	9 July
44057	P/O	BAYLISS, Gilbert Louis	40	26 August
741185	Sgt	BEALE, Frederick Allen	61	16-17 August
742726	Sgt	BEALES, Rex	83	2-3 August
C40663	P/O	BELL, Brian Stallard	50	31 July-1 August
39959	F/O	BERRY, Ernest Reginald	107	29-30 August
37373	S/L	BLACK, George Roderick Hartwell	77	14-15 October
40041	F/L	BLOM, Walter Michael, DFC	150	27 July
73028	P/O	BODY, John	149	11-12 August
580170	Sgt	BOWLES, Cyril	105	18-19 September
42390	P/O	BRAUN, Michael Ryves	75NZ	20-21 September
42187	P/O	BRAYNE, Ronald Percy	77	18-19 September
565447	F/Sgt	BROADHURST, Rodolphe Burford	40	2-3 September
742459	Sgt	BROOKER, Alec Albert	61	13-14 September
742131	Sgt	BROOKER, Francis John	50	5-6 October

Roll of Honour

Number	Rank	Name	Squadron	Date of loss
41560	F/O	BROWN, Ernest Henry	58	20-21 October
566550	Sgt	BROWN, George William	77	8-9 October
742961	Sgt	BROWN, John Herbert	144	16-17 October
745568	Sgt	BROWN, John Raymond	51	29-30 October
74328	P/O	BUFTON, John Raymond	49	27-28 October
75682	F/L	BULL, William Sharman	44	3-4 July
745279	Sgt	BUNKER, Anthony St. John	18	16 July
NZ 36237	P/O	CAMERON, Edward Colin Joseph	75NZ	20-21 July
742698	Sgt	CAMPION, Alfred Norman	10	13-14 August
74667	P/O	CARSON, Illtyd Thomas Holden	114	13 August
740975	Sgt	CARTER, Jonathan Wallace	144	5-6 September
768161	Sgt	CATTO, Patrick Tawse	149	9-10 October
NZ 43700	P/O	CAVE, Jack Milton	101	30-31 October
72328	F/O	CAZALET, Alexander Brise Travers	107	8-9 September
741349	P/O	CHARLES, Derek Elliot Stafford	149	16-17 August
28214	S/L	CHESTER, Hurll Fontayne	82	2 July
39183	F/L	CHIVERS, Eugene George Frederick	38	24-25 October
745257	Sgt	CLARKE, Charles Owen	144	5-6 September
741533	Sgt	CLAYTON, Gerald Lawrence	218	8-9 September
81027	P/O	CLEMERSON, William Herbert	61	16-17 October
72479	F/O	COBBE, Alexander William Locke	82	8 September
34232	A/S/L	COLLETT, Wilfred Ira	75NZ	4 August
563427	Sgt	COOKE, Charles William	101	8-9 September
81678	P/O	COONEY, Kenneth	10	14-15 October
580050	Sgt	CORNISH, Herbert	58	24-25 September
39502	F/L	COX, Anthony Howard Caldicott	9	29 September
37066	F/O	CRAIGIE-HALKETT, Lionel Montague	214	30-31 August
532141	Sgt	CROSSLAND, Albert Alfred Ellis	58	18-19 September
40680	P/O	CUNDILL, Thomas Cedric	61	12-13 August

Roll of Honour

Number	Rank	Name	Squadron	Date of loss
41560	P/O	CUNYNGHAME, Wilfred Bertram Stewart	214	30-31 August
37006	F/L	CURRY, Stephen Edward Frederick	51	19-20 July
C40162	P/O	D'ARCY-WRIGHT, Gerald	61	5-6 October
42592	P/O	DALLY, Paul Spencer	58	2-3 October
SA42203	P/O	DAVIES, Arthur Howell	50	14-15 October
742518	Sgt	DAVIES, John Harold	18	2 August
745882	Sgt	DAVIS, Francis William	38	24-25 October
745180	Sgt	DAWSON, Anthony Kyle	78	14-15 August
742008	Sgt	DAY, Harold	44	1-2 October
42487	P/O	DENCH, Francis George Hurlston	15	12-13 August
72148	F/O	DINGLE, Arthur Collings	37	29-30 September
745629	Sgt	DOBB, Kenneth Herbert	114	19-20 August
C43030	P/O	DOUGLAS, Walter Morrison	77	18-19 September
70191	F/O	DUCKER, Francis Edward Robert	101	18 July
42820	P/O	DUFTON, Charles Theodore	38	11-12 September
42822	P/O	DUNKELS, Cedric Owen	44	29-30 August
41685	P/O	DUNN, DFC, Andrew Woodrow	77	23-24 September
33473	P/O	EADIE, John	61	7-8 July
A41770	P/O	EARL, Raymond Patrick	61	26-27 September
C39784	A/F/L	EDWARDS, David Harold	144	20-21 July
41912	P/O	ELDRIDGE, Peter Ernest	77	18-19 September
C40292	F/O	ESPLEY, William Charles	58	2-3 October
78439	P/O	EVANS, William Rupert	40	30-31 August
565737	Sgt	FARMER, Edward Deryck	44	31 July-1 September
NZ41005	P/O	FAWCETT, Nicoll Brian	49	25-26 August
79542	P/O	FORD, Eric	58	18-19 September
37797	F/L	FOX, Charles Douglas	9	1-2 October
74673	F/O	FURNESS, Roy Giffard	149	9-10 October
748526	Sgt	FURZE, Luke James	78	14-15 September

Roll of Honour

Number	Rank	Name	Squadron	Date of loss
24208	S/L	FYFE, DFC, John Bernard	107	11-12 August
72558	F/O	GARDNER, Edwin Charles	61	16-17 October
741796	Sgt	GARVEY, Peter Keirn	15	15-16 August
C41013	P/O	GERRY, Reginald Torrance	115	2-3 August
81657	P/O	GIBBS, John Vicary Frank	106	29-30 October
41842	P/O	GILLING, Jack Humphrey	144	4-5 July
79180	P/O	GILLINGHAM, Maurice Hardy	82	13 August
745498	Sgt	GLADWIN, Kenneth Bruce	9	28-29 September
745606	Sgt	GOLDIE, Leonard George	115	30 September-1 October
40691	P/O	GOODE, John Douglas	114	1 August
80829	P/O	GOODE, Richard Gordon	44	17-18 September
40693	P/O	GOWER, Richard Francis	49	11-12 August
26011	S/L	GRANNUM, Clifton Winnington	105	28-29 October
741824	Sgt	GREEN, Alfred Joseph	75NZ	20-21 September
742028	Sgt	GREEN, Herbert Frederick	38	7-8 October
NZ79511	P/O	HADLEY, Ronald Arnold	58	8-9 October
C42219	P/O	HALE, Earl Robert	82	13 August
NZ43704	P/O	HALKETT, Charles de Vic	107	8-9 September
740620	Sgt	HALL, John Robert	214	27-28 September
07128	W/C	HARGROVES, Joseph Henry	101	5-6 July
741985	Sgt	HARTOP, Charles William	44	21 October
565332	Sgt	HENDERSON, Thomas Valentine	44	17-18 September
37805	A/S/L	HENDRY, Maxwell Frederick	139	24-25 September
SA42708	P/O	HERMON, William Duncan	61	26-27 September
742062	Sgt	HEYWARD, Clifford Charles	110	23-24 July
550068	Sgt	HILL, Christopher Grimwade	78	21-22 July
72024	F/O	HILL, James Jewill	106	29-30 October
741410	Sgt	HILL, Stanley Denys	83	12-13 August
566066	Sgt	HILLS, John Edwin	61	24-25 September

Roll of Honour

Number	Rank	Name	Squadron	Date of loss
36014	S/L	HINKS, John Olding	9	14-15 October
76582	P/O	HISSEY, Peter Bouch	114	29 October
566166	Sgt	HODSON, Dennis Derrick Raymond	105	9 September
741881	Sgt	HOPES, Denis Beach	58	1-12 July
33568	P/O	HOSSACK, Ian Milne	144	11-12 July
32197	S/L	HOUSE, Charles Constantine	218	22-23 August
37806	F/L	HOW, DFC, Douglas James	61	5-6 September
741337	Sgt	HUMPHREY, Keith Reginald	61	25-26 October
519997	Sgt	HUTTON, Frank	82	7 July
42840	P/O	JACKSON, Alan Kinnear	59	17 July
40831	P/O	JACKSON, George Hautville	37	1-2 September
565910	Sgt	JENNINGS, DFM, Robert James	49	6-7 August
740889	Sgt	JERRITT, Robert Anderson	149	8-9 September
70805	P/O	JONES, Cecil John Trevelyan	58	1-2 July
33061	S/L	JONES, Norman Clifford	82	13 August
C41296	F/O	KELLER, William Edmund Norman	99	13-14 October
36254	P/O	KIRDY, Matthew John Alexander	142	28-29 July
566117	Sgt	KIRKBRIDE, Sydney Chapman	37	14-15 July
40121	F/O	LANCASTER, Eric Bell	144	4-5 July
05102	W/C	LART, DSO, Edward Collis-de-Virac	82	13 August
41715	P/O	LAUNDERS, Oliver Harry	83	7-8 July
566470	Sgt	LEE, Cyril	83	1-2 July
C41716	P/O	LEEDS John Leeming	149	8-9 September
70399	A/F/L	LEWIS, Peter Humphrey	82	13-14 July
42134	P/O	LINDEN, Michael Cunningham Andrews	99	18-19 September
39018	F/O	LINDSAY, Douglas Weatherall	37	6-7 July
79207	P/O	LITTLEJOHN, John	37	29-30 September
740660	Sgt	LOADSMAN, Horace Cecil	61	25-26 October
517486	Sgt	LORD, Kenneth	105	2-3 October

Roll of Honour

Number	Rank	Name	Squadron	Date of loss
741604	Sgt	LORRIMAR, Francis Raines	101	25-26 September
566553	Sgt	LOVELUCK, James Gwyn	83	18-19 October
564908	Sgt	McCAULEY, John Francis	37	14-15 July
80827	P/O	McCAUSLAND, James Maxwell	82	8 September
39545	F/O	MCFARLANE, Laurence Herbert	58	1-2 July
SA41856	P/O	MACGREGOR, Robert Butler	77	14-15 August
36015	S/L	MACINTYRE, James Galt	44	28-29 July
79167	P/O	MACLEAN, Donald	38	30 September-1 October
42624	P/O	MASLIN, Thomas William	107	10 July
520314	Sgt	MERRETT, Jack Edwin	107	30 September-1 October
C39105	A/F/L	MIDDLETON, Douglas Davidson	9	19-20 July
42865	P/O	MILLER, John Garland	149	11-12 August
580343	Sgt	MONKHOUSE, Victor Clarence	78	21-22 July
41863	P/O	MONTAGU, DFC, Charles James Drogo	77	24-25 August
29098	S/L	MONYPENNY, John Blackwell Sinclair	9	19-20 July
NZ43708	P/O	MORGAN, Harry Wright	78	1-2 October
72027	F/O	MOSS, Brian Elwyn	12	31 July
745478	Sgt	MOSS, John Edward	21	5 September
42632	P/O	MUIRHEAD, George Hamilton	37	20-21 July
40636	P/O	MULLOY, DFC, William Arthur Coote	50	25-26 July
77613	P/O	MYLAND, Douglas Eric Charles	15	3-4 September
745300	Sgt	NEALE, Robert John	144	5-6 October
33492	P/O	NEWTON-CLARE, John Edward	144	5-6 September
42635	P/O	*NICHOLS, Michael Ivor	9	29 September
754920	Sgt	OGILVY, Allister Smith	139	14 October
42873	P/O	OTTERWAY, Francis James	47	4-5 September
37981	F/L	PALMER, Esmond John	101	8-9 September
42020	F/L	PALMER, John Harold Tearl	82	Lost 11 July died 6/12/42
42875	P/O	PARFITT, Douglas Alfred John	82	13 August

Roll of Honour

Number	Rank	Name	Squadron	Date of loss
SA740369	Sgt	PATRICK, William Ian Struan	40	8-9 September
42877	P/O	PAY, John Sydney	149	18-19 September
742651	Sgt	PEARCE, Edward Albert	142	22 August
79756	P/O	PHILLIPS, Richard Arthur	58	8-9 October
33201	A/S/L	PITCAIRN-HILL, DSO, DFC, James Anderson	83	18-19 September
42722	P/O	POOLE, Frank Twain	75NZ	25-26 July
C75988	P/O	POWER, Bruce Andrew	99	25-26 July
81070	P/O	PRESTON, Cyril	107	18-19 September
41060	P/O	PRICE, John Frederic Sydney Pritchard	110	30-31 August
41950	P/O	PROSSER, Ian	105	28-29 October
42723	P/O	PRYOR, Ronald William	115	2-3 August
42647	P/O	REA, John	214	27-28 September
37421	S/L	REBBECK, Peter Henry	144	16-17 August
41206	P/O	REDMAYNE, Douglas	83	1-2 July
A40059	F/L	REED, Robert James	50	10-11 September
550943	Sgt	RILEY, Eddie Andreas Hals	57	25-26 August
70873	P/O	ROBINSON, Charles Henry	15	25-26 July
A41471	P/O	ROBSON, DFC, Angus	144	21-22 August
C41323	F/O	ROBSON, Clarence Sydney	78	14-15 September
39174	F/L	ROGERS, Douglas John	44	10-11 September
40432	F/O	ROGERS, Mark Hubbard	102	16-17 August
42887	P/O	ROSE, John Alexander	149	11-12 July
740263	Sgt	ROSE, Robert Frederick	49	16-17 October
A40060	F/O	ROSS, DFC, Ellis Henry	83	12-13 August
740049	Sgt	ROSS, Thomas David Weston	107	18-19 September
42889	P/O	ROYLANCE, Peter William	50	10-11 September
42727	P/O	SANDERSON, Rex Martyn	75NZ	23-24 October
745096	Sgt	SAVILLE, Jack Herbert	18	8 August
37484	F/L	SCOTT, John Stanley	51	16-17 August

Roll of Honour

Number	Rank	Name	Squadron	Date of loss
NZ43711	P/O	SHANN, Winton Selwood	107	24-25 September
C42155	P/O	SHELDON, Harry Christie	61	12-13 August
742908	Sgt	SHELFER, Eric Henry William	106	26-27 September
NZ42770	P/O	SHORT, Rupert Edward	101	25-26 July
41877	P/O	SMETTEM, Kenneth Richard Killey	50	30-21 August
42901	P/O	SMITH, John Digby	58	22-23 July
42470	P/O	SMITH, Norman Henry Harwood	82	10-11/August
43143	A/F/L	SMYTHE, DFC, Thomas Laidlaw Scott	44	11-12 September
SA42366	P/O	SNOOKE, Dudley Delercourtte	83	27-28 September
39904	F/O	STENHOUSE, William Alan	77	14-15 August
32024	S/L	STEPHENS, John Frank	110	20-21 July
41330	P/O	STEWART, Alan	114	5-6 July
C42683	P/O	STEWART, Donald Eglinton	44	31 August-1 September
44486	P/O	STORROW, Arthur Raymond	110	10-11 August
745425	Sgt	STUBBS, Cecil Vernon	44	20-21 October
C40328	F/O	SWENSEN, Stanley Powell	51	14-15 August
34115	S/L	TAYLOR, John Cornelius	50	29-30 September
22092	S/L	TAYLOR, Rex Oliver Oxley	38	7-8 October
37332	A/S/L	THOMAS, Frank George Ralph	40	25-26 August
41222	F/O	THOMAS, Roy Haydn	10	6-7 September
745185	Sgt	THOMPSON, Neville William Gordon	115	30 September-1 October
745851	Sgt	THOMPSON, Ronald Edwin	9	1-2 October
37134	A/S/L	THWAITES, AFC, Evelyn Harry Toller	149	16-17 August
42162	P/O	TODD, Desmond Arthur	44	3-4 July
C42732	P/O	TORGALSON, Joseph Simon	149	11-12 July
C41224	P/O	TUDHOPE, William Frank	144	10-11 August
81339	P/O	TUPPEN, Donald Ralph	149	18-19 September
79576	P/O	TURNER, Gerald Percy	37	29-30 September
C40767	P/O	TWEDDELL, DFC, William Oliver Digby	83	25-26 July

Roll of Honour

Number	Rank	Name	Squadron	Date of loss
741308	Sgt	TYLDESLEY, Harold Edward	18	14-15 August
76457	P/O	*WALKER, Wilfred	44	19 July
741435	Sgt	WARD, James Walter	77	24-25 August
43130	P/O	WATKIN, Eric Thomas	106	18-19 September
74345	P/O	WATSON, Peter George Anthony	107	22-23 July
NZ77026	F/O	WATSON, Samuel Miles McKenzie	75NZ	20-21 July
C41638	F/O	WATTERSON, Arnold Irwin	58	24-25 September
742634	Sgt	WESSELS, Cyril	115	30 September-1 October
742136	Sgt	WHEELER, Frank Albert Roberts	114	26-27 September
79536	P/O	WIGLEY, Clive Warrington	82	13 August
745324	Sgt	WILLIAMS, Leslie Arthur	18	30-31 August
33470	P/O	WINGATE, David Leslie	144	21-22 August
754548	Sgt	WOOD, Maurice Ernest Laughton	99	18-19 September
25062	F/L	WORTHINGTON-WILMER, Ivor Chudleigh Bethune	18	4 July
42174	P/O	WRAY, Eric Aubrey	107	10-11 July
741930	Sgt	WRIGHT, Dennis Raymond	10	14-15 July
741086	Sgt	YEOMANS, Oswald Morris	15	13-14 September
517288	Sgt	YOUNG, Frederick	58	11-12 July

BOMBER COMMAND AIRCREW

Number	Rank	Name	Squadron	Date of loss
549202	Sgt	ABEL, Richard	83	12-13 August
580148	Sgt	ABRAHAMS, Frederick Joseph	102	28-29 October
513170	Sgt	AITKEN, Alexander	37	6-7 July
622419	Sgt	ALDOM, Douglas Ronald	61	12-13 August
970031	Sgt	ALGAR, Alan	61	5-6 October
649497	Sgt	ALLEN, Dudley Brooking	77	23-24 Sept. Died 26 September

Roll of Honour

Number	Rank	Name	Squadron	Date of loss
745535	Sgt	ANDREWS, Edgar James	50	14-15 October
751690	Sgt	ANGUS, John Henry	44	17-18 September
581136	Sgt	ANKERS, George Cyril	82	13 August
580923	Sgt	APPERSON, Eric Thomas	44	3-4 July
521409	Sgt	ARROWSMITH, Vincent	139	24-25 September
812247	Sgt	AUSTEN, Douglas William	58	18-19 September
751147	Sgt	BOGUE, James Joseph Aloysius	106	26-27 September
642862	Sgt	BAGULEY, John	77	18-19 September
552072	Sgt	BAILEY, Percy Fallows	144	4-5 July
581078	Sgt	BAINBRIDGE, George Henry	214	30-31 August
639105	Sgt	BAIRD, Arthur	44	3-4 July
751839	Sgt	BAKER, John	49	25-26 August
625671	Sgt	BALDWIN, DFM, Jack	44	14-15 October
647990	Sgt	BARBER, Peter William	37	1-2 September
905852	Sgt	BARRETT, Warren Seymour	18	2 August
542271	Sgt	BARROW, Victor St. George	114	1 August
78994	P/O	BARTLETT, John Edward	9	14-15 October
580629	Sgt	BATHO, Reginald Frank	49	6-7 August
581137	Sgt	BAUM, Alfred James	49	11-12 August
755028	Sgt	BAZELEY, Stanley Douglas	106	29-30 October
759127	Sgt	BEWS, Stanley	47	4-5 September
629952	Sgt	BEEBY, DFM, Augustus Spencer	82	13 August
624554	Sgt	BELL, William	44	6-7 September
581261	Sgt	BELTON, DFM, Spencer Lewis Smith	144	10-11 August
649294	Sgt	BENNETT, Benjamin Michael	58	11-12 July
549557	Sgt	BENNETT, Harry	144	5-6 October
969978	Sgt	BENNETT, Russell Gordon	44	20-21 October
552444	Sgt	BENTHAM, Henry	107	29-30 August
626342	Sgt	BEST, Herbert Henry	50	30-31 August

Roll of Honour

Number	Rank	Name	Squadron	Date of loss
651939	Sgt	BEVERLEY, Victor	99	18-19 September
650628	Sgt	BICHARD, DFM, Frederick James William	49	27-28 October
751016	Sgt	*BISSETT, William Stater	61	14 September
746887	Sgt	BLAZIER, John Kenneth	82	10-11 August
683207	Sgt	BLOOR, Gordon Elijah	101	18 July
43020	P/O	BOAK, Andrew Stenhouse	50	5-6 October
631257	Sgt	BOLAND, Alfred Edward	82	13 August
747801	Sgt	BOOTH, Philip Watson	101	25-26 September
550339	Sgt	BOOTH, Stanley Keable	101	8-9 September
743077	Sgt	BOWERS, Henry	15	15-16 August
581140	Sgt	BRADING, Ronald James	44	10-11 September
751046	Sgt	BROOKER, Sydney George	9	28-29 September
968371	Sgt	BROWN, Jack Leonard	149	8-9 September
970119	Sgt	BROWN, James	49	16-17 October
518807	Sgt	BROWN, Norman Wilson	75NZ	25-26 July
755318	Sgt	BRYANT, Kenneth Roy	18	2 August
987980	Sgt	BUCKLEY, Ronald John	83	12-13 August
A904181	Sgt	BULL, Nugent Joseph	149	8-9 September
580601	Sgt	BUNDOCK, Frank Vyvyan	105	2-3 October
648669	Sgt	BURNS, Angus John	40	2-3 September
551597	Sgt	BURROW, John	77	14-15 August
566634	Sgt	BURT, Leonard John	44	14-15 October
580867	Sgt	BURTON, Noel Huckman	78	12-22 July
755885	Sgt	BYRNE, Thomas Patrick Joseph	18	28-29 August
746944	Sgt	CAMERON, Alexander Douglas	115	30 September-1 October
533257	Sgt	CANDLISH, James Wilson	58	22-23 July
638518	LAC	CANN, Walter Ypres	150	27 July
746801	Sgt	CANNON, William Arthur	61	5-6 October
773S0	P/O	CARNEGIE, David Stuart	61	20-21 July

Roll of Honour

Number	Rank	Name	Squadron	Date of loss
75687	P/O	CARRELL, Ronald Mark	44	14-15 October
902238	Sgt	CARYLL-TILKIN, Marcel Cuthbert	58	20-21 October
614511	Sgt	CASSELLS, William Hogg	82	8 September
581374	Sgt	CASWELL, James John	10	14-15 October
632993	Sgt	CHAMBERS, Hunter	144	21-22 August
512011	Sgt	CHARNOCK, Leonard	107	8-9 September
751223	Sgt	CHEESMAN, Alfred Jack	58	2-3 October
966961	Sgt	CHETTER, Alan Ernest	58	2-3 October
81686	P/O	CHRISTOPHER, Henry Morton	82	8 September
624944	Sgt	CLARKE, Edmund John	83	2-3 August
759120	Sgt	CLARKE, Edwin Jack	77	24-25 August
743056	Sgt	CLARKE, James Cunningham	49	25-26 August
580869	Sgt	CLARKE, Roy Desmond Edward	51	16-17 August
77961	P/O	CLEAK, Frederick Bernard	75NZ	23-24 October
580946	Sgt	*COBURN, Alfred Robert	40	2 September
638760	Sgt	COCKBURN, Andrew McNab	61	20-21 July
642593	Sgt	COCKS, Ronald Joseph	149	11-12 August
581203	Sgt	COISH, Frederick Charles	218	8-9 September
580997	Sgt	COOK, Robert Donaldson	107	10-11 July
523013	Sgt	COOKE, Louis Charles	110	10-11 August
76007	F/O	COOMBES, Wilfred Francis Ernest	44	11-12 September
80556	P/O	COOPER, Walter Arthur	103	9-10 September
618707	Sgt	CORBETT, Frank	49	16-17 October
751198	Sgt	CORKER, William John Cheshire	101	25-26 August
629330	Sgt	COSGROVE, William	38	24-25 October
637463	Sgt	COTTHAM, Cleveland	77	8-9 October
628277	Sgt	COWELL, Walter Robert	9	19-20 July
580883	Sgt	COWLEY, Victor Charles	77	18-19 September
80848	P/O	COX, David Spencer	149	18-19 September

Roll of Honour

Number	Rank	Name	Squadron	Date of loss
743022	Sgt	CRAIG, John William	149	11-12 July
42947	P/O	CRANIDGE, Thomas Johnson	82	13 August
751938	Sgt	CRANSTON, Thomas George James	101	25-26 August
542430	Sgt	CRAVEN, Henry Eric Archibald	58	1-2 July
620421	Sgt	CRAWFORD, Frank	77	18-19 September
635759	Sgt	CROFT, Jack Miller	115	2-3 August
751554	Sgt	CROOKS, William Wilson	149	8-9 September
743076	Sgt	CUMMING, Gordon Murray	75NZ	20-21 July
749342	Sgt	DALL, James Mitchell	83	26-27 October
581504	Sgt	DALY, Kenneth Lavery	21	5 September
748206	Sgt	DANKS, Harry Edward	102	28-29 October
966854	Sgt	DAVIDSON, Kenneth McNab	149	9-10 October
580364	Sgt	DAVIDSON, Percival Matthew	139	24-25 September
553877	Sgt	DAVIES, Edward	10	14-15 October
552076	Sgt	DAVIES, Gordon	82	13 August
632374	Sgt	DAVIES, Harold	77	14-15 August
637484	Sgt	DAWSON, Raymond Carter	77	18-19 September
903467	Sgt	DAY, Cyril James	101	8-9 September
640266	Sgt	DEMPSEY, James.	115	2-3 August
652740	Sgt	DENNING, Randolph Frederick	99	13-14 October
755390	Sgt	DEVLIN, George James	44	1-2 October
580488	Sgt	DEWHURST, Joseph Langley	83	12-13 August
523204	Sgt	DICKINSON, Harry	144	16-17 August
525760	Sgt	DICKINSON, Richard Cuthbert, DFM	61	13-14 September
79372	P/O	DICKINSON, Robert James	10	14-15 October
626161	Sgt	DICKSON, George Middleton	40	25-26 August
581277	Sgt	DINGLE, Bryan Norman	144	20-21 July
746988	Sgt	DODD, Edward Laurence	101	18 July
632780	Sgt	DOWDS, John	75NZ	25-26 July

Roll of Honour

Number	Rank	Name	Squadron	Date of loss
650716	Sgt	DOWSETT, Colin	115	30 September-1 October
76599	P/O	DRAKE-CARNELL, Francis John	144	5-6 September
580431	Sgt	DREW, George Thomas	107	10-11 July
541979	Sgt	DRINKWATER, Fred	103	9-10 September
619755	Sgt	DUNBAR, Hugh	105	2-3 October
581442	Sgt	DUNCAN, Harry Horatio	105	1 September
521723	Sgt	DUNCAN, Thomas Samuel	142	22-23 August
765178	Sgt	EASTON, James Harley	107	8-9 September
640007	Sgt	EASTON, John Kerr	58	22-23 July
751841	Sgt	EDMEADS, Anthony Charles Henry	144	2-3 September
552585	Sgt	ELLICOTT, Reginald John Spurway	114	5-6 July
512499	Sgt	ELLWOOD, George Edward	114	29 October
642716	Sgt	EMMERSON, Normnan	58	11-12 July
78460	P/O	ETHERINGTON, Arthur Frederick	107	24-25 September
552163	Sgt	EVANS, Arfon	82	13-14 July
617444	Sgt	EVANS, Christopher Douglas	50	1 August
967877	Sgt	EVANS, Owen Prys	139	3-4 August
645352	Sgt	FERGUSON, John Adam	144	16-17 October
532927	Sgt	FLANAGAN, Dominick	61	16-17 October
743005	Sgt	FLEMING, Donald Bannerman	9	1-2 October
935733	Sgt	FLETCHER, Ronald Samuel	82	8 September
79236	P/O	FORD, George Reginald Michael	149	18-19 September
581328	Sgt	FOSTER, Brian Holmes	144	16-17 August
580739	Sgt	FRANCE, Eric Basil Hartley	144	11-12 July
522061	Sgt	FRANKLIN, William Henry James, BEM	150	27 July
551601	Sgt	FRASER, John McLean	106	18-19 September
747724	Sgt	FRIEND, Kenneth Charles	49	16-17 October
641321	Sgt	FUTCHER, John Vernon	149	11-12 July
552107	Sgt	GANDER, Owen Sandford	83	1-2 July

Number	Rank	Name	Squadron	Date of loss
78461	P/O	GARDENER, Donald Edwin	61	12-13 August
626245	Sgt	GEORGE, John Henry	101	19-20 August
745221	Sgt	GIBBONS, Derek Albert	77	23-24 September
625697	Sgt	GIBBS, Jack	75NZ	23-24 October
751217	Sgt	GIBSON, Alexander	57	25-26 August
905664	Sgt	GIBSON, Kenneth Victor	101	25-26 July
581092	Sgt	GILES, Alexander Joseph	144	20-21 July
552188	Sgt	GIRVAN, Thomas Eckford	82	13 August
614892	Sgt	GLEDHILL, Herbert Gresford	149	8-9 September
629156	Sgt	GLEN, Alexander	37	6-7 July
751954	Sgt	GOODERICK, Clifford John	101	30-31 October
620440	Sgt	GOODWILL, William	44	11-12 September
550891	Sgt	GORWOOD, John Ernest, DFM	83	23-24 September
522865	Sgt	GOTT, Merle	9	19-20 July
SA524674	Sgt	GOULD, Charles Terry	150	27 July
751434	Sgt	GRANT, Stanley Charles	149	8-9 September
581175	Sgt	GRAY, Angus Nigel	15	12-13 August
747715	Sgt	GREEN, Cyril Sidney Garrick	58	20-21 October died 23 October
965818	Sgt	GREEN, Rendle	105	9-10 September
532939	Sgt	GREENWOOD, James Edward	105	28-29 October
966648	Sgt	GREIG, John Creswell	78	14-15 September
581381	Sgt	GRIFFITHS, Arthur James	144	10-11 August
626994	Sgt	HAGGETT, Harry	51	16-17 August
551723	Sgt	HALDANE, Sydney John	214	30-31 August
755403	Sgt	HALL, Albert Richard Sidney	53	5-6 October
619068	LAC	HALL, George Arthur	150	27 July
900575	Sgt	HALL, George Edgar	58	8-9 October
566919	Sgt	HALLAM, Walter Thomas	149	28-29 September
564194	Sgt	HALLET, Cyril Richard	83	7-8 July

Roll of Honour

Number	Rank	Name	Squadron	Date of loss
78684	P/O	HALLOWS, Eric Stewart Isaacson	99	29-30 October
632830	Sgt	HALLS, Reginald	50	10-11 September
581214	Sgt	HAMILTON, Claude	82	10-11 August
627887	Sgt	HARDCASTLE, Jack	105	28-29 October
522533	Sgt	HARDY, Leonard William	9	28-29 September
936441	Sgt	HARVEY, Bernard	106	26-27 September
534211	Sgt	HARRIS, Aubrey John	51	19-20 July
77984	P/O	HARRIS, Edwin Arthur	49	11-12 August
581152	Sgt	HARRIS, Peter Raymond	18	16 July
538889	Sgt	HARRISON, Henry Herbert	149	18-19 September
903079	Sgt	HATCH, John Frederick	18	16 July
965765	Sgt	HAY, Colin	9	14-15 October
628965	Sgt	HAYWOOD, Walter Frank	102	16-17 August
647632	Sgt	HEARD, Douglas Thomas	99	18-19 September
551787	Sgt	HENRY, Bert Llewellyn	10	14-15 October
645617	Sgt	HETTLE, Robert McGregor	142	28-29 July
622581	Sgt	HEWITT, William Hutchinson	61	16-17 October
580871	Sgt	HEYWORTH, Ronald Macauley	78	14-15 September
688167	Sgt	HILL, Eric	58	22-23 July
567698	Sgt	HILL, Matthew	58	30-31 August
581219	Sgt	HILTON, Ronald	10	6-7 September
755307	Sgt	HINTON, Stanley Edward	107	10-11 July
510387	Sgt	HISTON, Herbert	82	2 July
937501	Sgt	HITCHEN, John Gregson	101	30-31 October
658978	Sgt	HITCHMOUGH, William Grice	75NZ	23-24 October
551722	Sgt	HOBSON, Alan Gordon	50	29-30 September
643610	Sgt	HOBSON, George John	44	11-12 September
749458	Sgt	HOLDSWORTH, John	15	7 July
745631	Sgt	HOLLAND, Charles Julius	107	22-23 July

Number	Rank	Name	Squadron	Date of loss
986848	Sgt	HOLLIDAY, George	88	7-8 October
966474	Sgt	HOLLINGSHEAD, Ronald Emes	15	13-14 September
746840	Sgt	HOOD, Claude Lionel Geoffrey	77	14-15 August
812340	Sgt	HOOKER, Donald	114	26-27 September
755811	Sgt	HOOPER, Cyril John	37	1-2 September
580957	Sgt	HORSFALL, Alan Albert	50	30-31 August
543161	Sgt	HORTON, Leslie John	15	25-26 July
77986	P/O	HOUSEMAN, Ridley Elgood	149	11-12 August
552504	Sgt	HOWARD, Leonard	83	7-8 July
644790	Sgt	HOWE, George Lawson	106	29-30 October
77937	P/O	HOWIE, Charles William	149	11-12 July
653137	Sgt	HUGHES, Alan Joseph	38	24-25 October
937392	Sgt	HUGHES, Dennis Victor	77	18-19 September
81069	P/O	HUGHES, Philip Leslie Norgrove	15	13-14 September
563882	Sgt	HUGHES, William Arthur	144	16-17 August
628383	Sgt	HUNTER, John Arthur	59	17 July
77988	P/O	HUTCHINS, David	144	16-17 August
748089	Sgt	IMBER, Dennis Sidney	49	16-17 October
550470	Sgt	ISHERWOOD, Leonard	58	11-12 July
746821	Sgt	JACKSON, James Joseph	144	16-17 October
749426	Sgt	JACKSON, Norman Halsall	22	28-29 October
755443	Sgt	JACOBS, Alec Victor	107	8-9 September
581513	Sgt	JAMES, Eric	38	11-12 September
637282	Sgt	JAMES, Raymond Wallace	38	24-25 October
937289	Sgt	JARMAN, Theos Geoffrey Scott	40	8-9 September
78762	P/O	JELLEY, Edward Arthur	75NZ	29-30 September
751725	Sgt	JELLEY, Percy William Norman	49	11 August
524198	Sgt	JERMOND, Sidney George	102	16-17 August
935192	Sgt	JOHNSON, Thomas Kenneth	114	26-27 September

Roll of Honour

Number	Rank	Name	Squadron	Date of loss
635088	Sgt	JOHNSON, William Aubrey	50	10-11 September
552521	Sgt	JOHNSTONE, James Ward	38	11-12 September
44074	P/O	JONES, Francis Herbert	15	30-31 July
590727	Sgt	JONES, Geoffrey Wyatt	83	25-26 July
565170	Sgt	JONES, Jack Bramwell	58	22-23 July
638740	Sgt	JONES, John	49	6-7 August
741975	Sgt	JONES, Maurice Herbert	51	4-5 September
905466	Sgt	JONES, Ralph Henderson Goff	18	30-31 August
965067	Sgt	JONES, William Henry	44	11-12 September
580962	Sgt	JOYCE, Denis Arthur	44	11-12 September
745998	Sgt	KEATS, Sidney Bertie	106	18-19 September
935752	Sgt	KELLY, James	78	14-15 September
562829	Sgt	KENMURE, Colin	106	18-19 September
966804	Sgt	KILGOUR, William	107	18/19 September
751190	Sgt	KINGSHOTT, Reginald Vincent	59	17 July
523885	Sgt	KINTON, Basil	83	7-8 July
746916	Sgt	KNIGHT, Charles John	61	5-6 September
82786	P/O	KNIGHT, Norman Arthur	105	28-29 October
528679	Sgt	LACEY, Herbert George	44	10-11 September
620368	Sgt	LACKENBY, Abraham	105	18-19 September
905836	Sgt	LAND, Victor Robert Thomas	18	8 August
76916	P/O	LANE, Tom Hwfa Nixon	61	13-14 September
A77944	P/O	*LEACH, Phillip Allen	38	21 July
569067	Sgt	LEAMY, Edward Dennis	144	11-12 July
43162	P/O	LEE, Terence Edward	102	24-25 October
78545	P/O	LEES, Harold Frederick Archdale	9	19-20 July
516225	Sgt	LEFEVRE, Percy Thomas	218	22-23 August
636576	Sgt	LEWIS, Ronald Norman	51	19-20 July
751309	Sgt	LIESHMAN, David	58	1-2 July

Number	Rank	Name	Squadron	Date of loss
638486	Sgt	LINDSAY, James Fenton	49	6-7 August
81036	P/O	LINSDELL, Arthur Peter	83	18-19 September
751534	Sgt	LITTLE, Frank	40	30-31 August
547515	Sgt	LITTLE, George Elliott	83	1-2 July
550254	Sgt	LIVERMORE, Robert Mark	101	5-6 July
580616	Sgt	LONG, Brian Conway	12	31 July
747748	Sgt	LONGCLUSE, Norman	142	28-29 July
649886	Sgt	LOWRY, Laurence Mortimer	142	22-23 August
749508	Sgt	McALISTER, William Gordon	51	9-10 September
627936	Sgt	MCALLISTER, Robert James	82	2 July
755640	Sgt	McCARTHY, Charles Gordon	83	18-19 September
580972	Sgt	McCONNELL, John Bretland	38	24-25 October
580801	Sgt	McCORMICK, Joseph Edward	75NZ	20-21 September
615278	Sgt	McCRORIE, William	78	21-22 July
936241	Sgt	McDONALD, Francis George Rae	149	9-10 October
755134	Sgt	MacDONALD, Norman	75NZ	20-21 September
551045	Sgt	MacKAY, Duncan	144	10-11 August
550348	Sgt	MacKAY, DFM, William Ian	144	5-6 September
755598	Sgt	McKEE, Jamnes	101	8-9 September
41439	P/O	MCKINNON, James Elmer	206	4 July
77985	P/O	McLAGGAN, Alexander Livingstone	15	25-26 July
751459	Sgt	MacMORLAND, William Goodall	77	8-9 October
755502	Sgt	MacNAIR, James George Campbell	115	30 September-1 October
615194	Sgt	MacPHERSON, Keith Dabray	82	29-30 July
749307	Sgt	MARSDEN, Arthur	40	2-3 September
580884	Sgt	MARSHALL, Charles Frederick	58	18-19 September
817286	Sgt	MARSHALL, James Douglas	50	5-6 October
746983	Sgt	MARTIN, Alfred Charles	149	8-9 September
C581164	Sgt	MATSON, George Enos	78	1-2 October

Number	Rank	Name	Squadron	Date of loss
552074	Sgt	MATTHEWS, Charles Ernest	38	11-12 September
580787	Sgt	MATTICK, Arthur Reginald	99	13-14 October
538737	Sgt	MAYDON, George Edwin	18	4 July
638466	Sgt	MEIN, Cuthbert	21	5 September
639880	Sgt	MERCER, Roy	107	10 July
755031	Sgt	MERRICK, Peter Anthony	50	29-30 September
547673	Sgt	MERRYWEATHER, George Edward	214	30-31 August
521578	Sgt	MIDDLETON, George Leslie	88	26-27 October
652446	Sgt	MILBOURNE, Richard Lindsley	44	20-21 October
74338	Sgt	MILES, Peter Fenton	40	9 July
551536	Sgt	MILLER, Reginald Talbot	44	19-20 July
742485	Sgt	MILLER, William Elliott	50	31 July-1 August
967458	Sgt	MILSOM, Edward John	9	28-29 September
610601	F/Sgt	MOORE, George Percy	82	13 August
653917	Sgt	MOORES, Leslie Edwin	114	13 August
965279	Sgt	MORRISON, Archibald Finlayson	82	13 August
653323	Sgt	MORRISON, Robert McCrindle	61	12-13 August
580414	Sgt	MORRISSY, Donald Patrick	114	13 August
NZ42759	P/O	MURFITT, Thomas Russell	102	24-25 October
532881	Sgt	MURPHY, Patrick	15	30-31 July
651567	Sgt	NEAVERSON, Kenneth Walter	82	13 August
976437	Sgt	NEILL, David	139	14-15 October
901772	Sgt	NEVILLE, Brian Walter	10	6-7 September
901776	Sgt	NEVILLE, Leslie Peter	10	14-15 October
742656	Sgt	*NEVILLE, Maurice William	61	11-12 October
631165	Sgt	NEVILL, William Eric	75NZ	25-26 July
626884	Sgt	NEWBERRY, James	82	13-14 July
755404	Sgt	NEWSON, Frederick Henry	40	25-26 August
543932	Sgt	NICOL, Andrew Isaac John	144	4-5 July

Number	Rank	Name	Squadron	Date of loss
968346	Sgt	NIELD, Eric	9	13-14 October
580671	Sgt	NIXON, Percy Dryden	44	19-20 July
902559	Sgt	NOAKES, Frederick Walter	38	11-12 September
550672	Sgt	O'BRIEN, John Barrie	51	14-15 August
643564	Sgt	O'HENEY, William Patrick	107	22-23 July
581525	Sgt	OLIVER, Ralston George	82	13 August
747713	Sgt	O'REGAN, Francis Patrick 3	8	7-8 October
748693	Sgt	OWLES, Aubrey Ernest	18	30-21 August
649968	Sgt	PALLETT, Denis Isiah	61	25-26 October
743071	Sgt	PALMER, Edward Bartle	105	9-10 September
748411	Sgt	PARKINSON, Jack	101	25-26 July
681118	Sgt	PARVIN, Frederick Finkill	18	8 August
681296	Sgt	PATCHETT, Arthur Homer	82	13 August
631112	Sgt	PATTERSON, James	102	16-17 August
902467	Sgt	PAYNE, Donald Mayston	149	8-9 September
612685	Sgt	PEGLER, Victor William	40	8-9 September
682154	Sgt	PEGRAM, Thomas Henry	102	28-29 October
581410	Sgt	PENNINGTON, Alan Jervis	116	30 September-1 October
751121	Sgt	PENNY, Ronald Trevor	77	24-25 August
629841	Sgt	PETRIE, Peter John	15	3-4 September
78668	P/O	PHILIPPE, Henri	37	1-2 September
567099	Sgt	PHILLIPS, Frank Herbert Edward	37	20-21 July
742976	Sgt	PICKERING, Charles William	82	7 July
751549	Sgt	PILLANS, Alexander Morrison	114	19-20 August
742311	Sgt	POLLARD, Maurice William James	102	16-17 August
966654	Sgt	POPE, William Roy	149	18-19 September
643788	Sgt	POTTER, Robert	49	16-17 October
902976	Sgt	POWELL, William Henry	107	24-25 September
641879	Sgt	POWELL, William Leslie	144	5-6 September

Roll of Honour

Number	Rank	Name	Squadron	Date of loss
581411	Sgt	POWYS-JONES, Hugh Arthur	15	3-4 September
638145	Sgt	PRICE, Thomas Oliver	107	11-12 August
751821	Sgt	PRITCHARD, Harold William	115	30 September-1 October
755485	Sgt	PUZEY, Arthur Burnham	214	30-31 August
580445	Sgt	RADFORD, Victor	105	18-19 September
646336	Sgt	RADLEY, Thomas James	12	31 July
533261	Sgt	RAMSAY, James Munro	58	8-9 October
748785	Sgt	RANDS, Edward Anthony Gaston	144	16-17 October
751803	Sgt	RAPER, John Alan	77	18-19 September
751840	Sgt	RAYMENT, Walter Benedict	61	5-6 October
580828	Sgt	READ, Charles Edward	37	14-15 July
626591	AC1	REAY, Gordon	49	25-26 August
746818	Sgt	REID, George	15	7 July
77040	P/O	RENDELL, Victor Arthur	83	18-19 September
747880	Sgt	REYNOLDS, Marcus Pete	149	9-10 October
581413	Sgt	RICHARDSON, Horace William	82	13-14 July
639639	Sgt	RICHMOND, Philip Hall	78	1-2 October
741996	Sgt	RILEY, Charles Peace	40	25-26 August
580587	Sgt	RIMMER, George	114	5-6 July
751060	Sgt	RIPLEY, Philip Watson	22	28-29 October
644958	Sgt	ROBERTSON, John Devine	9	1-2 October
751021	Sgt	ROBERTSON, Robert Forrest	49	27-28 October
900084	Sgt	ROGERS, John Aidan	82	7 July
615888	Sgt	ROLLS, Henry	15	15-16 August
683114	Sgt	ROSCOE, Arthur	78	1-2 October
631869	Sgt	ROSE, Clarence	144	11-12 July
900030	Sgt	ROSE, Maurice	102	28-29 October
359517	F/Sgt	RUFFELL-HAZELL, DFM, Richard James	115	2-3 August
633936	Sgt	SALISBURY, Robert Edward	58	18-19 September

Roll of Honour

Number	Rank	Name	Squadron	Date of loss
551589	Sgt	SALMON, Peter Duncan	51	16-17 August
935979	Sgt	SAMBROOK, Harry Edward	214	27-28 September
581475	Sgt	SAVILL, DFM, Bernard Leonard	772	3-24 Sept died on 25 September
548614	Sgt	SAYER, DFM, Kenneth Anthony	83	12-13 August
755254	Sgt	SCOTT, John James	149	11-12 August
615919	Sgt	SCRASE, Edgar Enoch	15	12-13 August
79000	P/O	SEARLES, Walter George	149	8-9 September
540186	Sgt	SEED, Harold Victor	10	6-7 September
743306	Sgt	SELLWOOD, Kenneth Reginald	99	25-26 July
755373	Sgt	SEXTON, Gerald Francis	99	5-6 July
536431	Sgt	SHERWOOD, Charles Alfred	83	5-6 October
619842	Cpl	SHARP, Dennis Harold	150	27 July
749466	Sgt	SHIMELLS, Kenneth	149	9-10 October
627701	Sgt	SHUTTLEWORTH, Bernard	99	13-14 October
640098	Sgt	SILLETT, Ernest Robert	44	1-2 October
905662	Sgt	SIMMS, Donald Brill	101	25-26 September
744969	Sgt	SINCLAIR, Donald	61	26-27 September
742286	Sgt	SKIDMORE, Albert Edgar	9	14-15 October
743057	Sgt	SKINNER, Eric William Joseph	50	30-31 August
747711	Sgt	SMART, Harold Edgar	99	18-19 September
366413	Sgt	SMITH, Ewart William	101	5-6 July
580884	Sgt	SMITH, Frederick Leece	18	14-15 August
755623	Sgt	SMITH, James Scott	40	25-26 August
580466	Sgt	SPENCER, Alan, DFM	40	9 July
680627	Sgt	SPENCER, Douglas Frederick	139	3 August
939190	Sgt	SPENCER, Robert Nettleton	101	8-9 September
581359	Sgt	STANLEY, Jesse George	18	4 July
749418	Sgt	STEPHENS, Reginald	38	7-8 October
77981	P/O	*STERLING, Robert Camac	149	23 July

Number	Rank	Name	Squadron	Date of loss
81060	P/O	STEVENS, Dennis Joseph Arthur	10	6-7 September
624161	Sgt	STEWART, Angus Lamont	50	25-26 July
638353	AC1	STEWART, Frederick	150	27 July
639949	Sgt	STILES, Royston Charles Edward	57	25-26 August
751322	Sgt	STUBBERFIELD, Lawrence Paul	51	14-15 August
536657	Sgt	SUGDEN, James	44	17-18 September
644680	Sgt	SUGGETT, Charles	149	11-12 July
581542	Sgt	SULLY, Alfred Peter	107	29-30 August
617486	Sgt	SULTER, James	78	21-22 July
903248	Sgt	SWEET, Reginald Philip	9	1-2 October
644387	Sgt	SWIFT, James Henry	149	11-12 August
42541	P/O	TAGG, Maurice Roy	61	20-21 July
526290	Sgt	TAILFORD, Donald	50	31 July-1 August
C751664	Sgt	TAIT, Richard Albert William	78	14-15 August
666130	Sgt	TANSLEY, John	51	19-20 July
644896	Sgt	TAYLOR, George Henry	37	29-30 September
965631	Sgt	TAYLOR, Gordon	218	8-9 September
581192	Sgt	TAYLOR, Leslie Hambleton	58	24-25 September
581862	Sgt	TAYLOR, Philip Bernard	107	11-12 August
77205	P/O	TAYLOR, Thomas Monks	50	25-26 July
662777	Sgt	TAYLOR, William Barrie	61	12-13 August
70666	F/O	TEDDER, Arthur Richard Brian	139	3-4 August
755298	Sgt	THOMPSON, Edward Francis	107	8-9 September
637847	Sgt	THOMSON, William	144	5-6 September
751512	Sgt	THROWER, Charles Edward	61	12-13 August
581125	Sgt	TOMLINSON, John	44	1-2 October
580075	Sgt	TOWNSEND, Douglas George John	83	25-26 July
581482	Sgt	TRUSCOTT, Granville Thomas	107	10-11 July
581552	Sgt	TUNE, Harold Arthur	110	30-31 August

Number	Rank	Name	Squadron	Date of loss
903333	Sgt	TURNER, Edward Victor	82	13 August
937492	Sgt	TURNER, Kenneth Victor	82	13 August
650773	Sgt	TURNER, William	114	29 October
626850	Sgt	UNDERWOOD, Arthur James	110	10-11 August
580685	Sgt	WAKE, Robert Leslie	144	16-17 August
615619	Sgt	WALKER, DFM, Albert Eric	144	2-3 September
581250	Sgt	WALKER, Bernard	139	14-15 October
755305	Sgt	WALKER, Leslie Alfred Nevison	110	23-24 July
581126	Sgt	WALSH, Edmond Ernest Raymond	18	4 September
635501	Sgt	WALTER, Frank Douglas	61	25-26 October
902245	Sgt	WALTER, James Le Blond Robert	115	30 September-1 October
626198	Sgt	WALTERS, Sidney	107	30 September
688850	Sgt	WALTHO, Frederick Stanley	61	20-21 July
858641	F/Sgt	WARD, Wilfred	61	12-13 August
938888	Sgt	WARDMAN, Joseph Reginald	77	8-9 October
516040	Sgt	WATCHOUS, Kenneth Harrison	50	29-30 September
631726	Sgt	WATERFALL, John Henry, DFM	37	6-7 July
42945	P/O	WATSON, Francis Joseph	83	23-24 September
580743	Sgt	WATSON, Fred	9	19-20 July
965301	Sgt	WATSON, Thomas	99	18-19 September
522273	Sgt	WATT, Gordon Reeves	50	25-26 July
755256	Sgt	WATT, John Archibald	40	30 August
650883	Sgt	WATTS, Henry Victor	115	22-23 August
647419	Sgt	WEBBER, Arthur Frank	77	24-25 August
533941	Sgt	WEST, DFM, James Victor	110	20-21 July
629457	Sgt	WESTHORP, Bernard Newman	44	10-11 September
805525	Sgt	WESTWOOD, Douglas Eric	115	30 September-1 October
751267	Sgt	WHELPTON, Harry	88	7-8 October
626218	Sgt	WHITE, DFM, Lewis Alan	75NZ	20-21 September

Roll of Honour

Number	Rank	Name	Squadron	Date of loss
755956	Sgt	WHITE, Reginald William Bryant	75NZ	23-24 October
76931	P/O	WILDE, Sidney John Scott	115	2-3 August
SA76932	P/O	WILK, Jack	149	16-17 August
580929	Sgt	WILL, Ernest Alexander	114	1 August
642147	Sgt	WILLIAMS, James Clough	61	26-27 September
751064	Sgt	WILMOT, Arthur Alexander	144	21-22 August
624190	Sgt	WILSON, Angus Stewart	102	24-25 October
755989	Sgt	WINBERG, Israel	110	23-24 July
640278	Sgt	WINCH, Frederick John Baulch	37	20-21 July
505501	Sgt	WISE, Charles Harold	50	5-6 October
79554	P/O	WISE, Stanley Cuthbert	44	11-12 September
688499	Sgt	WOOD, Cyril Edward Thomas	44	31 July-1 August
580689	Sgt	WOOD, George	144	5-6 October
751655	Sgt	WOOD, Sidney Metcalf	107	10-11 July
940148	Sgt	WOODS, Jack	9	28-29 September
746763	Sgt	WRIGHT, Albert	99	13-14 October
740280	Sgt	WRIGHT, Charles Austin	58	8-9 October
541172	Sgt	WYLIE, William.	144	20-21 July
532875	Sgt	YORATH, Philip Herbert	144	5-6 October
751187	Sgt	YOUNG, Kenneth Ernest	83	26-27 October
650682	Sgt	YOUNG, Peter Archibald	37	29-30 September
580690	Sgt	YOUNG, Robert Gilmour	144	16-17 October
580905	Sgt	YOUNGS, Leslie Reginald	82	13 August
749523	Sgt	ZAMEK, Ian Alexander	58	30-31 August

BELGIAN PILOTS

Number	Rank	Name	Squadron	Date of loss
81630	P/O	KIRKPATRICK, James Charles	235	9 October

ROYAL NEW ZEALAND AIR FORCE PILOTS

Number	Rank	Name	Squadron	Date of loss
39781	F/O	COLEMAN, DFC, William Harcourt	75NZ	25-26 July
891346	Sgt	DOUGLAS, Charles Harold	99	13-14 October
89911	P/O	FINLAYSON, William John	75NZ	23-24 October

ROYAL NEW ZEALAND AIR FORCE AIRCREW

Number	Rank	Name	Squadron	Date of loss
891321	Sgt	ANDERSON, Lindsay Douglas	75NZ	20-21 September
36139	F/Sgt	ANDERSON, Ronald Alexander John	75NZ	20-21 July
391377	Sgt	ANNAN, William Donald Francis	75NZ	25-26 July
40185	Sgt	BLATCH, Alfred Frederick	83	23-24 September
40199	Sgt	BRACEGIRDLE, James	44	6-7 September
40201	Sgt	BROWNE, Thomas Chamberlain Molineux	37	1-2 September
39964	Sgt	DALLAS, Arthur Fraser	105	28-29 October
40726	Sgt	NEWBERY, Charles Hugh Le Blanc	9	1-2 October
891882	Sgt	OWEN, John Lewis	75NZ	20-21 July
39971	Sgt	PHILPOTT, John Bernard	82	8 September
891870	Sgt	SCOULAR, Ian Cowie	102	24-25 October
39866	Sgt	MACDONALD, Stuart Hayden	204	28 October

CZECHOSLOVAKIAN PILOTS

Number	Rank	Name	Squadron	Date of loss
82557	P/O	LANDA, Bohumil	311	16-17 October
787416	Sgt	*LANG, Karel	311	16-17 October
787237	Sgt	*TOSOVSKY, Oldrich	311	16-17 October
82582	S/L	VESELY, Jan	311	16-17 October
787242	Sgt	ZAPLETAL, Frantisek	311	16-17 October

Roll of Honour

CZECHOSLOVAKIAN AIRCREW

Number	Rank	Name	Squadron	Date of loss
787410	Sgt	ALBRECHT, Josef	311	16-17 October
82605	P/O	JAROSEK, Hubert Zdenek	311	16-17 October
787141	Sgt	JIRSAK, Otto	311	16-17 October
787547	Sgt	KLIMT, Karel	311	16-17 October
787252	Sgt	KUNKA, Karel	311	23-24 July
82524	P/O	MATOUSEK, Jaroslav	311	16-17 October
82637	P/O	SLABY, Jaroslav	311	16-17 October
82538	P/O	VEJRAZKA, Miroslav Ervin	311	16-17 October

POLISH PILOTS

Number	Rank	Name	Squadron	Date of loss
76605	F/O	GEBICKI, Jan	300	13-14 October
76683	P/O	WARONSKI, Jozef	301	24-25 September

POLISH AIRCREW

Number	Rank	Name	Squadron	Date of loss
780231	Sgt	EGIERSKI, Tadeusz	300	13-14 October
76677	P/O	KULINSKI, Jozef	301	24-25 September
780113	Sgt	MORAWA, Edward	300	13-14 October
780445	Sgt	PALIWODA, Karol	301	24-25 September

MAINTENANCE COMMAND PILOT

Number	Rank	Name	Squadron	Date of loss
41543	P/O	BIRD, Charles Alex	5 M.U.	25 July

Roll of Honour

FLEET AIR ARM TRAINING

Number	Rank	Name	Squadron	Date of loss
78986	A/Leading Seaman	SEED, John Arthur	1 FTS	21 July

FLEET AIR ARM ATTACHED TO RAF BOMBER COMMAND

Rank	Name	Squadron	Date of loss
Sub-Lt	DE SANDOVAL-SIEVIER, Robert Adrian	103	9-10 September
Midshipman	HADINGHAM, David Arthur Charles	77	8-9 October
Sub-Lt	WILLIAMS, Peter Owen	77	18-19 September

DUTCH RNAS UNDER RAF COASTAL COMMAND

Rank	Name	Squadron	Date of loss
Off	DEN HOLLANDER, J. C.	320	26 July
Sgt Maj	DE KNEGT	320	26 July
Off	MARTARE, E.	320	26 July
Kpl	RAS, J. G.	320	26 July

NAVAL SQUADRONS UNDER RAF COASTAL COMMAND

Rank	Name	Squadron	Date of loss
Sub-Lt	EBORN Ralph Churchill	812	4 August
Naval Airman I	HOWE Grant Frederick Kerslake	826	30 September
Lt	JOHNSTON Timothy Armstrong , Royal Marines	812	4 August
Lt	KENNAWAY Charles Stewart Hamilton	826	30 September
Midshipman	LANE Richard John	826	30 September

Roll of Honour

NAVAL SQUADRONS UNDER NAVAL CONTROL

Number	Rank	Name	Squadron	Date of loss
77405	Naval Airman I	ADLAM Eric James	801	2 October
77498	Naval Airman I	BASS Sydney	801	26 July
79418	Naval Airman I	BREWSTER Basil Frederick Aubrey	821	26 October
80195	Leading Airman	BURT Harry William Victor	825	2-3 July
	Midshipman	CHAMBERS Richard Theodore	821	26 October
76535	Petty Officer	CLAYTON Alfred George	801	9 September
	Lt	FRYER William Arthur Francis	821	14 August
146121	Naval Airman I	GAYNON George Harry	821	22 September
	Sub-Lt	GRIGSON Barry Pawlet	825	2-3 July
	Sub-Lt	HARTOCH Alan	801	2 October
80151	Petty Officer	HARWIN Edward George Robert	801	13 September
76386	Petty Officer	KIMBER Henry Charles	801	9 September
	Sub-Lt	LAYCOCK Peter Bernard	821	26 October
	Sub-Lt	LEES Frederick Leonard	825	2-3 July
	Sub-Lt MARAIS	Derek John Theobald	821	23 September
152279	Naval Airman I	MAUNDER John Richard	801	13 September
	Sub-Lt	MOURILYAN Alec James	821	14 August
	Sub-Lt	MYERS John Edwin Howard	801	26 July
	Sub-Lt	SAUNDERS Frederick Christopher , DSG	821	23 September
76299	Petty Officer	TYLER Alfred Thomas	821	14 August
	Lt	VILLIERS-TUTHILL George	812	31 August

COASTAL COMMAND PILOTS

Number	Rank	Name	Squadron	Date of loss
74322	F/O	ACHESON, James Glasgow Irwin	206	14 October
C41539	P/O	ALLSUP, Charles James	220	1 August
42090	P/O	ARTHUR, Charles John	248	27 August

Roll of Honour

Number	Rank	Name	Squadron	Date of loss
44226	P/O	ATHER, William Laverick	253	21-22 July
43765	P/O	ATHERTON, Thomas	22	17-18 September
NZ36265	P/O	BALLANTYNE, Herbert Gregory	206	14-15 August
25095	A/F/L	BARTLETT, Ian Howard	53	8 September
59409	F/L	BENDELL, John Reginald	42	28 September
A42097	P/O	BENNETT, Clarence Charles	248	1 October
16216	W/C	BENNETT, Leslie Clive	21	9 July
81955	P/O	BEVAN-JOHN, Spencer Rhys	53	30 September
70074	F/O	BRACKENRIDGE, Gilbert Keith	233	5 October
480180	Sgt	BROCKLEHURST, Geoffrey Rainsford	42	26 October
84688	P/O	BROOME, Charles George	Heston	26 October
741269	Sgt	BROWN, John Barnet Mathieson	21	9 July
42556	P/O	BUCHANAN, Robert Munro	233	9 July
84916	P/O	BUCKLEY, Ronald Leach	53	27 October
36169	P/O	CAREY, Garth Wells, Fuller	220	13-14 July
78273	P/O	CARRICK, Alan Russell	224	25 October
72590	P/O	CLARK, Henry Alan	59	13-14 July
72466	F/O	CORBETT, Hugh Christopher	53	3 August
740172	Sgt	COX, Ronald Christopher	224	30 September
41260	F/O	CUTHBERT, Robert Guy	224	8 September
23538	P/O	DALZELL-McKEAN, Michael Hugh	210	2 September
42593	P/O	DAVIES, Ronald John	224	16 October
16 107	W/C	DAVIS, OBE, AFC, Edward Simeon Colbeck	204	21-22 July
72988	P/O	DAVIS, Henry Lawrence Newson	59	9 August
79166	P/O	DE KEYSER, John Lionel	206	15-16 October
42812	P/O	DELLOW, James	59	28-29 August
41264	F/O	DOLMAN, Ian Humphrey	224	8 September
79559	P/O	DREW, Deryck Allnutt	59	2 August
26199	S/L	DREW, Peter Edward	256	1 August

COASTAL COMMAND PILOTS

Number	Rank	Name	Squadron	Date of loss
05146	W/C	EDWARDS, Edward Cecil Theodore	53	31 August
C41160	F/O	EMENO, Lionel Burton	269	28 September
41274	P/O	EWING, Loris Jardine Ernest	233	9 July
42826	P/O	FINLAY, James Jackson	59	31 August
79540	P/O	FITZPATRICK, William Edward	53	28-29 August
NZ41277	P/O	FLEMING, James Tayne Tame	269	23-24 July
566110	Sgt	FLETCHER, Peter Howard	220	6 October
A37582	A/F/L	FLOOD, Frederick William	235	11 September
C41391	P/O	FORBES, Roy Bruce	224	7 August
42117	P/O	GANE, Sydney Russell	248	26 October
A741151	Sgt	GANNON, Benjamin Peter	206	3-4 August
740997	Sgt	GARFIELD, Walter James	248	13 September
748874	Sgt	GIBBS, Arthur James	224	30 September
A41399	P/O	GILBERT, John Allan	206	3-4 August
42404	P/O	GLADDIS, John Harry Herbert	224	25 October
526218	Sgt	GOLDSMITH, George Howard	206	4 July
740682	Sgt	GORDON, David Bruce	10 BC	21-22 October
40904	P/O	GORDON-PEINIGER, Anthony	217	11 August
78082	P/O	GREEN, Alexander William Valentine	235	11 September
580002	Sgt	GUNN, Robert Dick	22	9-10 September
NZ42749	P/O	HALL, Robert Gladstone	53	8 September
40823	P/O	HARRY, David Marwood	201	9th July
SA72482	F/O	HASWELL, Hugh	59	25 July
42344	P/O	HEATH-BROWN, John Alastair	21	9th July
40826	P/O	HENDERSON, Selby Roger, DFC	206	4 July
70305	F/O	HIGSON, Kenneth Hesketh	10 BC	15-16 August
81354	P/O	HIVES, Ernest Edward	59	17 October
36220	P/O	HOPKIN, Alan Dunn	59	9 July

Roll of Honour

Number	Rank	Name	Squadron	Date of loss
70324	P/O	HOPKINSON, Richard Adrian	57	9th July
41417	P/O	HORAN, James Henry	233	31 July
37971	F/O	HYDE-PARKER, Antony Edington	PRU Heston	14 September
745438	Sgt	ISMAY, Geoffrey Lucien	10 BC	30 September-1 October
82699	P/O	JOHNSON, Raymond Francis William	59	25 September
NZ41295	P/O	KEAN, DFC, Raymond Thomas	206	5 August
41030	F/O	LASCELLES, John Richard Hastings	206	14 October
41434	P/O	LESTER, Stanley John	206	4 July
740005	Sgt	LOCKTON, Eric Edward	236	20-21 July
C42067	P/O	MacDONALD, Gerald Edwin	204	21-22 July
A42137	P/O	McDONOUGH, Bryan Martin	236	1 August
42415	P/O	MACLEY, William Duncan	21	9 July
39237	F/O	MAHONY, John Edward	53	18 July
NZ42719	P/O	MALLON, John Charles	53	8-9 October
41603	P/O	MATHIAS, Anthony Ronald	500	11 July
41439	P/O	MCKINNON, James Elmer	206	4 July
33326	F/L	MIDDLETON, John Derek	201	9th July
740119	Sgt	MILLS, Frank George	57	9th July
37779	F/L	MOLE, Nigel Brook	269	24 October
05224	A/W/C	MORGAN-WELD-SMITH, Reginald Gilbert Squarey	59	1 August
43204	P/O	MORRISON, Victor Clement Robert	224	21-22 July
39559	F/L	MURRAY, John William David	21	9 July
700059	Sgt	OLIVER, John Morgan	224	7 August
42874	P/O	PALMER, Kenneth Victor	59	30 September
42076	P/O	PAREEZER, Reginald Tony	204	21-22 July
40012	A/F/L	PARRY-JONES, Peter Denys	210	2 September
NZ43370	P/O	PARSONS, DFC, Ernest Ian	10 BC	13-14 August
33441	P/O	PARVIN, John Hugh Keith	10 BC	26-27 August

Roll of Honour

Number	Rank	Name	Squadron	Date of loss
77529	P/O	PATTERSON, Robert Lawson	235	18 July
33442	P/O	PATTISON, Vincent James	254	6 July
39153	F/L	PHILLIPS, DFC, Allan Smith	10 BC	21-22 October
37827	A/F/L	PHILLIPS, DFC, Frank	204	21-22 July
33474	P/O	PHILLIPS, Ian Williams	210	2 September
42077	P/O	PIRIE, Herbert George Ross	500	9 August
37985	A/F/L	PRICE, Charles David Weaver	269	23-24 July
77124	F/O	PUSEY, Bertram Leopold Arthur	210	2 September
78982	P/O	REX, James	59	10 July
42528	P/O	REYNOLDS, Bruce	59	19-20 August
42149	P/O	RIGBY, Robert Harold	236	18 July
70584	F/O	ROCHFORD, Stephen Christopher	53	24-25 August
740667	Sgt	ROUND, James Henry	248	19 August
27146	F/L	ROWLEY, Louis Percy	233	14 October
42079	P/O	RUSTOM, Robin	206	5 August
741175	Sgt	RYLANDS, John Power	22	28-29 October
34055	F/L	SCOTT, Francis Cohn	224	16 October
33445	P/O	SEEDS, James	201	9 July
SA37266	F/L	SHEAHAN, Harold Wentworth Aylward, DFC	220	1 August
77920	P/O	SLATER, Peter Henderson	21	26 October
742822	Sgt	SMITH, Douglas Albert James	269	24 October
745231	Sgt	SNELL, Victor	10 BC	30 September-1 October
NZ41752	P/O	STARKY, David Bayntun	53	25 July
NZ41623	P/O	STEPHENSON, John Oscar Lloyd	206	14-15 August
90486	P/O	TEDEN, Derek Edmund	206	15-16 October
40031	F/O	THOMAS, Charles Raymond Delauney	236	18 July
NZ43050	P/O	TIBBITTS, Clarence Francis	53	19 September
42915	P/O	TURNBULL, Matthew Roy	59	25-26 July

Number	Rank	Name	Squadron	Date of loss
590984	Sgt	TWITCHIN, Sydney Gordon	22	9-10 September
41632	P/O	VARTAN, Phillip Knox	220	13-14 July
A83709	P/O	WEABER, William Owen	233	31 October
70731	F/O	WHITEHEAD, Arthur Wilfred Alexander	500	11 July
42929	P/O	WICKINGS-SMITH, Peter Claude	235	11 September
748404	Sgt	WILSON, James	500	10-11/ July
42666	P/O	WOODGER, David Noel	235	24 August

COASTAL COMMAND AIRCREW

Number	Rank	Name	Squadron	Date of loss
517434	Sgt	ALDRIDGE, Robert Edward	53	8 September
7467066	Sgt	ANDREW, John Gordon	57	9 July
42975	P/O	APPLEBY, William	269	23-24 July
581165	Sgt	BANN, Jack	53	28-29 August
78695	F/O	BARDOLPH, George Malcolm	53	11 August died 17 August
744953	Sgt	BEAUMONT, Barrington William	59	9 August
642035	AC1	BEAVIS, Kenneth William	204	28 October
751495	Sgt	BEER, Cyril Sydney Frank	22	9-10 September
552175	Sgt	BEESLEY, John Thomas	53	31 August
570289	AC1	BELDERSON, John Buchanan	201	9 July
751790	Sgt	BENJAMIN, Louis Lionel	53	31 August
570382	AC1	BENNETT, Leslie Charles	204	21-22 July
900253	Sgt	BETTIS, Leonard Edgar	59	28-29 August
572892	AC1	BLACKMORE, William Henry	210	2 September
535103	Sgt	BOLTON, William Henry	42	26 October
639109	Sgt	BRASH, George Brown	248	1 October
751402	Sgt	BRIGGS, William	53	24-25 August
648603	Sgt	BROOK, Dennis	53	24-25 August

Roll of Honour

Number	Rank	Name	Squadron	Date of loss
755766	Sgt	BROWN, Percy Sharp	269	28 September
536872	Sgt	BRUCE, Donald	233	5 October
629928	Sgt	BURT, Christopher James	21	9th July
546956	Sgt	BUSHELL ,Keith Stephen	206	4 July
548486	Sgt	CAMERON, William Gray	233	31 July
545658	Sgt	CAMPBELL, Alexander Whyte	269	24 October
543418	Sgt	CARSON, John Leadbetter	201	29 October
628721	Sgt	CARTER, Hughie William	10 BC	26-27 August
935081	AC1	CAUNTER, Leonard James	210	2 September
550636	Sgt	*CHRISTIE, Robert Craig	224	10 July
623619	AC1	CLARK, Peter	201	9 July
747818	Sgt	CLARKE, Gordon Stuart	248	1 October
643566	Sgt	CLAYTON, Frank	59	13-14 July
653790	Sgt	CLOSE, James Reuben	59	2 August
552142	Sgt	CONACHER, Murray Blair	53	8 September
581146	Sgt	COPCUTT, Richard	248	20 October
579958	Sgt	CORCORAN, Henry	236	20-21 July
742495	Sgt	COTTON, Edwin Arthur	224	21-22 July
41557	P/O	COULMAN, Richard Maxwell	217	11 August
619184	Sgt	COULTON, George Howey	59	9 August
747819	Sgt	COX, Ralph Cyril Rupert	248	27 August
523092	Sgt	CRABTREE, John James	233	21-22 July
526095	Sgt	CRANE, Kenneth Walter	53	3-4 August
551339	Sgt	CURRY, Samuel Walter	224	21-22 July
44271	P/O	DAVIS, AFM, David Henry	59	1 August
642917	Sgt	DEAN, Henry	233	31 October
649007	Sgt	DIGBY-WORSLEY, Maxwell Paul	248	19 August
610629	Sgt	DIXON, Denton Parcy	204	21-22 July

Roll of Honour

Number	Rank	Name	Squadron	Date of loss
900499	Sgt	DORRINGTON, Jack Brereton	21	9 July
626734	Sgt	*DOWLEY, Joseph Henry	22	23 September
526769	Sgt	DOWSON, John Douglas	224	25 October
570399	Sgt	DREWITT, Mervyn Arthur Frederick	210	2 September
551700	Sgt	DUCK, Gerald Ernest	21	9 July
741157	Sgt	DUDLEY, Laurence	220	6 October
546967	Sgt	DUFFIELD, Edwin	224	8 September
612371	Sgt	DUNNINGTON, Harry	53	28-29 August
745956	Sgt	EDWARDS, Kenneth Arthur	59	28-29 August
743044	Sgt	ELSDON, Harry Donald Buchanan	236	18 July
44190	P/O	ERSKINE, Basil Pollock	233	31 October
640689	Sgt	EXTON, George Edward	53	18 July
551873	Sgt	FALCONER, James	59	9 July
755909	Sgt	FARLOWE, James Thomas	206	14 October
641705	Sgt	FEATHER, John Leslie	22	17-18 September
545600	Sgt	FITZGERALD, Eddie	206	14-15 August
968419	Sgt	FITZGERALD, Reginald George	210	2 September
535408	LAC	FRAME, Dennis John	204	21-22 July
523417	F/Sgt	GADSDON, Victor William	42	26 October
616246	Sgt	GARSTIN, Richard Elleker	206	14 October
624628	Sgt	GENT, Victor George	220	13-14 July
751623	Sgt	GRACE, Robert William	53	19 September
539039	Sgt	GRANT, Stephen	224	7 August
78263	P/O	GREEN, Maurice David	248	20 October
551873	Sgt	FALCONER, James	59	9 July
581386	Sgt	HAMLYN, Willaim Arthur	21	9 July
536608	LAC	HAMMOND, Ronald Harry Frank	201	9 July
42706	P/O	HANKS, Robert Archibald	233	14 October

Number	Rank	Name	Squadron	Date of loss
805497	Sgt	HARROLD, Eric	53	19 September
581153	Sgt	HARTLEY, Willoughby	21	9 July
751693	Sgt	HARVEY, Cyril James	22	17 September
902456	Sgt	HEAD, Frederick Arthur Percy	236	1 August
519449	Sgt	HEATH, James William Clarke	269	28 September
755515	Sgt	HENDERSON, Cecil	53	27 October
749485	Sgt	HERBERT, Arthur Gordon	59	2 August
546994	LAC	HINDLE, John Frederick	201	9 July
625532	Sgt	HOPPERTON, Edgar	217	11 August
569978	Cpl	HOLLAND, Oliver Henry Selby	21	26 October
566374	Sgt	HOWARD, Harold George Herbert	10 BC	26-27 August
C625793	AC1	HUBBARD, William Charles	500	11 July
748737	Sgt	HUGHES, Trefor Alun	224	25 October
755799	Sgt	HULL, Frederick Herbert	206	2 August
C580545	Sgt	HUNT, Harry Walter	53	25 July
581339	Sgt	INSKIP, Ivor	53	11 August
529709	Sgt	IRELAND, Robert Glenday	233	9 July
570180	LAC	JAMES, William Thomas	210	2 September
530166	LAC	JARVIS, Melville John Ernest	201	9 July
581226	Sgt	JEFFREY, John Samuel	59	10 July
551360	Sgt	JERVIS, Terence James	57	9 July
580546	Sgt	JOHNSTON, Norman Reid	10 BC	26-27 August
759044	Sgt	JOHNSTON, William Logan	206	3-4 August
755459	Sgt	JONES, Bertram Dennis	59	17 October
967075	AC1	JONES, David Henry	210	2 September
546188	Sgt	JONES, Edward	59	17 October
638275	Sgt	JONES, Hywel	21	26 October
647610	Sgt	KAY, Archibald	248	13 September

Roll of Honour

Number	Rank	Name	Squadron	Date of loss
751079	Sgt	KEEL, George Ernest	235	9 October
747771	Sgt	KEETLEY, Denys Arthur	53	18 July
518350	Sgt	KENT, William	206	15-16 October
639811	Sgt	*KNOWLES, Henry	233	24 October
523170	Sgt	LAMONT, Albert William	233	21-22 July
623762	Sgt	LAND, Laurence	269	23-24 July
517249	LAC	LANE, Joseph Henry	201	9 July
507615	Sgt	LAUDER, Robert	201	29 October
751200	Sgt	LEONHARDT, Frederick John	59	31 August-1 September
746918	Sgt	LEWIS, Kenneth Everitt	206	4 July
638666	Sgt	LIDDLE, James William	59	10 July
538981	Sgt	LILLIE, DFM, William Gray	204	21-22 October
751506	Sgt	LOFTHOUSE, William Arthur	10 BC	21-22 October
524731	Sgt	McDONALD, John Norman	269	28 September
33546	P/O	MacFARLANE, Ruthven Arnold	22	17-18 September
541465	Sgt	McGHIE, John	224	25 October
A43289	P/O	McINTOSH, John	233	5 October
745470	Sgt	MCVEIGH, Robert Alexander	254	6 July
745928	Sgt	MACKINNON, Donald Duncan	236	18 July
522280	Sgt	MACNAUGHTON, John Allan	42	28-29 September
747938	Sgt	MacQUIRE, Stanley	53	30 September
41125	F/O	MacRURY, Archie	42	26 October
635470	Sgt	MAHON, Bernard Joseph	233	21-22 July
627225	Sgt	MANNION, Dennis	206	5 August
550436	Sgt	MAPPLETHORPE, Christopher Parker	10 BC	21-22 October
751104	Sgt	MARTIN, Raymond Bradshaw	59	25 July
622651	Sgt	MASSON, Charles Frederick	42	28-29 September
538451	Sgt	MATTHEWS, George Alexander	220	13-14 July

Roll of Honour

Number	Rank	Name	Squadron	Date of loss
969831	Sgt	MELLODY, Eric Kendrick	217	1 August
745987	Sgt	MESNER, Bertram William	248	13 September
551824	Sgt	MIDDLETON, Dennis	224	12-22 July
751326	Sgt	MILES, George Alfred	57	9 July
539583	Sgt	MORGAN, Samuel	233	31 July
615346	Sgt	MORIARTY, Bartholomew	53	25 July
581239	Sgt	MORTON, David Douglas	59	13-14 July
642718	Sgt	MORTON, James	21	9 July
625327	Sgt	MURRAY, James	22	9-10 September
552235	Sgt	MURRAY, John Charles	220	6 October
973249	AC1	NANGLE, George Allan	201	29 October
553802	Sgt	NAYLER, Alfred Valentine	224	16 October
749451	Sgt	NEALE, Percival Eric James	53	27 October
746922	Sgt	NEWCOMBE, Sydney James	57	9 July
77362	F/O	NOKES-COOPER, Benjamin	236	1 August
627424	Sgt	O'CONNOR, John Patrick	224	30 September
550833	Sgt	OVENS, Edward William	204	21-22 July
580975	Sgt	PALMER, David Denis	22	28-29 October
42954	P/O	PARKINSON, Herbert	220	6 October
42021	P/O	PATON, Bruce Campbell	233	31 July
747834	Sgt	PEDDIE, Andrew Liggat	59	31 August-1 September
747777	Sgt	PERRIN, William Ronald	42	26 October
644168	Sgt	PHELPS, Ronald Wilkie John	201	29 October
565653	Sgt	POSGATE, Kenneth	224	30 September
812244	Sgt	PRENTICE, Montague Adam	500	21-22 July
551852	Sgt	PRYDE, Peter	59	1 August
553164	Sgt	PURT, John Walter	233	14 October
581064	Sgt	RANDALL, John Dermot	53	8 September

Roll of Honour

Number	Rank	Name	Squadron	Date of loss
580595	Sgt	RAWSON, William Lloyd	21	9 July
747825	Sgt	REECE, Lawrence Hugh Murrell	235	18 July
637154	Sgt	REES, Michael	224	8 September
751028	Sgt	RIDDINGTON, Sydney Eric	53	3-4 August
629710	Sgt	RINGWOOD, Eric Alfred	248	27 August
755445	Sgt	ROSS, Malcolm Sydney	204	28 October
751202	Sgt	ROWE, Gilbert Peter	59	25-26 July
581474	Sgt	ROWLES, Thomas James	59	9 July
533654	Sgt	RUSSELL, Andrew	233	5 October
638724	Sgt	SAWYER, Frank Cyril	PRU Heston	27 August
613282	Sgt	SHACKLEFORD, Arthur Thomas	53	8-9 October
628218	Sgt	SHARP, Bruce Robertson	235	11 September
550430	Sgt	SHARVIN, John Edward Redmond	269	24 October
630002	Sgt	SHAW, Harold Arthur	53	30 September
551845	Sgt	SHELDRICK, Edward Denis	53	8 September
580983	Sgt	SHIER, William George	500	10-11/ July
78265	P/O	SHORROCKS, Norman Basil	235	11 September
755136	Sgt	SIMPSON, Derrick Barrie	59	25 July
615825	Sgt	SINCLAIR, Donald Clifford	233	9 July
623798	Sgt	SMITH, Sydney	220	1 August
935024	AC2	SNEYD, Eric	204	21-22 July
644325	Sgt	STEEL, James	206	15-16 October
550132	Sgt	STEPHENSON, Joseph William	10 BC	26-27 August
581538	Sgt	STEVENS, Claude Donald	21	9 July
552636	Sgt	STOCKS, Norman James	248	20 October
541918	AC2	STOKES, Lawrence Edward	210	2 September
546871	Sgt	STRIDE, Leslie Herbert	53	14 July
563808	Sgt	SUMMERS, Albert Thomas	21	9 July

Roll of Honour

Number	Rank	Name	Squadron	Date of loss
568173	Sgt	SUMNER, Gordon Clifton	206	4 July
551592	Sgt	SWANN, Stanley	224	30 September
620418	Sgt	SWINSON, Patrick William	206	3-4 August
550847	Sgt	TENNANT, George David	224	7 August
521431	Sgt	THOMAS, Arthur Frederick	224	16 October
82731	P/O	THOMAS, Richard Ceredig	235	9 October
74693	F/O	TISDALL, Anthony Beresford	224	16 October
744561	LAC	TOWE, Matthew Ewing	204	18 October
635359	LAC	TRICKEY, Trevor Percival Jack	204	21-22 July
552711	Sgt	TUCKER, Ronald Yeaman	235	18 July
628797	Sgt	WALLACE, David	59	25-26 July
568661	Sgt	WALLACE, James Andrew	233	31 October
642945	Sgt	WALTERS, Douglas Allan	59	20 September
745927	Sgt	WANT, William Hudson	248	19 August
746868	Sgt	WATTS, Reginald Douglas Haig	235	11 September
562350	Sgt	WHETTON, DFM, Wilfred Philip	53	8-9 October
967530	AC1	WHITE, John Alexander McLaren Gray	204	21-22 July
581252	Sgt	WHITING, William George Frederick	59	19-20 August
546143	Sgt	WILKINSON, William Gaston Jules	59	19-20 August
524023	Sgt	WILKS, John Jackson	253	14 October
638749	Sgt	WILLIAMS, Emyr	21	9 July
534498	LAC	WILLIAMSON, John Lindsay	206	4 July
969167	Sgt	WILLS, Ian George	10 BC	21-22 October
565451	Sgt	WOOLNOUGH, Cyril Kenneth	42	28-29 September
745453	Sgt	WORTHINGTON, Laurie Edgar	201	9 July
903377	Sgt	WORTON, Horace George	500	10-11 July
552618	Sgt	WRIGHT, Daniel Leslie	235	24 August
580992	Sgt	WRIGHT, Ernest Edward	59	20 September

Opposite page: The annual Battle of Britain ceremony at the Runnymede Memorial.

THEIR NAME LIVET
FOR EVERMORE

OFFICIAL SOURCES

My information was obtained mainly from official sources via the Public Record Office (National Archives) Kew, where I researched the Operation Record Books of the Squadrons and Groups involved. These can be found in the Classes Air 27 and Air 28.

The following files provided additional information:
Air 2/7355 - Air attacks on England - 8 August to 10 September
Air 2/5246 - Air attacks on England - 11 September to 31 October
Air 8/ 831 - Air Casualties - British and German
Air 22/51-52 - Daily Resumes of Air Operations

Additional information on aircraft losses came from the Archive Department of the Royal Air Force Museum, the Air Historical Branch of the Ministry of Defence and the Commonwealth War Graves Commission.

BIBLIOGRAPHY

Barker, Ralph - **Torpedo Bomber** - 1957 Chatto and Windus
Bowyer, M. J. - **The Battle of Britain** - Fifty Years on – 1990 Faber and Faber
Bowyer, M. J. - **2 Group** - Faber and Faber
Chorley, W. R. - **RAF Bomber Command Losses 1939/1940** - 1992 Midland Publishing
Collier, Basil - **The Defence of the United Kingdom** – 1957 HMSO
Deighton, Len and Hastings, Max - **The Battle of Britain** - 1998 Wordsworth Edition
Donnel. G. L. – **The Whitley Boys** – 1991 Air Research Publications
Foreman, John - **The Battle of Britain - Forgotten Months** -1988 Air Research Publications
Franks, Norman.L. R. - **RAF Fighter Command Losses - Vol. I 1939/1941** -. Midland Publishing
Halley, James J. - **RAF Aircraft Serials** – Air Britain (Historians) Ltd
Henry, Mike - **Air Gunner** – 1997 Crecy Publications
Jones, Geoffrey - **Attacker - The Hudson and its Fliers** - 1980 William Kimber
Mason, Francis K. - **Battle over Britain** - 1969 McWhirter Twins Ltd
Middlebrook, Martin and Everitt, Chris - **The Bomber Command War Diaries 1939/1945** - 2000 Midland Publishing
McNeill, Ross - **RAF Coastal Command Losses 1939/1941** - 2003 Midland Publishing
Moyle, Harry - **The Hampden File** - 1989 Air Britain (Historians) Ltd
Newton, Dennis - **A Few of The Few** - 1990 Australian War Memorial
Overy, Richard - **The Battle** - 2000 Penguin
Parry, Simon W. - **Intruders over Britain** – 1987 Air Research Publications
Pitchfork, Graham - **The Men Behind the Medals** -1998 Pen and Sword
Ramsey, Winson Ed. - **The Battle of Britain Then and Now** – 1980 After the Battle Publications
Ramsey, Winson Ed - **The Blitz Then and Now Volume 1** – 1987 After the Battle Publications
Ray, John - **The Battle of Britain - New Perspective** - Brackhampton Press
Roberts R. N. - **The Whitley File** – 1986 Air Britain (Historians) Ltd
Spooner, Tony DSO, DFC - **Coastal Ace, The Biography of Sqn.Ldr. Terrence Malcolm Bulloch, DSO*DFC*** - 1986 William Kimber
Tams F. A. B. - **Trenchard Brat** - 2000 Pentland Press
Terraine, John - **The Right of the Line** - 1997 Wordsworth Press
Roll of Honour - Westminster Abbey Library
Imperial War Museum Review No.6 - **The Role of Bomber Command in the Battle of Britain**